AUTONOMOUS LEARNING
FROM THE
ENVIRONMENT

AUTONOMOUS LEARNING
FROM THE
ENVIRONMENT

WEI-MIN SHEN

**Microelectronics and Computer
Technology Corporation**

Foreword by
Herbert A. Simon
Carnegie–Mellon University

**Computer Science Press
An imprint of W. H. Freeman and Company
New York**

Cover calligraphy by the author, in response to a request from the publisher for a Chinese character that means something like "knowledge through experience." Dr. Shen's explanation:

> This character has many meanings, most of them implicit when the character is used with other characters (so it makes readers think). The major meanings are (1) seek and search; (2) thinking and thought; (3) clue, hint; rope, chain; trial; (4) index for classifying; (5) thorough; (6) alone, autonomous. The meaning "knowledge" is vaguely implied.

Library of Congress Cataloging-in-Publication Data

Shen, Wei-Min.
    Autonomous learning from the environment / Wei-Min
    Shen.
        p.   cm.
    Includes bibliographical references and index.
    ISBN 0-7167-8265-0
    1. Machine learning.   2. Artificial intelligence –
Data processing.   3. Expert systems (Computer science)
I.   Title
Q325.5.S54   1994
006.3–dc20   93-33823
                                      CIP

Printed in the United States of America

Computer Science Press

An imprint of W. H. Freeman and Company
41 Madison Avenue, New York, NY 10010
20 Beaumont Street, Oxford OX1 2NQ, England

To the people, especially those in China.

CONTENTS

FOREWORD

BY HERBERT A. SIMON

Contemporary artificial intelligence (AI) systems depend heavily upon their programmers for their knowledge about the world in which they must act. Robotics is only beginning to provide the sensory and motor capabilities that are required when AI systems must interact with the physical environment. Even when such capabilities are in place or when interaction with the task environment is symbolic instead of physical, AI systems still need intelligent strategies for exploring their environments to acquire information about them and to build internal representations of these environments.

Dr. Shen's admirable book addresses these fundamental problems of how learning from and about the environment can be automated. It provides both a basic framework, within which Dr. Shen examines our present understanding of these matters, and an important example of a program, LIVE, that possesses novel and important capabilities for learning about its environment autonomously.

Tasks calling for intelligence fall into two broad categories. In the one case, the intelligent system knows the task situation exactly and so need not distinguish between the real world that its actions will affect and the mental world in which it plans its actions. In the other case, the intelligent system knows the actual situation only in part and so must be concerned with incompleteness and inaccuracies of its picture of reality; for its plans will frequently fail to reach the intended goals or have undesired side effects, and it must have means for recognizing these failures, remedying them as far as possible, and reestablishing its contact with the external reality.

Proving mathematical theorems belongs to the first category of AI tasks: The theorem prover is provided with the axioms and inference rules of its mathematical "world," never has to stray beyond that world, and can always be sure that its inferences will be valid in it. The domain of robotics belongs to the second category. There are always important differences between the world as perceived by the robot planner and the world upon which the robot acts. In this situation, an intelligent system must have means for gathering information about the world and correcting its picture of it. Of course, the category of systems that must handle uncertainty extends far beyond robotics, encompassing all intelligent systems that deal, physically or mentally, with the conditions of the world we live in. This book is concerned with this second, very broad and fundamental category of artificial intelligence tasks and with systems capable of coping with the uncertainties and incomplete information that are intrinsic to such tasks.

There is another way of dividing up AI tasks that is based upon a distinction between information the intelligent system is given and information it must acquire by some kind of learning process. A performance system is designed to work in a defined task domain, accepting particular goals and seeking to reach them by some kind of highly selective search. The system must be told what goal is to be reached and must be given a description of the structure and characteristics of the task domain in which it is to operate: its problem space. In real life, the problem space can only be a highly simplified and approximate description of the actual outside world.

In contrast, a learning system is capable of acquiring a problem space, in whole or in part, by interacting with the external environment and without being instructed about it directly. Learning, in turn, can be passive or active (or both). Passive learning uses sensory organs to gather information about the environment but without acting on the environment. Active learning moves about in the environment in order to gather information or actually operates on the environment to change it (performs experiments).

Since no intelligent system can grasp the whole of reality in its representation as a problem, it must build highly simplified and special problem spaces to deal with the special classes of situations it faces at given times. It must be able to alter its problem spaces frequently and sometimes radically. Clearly, systems that must distinguish between the real world and the world of thought, taking account of the differences between the actual and the expected, have to detect these differences and respond to them in adaptive ways. This book is concerned specifically with intelligent systems that have learning capabilities enabling them to correct their pictures of their environments and consequently to behave instrumentally in the world—the real world rather than the imagined one.

To build theory about complex systems, whether these systems be natural or artificial, we need to pursue both empirical and formal approaches; neither by itself is sufficient. Up to now most of what we have learned about artificial intelligence (and about human intelligence, for that matter) has been learned by building systems capable of exhibiting intelligent behavior. "The moment of truth," it has been said, "is a running system." At the same time, merely exhibiting such a system is not enough: We must discover how, why, and how well it works. That calls for a conceptual structure within which intelligent systems can be analyzed and compared.

This book indeed provides such a conceptual framework for addressing the general problem of learning from the environment. It emphasizes that if a system is to learn from its environment, it must have capabilities for induction—it must be able to assemble its observations into a coherent problem space that can serve as its model of the environment. As part of its modeling activity, it must be able to induce concepts and regularities and laws to describe the world it is living in. It must be able to make predictions and to modify its model when the predictions are shown to be false. It must be able to detect when the variables it can observe provide only an incomplete description of the external reality, and it must be able to respond to this incompleteness by postulating new hidden variables (theoretical terms).

A framework that encompasses all these requirements also encompasses many central topics in artificial intelligence: concept learning, heuristic search, law discovery, prediction and others. The first half of the book draws upon the research on all these topics, bringing this work into focus and exploring its implications for the design of systems that learn. It shows how a wide range of techniques—some drawn from AI, some from operations research, others from statistical decision theory and elsewhere—can be used for constructing models, for making predictions, for exploring the environment actively, and for correcting and elaborating upon the model. One major value of the book for me has been to put together in a principled way and as a single continent a large body of literature that had hitherto formed rather isolated islands.

Dr. Shen's book never loses sight of the fact that theory in AI is centrally concerned with what is computable and how it can be computed. Computability, from an AI standpoint, has almost nothing to do with Godel theorems that show that some valid propositions must always lie beyond the capabilities of any single formal system, or with the equivalence or inequivalence of certain languages or architectures with Turing machines. It has only a little more to do with those theorems on computational complexity that deal with worst cases as problem size increases without limit or with theorems that show that an algorithm will ultimately converge (after a computation of unspecified duration) to a desired result.

Computability in AI has to do with what can be computed over reasonable time intervals using the kinds of computing devices that are actually available or are likely to be available within a reasonable time. This is an imprecise criterion, but the only one of real interest and the only one that distinguishes AI from pure mathematics. Dr. Shen, while he does not ignore formal results, keeps this criterion clearly in mind in both his empirical and his theoretical work.

One way to study the computational capabilities of systems that learn from the environment is to construct robots to operate in a physical world. Another way is to construct two "worlds" within the computer—one in which actions are taken and consequences follow and one that represents the problem solver's representation of that real world, its problem space. A theory of autonomous learning from the environment can be developed and tested initially in either of these contexts, and the theory developed in this book applies to both. Ultimately, of course, the autonomous system must be tested in the real world, but simulation can provide a very effective and economical initial test platform.

The particular AI system, LIVE, that Dr. Shen has built and observed and that occupies much of the second half of the book, represents the second strategy. It is a conceptual rather than a physical robot; the world that LIVE learns about is stored in computer memory alongside (but separate from) its own problem space. The two worlds communicate only through the sensory capabilities with which LIVE is endowed and its capabilities for action.

This research strategy for studying learning from the environment avoids the arduous tasks of building physical visual and auditory sensors and mechanical arms and legs, but does not lose sight of the fundamental issue: the actual and possible discrepancies between the mental picture and the scene of action.

Research has shown that surprise—the accident, as Pasteur put it, that happens to the prepared mind—plays a frequent and important role in scientific discovery. Fleming's discovery of penicillin, Hans Kreb's discovery of the role of ornithine in the synthesis of urea, the Curies' discovery of radium are well-known examples. *Autonomous Learning from the Environment* shows clearly why surprise (the departure of expectations from observations) is useful for guiding the modification of the learner's problem space, and in particular how the formation of expectations enhances the knowledge obtainable from new observations.

Most readers, I think, will experience more than one surprise as they explore the pages of this book, and if they do not already know how to exploit surprise for purposes of discovery, they will find help on that topic too. On this and many other topics, Wei-Min Shen has provided us with an indispensable vade mecum for our explorations of systems that learn from their environments.

PREFACE

I decided to write a book on how machines learn from their environment after I finished my Ph.D. in 1989 while training under Herbert A. Simon. There were already many books on machine learning in general, but I felt that none of them addressed the questions that have motivated many researchers in the field of autonomous learning from the the environment: What does it mean that X learns from environment Y? Can we understand and duplicate such intelligent processes on man-made systems? These questions, although of interest to us all, have been addressed only by separated research areas with specific focuses. Yet the important inquiries, such as what the necessary tasks of autonomous learning are and what technologies we have today to accomplish these tasks (regardless of the field— mathematics, psychology, or computer science), can be addressed from a global view. This is what I have attempted to do in this book. The reader must judge whether I have succeeded.

The thesis of this book is that intelligent behavior of any creature, animal or machine alike, is rooted in its physical abilities to perceive and act in its environment. As Charles S. Peirce said more than a hundred years ago, "Our idea of anything is our idea of its sensible effects." We say ice is cold because we touch it and sense the effect. The secret of autonomous learning, I think, lies within the process of how each individual learns such sensible effects from its environment.

I hope the book will reach two groups of readers. For those who want to learn the subject of learning from the environment, the book should provide enough material to help them to become active researchers in the field. For those who already stand at the frontier of the research, the book, with lots of naive and sketchy ideas, should trigger some interesting thoughts of their own.

In attempting to address such an ambitious and broad subject, I am bound to miss some significant ideas, issues, and approaches, for which I ask the reader's forbearance. This book is more about the "mind" and less about the "body" of autonomous systems. Most discussions in the book are on computational methods and nothing is said about their hardware, such as cameras or manipulators.

The research in autonomous learning from the environment is still in its infancy today. This book is only a sprout, whose seed can be found in my Ph.D. dissertation completed at Carnegie–Mellon University and whose roots now stretch out into many scientific fields seeking better nutrition. Although there is a long way to go before the sprout grows into a standing tree, I believe the future of this research is bright. Truly autonomous learning systems, once they are built, can bring humanity endless benefit and prosperity.

I want to thank many of my great teachers and friends at Carnegie–Mellon University. I owe a great deal of gratitude to my advisor, Herbert A. Simon, who opened for me the doors to Western science and guided me through the maze of scientific research. To me, he is both my academic advisor and a noble man who has dedicated himself to science. This book is only a by-product of what I have learned from him. Professor Jaime G. Carbonell, Tom Mitchell, and Chuck Thorp, who were my coadvisors, showed great support. In our many pleasant meetings, they always understood the ideas that I was trying to explain better than I understood them myself. When I was writing my dissertation, Professor Allen Newell gave me valuable advice. It is sad that we have lost such a great pioneer in our field. I'll never forget his unique and warm handshakes. In those CMU years, I also overcame my Confucian diffidence and learned how to discuss ideas with people (even if I don't know what I'm talking about). Among the valued participants in these discussions were Jerry Burch, Murray Campbell, Jill Fain, Allan Fisher, Yolanda Gil, Klaus Gross, Angela Hickman, Peter Highnam, Peter Jansen, David Long, Ken McMillan, PengSi Ow, Jeffrey Schlimmer, Peter Shell, Han Tallis and many others.

Working at the Microelectronics and Computer Technology Corporation has made me much more mature as a researcher and as a citizen. While writing this book, I had numerous discussions with Mark Derthick, Michael Huhns, and Avi Saha, who broadened my view of machine learning and reinforced my confidence when I needed it most. Special thanks to Phil Cannata, who knows how to bring out the best in people. Working with him is a great pleasure.

The editors at Computer Science Press, W. H. Freeman and Company—Gary Carlson, Burt Gabriel, William Gruener, and Penny Hull—provided much help. William Gruener gave me the courage to start the project. I want to thank Jeffrey Ullman, Paul Rosenbloom, David Chapman, Richard Sutton, and several anonymous reviewers for their valuable criticisms and suggestions on the earlier drafts of this book. I am, however, still responsible for the errors and mistakes in this book.

Finally, I think no man can stand alone. My earlier teachers, Wang Jian, You Juin-Hong, and Lou Chi-Ming taught me that life can be meaningful. My beautiful wife, Sai Ying, and lovely sons, Ted and Lucas, have made me complete. My parents and sister in China have supported me unconditionally and sacrificed a great deal to make me who I am now.

Wei-Min Shen
February 1994

CHAPTER 1

INTRODUCTION

This book is about building systems that can learn autonomously from their environments. We say that a system is capable of learning autonomously if it can accomplish tasks without guidance from any other systems. You tell the system what to do, and it will figure out how to do it and have it done. With such a system, you could simply tell your lawn mower to mow your lawn without worrying that it might destroy your fence or drive into your neighbor's house.

1.1 Why Autonomous Learning Systems?

Why should we care about such autonomous learning systems? The reasons are simple: They are useful and interesting. As we know, today's machines, like computers, can perform many tasks better than humans. They can be much faster and much smaller. However, they are not as smart. For example, machines must be told at every step how to do a task. They don't learn from their experience. Even the slightest mistake in their instructions will cause them to fail at their tasks. Unless the bugs are removed from their "brain" by some kind of "surgery," they will repeat a silly mistake forever. Autonomous learning is one way to make machines smarter. If machines can correct their mistakes automatically, they will be much easier to use.

Autonomous learning systems are also interesting. Building them can help us to understand what intelligence is about. There are many aspects of intelligence, but the most important one is the ability to learn. It is because of this ability that intelligent creatures can build cause-and-effect models of the world surrounding

1

them and therefore *live* in that world. If we can build artificial systems that have such abilities, then we can say that we have found satisfactory answers for the mystery of intelligence.

1.2   What Is Autonomous Learning?

To put the research of such systems on a firm ground, we need to be more precise about what autonomous learning is. Clearly, autonomy itself does not imply learning. Rocks can exist autonomously, but they don't learn. On the other hand, learning need not be autonomous. One can learn by being told. In saying "autonomous learning," we emphasize a special kind of learning. Such learning is active. It is learning by doing, it is interacting with the environment, and it has purposes. Abstractly speaking, an autonomous learning system must satisfy at least the following requirements:

- An autonomous system must have its own way to interact with the environment. That is, it should have its own actions and perceptions. Everything that is built must be built upon these actions and percepts. Every concept or idea of that system must eventually have meaning in terms of these actions and percepts. A system says ice is cold, because it can touch ice and sense the effect of that action.

- An autonomous system must learn from its experience, especially from its mistakes. No matter how thoughtful its creator is, an autonomous system is bound to meet situations in its own world that are not specified in its built-in instructions. Because of this, mistakes are inevitable. An autonomous system must be able to correct mistakes as they happen, not repeat them forever.

- An autonomous system must decide what to do by itself. Actions must have purposes: either making progress toward the goals or exploring the environment to gather more information. There is no teacher to tell a system what to do. The only source of learning is the consequences of its actions.

- An autonomous system must be able to adapt to different environments and tasks. The system must be flexible and general. It should be able to learn from any environment in which it can "live." For example, an autonomous lawn mower should be able to mow your front yard or a soccer field.

- Finally, autonomy does not mean refusing any external help. In fact, an autonomous system should always be able to assimilate advice. For example, one might tell an autonomous system what the life-threatening situations are so that the system will not jump off a cliff or plunge into acid. However, advice should not be taken in a blind fashion. Whether a piece of advice is good or bad will ultimately be judged by the system itself. This does not necessarily mean that the system will try these irreversible actions itself. It can watch and learn from the experience of other systems.

1.3   Approaches to Autonomous Learning

We just outlined a type of system that sounds wonderful. How do we go about making such a dream come true? Our philosophy is to divide an autonomous system into three parts: the action part, the perception part, and the thinking part. Actions and perceptions are innate to systems. When a creature is born, the physical abilities that enable it to act and see are fixed. A tree cannot move, a bat cannot see the light. The thinking part is the building process that uses the innate actions and percepts to build a mental model of the world. Although the thinking process must use actions and perceptions, the study of the building process can be abstracted from any particular kind of action or sense. The hope is that if we figure out the principles of this crucial "software" of autonomous systems, we can then link the results with any kind of action or percept.

Following this philosophy, the next step is to identify the problems and challenges of this software and study them at an abstract level. This leads to the study of learning from the environment, the main topic of this book.

To explain what learning from the environment is, let us start with a simple example. Imagine yourself just learning how to swim. You may ask your friends for advice or even read books about it, but when you are actually in the water, the first thing you will probably do is to move your arms and legs to see what really happens. After noticing that rowing your arms backward causes your body to move forward, you may deliberately move your arms in order to move your body. Meanwhile, you may choke once or twice when you accidentally breathe water. You thus learn that you should never breathe under water. After a while, you gradually become familiar with the environment of the water and may be able to swim one or two meters. This process — the explorations, the mistakes, and the experimentation — is the process of learning from the environment.

Learning from the environment is an abstraction of autonomous learning. It emphasizes that the internal knowledge of an autonomous system should grow out of its own ability to see and act. From a learner's point of view, it is also a problem. It is about how to construct actively a model of the environment and use the model to satisfy desires.

Learning from the environment is a very complex process involving many activities. The machine learner must explore the environment to identify the correlations between the learner's percepts and actions. It must organize its experience in such a way that it can predict the future. It must plan its actions to drive the environment into states that satisfy its desires. It must improve its model of the environment when mistakes are identified. Finally, it must coordinate all these activities in a coherent way so that activities happen at the right time and do not interfere with each other.

The objective of this book is to abstract these tasks and study them in an integrated way. In particular, we wish to identify which tasks must be done to learn from the environment and which technologies are already available today.

1.4   What Is in This Book?

The purposes of this book are to give a fairly thorough presentation of the issues and approaches that are related to learning from the environment and then to use a particular system called LIVE to illustrate a coherent subset of these issues and approaches.

Guided by these purposes, this book is organized in three parts. The first part tries to answer the question "What tasks must be done in order to have an autonomous learning system?" This part consists of two chapters. Chapter 2 gives the basic definitions of components of learning from the environment, and Chapter 3 identifies the three major tasks of learning from the environment: (1) abstracting a model that approximates the environment, (2) applying the model to determine actions for the learner to perform, and (3) integrating the control between the first two tasks. We will discuss each of these tasks in detail and relate them to many scientific disciplines, including mathematics (function approximation and optimization), system sciences (dynamic systems and chaos), symbolic computation (system identification and data classification), control theories (adaptive control and reinforcement learning), and psychology (the theories of Piaget and Gibson).

The second part of the book (Chapters 4 through 7) attempts to answer the question "What has been done to accomplish the tasks?" We will survey many different approaches and point out how they are related to the three tasks of learning from the environment. For model abstraction, we will discuss learning finite state machines, learning hidden Markov models, learning symbolic concepts, learning models using neural networks, learning with Bayesian probability theory, and learning action/prediction rules. For model application, we will describe approaches that seek optimal solutions, such as dynamic programming, the A^* algorithm, and reinforcement Q-learning, as well as approaches that look for "satisficing" solutions, such as the General Problem Solver, the real-time A^* algorithm, and neural networks that do distal supervised learning. For integration, we will introduce Simon–Lea's two-space paradigm and some solutions in control theory for solving the dual control problem.

The third part of the book (Chapters 8 through 12) presents a prototype system, called LIVE, that illustrates some coherent subset of the issues and the approaches described in the second part of the book. For model abstraction, this part of the book illustrates LIVE's representation and learning of action/prediction rules (a type of model) and, more interestingly, LIVE's discovery of hidden features from its environment for building action/prediction rules. For model application, this part illustrates LIVE's goal regression (a special case of the General Problem Solver), exploration, and experimentation based on models. For integration, these chapters illustrate how LIVE uses the two-space paradigm to integrate all the activities autonomously. Overall, the purpose of presenting the LIVE system is to inspire new ideas rather than proclaim solutions.

Chapter 13 concludes the book with a set of future research problems. For those who have made themselves familiar with the material presented here and for those who already stand at the frontiers of autonomous learning, these problems may serve as triggers for new and possibly breakthrough ideas.

CHAPTER 2

THE BASIC DEFINITIONS

2.1 Learning from the Environment

Learning from the environment can be described as follows:

> An agent L learns through experience what it can do and see in an environment $\mathcal{E}$ to the point that L can drive $\mathcal{E}$ into a set of states that L wants $\mathcal{E}$ to be in.

As we can see, learning from the environment involves two actors: the learner L and the environment $\mathcal{E}$. The learner is an active system. It is purposeful and adaptive. It has some goals to achieve and can change the environment through its actions and observe the environment through its perceptions. Its objective is to construct a model of the environment or adapt itself to the environment so that it can drive the environment into some states to satisfy its goals.

The environment is a passive but persistent system. It changes its internal states only when it is acted on. Actions on an environment can come from more than one source. If there are action sources other than the learner itself, an environment may seem active to the learner. For example, if you are rowing a boat across a river, the position of the boat may change even if you do not row at all. An environment has its own states, and its states change according to some secret rules that are not visible from outside. Furthermore, the change of states may or may not be visible to a particular learner. It all depends on the perceptual ability of the learner. For example, colors of objects may change, but this may not be visible to a color-blind learner.

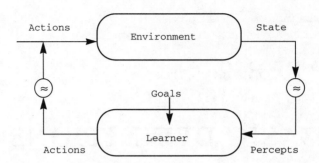

Figure 2.1   The basic definition of learning from the environment.

The relation between a learner and an environment is illustrated in Figure 2.1. The learner has some goals (either built in or given), and affects the environment through its actions and perceives state information from the environment as percepts. The symbol $\approx$ reflects the fact that the apparatus that delivers actions and receives percepts may not be perfect. This apparatus can be disturbed by noise.

2.2   The Learner and Its Actions, Percepts, Goals, and Models

As indicated in Figure 2.1, the learner operates in terms of three basic elements: actions, percepts, and goals. Let us define them precisely before we give the definition of models and the structure of the learner.

An *action* is a physical change that occurs inside the learner, such as a muscle contraction inside a human body or an electrical signal sent to some switch in a robot. Actions so defined have two interesting properties. First, actions are innate to the learner. When a learner is born, the set of actions it can perform is fixed. Second, actions are separated from their consequences in different environments. A learner can execute its action in any environment regardless of which consequence the action might cause. For instance, a contraction of one's arm muscle can be executed regardless of whether the arm will hit something or not. This separation provides a clear boundary between a learner and an environment, and it is crucial to learn the effects of actions in different environments.

A *percept* is a representation inside the learner about the state information of the environment. Like actions, the apparatus for creating such an internal representation from external information are innate to the learner. This device is the only channel that allows information from the environment to flow into the learner. For humans, such devices are the sensing organs, and percepts are the signals that are sent to the brain from the sensing organs. Percepts need not be in any restricted form. They can be a reading from an instrument (e.g., a real number), an object (e.g., a book), a feature (e.g., blue), a function (e.g., *Color: object → feature*), or even a relation (e.g., *On: object × object*). A percept can also be a representation of the learner's own features, for example, whether its hand is open and how much its left arm is bent. At any time t, the learner perceives a set of percepts from the environment. We shall call this set an *observation* at time t.

A *goal* is defined as a set of percepts that the learner wants to receive from the environment. We say that a goal is satisfied by an observation if the observation is a superset of the goal (they are both sets of percepts). For example, if a goal is defined as {"blueTriangle"}, then any observation that contains the percept "blueTriangle" will satisfy the goal.

With actions and percepts as building blocks, the learner is to construct a *model* of the environment so that it can predict the consequences of its actions and direct its actions towards the goals. A model is a set of specifications that predict future observations from previous experience (previous observations and actions). A typical notation for a model M is a six-tuple:

$$M \equiv (A, P, S, \phi, \theta, t)$$

where A is the set of basic actions, P is the set of percepts, S is a set of model states (the internal representation of experience), ϕ is a state transition function $S \times A \to S$ that maps a state and an action to the next state, θ is an appearance function that maps states to observations $S \to 2^P$ (2^P denotes the power set of P), and t is the *current model state* of M. When a basic action $a \in A$ is applied to M, the current state t is updated to be $\phi(t, a)$ and the predicted observation (a *prediction*) is $\theta(\phi(t, a))$.

In order to build complex model states from basic percepts and actions, the learner is given a set of *m-constructors*. Typically, m-constructors are relations (e.g., $=$), logical connectives and quantifiers (e.g., $\wedge$ and $\exists$), and functions (e.g., $+$ and $*$). These constructors, together with actions and percepts, are the vocabulary of the learner's mental language to build model states.

To illustrate these basic definitions, let us consider the little prince's world [92] as a simple example. The little prince lives on a tiny two-dimensional planet, shown in Figure 2.2, where there are four regions: north, south, east, and west. There is a rose in the east region, a volcano in the west, a whale in the south, and a polar bear in the north. On this planet, the prince can move forward, backward and turn around, but he cannot see anything in his world except the rose and the volcano. Due to his limited percepts, he cannot see the whale or the bear, nor can he sense the region or the direction. The prince has a goal to reach: He wants to find the rose from anywhere on the planet. The model of the planet, from the viewpoint of the little prince, is shown in Figure 2.3. Using the six-tuple notation, this model

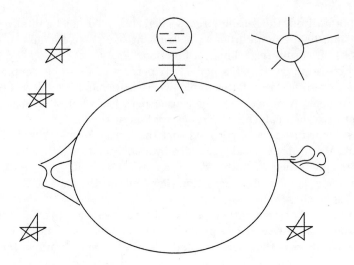

Figure 2.2   The little prince's perceived environment.

can be specified as follows:

$$A \equiv \{\text{forward, backward, turn-around}\}$$
$$P \equiv \{\text{rose, volcano}\}$$
$$S \equiv \{s_1, s_2, s_3, s_4\}$$
$$\phi \equiv \phi(s_0, \text{forward}) = s_3, \phi(s_0, \text{backward}) = s_2, \ldots$$
$$\theta \equiv \theta(s_1) = \{\text{volcano}\}, \theta(s_0) = \{\text{rose}\}, \theta(s_2) = \theta(s_3) = \{\}$$

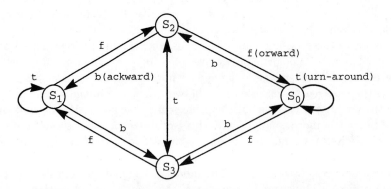

Figure 2.3   The little prince's model of his world.

It is important to notice that a model need not be exactly the same as the environment as long as it behaves the same as the environment from the learner's point of view. For example, compared to the "real" planet (discussed in Section 2.3), the model here has fewer states. This is because the little prince's percepts are limited, and he cannot see the difference between the north region and the south region. Notice also that the states in a model reflect the information contained in the learner's experience, that is, sequences of actions and observations in the environment. For example, s_2 in the little prince's model represents the sequence {rose}, backward, {}, and s_1 represents the sequence {volcano}.

In general, the format of a model can be arbitrary. It can be a state machine, a polynomial function, or a grammar of language. However, because a learner is limited by its actions and percepts, there can be only one set of possible models for a particular learner to consider. This set is called a *model space*. The learner will model the environment by searching for an appropriate model in this space. The model space can be thought of as a mental language that is used by the learner to describe the environment. A model for a particular environment is just a sentence composed in this language. For example, the model space in our little prince example is all the finite deterministic state machines that can be constructed from the three actions and two percepts. The model illustrated in Figure 2.3 is one of those. A model space presupposes that the learner has knowledge about certain mental operations. For example, if a learner's model space is all the polynomials, then we suppose the learner knows addition, subtraction, and multiplication. If a learner's model space involves logical expression, then we assume it knows the basic logical connectives such as $\wedge$, $\vee$, and $\neq$. These mental operations are the m-constructors defined earlier.

No matter what the model space is, one important constraint on the model is that it must function with a bounded memory or time (in contrast with Turing machines, which require an infinite amount of memory or time). Thus, the number of model states is bounded by the capacity of memory (how much experience the learner can remember), and predictions from the model must be made within a certain amount of time. Because of this constraint, the learner's model is almost always an approximation (or abstraction) of the environment. We will come back to this point in Chapter 3.

Having defined the basic elements of a learner, we now discuss the learner's structure, shown in Figure 2.4. This structure is designed to support the objectives of learning from the environment, and it has two main components: the model abstractor and the model applicator.

The *model abstractor* constructs and revises a model of the environment based on monitoring the performance of the current model (actions and predictions) and the actual consequences that are perceived from the environment. It has a full right for changing the model (indicated by the cross arrow shown in Figure 2.4), and its major tasks are detecting the deficiencies of the model and revising the model to improve performance.

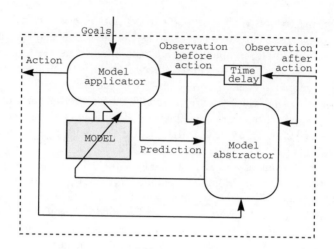

Figure 2.4   The basic structure of a learner.

The *model applicator* decides actions for the goals based on the current model. Its major tasks include selecting actions for achieving the goals and making predictions for actions that will be performed. The goals can come from external sources or from the model abstractor when explorations and experiments are needed.

The structure shows that the information flow occurs inside the learner, but the coordination or integration of the model abstractor and the model applicator can be flexible. For example, one can let the model abstractor control the model applicator. Whenever a new observation is perceived, the model abstractor checks to see if it has anything to do before it passes the control to the model applicator. The advantage of this approach is that the model is updated whenever necessary. Another possible way of coordination is to put the model applicator in charge. This allows the model applicator to carry out an entire sequence of actions without interruption. Nevertheless, integration itself is an important problem in autonomous learning, and we will have a lengthy discussion of this topic in Chapter 7.

2.3   The Environment and Its Types

An environment is a black box that maps its inputs to its outputs. Since the box's internal mapping mechanism cannot be seen, we care only about the inputs and outputs and denote the environment as a triple (Σ, ρ, Δ), where Σ is a set of *inputs*, Δ is a set of *outputs*, and ρ is the *environmental mapping function* that governs the mapping from the current input to the output. Such mapping may use states that are internal to the environment and not visible from outside. Since the mapping may be invisible from outside, we do not and cannot presuppose the nature of the environment's internal structure. It may be a function, a grammar, or a stochastic machine with infinitely many internal states.

The outputs of an environment may or may not be completely perceived by a learner. This depends on the perceptual ability of the learner and has no relation to the environment. Likewise, the environment does not care where its inputs are from. A single environment can be manipulated by several learners or actors.

If an environment is indeed a state machine, it may or may not have hidden states. An environment has no hidden states if each of its internal states emits a different output. In this case, the output signals faithfully represent the internal states. An environment has hidden states if the emission from internal states to outputs is many-to-one. In this case, two different internal states may look the same from the outside. Of course, whether the emitting function is one-to-one or many-to-one is unknown to the learner *a priori*. It is the learner's task to detect this fact through experience.

Let us again consider the little prince's world as an example. The environment (the planet) can be represented as the deterministic state machine shown in Figure 2.5. The states are represented by two variables. The first variable represents the region where the prince is, and the second represents his facing direction: clockwise (cw) or counterclockwise (cc). Of course, this "real" environment is considerably different from the model constructed by the little prince. This illustrates an important difference between the *objective environment* (the real environment out there) and the *subjective environment* (the perceived environment internal to the learner).

Although the term environment is used here, the black box is not restricted to the physical world. An environment can be a room, a planet, or an underwater working site, or it can be a puzzle, a machine under diagnosis, a factory to be controlled, a teacher, a communications partner, or simply a discrete or continuous function. As an example, if the environment is a communications partner, then the inputs and the outputs of the environment are messages. To learn from such an environment means to build a model of the other agent such that one can do the

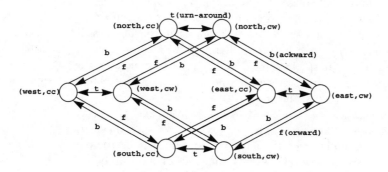

Figure 2.5   The little prince's actual environment.

minimal number of actions (i.e., sending as few bits as possible) and get the desired percepts (i.e., having the partner understand what you want to say).

The nature of the internal structure of the environment, for example, whether it is a state machine or whether the function ρ is deterministic or stochastic, is not in the control of the learner. However, it is interesting to note two different views of this point.

One view is that the internal structure of environment is always deterministic. The nondeterminism or uncertainty is in our head. Two typical examples are Einstein's statement "I cannot believe that God plays dice with the cosmos" and the Bayesian definition of probability (see Section 4.12). In this view, an environment can appear nondeterministic to a learner only because the learner does not know the whole picture of what is inside. The environment may have hidden states, or it may accept actions from sources other than the learner (i.e., it has actions that the learner cannot control).

The other view is that the internal structure of environment is fundamentally nondeterministic and the uncertainty is in the nature of the environment. Two notable examples are quantum mechanics and fuzzy logic [45]. In this view, there is a demon with a "pure random" device hiding behind the curtain of the environment. Every time an action is received by the environment, this demon shakes his device and determines the output of the environment according to the output of his device.

Whether one view is more correct than the other is not important to us. The important thing for a learner is to be prepared to accept uncertainty, regardless of whether the uncertainty is in the learner's head or in the environment. In the context of learning from the environment, however, it is better for the learner to place the uncertainty in its head so that learning can be used to reduce this uncertainty as much as possible.

As an example, consider the situation where a learner sees a nondeterministic behavior of the environment as follows: At time t_i, applying an action a to a state s results in an observation o_i, but at time t_j, applying the same action a to the same state s results in a different observation o_j. This phenomenon may be caused by one of the following two conditions: The environment mapping function ρ is stochastic, or the environment has hidden states so that s is not the same state at time t_i and t_j although they look the same. The challenge for the learner is to decide which condition is more appropriate at any given time.

Finally, it is worthwhile to point out that the only means for changing the environment is through its input channel. As a consequence, one cannot ask the environment to "jump" to some desired state. To maneuver the environment into a desired state, one must determine what the current state is and design a sequence of actions according to the transition function.

When a learner is connected to an environment, the process of learning from the environment begins. This process is driven by the learner, and it involves abstracting a model from the environment and driving the environment into a set of states where observations satisfy the goals of the learner.

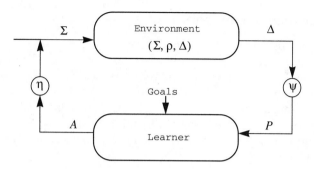

Figure 2.6   The connection between the learner and the environment.

The learner and the environment are connected through two interface mappings, ψ and η, as shown in Figure 2.6. The *perception interface mapping* ψ maps the outputs of the environment to the learner's observations. It reflects the degree to which outputs of the environment can be perceived by the learner (e.g., the nature of the sensors). The *action interface mapping* η maps the learner's actions to the inputs of the environment. It reflects how the actions of the learner are delivered to the environment (e.g., the nature of the learner's physical body). These two mappings are not determined by any third party. For any given pair of learner and environment, the ψ mapping is determined by the learner's percepts and the environment's outputs, and the η mapping is determined by the learner's actions and the environment's inputs.

With these connections established, abstracting a model from the environment can be viewed by the learner as building a causal relation between its own actions and its own observations in the context of the current environment.

Depending on the nature of the interface mappings and whether the environment receives actions from sources other than the learner, there are four basic types of learning from the environment. It is important to identify these types because different learning methods may only work for different types of configurations.

2.3.1   Transparent Environment

In the first type of learning from the environment, the environment has no hidden states and the perception interface mapping ψ is one-to-one. We call this type of learning "learning from a *transparent* environment" because the learner can clearly see the inside of the environment. Learning from a transparent environment is not always easy. The size of the environment may be very large, and there may be too much for the learner to see. In order to act effectively in this type of environment, a compact, high-level model must be abstracted from the environment.

2.3.2   Translucent Environment

In the second type of learning from the environment, the environment has hidden states or the perception interface mapping ψ is many-to-one. We call this type of learning "learning from a *translucent* environment" because the learner cannot see all the states of the environment at once (but can infer them through experience). Clearly, learning from a translucent environment is more difficult than learning from a transparent environment. The learner is bound to experience nondeterminism and it must look into the history of its actions and observations in order to construct appropriate hidden model states.

2.3.3   Uncertain Environment

In the third type of learning from the environment, the interface mappings are noisy. This means that the observations of the learner do not truly reflect the outputs of the environment, and the actions of the learner are not delivered to the environment undisturbed. This kind of learning occurs frequently in the real world because the sensors and the effectors (devices that carry out actions) cannot be built so that they are completely precise. We call this type of learning "learning from *uncertain* (or *noisy*) environments." To learn from such environments, the learner must abstract models that can filter out the noise or that best estimate the uncertainty.

2.3.4   Semicontrollable Environment

In the fourth type of learning from the environment, the environment receives actions from sources other than the learner. From the learner's point of view, the action interface mapping η seems to be a one-to-many mapping and the environment changes its outputs by itself. We call this type of learning "learning from a *semicontrollable* environment" because the environment receives actions that the learner cannot control. An extreme of this type of learning occurs when the learner's actions have no effect at all on the behavior of the environment yet the output of the environment keeps changing. The learner cannot control the environment but observes the changes of the outputs. We call this type of learning "learning from an *observation-only* environment." In general, we will refer to the type of environment that changes without the actions from the learner a "*time-variant* environment." The reasons for the changes in the environment may vary, but these reasons have no significance from the learner's point of view. To learn from this type of environment is even more difficult. The learner must model not only the environment but also the sources of other actions (e.g., other agents).

Learning from the environment may be a combination of these basic types. For example, it can be both translucent and noisy, or even semicontrollable. However, the learner does not know what kind of learning task it faces a priori. This makes learning from the environment in general a very challenging problem.

2.4 Examples of Learning from the Environment

To illustrate the definitions in this chapter, let us look at some more examples of learning from the environment.

The little prince's planet

Since we have already discussed this example in detail, a summary here will be sufficient. The learner's actions, percepts, and goals are shown in Table 2.1. The environment is translucent. The prince cannot see the difference between the north region and the south region (he cannot see the bear and the whale), nor can he see the difference between clockwise and counterclockwise.

The Tower of Hanoi

The Tower of Hanoi is a puzzle game. In the most common form, the puzzle has three pegs and three disks. The object of the game is to move all the disks from one peg to another without violating the three rules listed in Figure 2.7. There are many variations of this puzzle. For example, instead of moving disks between pegs, one might move balls between plates. The constraints on the sizes of the disk on a peg can be applied to the sizes (or colors) of the balls on a plate.

To make this puzzle an example environment to learn from, we suppose that the three rules are not given to the learner at the beginning; instead the environment enforces the rules by giving unexpected results for any illegal actions. For example, if the learner tries to put a disk on a peg that has smaller disks, it may find the disk is dropped onto the table instead of onto the peg.

Many learners can be designed to learn from this environment. Different learners use different actions and percepts and face different difficulties. For illustration, we define three typical learners: the LOGIC1 learner, which perceives relational pred-

Percepts	rose, volcano
Actions	forward, backward, turn-around
M-constructors	finite deterministic state machines
Goals	{rose}
Environment	little planet in Figure 2.5

Table 2.1 The little prince learner.

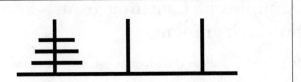

Rule 1: Only one disk can be moved at a time.
Rule 2: Only the smallest disk on a peg can be moved.
Rule 3: A disk can only be put on top of a larger disk.

Figure 2.7 The Tower of Hanoi puzzle.

icates and performs high-level actions; the HAND-EYE learner, which perceives features of objects and controls its hand; and the "size-blind" LOGIC2 learner, which is the same as LOGIC1 except that it cannot see the size relation between objects.

The LOGIC1 learner is defined in Table 2.2. It has three types of percepts: percept ON(D, P) if disk D is on peg (or table) P, percept SIZE>(D1, D2) if disk D1 is larger than disk D2, and percept INHAND(D) if disk D is in the hand of the learner. The two actions Pick and Put are as follows. The Pick(D, P) action picks up disk D from peg P and the Put(D, P) action puts disk D on peg P.

For the learner LOGIC1, the Tower of Hanoi environment is transparent. This learner has the task of abstracting a model of the three rules in Figure 2.7 in terms of its actions and percepts and uses the model to move all the disks to the rightmost peg.

Percepts	ON($disk$, $peg/table$) SIZE>($diskx$, $disky$) INHAND($disk$)
Actions	Pick($disk$, peg) Put($disk$, peg)
M-constructors	$\wedge$ and $\neg$
Goals	all disks on the rightmost peg
Environment	the Tower of Hanoi in Figure 2.7

Table 2.2 The LOGIC1 learner.

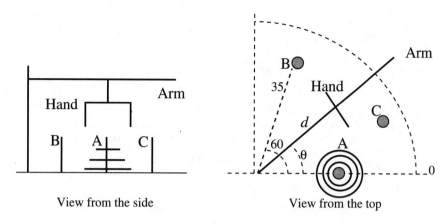

View from the side   View from the top

Figure 2.8   The HAND-EYE environment.

Percepts	feature(object): shape(x), size(x), direction(x), distance(x), altitude(x)
Actions	Rotate(θ), Slide(d), Pick(x), Put(x)
M-constructors	$>$, $=$, $-$, $\wedge$ and $\neg$
Goals	all disks have the same location as pegC
Environment	see Figure 2.8

Table 2.3   The HAND-EYE learner.

The HAND-EYE learner, whose environment is in Figure 2.8 and definition in Table 2.3, is more like a hand–eye robot. Compared to the LOGIC1 learner, this learner cannot perceive any relations between objects, but it can perceive features of individual objects, such as shape (disk or peg), size, location (measured in direction and distance), and altitude. The actions are more primitive. They control the movement of the learner's arm and hand. Its task is more difficult than that of LOGIC1 because it has a larger model space to search (i.e., it has more primitive actions and percepts). For example, it must investigate the relations between an object's features and the position of its hand. Notice that the HAND-EYE learner is independent from the environment. It can learn from any environment in which it can move its arm and hand, while the LOGIC1 learner can learn only from environments where disks are moved from peg to peg. In general, the more independent a learner is from the environment, the more general the learner is. Naturally, the more general the learner is, the more difficult the learning task will

Percepts	ON(*disk, peg/table*) INHAND(*disk*)
Actions	Pick(*disk, peg*) Put(*disk, peg*)
M-constructors	$>$, $=$, $\wedge$ and $\neg$
Goals	all disks on the rightmost peg
Environment	the Tower of Hanoi in Figure 2.7

Table 2.4 The LOGIC2 learner.

be. Nevertheless, the Tower of Hanoi environment is transparent for both LOGIC1 and HAND-EYE.

The LOGIC2 learner (Table 2.4) is exactly the same as LOGIC1 except that it cannot see differences in size in the objects and it has two extra mental relations: $>$ and $=$. For this learner, the Tower of Hanoi environment is *translucent*. Because disks look identical to this learner, the environment may appear nondeterministic. For example, putting disk D1 on top of disk D2 looks the same as putting disk D2 on top of disk D1, yet these two actions have different consequences. To learn from this translucent environment, the "size-blind" LOGIC2 learner must construct internal model states.

Child learning to use a lever

Another example of learning from the environment is from an experiment in developmental psychology [46]. Figure 2.9 illustrates this environment. A bar is placed on a rotatable circular platform that is mounted on a table. An interesting toy is fastened at one end of the bar. The bar and table are so arranged that a child cannot reach the toy at his or her side of the table without rotating the bar. The goal of the learner is to reach the toy. The key property of this environment is the rotatability of the bar. Properties like this can be viewed as the key that enables an object to become a *tool* to reach goals.

The learners are young toddlers (between 12 and 24 months) who presumably have no experience in using levers that can be rotated. Based on their limited knowledge about the environment, they first try to reach the toy directly. They lean across the table; they pull or push the bar directly towards or away from them; they touch or lift the bar and even pull the table. Since none of these actions fulfills their expectation, they begin to explore the environment by playing with the device. They soon discover that the bar can be rotated, thus affecting the location

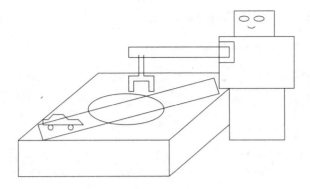

Figure 2.9   Learning to use a lever.

of the toy. They keep playing with the lever (maybe building a model of it) until they purposefully rotate the bar to get the toy.

In the environment, it is clear that the learner's percepts are the positions of the objects, and its actions are all those a toddler can do on the spot: stamping feet, pushing the table, moving hands, or crying for mother. It is not clear, however, what model space a toddler uses or what model a toddler already has about the environment when the child starts the experiment.

Learning to drive a boat

In this example, the environment, modified from [4], consists of a boat and a series of gates on a lake, as illustrated in Figure 2.10. At any time, the state of the boat

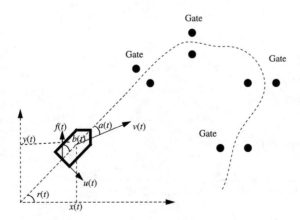

Figure 2.10   Learning to drive a boat.

is determined by the following parameters:

$x(t)$: x-coordinate of the boat center

$y(t)$: y-coordinate of the boat center

$r(t)$: bow direction of the boat relative to the x-axis, $-\pi \le r(t) \le \pi$

$v(t)$: speed of the boat

$a(t)$: direction of $v(t)$ relative to $r(t)$, $-\pi \le a(t) \le \pi$ (a positive number indicates sideways movement towards the left, a negative number movement to the right)

$u(t)$: speed of rotation around the center of the boat, measured at the stern of the boat; the direction of this speed is always perpendicular to the bow direction (a positive number indicates right of perpendicular, a negative number left)

Based on the nature of this environment, one can define a learner as in Table 2.5. Notice that the environment is translucent (i.e., has hidden states) to the driver because the driver can perceive only the parameters $x(t), y(t)$, and $r(t)$.

To elaborate on this example, let us take a look inside this environment. For simplicity, we ignore the friction and assume that $f(t)$ and $b(t)$ do not change during the period from time t to $t+1$. We also assume that there is a constant c, $0 < c < 1$, such that the force $f(t)\sin(b(t))$ is distributed into two parts: $cf(t)\sin(b(t))$ affects the direction of the boat speed, and $(1-c)f(t)\sin(b(t))$ affects the rotation of the boat. Under these assumptions, we can represent the state transition of the boat from time t to $t+1$ by the following equations:

$$
\begin{aligned}
x(t+1) &= x(t) + v(t)\cos(a(t)+r(t)) \\
y(t+1) &= y(t) + v(t)\sin(a(t)+r(t))
\end{aligned}
$$

Percepts	$x(t), y(t)$, and $r(t)$
Actions	$f(t)$, force at the stern (e.g., the motor) $b(t)$, direction of $f(t)$ relative to $r(t)$
M-constructors	$=, >, \wedge, \neg, \ldots$
Goals	going through all the gates
Environment	see Figure 2.10

Table 2.5   The boat driver.

$$
\begin{aligned}
r(t+1) &= r(t) + f(t) \\
v_1(t+1) &= v(t)\cos(a(t)) + f(t)\cos(b(t)) \\
v_2(t+1) &= v(t)\sin(a(t)) + cf(t)\sin(b(t)) \\
v(t+1) &= \sqrt{(v_1(t+1))^2 + (v_2(t+1))^2} \\
a(t+1) &= \arctan(v_2(t+1)/v_1(t+1)) \\
u(t+1) &= (1-c)f(t)\sin(b(t))
\end{aligned}
$$

In this environment, the learner's task is to learn how to control the boat and drive it through the series of gates. This environment requires the learner to construct a model that approximates the environment for achieving its goals. Psychological experiments [4] have shown that humans construct a model of this environment at a much higher-level than the exact transition functions. Their models incorporate high-level features, such as the trajectory of boat motion, mental gates, and the relations between the positions of the boat and the goals. How to construct these high-level mental features is a challenge for learning from the environment.

2.5   Summary

In this chapter, we have defined learning from the environment as a problem for the learner to abstract a model from the environment and to apply its actions towards its goals. The learner must build the model in terms of its own actions, percepts, and m-constructors. Since such physical resources are bounded for each learner, the built model is often an approximation of the environment. This subjective model behaves the same as the environment from the learner's point of view, but it need not to be identical to the objective real environment. Depending on the nature of each learner and the interface mappings between the learner and the environment, there are four basic types of learning from the environment: learning from transparent environments, learning from translucent environments, learning from uncertain environments, and learning from semicontrollable environments.

CHAPTER 3

THE TASKS OF AUTONOMOUS LEARNING

By definition, autonomous systems that learn from their environments must be able to predict the consequences of their actions so that they can purposefully direct their actions to achieve their goals. This demands three major tasks: actively modeling the environment (model abstraction), purposefully applying the model (model application), and coherently controlling the balance between learning and problem solving (integrated control). This chapter describes these tasks in detail and shows their importance in a number of scientific disciplines.

3.1 Model Abstraction

The task of model abstraction is to construct a model based on the interactions between the learner and the environment. This is essentially a loop process of generate-and-test: One starts with a model, tests the model by observing its performance, and generates a new model if the current one is not good enough. With this in mind, model abstraction can be decomposed into three subtasks: the choice of model forms, the evaluation of models, and the revision or generation of models.

3.1.1 The Choice of Model Forms

The choice of model form (or model representation) determines the space of all possible models that can be considered by the learner. In learning from the environment, this is an extremely difficult task, since the learner must dynamically balance generality and efficiency. The uncertainty of the environment (i.e., the learner cannot know the environment a priori), on the one hand, demands the most general and flexible model form so that the learner can construct an adequate model regardless of what environment it is in. The bounded computational resources, on the other hand, require the model form to be as simple as possible so that the learner can learn the environment efficiently. At present there is no satisfactory solution known for autonomously performing such a balance. Most autonomous systems choose the model form at design time and it is fixed thereafter.

Nevertheless, the choices of model forms can be classified along several dimensions, such as the degree of determinism and the degree of discreteness (or continuity). Along the dimension of determinism, model forms can range from deterministic (such as deterministic finite state machines, classic logical systems, or neural networks) and nondeterministic (such as nondeterministic finite state machines) to stochastic (such as stochastic state machines or hidden Markov models). Along the dimension of continuity, model forms can have continuous states (such as real numbers) or discrete states (such as symbols or classic logical expressions). Discrete states can be further divided into *atomic* states (those represented as symbols) and *penetrable* states (those represented as compound expressions).

Whatever model form the learner chooses, it is useful to think of the process of model abstraction as an approximation. This is evident for at least the following three reasons:

- A learner has only a fixed number of resources (its actions, percepts, and memories), and it is very likely that building a precise model of the environment is beyond the capacity of the learner. For example, precise weather forecasting requires more computational resources than what we can afford today, so the best we can do is to build a model as similar as possible to the environment. Without the ability to build and use imperfect models, the learner would be useless in such an environment.

- A learner can have so many actions and percepts that a model for every action and every percept would be beyond the learner's computational abilities. For example, if a learner's percepts are images of 32×32 bits, then the number of states of a precise model will be $2^{32 \times 32}$. Therefore, the learner must approximate or generalize its own percepts and actions, focusing its attention on useful information and selecting its actions to explore and experiment with the useful states of the environment.

- A learner's interface mappings are bound to have some randomness because real-world sensors and effectors cannot be perfect. Approximation offers a nice way to model the environment when randomness cannot be avoid.

Therefore, the best approach to choosing model forms is to start with the most general ones (such as stochastic, continuous models) and quickly converge to the simplest model form (such as deterministic, discrete models) as more information becomes available from the environment. With this approach, the learner can tolerate uncertainty during learning yet have a certain model after learning. Of course, how deterministic the final model is depends on how much information can be gathered from the environment.

3.1.2 The Evaluation of Models

In order to find a better model for the current environment, the learner must evaluate its current model. Since there is no teacher to tell the learner what part of its model is incorrect, the learner must be self-sufficient in this task. In learning from the environment, the only information the learner gets is from observations of the consequences of its actions on the environment. To use these observations for model evaluation, the learner must make predictions each time it performs an action. Since predictions are based on the current model and reflect the status of the model, a failure of prediction (a discrepancy between the prediction and actual observation) is a very useful indication that the current model has flaws.

Predictions are defined in terms of observations. A *prediction* is a set of key percepts that the learner expects to see after an action is applied to the current environmental state. Let the state before an action be called the *condition* and the observation after the action be the *actual consequences*; then a *prediction failure* occurs when a prediction is not a subset of the actual consequences. For example, if a prediction of the little prince is {rose}, but he actually observes {volcano}, then this is a prediction failure.

A prediction failure should not be confused with the general meaning of failure or success. In the general sense, a failure or a success is measured relative to some goals. Here the term failure is measured relative to the prediction. Therefore, an action can be successful in achieving a goal by accident (i.e., the actual consequences satisfy the goal) but prediction can still fail (i.e., the prediction is not included in the actual consequences). So learning from prediction failures actually includes both learning from failures and learning from successes in the normal sense.

Learning from prediction failures can be viewed as a special way of learning from a very lazy teacher. To learn anything from the teacher, the student must keep asking the same question: "What happens after X?" The teacher responds to the question with plain facts but no explanation. It is the student's responsibility to figure out whether his or her current understanding is correct, and if not, why not. Due to this fact, one can see that the process of model abstraction is an active process.

One important aspect of model evaluation is to decide when a good-enough model has been learned. That is the termination criterion for model abstraction. In many traditional learning paradigms, *enough* means that the model is exactly the same as the environment. However, in learning from the environment, this *environment-oriented* termination criterion may not be possible to confirm because the learner has no access to the inside of the environmental black box. (For the same reason, determining whether the learner has visited all the states in the environment is also a difficult problem.)

One can relax the environment-oriented criterion to be goal-oriented. Under this criterion, we say that the learner has learned enough of the environment as long as the model can correctly predict the consequence of actions that are used in achieving the goals. For example, when a child learns how to use a lever, she is considered to have learned enough if she can grasp the toy successfully, even though the model may not describe the physics of the lever completely.

A model learned under the goal-oriented criterion may have a degree of confidence, for it may fail to achieve the goals from some initial states (or fail to achieve different goals from the same initial state). One way to ensure the usefulness of a model is to test it in as many initial states (or goal states) as possible. The confidence of a model is thus proportional to the number of tested initial states (or goal states). It can be measured probabilistically by the length of time during which the learner's predictions are all correct.

Of course, if this criterion is used, the learner's actions may not be optimal. The current model may provide solutions to the current goals, but such solutions may not be optimal because the model may not be perfect. What is guaranteed is that the solution is optimal according to the current model.

In the long run, the goal-oriented criterion converges to the environment-oriented criterion, and a perfect model of the environment will be built. However, the goal-oriented objective is more practical in learning from the environment, for the objective of the learner is to achieve goals.

3.1.3   The Revision of Models

When the current model causes a prediction failure, how does the learner generate a better model? This requires the learner to identify and rectify the deficiency in the current model. This task has many degrees of difficulty. Sometimes one can easily identify the reason for a failure, but at other times one has to experiment, to explore, or to define hidden state variables. In all cases, the model must be open for inspection and modification.

Experimentation is an essential part of model abstraction; it is a way to refute or confirm a hypothesis in order to identify a model deficiency. A typical hypothesis is that "X in the model is wrong." To confirm this hypothesis, the learner can design a sequence of actions and hope that executing these actions will cause some prediction failures due to the incorrectness of X. In this sense, an *experiment* represents a sequence of actions whose predictions are known, but the learner wishes them to be refuted by the actual consequences. In other words, an experiment is a sequence of actions that seeks counterexamples to the current model.

Exploration is a way to augment an incomplete model, and it works just as learning from a prediction failure does. When the learner has never applied an action under a particular set of conditions before, it sets the prediction to be a prediction that always fails. Such a prediction can be a special symbol that can never be observed from the environment. Thus performing an action with such a *false prediction* will always lead to a model revision. Such revision augments the current model; if the same action is applied again, the learner will have something to predict. This approach puts exploration in the same category as experimentation. That is, exploration is yet another hypothesis that needs to be confirmed or refuted. Thus, an exploration is a sequence of actions that contains some predictions that are bound to fail.

Model revision sometimes involves defining hidden states. In a translucent environment, two states may look the same to the learner but actually be different in the environment. Thus, the learner's prediction of the same action under the "same" conditions may succeed at one time but fail at another. For example, from a state where the little prince sees nothing, his prediction to see a rose by forward action will succeed if he is at the north pole but fail if he is at the south pole. Yet these two poles look exactly the same to him.

Similar to hidden states, an environment may receive actions that are not from the learner. Thus, depending on whether these invisible actions are active or not, an action of the learner in any particular state can have different consequences. In general, it is impossible to distinguish whether the environment has hidden states or invisible actions. In both cases, the learner must augment the model with new states. Such states represent the difference between these surprising experiences. We call the process of detecting and postulating these kinds of states as *discovering hidden states*.

3.1.4 Active and Incremental Approximation

So far we have described model abstraction as a process of three subtasks: model representation, model evaluation, and model revision. What can we say about this complex process in general? In this section, we shall argue that the process of model abstraction must be an incremental and active process of approximation.

We already mentioned why model abstraction is an approximation process when we discussed model representation: (1) The learner has bounded resources compared to the unlimited size of environments; (2) it is computationally infeasible to model every percept and every action in the model; and (3) the interface between the learner and the environment is intrinsically noisy.

There are at least two reasons why model abstraction is an incremental process: The learner's experience can only be accumulated incrementally, and the model being constructed must be ready for use in attempting to reach the goals. The first reason seems self-evident. The learner can only observe the environment state by state. So the model must be constructed gradually, using whatever information is available at the time. One cannot wait for all the information from the environment to be gathered before constructing the model. The second reason applies particularly to systems that must interleave model abstraction with model application. Because the purpose of the learner is to achieve its goals, the constructed model must be in some usable form even if it is not yet completed.

Model abstraction is also an active process. By active, I mean the learner must choose actions to perform. In model abstraction, each action can be either an exploration for gathering more information or an experiment for evaluating the model and revealing the reasons why the current model is not perfect.

The term *active learning* should not be confused with the terms *supervised learning* or *unsupervised learning*. Supervised learning means the learner is under the guidance of some teacher. It does not distinguish between passively waiting for instructions from the teacher and actively asking questions. Likewise, unsupervised learning means that the student must find the best answer to whatever question it has. If it is a classification problem, then the learner must decide not only what the class description is but also how many classes there should be. However, activeness has no meaning for unsupervised learning because the learner has no teacher and is always active in some sense. (On the other hand, unsupervised learning can be viewed as passive, too, because the learner is passively waiting for all the data to be ready before it starts its guessing or learning.)

Active learning emphasizes the fact that the learner must ask questions actively. In learning from the environment, the learner is the driving force of the learning process. If it performs no action, it will never develop a model of the environment and it will never achieve its goals. The environment can be viewed in some sense as a teacher, but it is a passive teacher. If the learner does not do anything, the teacher will not do anything. If you don't ask questions of the environment, the environment will never teach you anything. For this reason, it is inappropriate to classify learning from the environment as either supervised or unsupervised learning.

3.2   Model Application

Since the ultimate object of a learner is to solve problems, another major task of learning from the environment is *model application*, which is using the learned model for selecting actions to achieve the learner's goals. This task has two subtasks: searching for a solution to a given goal and generating new goals based on the desires of the learner.

Like model abstraction, model application can be viewed as a search problem. If model abstraction is a search in a model space, model application is a search in a state space. In particular, the state space is defined by the learned model where actions are operators that take you from one state to another. The goal expression specifies a set of states in this space that satisfy the learner's desire. The task is to select a sequence of actions to drive the environment from the current state to one of the goal states.

In addition to the standard problems of search, such as how to search a solution path efficiently, model application also faces the problem that the current learned model is not guaranteed to be complete and correct. This introduces two extra complications. The first is that the solution that results from the mental search activities (searching in the space defined by the current model) may not work in the environment. To deal with this problem, a problem solution must have some extra information. Instead of just a sequence of actions, a solution must also provide predictions for each of its actions. With these predictions, the learner can check if the solution really works in the environment. If any prediction fails when the solution is executed, the learner will know there are flaws in the current model.

The second complication is that the optimality of a solution is relative to the current model. So one must decide if one is spending too much of a resource (e.g., time) to find an optimal solution when the model may not be a perfect one. One alternative is to search for a "satisficing" solution rather than an optimal one.

The imperfection of a model also poses the challenge of when to start learning so-called search control knowledge (knowledge that helps in finding solutions quickly). If a learner commits itself to learning such knowledge too soon, such knowledge may be wasted if the model is not perfect and must be revised.

Model application also includes *goal generation*. This is the problem of reducing large, long-term problems into small, short-term problems. When the learner is "born," it has a set of innate, lifetime goals, for example, to increase its well-being. However, when it starts its life, it has no idea how that can be achieved. As its model of the environment becomes more complete, it may know that to be rich or to be powerful contributes to the ultimate goal of well-being, so it then works to achieve these new goals. This is indeed a model application, because without the model these new goals cannot be generated.

The task of goal generation requires that the model be used backwards. Instead of predicting future events based on the current state and action, goal generation is to regress future events into the current state and actions. This requirement must be considered when the form of the model is chosen. Models that are only good for one-way use are not suitable for learning from the environment.

3.3   Integration: The Coherent Control

We have introduced two major tasks in learning from the environment: model abstraction and model application. However, to be an autonomous learning agent, these two tasks must be integrated in a coherent way. This integration is the third and last major task of the learner.

As we have seen, model abstraction and model application are rather different activities. The main difference is in the purposes of the actions. In model application, an action may be a step toward reaching the goals, while in model abstraction, an action may be an exploration to gather more information or part of an experiment to seek counterexamples for improving the model. At any moment, the learner must make conscious decisions about the purpose of its actions. If these purposes are not organized coherently, then actions might interfere with each other.

Nevertheless, these differences are superficial. Model abstraction and model application are really two processes that are mutually beneficial. Actions for model abstraction can result in a better model, which can make future model application more accurate. Conversely, actions for achieving the goals are evaluations of the learned model, and they provide the information resource for improving the model.

Integration can be thought of as intelligently switching between model abstraction and model application. This switch mechanism must (1) interleave model abstraction and model application and (2) trigger the appropriate activity at the best time.

It is a requirement, not a choice, to interleave model abstraction with model application. The reason is obvious. One cannot finish all actions for model abstraction before starting actions for the goals because approximation would never finish. Similarly, one cannot seek the goals without building an accurate model. It would be like randomly looking for a needle in a haystack. A model, or at least some memory of previous experience, must be available to facilitate problem solving.

It is very important to trigger the right activity at the right time, otherwise opportunities for improving the model and approaching the goals may be lost. For example, if a prediction failure occurs during the execution of a solution, the learner should switch to model abstraction using the information that is available at that time to improve the model. Recognizing such opportunities is a key component of a successful integration.

Based on this switch metaphor, the problem of integration can be illustrated in the control loop shown in Figure 3.1. There are two layers in the loop. The outer loop generates new goals based on the learner's current model and its innate desires. This loop calls the inner loop to reach these goals. The inner loop generates appropriate actions either for achieving the goals or for gathering information to improve the model (A and B, respectively, in Figure 3.1). It then carries out those actions and perceives the actual consequences from the environment. It also revises the model based on the feedback generated from these activities. As we can see, this loop includes all the tasks of the learner: goal generation, problem solving,

LOOP FOREVER:
1   Generate goals based on the innate goal and the current model,
2   WHILE the goals are not accomplished:
3   Choose one of the following two activities:
4   A. Generate actions for achieving the goals,
5   B. Generate actions for model abstraction,
6   Execute actions in the environment,
7   Perceive information from the environment,
8   Improve the model based on the feedback.

Figure 3.1   The integration loop.

model abstraction, acting, and sensing. Since the loop is only an illustration of the integration task, it does not specify how the actions should be chosen or what the details of model abstraction are. (Actions for model abstraction can be either explorations or experimentations.)

Nevertheless, there are only five strategies for determining the choice between A and B: (1) always choose A, (2) always choose B, (3) randomly choose A or B, (4) statically determine two numbers a and b, and choose A for a times and B for b times, and (5) dynamically determine the values of a and b and choose A and B according to a and b. It is the learner's task to adopt a strategy and carry it out. We will discuss the pros and cons of these strategies in Chapter 7.

3.4   Views from Other Scientific Disciplines

The problem of learning from the environment is highly multidisciplinary. The tasks specified here are not just one person's opinion; they are actually research topics in many disciplines. This section describes some of this research, and in doing so, I hope readers can see the links between these areas so that ideas in one area can be beneficial to all.

3.4.1   Function Approximation

Function approximation is a branch of mathematics in which functions are approximated by other functions [79]. This is the oldest and probably most abstract form of learning from the environment and can be traced back to Euler and Bernoulli in the eighteenth century. Let us begin with a simple example.

Suppose we want to approximate the sine curve $y = \sin x$ on $[0, \pi]$ by another function of the form $P(x) = a_0 + a_1 x + \cdots + a_n x^n$. This form is known as an algebraic polynomial, and the a_k are constants that are independent of x. Suppose we have chosen to evaluate the sine function at three points, $x = 0$, $\pi/2$, and π, and observed the values $y = 0$, 1, and 0. Since we know that $P(x)$ must agree with $\sin x$ at these points, we have the following equations:

$$
\begin{aligned}
P(0) &= a_0 + a_1 0 + a_2 0^2 = 0 \\
P(\pi/2) &= a_0 + a_1(\pi/2) + a_2(\pi/2)^2 = 1 \\
P(\pi) &= a_0 + a_1 \pi + a_2 \pi^2 = 0
\end{aligned}
$$

Solving these equations, we have $a_0 = 0$, $a_1 = \frac{4}{\pi}$, and $a_2 = \frac{-4}{\pi^2}$, and obtain the approximation

$$
P(x) = \frac{4}{\pi^2} x(\pi - x) \approx \sin x
$$

The above example illustrates a well-known method for function approximation called interpolation. Even though the example is simple, we can already see many of the similarities between function approximation and learning from the environment. From the point of view of function approximation, the environment is the function to be approximated, the model space is the type of approximating function (e.g., the polynomial in the above example). The model is the actual formula of approximation, the actions are choosing points to evaluate the unknown function, and the percepts are the values of these evaluations.

The important classes of approximating functions include algebraic polynomials, trigonometric polynomials, and more recently, various types of neuron networks such as radial based functions. These classes of functions have proven to be, under certain conditions, a natural means of approximating other more or less arbitrary functions.

There are a number of methods for function approximation. The most important two methods are interpolation and Fourier series. As illustrated in the example above, interpolation is a method for constructing an algebraic polynomial of degree n whose value at the chosen points is the same as the value of the target function. (Interpolation can also be applied to trigonometric polynomials.) Lagrange proved that the desired polynomial may be written in the form

$$P_n(x) = \sum_{k=0}^{n} \frac{(x - x_0)(x - x_1) \cdots (x - x_{k-1})(x - x_{k+1}) \cdots (x - x_n)}{(x_k - x_0)(x_k - x_1) \cdots (x_k - x_{k-1})(x_k - x_{k+1}) \cdots (x_k - x_n)} f(x_k)$$

and further that this polynomial is unique. The method of interpolation is a universal means for approximating functions. The function to be approximated need not have any specific properties.

Using Fourier series is a method for approximating continuous periodic functions using trigonometric polynomials:

$$f(x) = \frac{a_0}{2} + \sum_{k=1}^{\infty} (a_k \cos kx + b_k \sin kx)$$

The constants a_k and b_k can be determined by the integrals

$$a_m = \frac{1}{\pi} \int_{-\pi}^{\pi} f(x) \cos mx\, dx \quad (m = 0, 1, \cdots)$$

and

$$b_m = \frac{1}{\pi} \int_{-\pi}^{\pi} f(x) \sin mx\, dx \quad (m = 0, 1, \cdots)$$

Interestingly enough, many function approximation methods are incremental and active. One can choose points one at a time and construct the approximation formula of degree n based on the formula of degree $n - 1$. These methods are also active, in the sense that they tell you how many points to choose and where the points should be. These "actions" sometimes determine whether the approximation will succeed or not. For example, it is known that if the points for interpolation are chosen uniformly along the whole domain, then the approximating function will not converge to the target function as n goes to infinity. However, if "actions" are chosen properly, such as by the Čebyšev formula

$$x_n = \cos \frac{2k+1}{2(n+1)}\pi, \quad (k = 0, 1, \dots, n)$$

then the approximating polynomial that agrees with the target function at these points will be uniformly convergent to the target function, provided that the target function is a smooth one (i.e., is continuous and has a continuous first derivative).

There is a great deal of information in the field of function approximation that can be applied to building autonomous learning systems. This information helps us ask the key questions in learning from the environment. For example, just as universal approximating functions can approximate arbitrary functions, are there any universal approximating models for arbitrary environments? What methods can be used to construct these models? Under what conditions is one method better than another?

Although function approximation can provide solutions to many important problems, it cannot solve all problems in learning from the environment. For example, environments are not necessarily functions. Methods involving function approximation may not be the best for dealing with time sequences since they cannot select a point from anywhere at any time. Furthermore, there is no notion of goals or model application in function approximation.

It is interesting to consider how the notion of goals can be introduced in function approximation. The goals can be thought of as some particular value d for $f(x)$. Achieving a goal can be thought of as determining a point a (an action) such that $f(a) = d$. This requires not only approximating the target function but also an inverse function g of f. This inverse function is used in model application to determine the desired point a to obtain the value d, as $a = g(d)$.

3.4.2 Function Optimization

Function optimization is a branch of mathematics studying the following problem: Given a function $f(x)$, find a point x^* such that $f(x^*)$ is the minimum value for all $f(x)$. On the surface, this problem seems unrelated to learning from the environment. But closer examination reveals that function optimization is a twin problem of function approximation. Their interesting relation was first discovered by Čebyšev [79].

Suppose that you are approximating a function $f(x)$ on an interval $[a, b]$ using a "mechanism" ϕ that is completely specified by a set of parameters $\alpha_0, \alpha_1, \cdots, \alpha_m$. Let the magnitude $\|f - \phi\|$ be the maximum deviation of the function $f(x)$ from the approximating function $\phi(x; \alpha_0, \alpha_1, \cdots, \alpha_m)$ on the interval $[a, b]$. The quantity $\|f - \phi\|$ is obviously a certain function $F(\alpha_0, \alpha_1, \dots, \alpha_m)$ of the parameters $\alpha_0, \alpha_1, \dots, \alpha_m$. So the problem of finding the best approximation of $f(x)$ using ϕ

with $m+1$ parameters now becomes a problem of finding the minimum value of F. Therefore, the problem of approximation is reduced to the problem of optimization.

In addition to function approximation, optimization is very closely related to the problem of finding a value of x such that the value of a given function $f(x)$ will be equal to some desired goal value g. The reduction is obvious. Let the difference between $f(x)$ and g be a new function $F(x) = |f(x) - g|$. Then the problem of finding a value of x^* such that $f(x^*) = g$ becomes the problem of optimizing $F(x)$, or finding the value of x^* such that the value of $F(x^*)$ is zero, which is of course the minimum.

Therefore, learning from the environment can be viewed as an optimization problem. The environment is the function to be optimized, the actions are choosing points to evaluate the function, the percepts are the values of these evaluations, and the goal is the minimum value of the function.

3.4.3   Classification and Clustering

The problem of classification is to construct descriptions of target classes based on examples from each class. For instance, to classify "tables" and "chairs," a learner may examine some examples of tables and chairs and come up with a description. When a new object is presented, the learner should be able to tell whether it is a table or a chair.

In classification, each object is normally represented as a set of predetermined features, such as color and length, and each feature has a value from some predetermined sets. For example, the value of color may be red, green, or yellow. The value of length may be any real number greater than zero. Classes are described as sets of objects. For instance, one class may be the set of all objects that are red and less than ten feet in length. Examples are presented by a teacher. Each example consists of an object and the name of the class to which it belongs.

Technically, the features and their possible values constitute a feature space, in which each object is a point. All the points that have been presented to the learner are the *data points*. The problem of classification is to identify a set of points in the space that corresponds to the true classification or that at least agrees with the true classification at all the data points. A class can be a continuous region in the space or a collection of discrete points.

The problem of clustering is the same as the problem of classification except that the examples seen by the learner have no predetermined classes. The learner's task is still to construct class descriptions except that it has the freedom to determine the classes by itself. Thus, classification is sometimes called supervised learning, since a teacher must tell the learner what class an object is in; clustering is sometimes called unsupervised learning, because it does not require such a teacher. However, clustering requires a predetermined "distance" function to tell whether two points should be considered similar. In a sense, this distance function is a supervisor who tells the learner whether the current way of classifying the data points is good or bad.

Both classification and clustering can pose a problem called *overfitting*. That is, the learner may have the tendency to construct classes or clusters that cover just the data points and nothing else. For example, a cluster learner may decide that each data point is a cluster unto itself. The result of such learning has no predictive power: The description of classes or clusters says nothing about new points.

Classification and clustering are restricted forms of learning from the environment. In the case of classification, the environment is the teacher who knows the true classification and who provides training examples. The model that the learner develops is an approximation of the teacher's classification. The model of the environment is the class description constructed by the learner. The learning is passive in the sense that the learner has no actions but passively observes the examples as presented.

In the case of clustering, the environment is the distance function that evaluates the compactness of a particular clustering of all the points that have been evaluated. The model of the environment is a cluster of all the data points that minimizes the distance function. In this case, the environment serves as a critic of the model. Whenever the learner constructs a new cluster, it can perform the action of asking the environment how good the new cluster is. The task of the learner is to find the best cluster, similar to finding the x^* point in function optimization.

Notice that the environment and the model in both classification and clustering have no states. Making a new classification or a new cluster depends only on what the data points are, not on how the data points were presented. However, the environment and the model can easily be extended to deal with states because states can be viewed as a set of points in some space. From this point of view, a classifier/cluster can learn a state transition function for each action as a triple (class1, action, class2), where class1 is the condition state and class2 is the result state.

Classification and clustering are fundamental problems that have been subjects of research in many areas. Different areas use different representations of the data and the model.

In artificial intelligence, classification is called *concept learning*. Typically, the data and the model are represented symbolically (in contrast to numerical functions). The data are feature vectors with symbolic values, and the model is an expression of the features in some logical language, for example, the first-order predicate calculus. A typical method for this kind of classification is search: finding an expression in the language that consistently classifies the data points.

Classes and clusters can also be represented as functions, especially probability density functions. In this sense, classification and clustering is a problem of statistical density estimation. In this paradigm, the data are viewed as samples from a random variable (an environment), and the model is the estimated density function that governs the random variable. The action of the learner is to select samples, and the percepts are the values of the samples. One major advantage of this approach is that noise can be dealt with easily.

3.4.4   Inductive Inference and System Identification

Inductive inference is the process of hypothesizing a general rule from examples. Imagine yourself standing in front of a black box that displays a sequence of pairs [question, answer], where the answer is generated from the question based on a rule hidden inside the box. For example, if the rule is a numerical function $f(x)$, then the sequence may be $[1, f(1)], [2, f(2)], [3, f(3)], \ldots$. If the rule is a predicate that checks whether a string is consistent with a grammar, then the sequence may be [string1, yes], [string2, no], ... Your task is to predict the answer for each question before you see the answer.

According to Angluin and Smith [3], to define an inductive inference problem, five items must be specified:

1. the class of rules being considered, usually a class of functions or languages,

2. the *hypothesis space*, which is a set of descriptions such that each rule in the class has at least one description,

3. a set of examples for each rule, and the sequences of examples that constitute admissible presentations of the rule,

4. the class of inference methods under consideration, and

5. the criteria for a successful inference.

For example, to define the problem of inferring a regular expression $(00)^* + 0^*11$, the first item above corresponds to all the regular sets over the alphabet {0,1}. The hypothesis space, the second item, may be the set of all regular expressions over the same alphabet. (Other choices include deterministic finite state acceptors, nondeterministic finite state acceptors, or context-free grammars.) An example of a regular language L may be a pair $[s, d]$ such that d is Y(es) or N(o), according to whether the string s is in L or not. An admissible presentation of L, the third item, is an infinite sequence of examples of L such that every string over the alphabet {0,1} appears at least once in some example in the sequence. So an admissible presentation of the language of the expression 0^*11 might begin

[00011, Y], [00, N], [11, Y], [011, Y], [1, N], [0111, N], [1, N], ...

(Note that repetitions are permitted.) The method for inferring the grammar, the fourth item, can be a computer program that takes a finite initial segment of a presentation of any regular language as input, always halts, and produces as output a regular expression. The criteria for success, the fifth item, can be *identification in the limit*; that is, there exists a constant N such that after N pairs are seen in any admissible representation, the method outputs (or identifies) the language.

As we can see, inductive inference is very similar to learning from the environment. In fact, the five items listed above can be expressed using the terminology of learning from the environment directly:

1. the environment,

2. the representation of the learner's model (or the model space),

3. the interface with which the learner sees and acts in the environment,

4. the learner's model abstraction method, and

5. the termination criteria.

The differences between inductive inference and learning from the environment are the following: (1) Inductive inference has no goals to reach. (2) In inductive inference, a learner can observe only the behavior of the box (the box decides what to feed to itself next), while in learning from the environment, a learner can affect the inputs to the environment as well. (3) Inductive inference allows infinite models, while learning from the environment allows only bounded models. (4) In inductive inference, the box may provide an extra service for the learner. For example, to check whether a string belongs to a grammar, the box must reset itself to an initial condition before it works on the string. In learning from the environment, the environment will not assist the learner in any way, and it will not change its state unless it is acted upon.

Overall, we can view inductive inference as a version of learning from the environment in which there are no goal states to reach, the learner can only observe, and the environment is more cooperative.

3.4.5 Learning Finite State Machines and Hidden Markov Models

The problem of learning state machines is to construct a finite, and typically discrete, state machine based on the observation of the input/output behavior of another machine whose internal structure is unknown. This is a type of inductive inference where the learner can control the inputs of the environment.

Learning state machines can be viewed as learning from the environment without model application. The unknown machine is the environment, and the machine to be constructed is the model of the environment. The process of model abstraction is active and incremental, but the objective is not to make an approximate but a perfect model of the unknown machine. There are no goal states in this type of learning; the objective of this type of learning is not to go into some desired states but to construct a correct model for the whole environment.

Learning state machines are especially interesting for our needs because state machines, with certain conditions, are universal approximators. According to the thesis of Turing and Church, state machines with an infinite amount of read/write memory (i.e., Turing machines) can be used to model any kind of environment. That is, anything that is computable can be computed by a Turing machine. Since an autonomous agent cannot a priori know the type of environment (whether it is a function, a grammar, a set of rules, or a state machine), it is important to have a general model space to start with.

To get some concrete feeling about how state machines are related to learning from the environment, let us look closely at a special type of state machine called hidden Markov models (HMMs) [90]. (Other types of state machines are automata, push-down automata, and Turing machines [36].) Hidden Markov models are used to explain and characterize the occurrence of a sequence of observable symbols generated by an unknown process (the environment). The model is very much like the model defined in Section 2.2. An HMM is a stochastic process with a hidden underlying stochastic process (corresponding to the states S and the state transition function ϕ in Section 2.2). The hidden process can only be observed through the stochastic process that produces the sequence of the observed symbols (corresponding to the appearance function θ in Section 2.2).

For example, suppose you are told the results of tossing coins by someone else in another room. What you hear is a sequence of "heads" and "tails," but you don't know how this sequence is produced. The experimenter may have more than one coin, and the coins may be biased. To best model the sequence, you may choose to construct a stochastic state machine with more than two, say three, states. In this case, the states in your machine are hidden because they do not correspond one-to-one to the observed symbols "heads" and "tails."

HMMs have three major tasks. First, given a sequence of observations O and an HMM M, one must compute the probability $P(O|M)$ that the observation is generated by the model. Second, given the observation and the model, one must identify a sequence of states that best matches the observations according to some criteria. For example, if you heard a segment of speech, finding the state sequence may correspond to the words in the speech. Third, one must adjust the model parameters to maximize the probability $P(O|M)$.

As we can see, these tasks correspond closely to the tasks of learning from the environment, although the HMM learners perform no actions themselves (they can only observe the results of actions by somebody else). The first task is model evaluation (a part of model abstraction), the second task is model application, and the third task is model revision (another part of model abstraction). The environment is the experimenter, and it is translucent because it hides its internal states from the learner.

3.4.6   Dynamic Systems and Chaos

Dynamic systems are generalizations of state machines. They allow not only finite and discrete states but also infinite and continuous states. A dynamic system consists of two parts: a state space that captures the information about the system, and a state transformation that describes how the state evolves with time.

The problem of learning dynamic systems is as follows. The learner observes a sequence (continuous or discrete) of outputs from an unknown system and constructs a dynamic system that can predict the future output of the unknown system. To do so, the learner must determine whether the state is continuous or discrete. It must decide the dimension of the underlying state space (i.e., how many state variables are necessary). It must identify the transformation function, whether linear or nonlinear, time varying or time invariant, deterministic or stochastic.

Learning dynamic systems is very closely related to learning from the environment. The environment is the unknown system, and the learner's main objective is to construct a model for the system based on his perception (the observation of the system). The difference between learning dynamic systems and learning from the environment is that the learner of dynamic systems does not perform actions to control the system, and so the learning is not really active. Also, learning dynamic systems does not have any goals to reach, so it emphasizes model abstraction and does little model application (e.g., the model is used only for prediction, not problem solving).

Recently the rediscovery of chaos [18] has revolutionized the theory of dynamic systems (chaos was discovered by Henri Poincare about 80 years ago). The classical approach to predicting the future is to build an explanatory model from first principles and measure initial data. However, a chaotic system is an error amplifier: A tiny error in the measurement of the current state can have tremendous effects on future events. Since we cannot measure a system without any error, predicting the long-term behavior of a chaotic system is impossible.

The impossibility of making long-term predictions is not necessarily bad news for learning from the environment, however. Chaos has a bright side, too. Many systems previously considered to be random are found to be governed by some simple, deterministic chaotic models. As a result, even if the environment seems random, the learner can still build models to make short-term predictions that are accurate enough. The only requirement is that the learner must *interact* with the environment frequently. That is exactly the philosophy behind our study of learning from the environment.

3.4.7   Problem Solving and Decision Making

Up to now, the areas we have discussed do not take goals or model applications into consideration. Problem solving and decision making, however, are two areas where model application is the main concern.

The problem in these areas is, given a model and a set of constraints, to find a set of optimal actions with respect to the constraints. The constraints may include reaching a goal state (for problem solving) or gaining the maximal utilities (for decision making).

Thus, learning from the environment can be viewed as problem solving or decision making in a special context. That is, the model and the constraints are not fixed but evolve with time. This has a profound implication on the criteria of problem solving and decision making: Optimal solutions are relative to the current model. One should prefer satisficing solutions over optimal solutions because the model is not guaranteed to be perfect.

3.4.8 Reinforcement Learning

Reinforcement learning is a learning paradigm that takes both learning and the value of goals into consideration. The problem of reinforcement learning can be formalized as follows: Given a set of actions A, a set of states S, and a function $r(s)$, $s \in S$, that specifies a reinforcement value for each state, construct a set of rules $q(s, a) \to c$, where s is a state, a is an action, and c is a real number, such that you can maximize the reinforcement if you always choose, in any state s, the action $a_m = \max_{1 \leq i \leq p}(q(s, a_i))$, where p is the number of possible actions in state s. Stated in English, the rules tell you what action you should take in any state and guarantee that if you do so, your long-term rewards (the sum of rewards from all the states that you will visit) will be maximized.

The values of various goals are embedded in the function $r(s)$. For example, one can give the goal states high reinforcement values, while other states are assigned low values. The current known learning algorithms (see for example Section 6.1.3) can "back propagate" the reinforcement values from the goal states to the nongoal states. Thus, the learner's actions are driven by the goals. However, this setting differs from the tasks specified in this book. The function $r(s)$, which can be considered as a model evaluation function, is not considered to be a part of the learner itself. Furthermore, the model learned in this fashion is specific to the goal states. If the goal states change, then the whole set of rules must be learned again.

Notice that the model of the environment learned in this fashion is in the form of states to actions, $(S \to A)$, rather than states and actions to next states ($S \times A \to S$). A system that learns only an $S \to A$ mapping may have to change this mapping completely for a small change in the world. For example, suppose you are learning to find cheese in a maze. After you have succeeded, suppose the cheese is moved to a new location. Usually this will completely change the $S \to A$ mapping but require little change in the $S \times A \to S$ mapping, because the immediate consequences of most actions would be unchanged (the structure of the maze itself would be unchanged). A similar thing happens if the agent is thirsty at a later time rather than hungry and has to travel to a different place. In both cases, the $S \to A$ learner will have a harder time adjusting to the change.

Nevertheless, reinforcement learning is nice combination of model abstraction (active and incremental) and goal achievement, although the integration is not emphasized in the literature and the representation of the model may not scale well to large environments.

3.4.9 Adaptive Control

Adaptive control is a branch of control theory whose objective is to infer a model of a complex system in the process of driving the system into some desired states. Traditional control theory uses the following equation to model systems:

$$A\vec{y}_t + B\vec{u}_t + \vec{n} = \vec{y}_{t+1} \qquad (3.1)$$

The variables $\vec{y}_t$ and $\vec{y}_{t+1}$ are state vectors at times t and $t+1$, respectively, the variable $\vec{u}_t$ is the input vector to the system at time t, and the variable $\vec{n}$ is a disturbance factor used to model the interface noise between the observer/controller and the underlying system. The constants A and B are two matrices. The equation is essentially a state transition function. It specifies how the system changes its state based on the input. Initially, the model may not predict the actual behavior of the system, but as more and more feedback is received from the system, the learner adapts the system by adjusting A and B.

Adaptive control addresses almost all the tasks of learning from the environment. The system to be controlled is the environment, and the matrices A and B comprise the model of the environment. The inputs are the actions of the learner, and the state variables are the observations. The controller must approximate the system using the formula and should be able to adjust A and B to revise the model toward the true underlying system. The adaptation process is active and incremental because the learner must decide the inputs and receive observations one at a time.

The equation above provides not only a model for predicting the behavior of the system but also a means for determining which action must be taken to drive the system into some desired state y^*. This can be done by rearranging the equation as follows:

$$\vec{u}_t = B^{-1}(y^* - A\vec{y}_t - \vec{n})$$

The equation says that if A and B are known and B has an inverse B^{-1}, then the best action $\vec{u}_t$ for the desired state y^* can be calculated mathematically.

Note that this kind of model application involves no search as long as the underlying system can accept any input value at any time. If the system does not have this property, then model application might involve search for a sequence of actions in order to reach a particular state as specified in the task of model application in Section 3.2.

Since actions serve a dual purpose here (either to gain feedback or to reach the desired state), adaptive control also faces the problem of integration. The problem is called *dual control* in control theory. There is no satisfactory solution known for the problem yet [29].

As we can see from equation 3.1, adaptive control can deal with a noisy environment to a large extent. The general approach to dealing with noise is to assume a model of the noise (e.g., Gaussian distribution) and then use the model to filter out the noise.

We should point out that equation 3.1 can have a different form. Depending on the content of matrices A and B, the equation can be linear or nonlinear. However, most known results about convergence are limited to linear models. When the model is nonlinear, many of the nice properties of the equation disappear and analysis becomes very complex. However, recent research has used neural networks as a modeling tool. The advantage of these networks is that they can represent both linear or nonlinear functions uniformly, and there exist powerful learning methods for adapting a network to a particular environment.

Adaptive control theory [29] offers many mathematically sound tools for learning from the environment when the environment is a system that can be described as a set of continuous functions with certain properties. However, one of the problems of adaptive control is how to determine the *structure* of the matrices A and B. Most existing methods assume the structure is predetermined, so adaptation involves adjusting only the parameters, not the structure of the model.

3.4.10   Developmental Psychology

As far as we know, humans are the most intelligent learning machines. Understanding human learning ability may provide keys to building autonomous learning systems.

Developmental psychology studies how children learn from their environments to build a model of the physical world; the objective of this research is not to build a learning machine. Nevertheless, such studies provide a "third-party" viewpoint of the problem of learning from the environment.

In developmental psychology, the learner is a child, and the environment is the physical world. A child, just as the learner we defined here, uses actions to affect the world and uses his or her sensing organs to perceive the world. Although we have no idea what the internal model looks like, several widely accepted theories do provide some insights into the functionality of such internal models.

The most relevant psychological theory is the "ecological" approach to visual perception, developed by Gibson [27] and his colleagues [130]. The main hypothesis is that humans perceive the environment (objects and events) in terms of the actions the environment *affords*. For example, stairs afford climbing, apples afford grasping and chewing. Unfortunately, Gibson never addressed the problem of how to compute invariants in the perceived environment that correspond to the afford functions. Nevertheless, this view is very consistent with our view that the environment is passive but provides information about its changes through a learner's perception. It supports the hypothesis that actions and perceptions must be considered together to build a model of the environment.

The most celebrated work in developmental psychology is that of Piaget. He speaks not only of how perceptions and actions are related but also about the construction of reality in a child [82, 83]. To some extent, we can say that building autonomous learning machines tests whether these psychological theories can be implemented in a computational way. If so, how do we do it? If not, what are the limitations of computation?

3.5 Summary

Autonomous systems that learn from their environments must be able to predict the consequences of their actions so that they can purposefully direct their actions to achieve their goals. This demands three major tasks: actively modeling the environment, purposefully applying the model, and coherently controlling the balance between learning and problem solving.

Modeling of the environment must be based on the learner's own actions and percepts, and the model must be approximate because the learner has only limited resources. The learned model, no matter how approximate it is, must be used to direct the learner's actions toward the goals. Thus the model must always be in a usable form (i.e., constructed in an incremental fashion), and the activities of model abstraction and model application are interleaved. To integrate all the activities coherently, the learner must consciously determine the purposes of any action: whether it is to explore, to experiment, or to progress toward the goals.

Because of the diversity of tasks and environments, the discussion of existing methods can be organized either by the tasks they perform (model abstraction, model application, or integration) or by the types of environment in which they function (transparent, translucent, uncertain, or semicontrollable).

In the next four chapters, our discussion of existing methods will be organized according to the tasks they deal with. Chapters 4 and 5 deal with model abstraction in transparent and translucent environments, respectively. Chapter 6 discusses model application in all four types of environments, and Chapter 7 discussses integrated control, also in all four types of environments. This organization seems better than classifying methods by the type of environment in which they can function, because many methods can be used in different types of environment. However, whenever necessary (such as in the discussion of integration), we shall classify according to environment types.

CHAPTER 4

MODEL ABSTRACTION IN TRANSPARENT ENVIRONMENTS

We now begin to discuss the problems and the methods for model abstraction. The subject will be treated in two chapters. This chapter focuses on model abstraction in transparent environments, and the next chapter focuses on translucent environments.

4.1 Experience Spaces and Model Spaces

The task of model abstraction is to build a model from the experience of the learner to predict future observations from the environment. The format of the model may vary with the method, but experience E is always represented as a sequence of actions and observed consequences up to the present, as follows:

$$E \equiv \{\ldots, o_{-n}, a_{-n}, \ldots, o_{-i}, a_{-i}, \ldots, o_{-2}, a_{-2}, o_{-1}, a_{-1}, o_0\}$$

where each o_i is an observation, each a_i is an action, and o_0 is the current observation.

In theory, the experience of a learner in an environment is infinitely long. In practice, however, since the capacity of a learner's memory is always limited, we regard an experience as a finite sequence of actions and observations:

$$o_{-C}, a_{-C}, \ldots, o_{-i}, a_{-i}, \ldots, o_{-2}, a_{-2}, o_{-1}, a_{-1}, o_0$$

where C is the capacity of the learner's memory.

Given a learner and its environment, we call the set of all possible experiences the *experience space*. We call the power set of the experience space the *model space*, because a model of an environment is essentially a set of all the experiences that are possible in the environment. For example, a deterministic finite automaton can be viewed as an expression about a set of experiences. From this point of view, model abstraction is essentially partitioning the experience space into classes so that the learner can predict what experience is possible and what is not.

The size of both spaces can easily be estimated. Given a set of actions A, a set of percepts P, and the memory capacity C, the experience space is the set of all possible sequences of the form

$$\underbrace{P \times A \times \cdots \times P \times A}_{C \text{ terms}} \times P$$

and the size of this space is $(PA)^{C/2}P$. For example, in the little prince environment, the number of possible percepts is 2 (i.e., rose and volcano), the number of actions is 3 (i.e., forward, backward, and turn-around). If we assume that C is 4, then the number of possible experiences is $(2 * 3)^2 * 2 = 72$. In the environment of the Tower of Hanoi, there are 125 different observations and 8 actions. If we assume that C is 2, then the number of possible experiences is $125 * 8 * 125 = 125,000$. Thus, the experience space can be infinitely large when the learner has infinitely many actions and percepts.

The size of a model space is exponentially larger than the size of the experience space, for a model space is the power set of the experience space. Thus, if $|E|$ is the size of the experience space, the model space defined on it has the size of $2^{|E|}$.

With the experience space and the model space so defined, the task of model abstraction is to construct a model M such that, given an action a_0 and the most recent m elements in the observed experience, $E' = (o_{-m}, a_{-m}, \ldots, o_{-1}, a_{-1}, o_0)$, where m is a constant depending on the environment, the model M returns a description of observation, $p = M(E', a_0)$, that predicts the consequence of the action a_0 in the current situation.

There are two extreme approaches for model abstraction. One is to use the whole experience sequence itself as the model. With this approach, the model is constructed (not abstracted) by simply remembering all the experience that has occurred. To make predictions based on this model, one searches through the entire experience to find a piece of experience, say $(o_{j-m}, a_{j-m}, \ldots, o_j, a_j)$, that is most similar to (E', a_0) according to some criteria, and then uses o_{j+1}, the observed consequence of a_j in the experience, as the prediction for now. This approach requires a considerable amount of memory and is often called *memory-based prediction and control* [6].

The other extreme is to condense or abstract the information in the experience into a concise model. Conceptually, such a model M specifies a set of prediction rules as follows:

$$M = \begin{cases} (O_{-m}, a_{-m}, \ldots, O_{-1}, a_{-1}, O_0, a_0) \rightarrow P_0 \\ \qquad\qquad\qquad \vdots \\ (O'_{-m}, a'_{-m}, \ldots, O'_{-1}, a'_{-1}, O'_0, a'_0) \rightarrow P_n \end{cases}$$

Each prediction rule maps a sequence of observations/actions into a prediction. For example, $O_{-m}, \ldots, a_{-1}, O_0, a_0$ are mapped into P_0. The O_j, $-m \leq j \leq 0$, and P_i are descriptions of observations, each of which specifies a set of observations. The a_j, $-m \leq j \leq 0$, are actions. The number m depends on the nature of the environment but usually is small. For example, $m = 0$ for transparent environments. To make a prediction for (E', a_0), this approach searches through the model M to find a rule whose left-hand side matches (E', a_0) (i.e., each description O_j is satisfied by its correspondent o_j in E', and the sequence of actions $a_{-m}, \ldots, a_{-1}$ in the rule are the same as the actions in E' and a_0 is the same as a_0), then uses the rule's prediction P_0 as the prediction for now. Clearly, in this approach, a concise model must be generalized or abstracted from the learner's experience. For this reason, we shall call this approach *generalization-based*.

To illustrate these two extremes, consider a simple environment that maps its input x to its output $f(x) = x + 1$. Suppose the learner decides to feed the environment natural numbers from 1 to infinity. In this environment, the memory-based approach will simply remember the following sequence:

$$1, f(1), 2, f(2), 3, \ldots, f(n)$$

where n is the last action taken. To predict the result for input $n + 1$, the most similar experience is $n \rightarrow f(n) = n+1$, so the prediction for $f(n+1)$ is $(n+1)$. On the other hand, the generalization-based approach may build a function (model), say $(x) \rightarrow (x+1)$, to approximate the environment. To predict the result of $f(n+1)$, the model's prediction will be $((n+1)+1)$. (Note that this example illustrates the basic idea; it does not imply that one approach is superior to the other.)

With these two extremes, all methods for modeling an environment can be characterized along the spectrum between them. Since a memory-based approach is essentially model-free (the complexity of the approach lies in picking the relevant experience), our discussions concentrate on approaches that indeed construct models. Furthermore, since we are concerned with transparent environments in this chapter, all models in this chapter have the constant $m = 0$. This is because in a transparent environment, the learner's observations can uniquely distinguish the states of the environment; consequently, there is no need to look back into the history. The learner's current observation determines the current environmental state.

Finally, the size of the learned models is also important. We say that a system is doing *model abstraction* if it learns models that are much more compact than the environment. On the other hand, we say that a system is doing *model construction* if it can only learn models that are the same size as the environment.

4.2   Model Construction via Direct Recording

Model abstraction in transparent environments can be quite straightforward if the size of the environment is relatively small compared to the resources of the learner. In this case, the learner can construct a perfect model of the environment by faithfully recording its experience into a model. This is a case of model construction because the learned model will always have the same size as the environment. To make the idea concrete, we consider in this section the models of finite state machines.

More specifically, a model M of the environment $\mathcal{E}$ is defined as a variation of a Moore machine $(A, P, S, \phi, \theta, t)$, where

- A is a set of basic actions. We assume that the environment can be totally controlled so these actions are the only means for changing the environment.

- P is a set of percepts. Since the environment is transparent, these percepts and the states in the environment have a one-to-one correspondence.

- S is a set of atomic model states.

- ϕ, a function from $S \times A$ to S, is the transition function of M.

- θ, a function from S to P, is the appearance function of the model.

- t is the current model state of M. When a basic action a is applied to M, t is updated to be $\phi(t, a)$.

For simplicity, we assume that the environment $\mathcal{E}$ is also a finite state machine $(A, P, Q, \delta, \rho, r)$, where

- A is a finite set of input actions.

- P is a finite set of output symbols.

- Q is a finite set of environmental states.

- δ, a function from $Q \times A$ to Q, is the transition function of the environment.

- ρ, a function from Q to P, is the appearance function of the environment. (If the environment is transparent, then $Q \equiv P$.)

- r is the current state of $\mathcal{E}$. Initially r can be any state in Q. When an action a is received, r is updated to be $\delta(r, a)$.

We denote the set of all finite action sequences by $B = A^*$, and extend the domain of the function $\delta(q, \cdot)$ to B as follows: $\delta(q, \lambda) = q$, and $\delta(q, ba) = \delta(\delta(q, b), a)$ for all $q \in Q, a \in A, b \in B$. Here, λ denotes the null action. Thus, $\delta(q, b)$ denotes the environmental state reached by executing sequence b from an environmental state q. We note that all these extensions and notations on δ also apply to M's transition function ϕ.

We assume that the learner can apply any basic action $a \in A$ to the environment (and to the model as well) and can observe the current output $p = \rho(r)$ ($p \in P$) from the environment. We say that a model state s is *visibly equivalent* to an environmental state q if $\rho(q) = \theta(s)$, where $q \in Q$ and $s \in S$. Furthermore, we say that M is *perfect* and *synchronized* with respect to $\mathcal{E}$ if the current model state t is visibly equivalent to the current environmental state r, and for all sequences of actions $b \in B$, the model state $\phi(t, b)$ is also visibly equivalent to the environmental state $\delta(r, b)$. The objective of model construction is to learn a perfect and synchronized model of the environment.

As defined in Chapter 2, an environment is transparent if its appearance function ρ is a one-to-one mapping. In this case, all environmental states are visibly different, and we can treat $q \equiv p$ and build $\phi(p, a)$ by simply executing a and observing the state reached. If $\phi(p, a)$ is already known for all the basic actions, then either we can find a path based on what is already known about ϕ to a state for which this is not the case, or we have finished learning a perfect and synchronized model of $\mathcal{E}$. Since the percepts of the learner are equivalent to the states in the environment, the number of states in the model is equal to the number of difference percepts, and what you see is where you are. The algorithm that learns from a transparent environment is listed in Figure 4.1. For reference, we shall call this algorithm the D *algorithm*. It can be proven that the D algorithm takes at most $O(|A||Q|^2)$ actions to learn a perfect and synchronized model of a transparent environment [93].

Notice that the model constructed in this fashion is as large as the environment. That is, the number of model states is equal to the number of difference percepts. We call this type of model a *direct* model.

1   Initializing $S = P$ and $\phi = \{\}$

2   Repeat:

3   Let the current model state $t = z_0$, where z_0 is the current observation $\rho(r)$

4   Select actions ba (possibly $b = \lambda$) such that $\phi(\phi(t, b), a)$ is unknown,

5   Execute ba,

6   Record $OS(r, ba) = [p_0, \ldots, p_{|b|}, p_a]$,

7   Insert $\phi(p_{|b|}, a) = p_a$ into ϕ,

8   Until $\phi(p, a)$ is known for all $p \in P$ and $a \in A$,

9   Return ϕ and $t = p_a$.

Figure 4.1   The D algorithm for model construction in transparent environments.

4.3   Model Abstraction via Concept Learning

In most real-world situations, constructing a direct model of the environment is beyond the capacity of a learner. For example, in the environment of the Tower of Hanoi, a direct model must have $125 \times 8 = 1000$ transitions. (The environment has 125 states — each disk can be on one of the three disks, in the hand, or on the table — and 8 possible actions — 4 possible places to pick up a disk and 4 possible places to put one down.) In learning how to drive a boat, the number of states and actions in the environment is essentially unbounded. A model that directly records all experience is thus quite impractical.

Therefore, more compact models, or *abstract models*, are often preferred. An abstract model is a compact representation of the essence of the environment for the purposes of the learner. Such models need not be exactly the same as the environment, but adequate enough to allow the learner to accomplish its goals. Specifically, instead of building transitions from a single observation to a single observation, an abstract model specifies transitions from a set of observations to another set of observations through a set of actions. For example, an abstracted model in the Tower of Hanoi environment needs only the following four transition rules to govern all 1000 transitions in the environment:

- Rule 1: If a disk x is the smallest one on a peg p and the hand is empty, then applying action $\text{Pick}(x, p)$ will result in a state where x is in hand and x is not on p.

- Rule 2: Otherwise, x will still be on peg p.

- Rule 3: If a disk x is in hand and a peg p does not contain disks that are smaller than x, then applying action $\text{Put}(x, p)$ will result in a state where x is on peg p and x is not in hand.

- Rule 4: Otherwise, x will still be in hand.

Since direct models and abstract models are very different in nature, they require different methods to set up. Interestingly enough, constructing abstract models is very closely related to a machine learning research field called *concept learning*.

Concept learning is learning a concise description of some concepts from examples. This learning can be either supervised or unsupervised. In supervised learning, the task is to learn the description of some unknown classes from a set of preclassified instances, so that one can predict the classifications of new and unclassified instances. The preclassified training instances are called *examples*, and they are in the form of (instance, class name). For example, in learning what are tables and chairs, examples may be (object1, table) and (object3, chair). The supervision comes from the fact that each example contains the name of a class to which the instance in the example belongs.

In unsupervised concept learning, on the other hand, the task is to cluster a set of given instances into a set of classes without preclassified information. The clustering is subject to some criteria for measuring the similarity between instances that must be input or assumed. For example, given a set of office equipment, one may divide them into tables, chairs, and lamps. This task is unsupervised in the sense that the training instances contain no information about how many classes or clusters there should be or what they should be called.

To see how model abstraction is related to concept learning, recall that a model is essentially a set of transition rules in the form of (history, action, prediction). The history is the condition in which the action is executed, and the prediction is the expectation of the environmental state after the action. Now suppose that for each action a, we use unsupervised concept learning to cluster all possible consequences of the action into a set of finite categories $\{r_1, r_2, \ldots, r_n\}$. Then the set of transitions about the action a can be specified as the following set:

$$(\text{history}1,\ a) \rightarrow r_1$$
$$(\text{history}2,\ a) \rightarrow r_2$$
$$\vdots$$
$$(\text{history}n,\ a) \rightarrow r_n$$

Then, learning the transitions for the action a can be accomplished by supervised learning of each history$i$, where $0 \leq i \leq n$, using (a, r_i) as the class name. Here, the relation between concept learning and model abstraction is clear: The experience observed by the learner is the training instance, and the descriptions of each history$i$ in the rules are the concepts to be learned.

4.4   Aspects of Concept Learning

Before discussing different methods, it is beneficial to take a look at three important aspects of concept learning at a high level: the partial order of models, the biases of restricted model spaces, and the termination criteria of concept learning.

4.4.1   The Partial Order of Models

Given a language, the set of all possible instances is called *instance space*, and a subset of the instance space is called a *concept*. Searching for the correct description of an unknown concept is not a trivial problem, especially when the space of all possible concepts, which is called the *concept space* or *model space*, is large. However, there is an intrinsic property of the model space — the partial order of models — that can used to perform the search in a systematic way.

Models in a model space are partially ordered because they are sets of the experience. The partial order is determined by size. This partial order is best illustrated by a simple example. Suppose the percepts of the learner are *color* (with values *red*, *yellow*, and *blue*), *shape* (with values *square*, *triangle*, and *circle*), and *size* (with values *small* and *large*), and the memory capacity is $C = 2$. Then the experience space contains all possible combinations of

$$(color, shape, size), action, (color, shape, size)$$

If there is only 1 object, then the number of different observations is $3 \times 3 \times 2 = 18$. If there are 5 actions, then the size of this experience space is $18 \times 5 \times 18 = 1620$.

Suppose further that we use Boolean expressions to describe sets of experiences. For example, $color = red$ represents the set of all observations for which the color of the object is red. Then the transitions made by an action a_1 that changes the color of the object from anything to red can be expressed as

$$m1 = (\bullet, \bullet, \bullet), a_1, (red, \bullet, \bullet)$$

where $\bullet$ means "don't care." The number of experiences that are covered in this set is $(3 \times 3 \times 2) \times 1 \times (1 \times 3 \times 2) = 108$. Similarly, for an action a_2 that changes the size of red objects from any size to *small*, the following expression specifies a set of $(1 \times 3 \times 2) \times 1 \times (1 \times 3 \times 1) = 18$ experiences:

$$m2 = (red, \bullet, \bullet), a_2, (red, \bullet, small)$$

The partial order of all the models is based on the subset relations between models. In the above example, $m1 > m2$ because $m1$ covers a superset of the experiences of $m2$. In general, if a model m is a proper superset of a model n, then we say that m is more *general* than n, and n is more *specific* than m. Because of this partial order, we can put all the models in a lattice. The more general the models are, the higher they are in the lattice. For example, the lattice of models for our example experience space is shown in Figure 4.2, which contains 2^{1620} models.

Given the partial order of concepts (models), learning algorithms can be designed to search for the target concept systematically. Three typical search strategies are searching from more specific concepts to more general ones, searching from more general ones to more specific ones, and searching from both ends towards the middle. The details of these strategies will be illustrated shortly when we discuss various methods for learning concepts.

4.4.2   Inductive Biases: Attribute Based and Structured

The partial order of models (or concepts) enables the search for the target concept to be systematic. However, the size of a complete concept space is normally too large to be searched exhaustively. Given an instance space of size n, a *complete* concept space on the instance space contains 2^n concepts. For example, consider an instance space that has a set of objects specified by *shape* (with values *circle*,

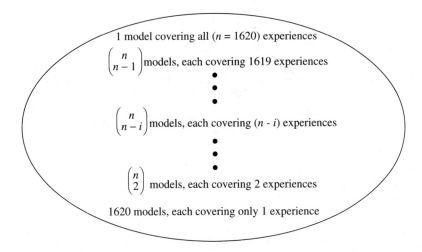

Figure 4.2 The hierarchy of complete model space.

square, and *triangle*) and *size* (with values *small* and *large*). This instance space contains 6 possible instances:

Instance 1: (*small, square*)
Instance 2: (*large, square*)
Instance 3: (*small, circle*)
Instance 4: (*large, circle*)
Instance 5: (*small, triangle*)
Instance 6: (*large, triangle*)

The complete concept space on this instance space, shown as the lattice in Figure 4.3, contains $2^6 - 1$ nodes (each instance is represented by its number). The top of this lattice is a single set that contains all the instances. The bottom of the lattice is a set of singleton sets, each containing a single instance. Clearly, the overhead for systematically searching such a complete concept space can be exponentially large with respect to n.

Therefore, the complete concept space is rarely used in practice. Instead, some restricted concept space is used. The most natural way to restrict the space is to use some concept description language that can describe only a subset of the complete concept space. For example, if we choose a concept language that allows only the conjunctions of attributes, then the concept space in Figure 4.3 is restricted to the concept space in Figure 4.4. The bottom line of this lattice contains all possible conjunctions of two attributes, the middle line contains concepts that use one attribute (the symbol • means "don't care"), while the top of the lattice is the set of all instances.

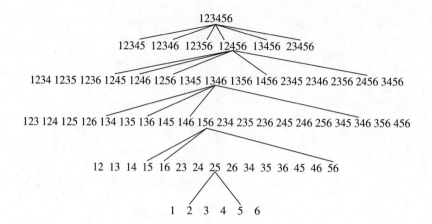

Figure 4.3   A complete concept space for the instance space {1,2,3,4,5,6}.

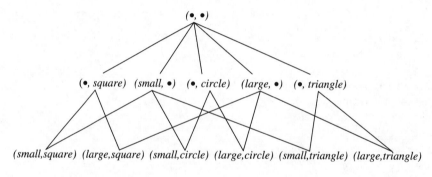

Figure 4.4   A restricted concept space.

The use of a restricted concept language (or restricted concept space) is called *inductive bias* [68, 123]. Such biases make concept learning more efficient. Clearly, the more biased a concept space is (assuming it still contains the target concept), the easier the target concept can be learned and hence the faster learning algorithms can learn it.

The down side of using a restricted concept space is that it must be chosen a priori, and there is a danger that the target concept might not be in the space. For example, suppose the target concept in the above example is $(\bullet, circle) \vee (\bullet, square)$ (i.e., $C = \{1234\}$), but the concept space is restricted as in Figure 4.4; then a learning algorithm may fail to learn the target concept completely.

Nevertheless, the bias of a concept space is one measure of how difficult a concept learning task is. Given an instance space I and a concept space H defined on I by some concept description language, we can quantitatively measure the bias of H with respect to I. Let $\mathcal{I} = 2^I$ be the complete concept space of I; then, roughly speaking, the bias of H on I, denoted as $B_I(H)$, is how large a subset of $\mathcal{I}$ can be described by H. This quantity can be measured in two ways. The simpler way is to use the cardinality of H. That is, $B_I(H) = |H|$.

The other way is to use the *growth function* of H relative to the subsets of I, defined as follows (see [33] for more details). Let S be a subset of I, and define $\prod_H(S) = \{S \cap h | h \in H\}$, the set of all subsets of S that can be obtained by intersecting S with a concept in H. Equivalently, one can think of $\prod_H(S)$ as the set of all ways in which the instances in S can be divided into positive and negative instances so as to be consistent with some concept in H, that is, the set of all dichotomies of S induced by concepts in H. For every $m \geq 1$, let $\prod_H(m)$ denote the maximum of $|\prod_H(S)|$ over all S of size m. Thus $\prod_H(m)$ is the maximal number of dichotomies induced on any m instances by the concepts in H. We will refer to $\prod_H(m)$ as the growth function or *capacity* of H. The largest m such that $\prod_H(m) = 2^m$ is called the *Vapnik–Chervonenkis dimension* of H, notated as VCdim(H).

With biases so defined, let us now look at some of the languages that are commonly used. We first consider attribute-based instance spaces and then structured instance spaces.

When instances are attribute based, they are characterized by the values of a finite set of finitely valued attributes. Some common languages in this category and their biases are listed as follows:

- *Pure conjunctive atoms.* Formulae of the form *attribute* = *value* and their conjunctions. The language used in Figure 4.4 is an example of this type.

- *Pure disjunctive atoms.* Formulae of the form *attribute* = *value* and their disjunctions.

- *Pure conjunctive concepts.* This is an extension of pure conjunctive atoms. In this language, values of an attribute are organized in a tree structure (which may contain abstract values) or in a linear order. For example, a value for *shape* could be *polygon*, which subsumes *triangle* and *square*. Similarly, the value of size may be (5 < *size* < 10). Atoms in this language are allowed to have the form *attribute* = *abstract-value* for tree-structured attributes and *value1* $\leq$ *attribute* $\leq$ *value2* for linear attributes. For this language, the bias $\prod_H(m) \leq (em/2n)^{2n}$ for all $m \geq 2n$, where e is the base of the natural logarithm and n is the number of attributes. If no more than s atoms are allowed in any conjunction, then $\prod_H(m) \leq n^s m^{2s}$ for all $m \geq 2$.

- *Pure disjunctive concepts.* The atoms in this language are the same as those in pure conjunctive concepts, but only disjunctions of atoms are allowed. If no more than s atoms are allowed in any disjunctive, then $\prod_H(m) \leq n^s m^{2s}$ for all $m \geq 2$.

- *k-DNF (disjunctive normal form) formulae.* Arbitrary disjunctions of pure conjunctive concepts, with each pure conjunctive concept using at most k atoms (bias unknown).

- *k-term DNF formulae.* Disjunctions of at most k pure conjunctive concepts, each using an unlimited number of atoms. If no more than s atoms are allowed in any conjunctive concept, then $\prod_H(m) \leq n^{ks}m^{2ks}$ for all $m \geq 2$.

- *k-CNF (conjunctive normal form) formulae.* Arbitrary conjunctions of pure disjunctive concepts, with each pure disjunctive concept using at most k atoms (bias unknown).

- *k-clause CNF formulae.* Conjunctions of at most k pure disjunctive concepts, each using an unlimited number of atoms. If no more than s atoms are allowed in any disjunctive concept, then $\prod_H(m) \leq n^s m^{2s}$ for all $m \geq 2$.

- *Unrestricted formulae.* This language allows arbitrary conjunctions and disjunctions of atoms. It is expressive enough to cover the complete concept space, thus $\prod_H(m) = 2^m$ for all m.

Most of the languages listed are in the logic framework. However, there are many other languages for representing the concept space. For example, there can be functions, grammars, Turing machines, deterministic or nondeterministic finite automata, production systems, neural networks, and just the sets of instances. Even inside the logic framework, we can introduce quantifiers on variables. This is necessary when instances must be represented by both attributes and relations.

In addition to attribute-based instances, instances can be structured. For example, observations from the environment include not only attributes of objects but also *relations* between objects. In the environment of the Tower of Hanoi game, disks are *on* pegs or *in* the hand. To learn from these observations, we must not only represent the attributes of the objects but also the relations between them. We will refer to such observations as *structured* instances [34].

Here we will restrict ourselves to binary relations. To be consistent with attributes, these relations can take normal values, abstracted values in a tree structure, or values in a linear order. To illustrate the idea, consider some binary relations that might be used to characterize the spatial relationship between an ordered pair of objects in a 2-dimensional scene. In Figure 4.5, the relation *dist-between* is defined as a linear binary relation in analogy with the attribute *size*, perhaps using the Euclidean distance between the centers of mass. In addition, the relation *rel-pos* is defined by tree structure values that qualitatively specify the relative positions of two objects.

Following Haussler [34], we assume a fixed set R of relations consisting of n attributes $A_1, \ldots, A_n$ and l binary relations $B_1, \ldots, B_l$. We also assume a fixed upper bound k on the number of objects per observation. Thus an observation

Attributes: *size* (linear): 1,2, . . ., 5
shaded (boolean): *yes, no*
shape (tree-structured as follows):

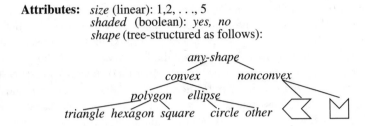

Binary Relations: *dist-between* (linear): *touching, close, far*
rel-pos (tree-structured as follows):

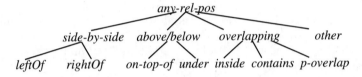

Figure 4.5   The value structures for attributes and relations.

with t objects, $0 \le t \le k$, can be represented as a complete directed graph on t nodes, such as the one shown in Figure 4.6, with each node representing an object in the observation. Each node is labeled by the n-tuple that gives the observed value of each attribute of that object, and between each pair is a directed edge from the node representing obj_1 to the node representing obj_2 labeled with an l-tuple that gives the observed values of each binary relation on the ordered pair (obj_1, obj_2). A graph of this type is called an *instance graph*. In Figure 4.6, the triples in the nodes

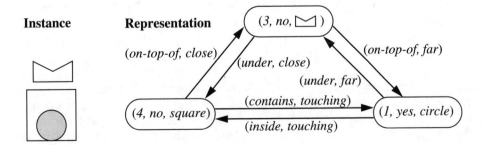

Figure 4.6   An instance graph.

give the values of the attributes *size*, *shaded*, and *shape*, respectively, and the pairs on the edges give the values of the relations *rel-pos* and *dist-between*, respectively.

The *instance space* of structured instances is defined as the set of all instance graphs. As before, a subset of this space is called a *concept*, and the power set of this space is the complete *concept space* on the instance space. Various restricted concept spaces can be defined by using different concept languages. In the following discussion, we will discuss one such restricted concept space, called *existential conjunctive concepts*, which is defined by a language called *existential conjunctive expressions*.

The basic elements of this language are *atomic formulae* over R defined as in [64]. Atomic formulae are either *unary* or *binary*. A unary atomic formula $f(x)$, where x is a variable, is in one of the following two forms:

- $(A(x) = v)$, where A is a tree-structured attribute in R and v is a value of A, or

- $(v_1 \leq A(x) \leq v_2)$, where A is a linear attribute in R and v_1 and v_2 are values of A such that $v_1 \leq v_2$.

We say that an object *satisfies* $f(x)$ if its value for the attribute A is below v in the tree when $f(x)$ is in the first form or between v_1 and v_2, inclusively, with respect to the linear order of A when $f(x)$ is in the second form.

Similarly, a binary atomic formula $f(x, y)$, where x and y are variables, is in one of the following two forms:

- $(B(x, y) = v)$, where B is a tree-structured binary relation in R and v is a value of B, or

- $(v_1 \leq B(x, y) \leq v_2)$, where B is a linear binary relation in R and v_1 and v_2 are values of B such that $v_1 \leq v_2$.

We say that an ordered pair of objects (obj_1, obj_2) *satisfies* $f(x, y)$ if the binary relation between these objects has the appropriate value, as defined above for unary relations.

With the atomic formulae so defined, an *existential conjunctive expression* over R is a formula ϕ of the form

$$\exists^* x_1, \ldots, x_r : f_1 \wedge f_2 \wedge \cdots \wedge f_s$$

where $s \geq 1$, each $x_j, 1 \leq j \leq r$, is a variable, and each $f_i, 1 \leq i \leq s$, is an atomic formula over R involving either a single variable from $\{x_1, \ldots, x_r\}$ or an ordered pair of distinct variables from this set. The symbol $\exists^*$ indicates that all the variables $\{x_1, \ldots, x_r\}$ must be bound to *distinct* objects. Thus, an instance graph satisfies ϕ if it contains r distinct objects $obj_1, \ldots, obj_r$ such that every f_i, $1 \leq i \leq s$, is satisfied.

As an example, the instance graph in Figure 4.6 satisfies the following existential conjunctive concept:

$$\exists^* x, y : \quad (shape(x) = circle) \land (1 \leq size(x) \leq 3)$$
$$\land (shape(y) = convex) \land (rel - pos(x, y) = inside)$$
$$\land (rel - pos(y, x) = contains)$$

Since each existential conjunctive concept represents a set of instance graphs, the space of existential conjunctive concepts has a partial order. Namely, a concept ϕ_1 is more general than another concept ϕ_2 if the set of instances represented by ϕ_1 is a proper superset of the set of instances represented by ϕ_2.

In later chapters (in particular, Chapter 8), we will see an example of such a language used in the LIVE system. In essence, the observations of environments made by LIVE are represented as graphs of relations and features of objects. LIVE uses this language to build a set of prediction rules to model the environment and to direct its actions towards solving problems.

4.4.3   Correctness Criteria: PAC and Others

When has one learned enough in concept learning? This problem is not only practical, because the result of learning must eventually be available for use, but also theoretically interesting, because with different learning criteria different learning algorithms can be designed.

The most obvious criterion is *exact identification*. That is, the learned concept is exactly the same as the target concept. A less objective criterion is *identification by examples*. In this criterion, the learned description identifies a set of concepts that are (nearly) consistent with the given training examples. Such concepts are called *(nearly) consistent concepts* (or hypotheses).

The exact identification criteria can be relaxed in a number of ways. For example, one may look only for either a *reliable and useful* concept description [95] or a *probably approximately correct* concept description. The former criterion requires predictions about new instances to be reliable but allows "don't know" as a prediction. This criterion is sound but not complete. The second criterion requires that *most* predictions about new instances be correct.

Frequently the correctness criteria on the learned concept also include the kind of information that is available to the learner. For example, some criteria require learning the concept regardless of which examples are given (i.e., the learner can learn from any distribution of examples drawn from the instance space). Other criteria may require the examples to be of high quality (i.e., the learner can learn from certain distributions).

With the probably approximate criterion, the goal of a learning algorithm is to produce a concept in the concept space based on a sequence of examples that are randomly drawn from the instance space according to an unknown but fixed *training distribution*. The learned concept need not be consistent with all the training examples. Rather, the learning is successful if the learned concept performs well on most further random examples drawn according to an unknown but fixed *testing distribution*. More formally, we define the *error* of a concept as the probability that it disagrees with the target concept on a randomly drawn instance according to the testing distribution. With this definition, a successful learning algorithm is one that, from random examples of any target concept in the concept space, finds with a high probability a concept that has a small error.

We can supplement this correctness criterion with the following requirements:

- The learning algorithm produces with a high probability a concept with a small error for *any* fixed training distribution and testing distribution.

- The learning algorithm uses sample size and computation time that is a polynomial function of the following three quantities: (1) the complexity of the target concept (i.e., how difficult it is to define the concept in the given concept language), (2) the inverse of the *accuracy* parameter ϵ, and (3) the inverse of the *confidence* parameter δ. Note that learning with accuracy $1 - \epsilon$ and confidence $1 - \delta$ means getting a concept with error at most ϵ with probability at least $1 - \delta$.

If we use the correctness criterion and the preceding requirements, we get the learning framework defined by Valiant [127]. This has been called *probably approximately correct* (PAC) learning.

Since it is conceivable that one could find a concept with a small error without fitting the training examples exactly, at first glance there appears to be some hope that this PAC framework, by itself, could considerably relax the exact correctness criterion. However, results show that finding concepts with a small error for an arbitrary probability distribution on the instances is at least as hard as finding a consistent hypothesis [84]. In fact, adopting this PAC correctness criterion only makes matters worse: Even if we did find a consistent (or nearly consistent) concept, we have no guarantee that it would have a small error for any training distribution.

However, other results show that any concept that is (nearly) consistent with a large enough set of training examples is guaranteed to have small errors with respect to the target concept [34]. Here we assume that the training distribution and the testing distribution are the same.

Formally, let I be an instance space, H be a concept space on I, and $0 < \epsilon < 1$. If Q is a sequence of m independent random examples chosen according to some fixed probability distribution D on $I \times \{+, -\}$, then the probability that there is any concept in H that disagrees with a fraction less than $\epsilon/2$ of the examples in Q, yet has error more than ϵ with respect to D, is less than

$$8 \prod_H (2m) e^{-\epsilon m/16}$$

Using this result, one can calculate how many examples are needed to find a consistent concept in a given concept space with a small enough error. For example, if the concept space is the set of existential conjunctive concepts defined on a structured instance space X, the number of objects in an instance is at most k, and both the number of attributes defined on objects and the number of relations defined between pairs of objects in an instance is at most n, then for any s, $1 \leq s \leq nk^2$, there is a set of samples, drawn according to an arbitrary but fixed distribution D on $X \times \{+, -\}$, with size

$$m = O\left(\frac{s}{\epsilon} \log \frac{kn}{\epsilon}\right)$$

that is sufficient for learning existential conjunctive concepts over X in the following sense: Given m independent random examples from D, any algorithm that succeeds in finding an existential conjunctive concept with s atomic formulae that disagrees with at most $\epsilon m/2$ of these examples has, with probability at least $1 - O(ke^{-\epsilon m})$, found a concept with error less than ϵ.

Similar calculations can be done for other concept spaces. This result indicates that any (nearly) consistent concept will be good enough according to the PAC criterion. So the only barrier to efficient learning is finding a consistent concept quickly. This opens the door for *heuristic algorithms*, which search the concept space efficiently but not systematically.

As we have seen, PAC learning is still a very strong criterion for learning. It requires a learning algorithm to work under *any* training distribution. Alternatively, we can define a more relaxed criterion that takes the training distribution into consideration. Intuitively it is easy to see that the more closely the training distribution is related to the target concept, the easier it will be to learn the target concept. In this framework, we can measure how good a training distribution is with respect to the target concept. Consequently, the error of learning will be defined according to the uniform testing distribution instead of any testing distribution.

The reason we list this alternative is to provide a theoretical foundation for *active* learning. An active learner does not passively receive examples but actively chooses examples. In this sense, learning algorithms that are sensitive to the order of training examples may choose the examples that provide more information for learning the target concept.

There are three basic types of active queries: *membership queries, subset queries,* and *equivalence queries.* In a membership query, the learner presents an instance to a teacher and asks if the instance belongs to the target concept. The answer to such a query is usually binary (i.e., either yes or no). In a subset query, the learner presents its best hypothesis to a teacher and asks if the hypothesis is a subset of the target concept. Again, the answer to such a query is binary. In an equivalence query, the learner asks if its best hypothesis is the same as the target concept. The answer to such a query is either a yes or a counterinstance that belongs to the target concept but not to the hypothesis.

Using these active queries, it is hoped that effective learning algorithms can be found for learning concepts that are difficult to learn by traditional learning criteria. Some of the algorithms discussed in the following sections can be extended to active. But truly active algorithms will be discussed in the next chapter, where the environments are assumed to be translucent.

4.5   Learning from Attribute-Based Instances: Version Space and Related Algorithms

Using the aspects of concept learning just discussed, we now turn our attention to algorithms that learn from attribute-based concepts. We start with the version space [67], because it represents a family of learning algorithms that have been well studied; it also has implications for many recent developments in learning algorithms. Of course, there are many other algorithms that can also learn from attribute-based instances. Interested readers may find descriptions of ID3 in [85], the AQ family algorithms in [65], and the COBWEB algorithm in [24].

Version space is an algorithm that searches for the target concept from both ends of the partial order of concept space, and it terminates with the exact identification criterion. The idea of this algorithm is to maintain two boundaries, starting from both ends of the partial order, that enclose a set of concepts (i.e., the version space) that are consistent with all the training examples. A concept C is considered to be *consistent* with a set of examples if and only if all examples that are labeled with the target concept are included in C and all examples that are labeled with the nontarget concept are excluded from C.

The frontiers of the search are represented as two sets of concepts: the set S that delimits the more specific end of the version space and the set G that delimits the more general end. More precisely, the sets S and G are defined as follows:

$S = \{ s \mid s$ is a concept that is consistent with the observed examples and there is no other concept more specific than s that is consistent with the observed examples$\}$

$G = \{ g \mid g$ is a concept that is consistent with the observed examples and there is no other concept more general than g that is consistent with the observed examples$\}$

The set of all concepts that are between G and S with respect to the partial order is the *version space*. Whether a given concept m is in the version space delimited by G and S can be determined by the following criteria:

1. m is more specific than or equal to some member of G, and

2. m is more general than or equal to some member of S.

1   For each new instance i,
2   If i is a negative example, then
3   Retain in S only those concepts which do not cover i,
4   For each $g \in G$ that covers i, do:
5   Specialize g so that it no longer covers i,
6   Remove from G any concept that is more specific than some
                        other concept in G or every $s \in S$,
7   Else (i.e., i is a positive example)
8   Retain in G only those concepts that cover i,
9   For each $s \in S$ that does not cover i, do:
10   Generalize s so that it no longer covers i,
11   Remove from S any concept that is more general than some
                        other concept in S or every $g \in G$,
12   If either G or S is empty, then
13   Declare that no concept in the concept space is consistent
                    with the examples.

Figure 4.7   The version space learning algorithm.

Notice that the relation of general to specific is defined by the partial order of the concepts (see Section 4.4.1).

Initially the sets S and G are the sets of the maximally specific and maximally general concepts, respectively, that are consistent with the first observed positive example. As more examples become available, the sets S and G are updated according to the algorithm illustrated in Figure 4.7. As we can see, the G set is made more specific every time a negative example is observed, while the S set is made more general every time a positive example is observed. Eventually the two frontiers meet each other ($G = S$), and the target concept is identified.

Given the concept lattice, specializing a concept $g \in G$ to exclude a negative instance i (line 5) is accomplished by going *down* in the lattice to the first concept that does not cover i. For example, suppose $g = \{23456\}$ (the set covers instances 2, 3, 4, 5, and 6) and the negative instance is 5. Then the g is specialized to become $\{2346\}$. Similarly, generalizing a concept $s \in S$ to cover a new positive instance i (line 10) is accomplished by climbing *up* in the lattice to the first concept such that C' covers i as well. For example, suppose the current concept is $s = \{23\}$; to cover a new positive instance 6, the concept is generalized to $\{236\}$.

To illustrate the algorithm, consider the task of learning the target concept (*shape = circle*) (i.e., ($\bullet$,*circle*)) in the concept space shown in Figure 4.4. Suppose that the given examples are ((*small*, *circle*) +), ((*large*, *triangle*) −), ((*large,circle*) +), and ((*large,square*) +), where + means the example is positive and − means negative. Version space can learn the concept in three steps as shown in Figure 4.8.

After seeing $((small,\ circle)\ +)$, initialize the version space:

G: $(\bullet, \bullet)$
            $(small, \bullet)$ $(\bullet, circle)$
S: $(small, circle)$

After seeing $((large, triangle)\ -)$, update G:

G: $(small,\ \bullet)$ $(\bullet, circle)$
S: $(small,\ circle)$

After seeing $((large, circle)\ +)$, update S:

G = S: $(\bullet, circle)$

Figure 4.8   An example of version space learning.

As you may have noticed, the version space algorithm is rather resource demanding. The size of G or S can grow exponentially large with respect to the number of instances in the instance space. In the above example, for instance, if the concept space is not restricted (e.g., using Figure 4.3 instead of Figure 4.4), the algorithm will take much longer to converge.

From the above example, one can also see that some inductive biases may have devastating effects on version space. If the target concept is $(\bullet, circle) \vee (\bullet, square)$ instead of $(\bullet, circle)$, then after the first three examples are processed, the version space jumps to the conclusion $(\bullet, circle)$ even though it has never seen an example of squares. When the fourth positive instance $(large, square)$ is presented, the version space becomes empty and fails to learn anything further. This failure is due to the choice of a poorly biased concept space that does not include the target concept at all.

Furthermore, applying version space directly to learning existential conjunctive concepts from structured instances is too expensive in computation. In particular, it has been proved that such an application is NP-complete [34] because a special case of this task is equivalent to the problem of subgraph isomorphism for directed graphs, which is known to be NP-complete.

Moreover, even if no binary relations are defined, each attribute is Boolean valued, and each example contains exactly two objects, finding an existential conjunctive concept that is consistent with a sequence of m examples over an instance space defined by n attributes (where m and n are variable) is still NP-complete [34]. The proof is based on the reduction of a known NP-hard problem, SAT [26], to this problem.

As we pointed out earlier, version space takes advantage of the partial order of concepts using a bidirectional search. However, one-way search strategies are also possible. If the search in the lattice is conducted one way from the specific to

1   For each new instance i,
2   If i is a negative example,
3   Then remember i in a list,
4   Else for each $s \in S$ that does not cover i, do:
5   Generalize s to cover i,
6   Remove from S any concept that is more general than some other
                    concept in S;
7   After all examples are seen, do:
8   If any negative example is included in the concepts in S,
9   Then declare that no concept in the concept space is consistent with
                the examples,
10   Else return a concept in S.

Figure 4.9   The S-to-G version space learning algorithm.

1   For each new instance i,
2   If i is a positive example,
3   Then remember i in a list,
4   Else for each $g \in G$ that covers i, do:
5   Specialize g to exclude i,
6   Remove from G any concept that is more specific
                    than some other concept in G;
7   After all examples are seen, do:
8   If any positive example is not included in the concepts in G,
9   Then declare that no concept in the concept space
                is consistent with the examples,
10   Else return a concept in G.

Figure 4.10   The G-to-S version space learning algorithm.

the general, then we have the S-to-G version space algorithm shown in Figure 4.9. This algorithm is the same as version space except that only the S set is updated. Compared to version space, this algorithm is not completely incremental because it must remember all the negative examples and be told when all the examples have been seen.

Similarly, we can also design algorithms that search the concept lattice from the general to the specific. This algorithm, G-to-S version space, is listed in Figure 4.10. The algorithm should be self-explanatory because it is symmetric to the S-to-G version space.

Both S-to-G and G-to-S are more efficient than version space in many circumstances. For example, in learning concepts of conjunctive attributes, the S set in the S-to-G version space will never become exponentially large. In fact, in the

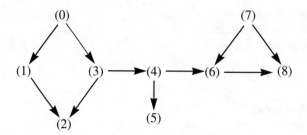

Figure 4.11   A small network illustrating structured instances.

above example of learning ($\bullet$, *circle*), this algorithm updates S only twice to find the target concept (*shape* = *circle*), and the S set contains only one concept during the entire learning process.

4.6   Learning from Structured Instances: The FOIL Algorithm

In this section, we use Quinlan's FOIL algorithm to illustrate the process of learning relational concepts from structured instances. Naturally, other algorithms are also available that can learn from structured instances [47, 128].

Unlike attribute-based concepts that describe properties of single objects, relational concepts are expressions about relations between objects. The instances of a relational concept, therefore, are tuples of objects that satisfy the relation. For example, suppose we are interested in the relation $LinkedTo(x, y)$ in the network shown in Figure 4.11; then the positive instances of this relation are the following tuples:

[0,1], [0,3], [1,2], [3,2], [3,4], [4,5], [4,6], [6,8], [7,6], [7,8]

Notice that the relation $LinkedTo(x, y)$ in this case is defined *extensionally*. That is, it is defined by a set of instances. These instances are positive examples of the relation (they all satisfy the relation). In general, extensionally defined relations also have negative examples (those that do not satisfy the relation). For example, the negative examples of $LinkedTo(x, y)$ in Figure 4.11 are the following tuples:

[0,0], [0,2], [0,4], [0,5], [0,6], [0,7], [0,8], [1,0], [1,1], [1,3], [1,4], [1,5], [1,6], [1,7], [1,8], [2,0], [2,1], [2,2], [2,3], [2,4], [2,5], [2,6], [2,7], [2,8], [3,0], [3,1], [3,3], [3,5], [3,6], [3,7], [3,8], [4,0], [4,1], [4,2], [4,3], [3,4], [4,7], [4,8], [5,0], [5,1], [5,2], [5,3], [5,4], [5,5], [5,6], [5,7], [5,8], [6,0], [6,1], [6,2], [6,3], [6,4], [6,5], [6,6], [6,7], [7,0], [7,1], [7,2], [7,3], [7,4], [7,5], [7,7], [8,0], [8,1], [8,2], [8,3], [8,4], [8,5], [8,6], [8,7], [8,8]

Quinlan describes an algorithm called FOIL that learns relational concepts from structured examples [89]. In FOIL, relations are represented as function-free and constant-free *Horn clauses* in the form

$$R \leftarrow L_1, L_2, \ldots, L_n$$

where R is a predicate to be learned and each *literal* L_i is either a predicate or the negation of a predicate. These predicates are selected from a given set of background predicates all defined extensionally; they can have variables but not functions or constants. The clause is interpreted as "if L_1 and L_2 and ... and L_n, then R." For example, a concept "node x can reach node y" in the above network can be represented as

$$CanReach(x,y) \quad \leftarrow \quad LinkedTo(x,y) \tag{4.1}$$
$$CanReach(x,y) \quad \leftarrow \quad LinkedTo(x,z) \wedge CanReach(z,y) \tag{4.2}$$

It is interesting to compare the Horn clauses with the existential conjunctive expressions discussed in Section 4.4.2. We can see that predicates in existential conjunctive expressions do not allow negations, but they can have constants or regions of values. The Horn clauses defined here, however, contain no constants but do permit negations and recursive definitions of predicates.

Since all predicates are extensionally defined, what it means for an instance i to satisfy a clause $R \leftarrow L_1, \ldots, L_i, \ldots, L_n$ must be carefully defined. Suppose that R and L_i are defined by sets of object tuples T and Q_i, respectively. Suppose further that R has k variables and L_i has variables $X \cup Y_i$ (X and Y_i are sets of variables) such that X is shared by L_i and R. Then we say that a given instance i (a tuple of k objects) satisfies the clause if and only if there exist variable bindings of X to i that make R true in T and *thereafter*, for each L_i, there exist variable bindings of Y_i to make L_i true in Q_i.

For example, in the above network the predicate $CanReach(x,y)$ is extensionally defined by the following positive and negative examples:

Positive examples of $CanReach(x,y)$:

[0,1], [0,2], [0,3], [0,4], [0,5], [0,6], [0,8], [1,2], [3,2], [3,4], [3,5], [3,6], [3,8], [4,5], [4,6], [4,8], [6,8], [7,6], [7,8]

Negative examples of $CanReach(x,y)$:

[0,0], [0,7], [1,0], [1,1], [1,3], [1,4], [1,5], [1,6], [1,7], [1,8], [2,0], [2,1], [2,2], [2,3], [2,4], [2,5], [2,6], [2,7], [2,8], [3,0], [3,1], [3,3], [3,7], [4,0], [4,1], [4,2], [4,3], [3,4], [4,7], [5,0], [5,1], [5,2], [5,3], [5,4], [5,5], [5,6], [5,7], [5,8], [6,0], [6,1], [6,2], [6,3], [6,4], [6,5], [6,6], [6,7], [7,0], [7,1], [7,2], [7,3], [7,4], [7,5], [7,7], [8,0], [8,1], [8,2], [8,3], [8,4], [8,5], [8,6], [8,7], [8,8]

We can see that the instance $[0, 8]$ satisfies the clause in equation 4.2 because there exist variable bindings $x = 0$, $y = 8$, and $z = 3$, such that $[x, y] = [0, 8]$ is in the set of positive examples of *CanReach*. Specifically, $[x, z] = [0, 3]$ is in the set of positive examples of *LinkedTo*, and $[3, 8]$ is in the set of positive examples of *CanReach*. On the other hand, the instance $[1, 8]$ does not satisfy equation 4.2 because there are no such bindings.

Given a set of positive and negative examples for some relational concept R and a set of background predicates that are extensionally defined, FOIL inductively generates a set of Horn clauses for the concept as shown in Figure 4.12. The algorithm repeatedly creates a new clause until all the positive examples satisfy some learned clauses. A new clause, created by calling the LearnClauseBody procedure, is guaranteed not to be satisfied by any negative examples. A new literal added to the body must be *connected* (i.e., share variables with the existing body). Among all the connected literals, FOIL selects the one that is satisfied by the most number of positive examples in E^+ and the least number of negative examples in E^-. (See [89] for the detailed mathematical formula.)

Let R be the relational concept to be learned.
Let G be a given set of background predicates.
Let POS and NEG be the positive and negative examples of R, respectively.

Procedure FOIL(POS, NEG):
1 VARS ← the variables used in R,
2 E^+ ← POS,
3 Until E^+ is empty, do:
4   (BODY, VARS) ← LearnClauseBody(NEG, E^+, VARS),
5   Create a Horn clause R ← BODY,
6   Remove from E^+ all examples that satisfy BODY,
7 Return all Horn clauses created.

Procedure LearnClauseBody(E^-, E^+, VARS):
1 Let BODY be empty,
2 Until E^- is empty, do:
3   Select a *connected* literal L that is satisfied by the most number
        of examples in E^+ and the least number of examples in E^-,
        (L is connected if its predicate is in G and its variables overlap with VARS)
4   Add the new variables in L to VARS,
5   Conjoin L with BODY,
6   Remove from E^- all examples that do not satisfy BODY,
7 Return BODY and VARS.

Figure 4.12   The FOIL algorithm.

To illustrate the algorithm, consider an example of learning $CanReach(x, y)$ from the network in Figure 4.11, where the background predicates $LinkedTo$ and $CanReach$ are defined extensionally as above.

FOIL is called with POS equal to all the positive examples of $CanReach$ and NEG equal to all the negative examples of $CanReach$. Initially, then, we have

$$
\begin{aligned}
E^+ &= \text{all positive examples of } CanReach \\
E^- &= \text{all negative examples of } CanReach \\
\text{VARS} &= \{x, y\}
\end{aligned}
$$

Then LearnClauseBody is called to construct a clause. If the first literal selected is $LinkedTo(x, y)$, then none of the examples in E^- satisfies this literal and LearnClauseBody returns $LinkedTo(x, y)$. So FOIL builds a new clause

$$CanReach(x, y) \leftarrow LinkedTo(x, y)$$

and updates the set E^+ (positive examples not yet satisfying the existing clauses) as follows:

$$E^+ = [0,2], [0,4], [0,5], [0,6], [0,8], [3,5], [3,6], [3,8], [4,8]$$

When LearnClauseBody is called again, VARS is still $\{x, y\}$. Suppose on the first iteration the procedure selects the literal $LinkedTo(x, z)$, then the examples $[2, \cdot]$, $[5, \cdot]$, and $[8, \cdot]$ in E^- will be deleted because they do not satisfy $LinkedTo(x, z)$. On the second iteration, the procedure LearnClauseBody can choose either $CanReach(z, y)$ or $LinkedTo(z, y)$. However, $CanReach(z, y)$ is selected because it is satisfied by more positive examples in E^+ than $LinkedTo(z, y)$. In particular, notice that the instance $[0, 8]$ in E^+ does not satisfy $LinkedTo(z, y)$ because after binding $x = 0$ and $y = 8$, there is no binding for z such that $LinkedTo(0, z)$ and $LinkedTo(z, 8)$ can both be true according to the predicate's extensional definition. On the other hand, the instance $[0, 8]$ can indeed satisfy $CanReach(z, y)$ because there is a binding $z = 3$ (after x and y are bound as above) so that both $LinkedTo(0, z)$ and $CanReach(z, 8)$ are true according to their extensional definitions. Since the new body $LinkedTo(0, z) \wedge CanReach(z, 8)$ now eliminates all the negative examples in E^-, it is returned from the procedure LearnClauseBody. FOIL then builds the second clause

$$CanReach(x, y) \leftarrow LinkedTo(x, z) \wedge CanReach(z, y)$$

At this point, all the positive examples in E^+ satisfy this new clause and FOIL terminates.

4.7 Complementary Discrimination Learning (CDL)

Most concept learning algorithms share a common property: Their search strategies are monotonic. For example, as more examples become available, both boundaries of a version space move monotonically along the partial order of the concepts; the S set becomes monotonically more general and the G set becomes monotonically more specific.

In the literature of machine learning, the monotonic search strategy is represented by two basic learning approaches: learning by generalization and learning by discrimination. In learning by generalization, search for a target concept proceeds in a hypothesis space from specific to general, guided by similarities between instances. Winston's work on learning the concept of arch is a typical example [135]. In learning by discrimination, on the other hand, search proceeds from general to specific guided by differences between instances. Feigenbaum and Simon's EPAM [22] and Quinlan's ID3 [85] serve as good representatives. Although many algorithms, such as version space [69], counterfactuals [128], and STAR [64], have used both methods, few of them have revealed the relations between these two seemingly very different approaches and the usage of such relations for designing better learning algorithms.

In this section, we introduce a framework called *complementary discrimination learning* (CDL) for unifying generalization and discrimination. The key observation is that generalizing a hypothesis is equivalent to discriminating its complement, and vice versa. Thus, in order to generalize a hypothesis, one discriminates its complement. In order to generalize the complement, one discriminates the hypothesis. In light of this framework, learning a target concept can be viewed as adjusting or moving the boundary between a hypothesis and its complement until the hypothesis boundary converges to the boundary between the target concept and its complement. Notice that the search pursues nonmonotonically, for the current hypothesis concept may become either more general or more specific, depending on the nature of the new examples.

Like other concept learning algorithms, CDL learns from instances. As we now know, instances can be viewed as points defined in the instance space and concepts (hypotheses) as regions in such a space. To learn a target concept C, CDL maintains a current hypothesis boundary, represented by the two sides of the boundary H and $\overline{H}$, and adjusts or moves this boundary until it converges to the boundary between the target concept C and its complement $\overline{C}$. To fulfill this objective, CDL must accomplish three tasks for every training instance it processes: (1) determining whether and in which direction to move the boundary, (2) finding out how much the boundary should be moved, and (3) actually moving the boundary.

Before discussing these three tasks, let us first set up a simple learning task as an illustration. Consider a set of instances that are represented by binary feature vectors (x_1, x_2, x_3, x_4): 0000, 0001, 0010, ..., 1110, and 1111. We can use Boolean

Inputs: A set of previous examples E, and a new instance i.
Outputs: The minimal differences to distinguish E from i.
Procedure DIFFERENCES(E, i):
1   Let D be $\{e \backslash i \mid e \in E\}$ where $e \backslash i$ is the set of features that are in e but
       not in i,
2   Order the elements in D by their length,
3   Return elements from the beginning of D until *all* examples in E are
       distinguished from i.

Figure 4.13   Finding the minimal differences.

formulas of these features to represent sets of instances (i.e., concepts and hypotheses). For example, the singleton instance set $\{1101\}$ is represented as $x_1 x_2 \overline{x_3} x_4$, and the set of instances whose first two features are 10 or whose third feature is 1 is represented as $x_1 \overline{x_2} \vee x_3$. We say that an instance i belongs to or is covered by a concept C (or hypothesis H) if $i \in C$ (or $i \in H$). In the following discussion, we assume the concept to be learned is $C = (x_2 \vee x_3) x_4$.

For the first task, that is, determining the direction of boundary movement, CDL uses the following strategy. When a new training instance is processed, CDL predicts that the instance belongs to one of the hypothesized complements, either H or $\overline{H}$, depending on which side of the boundary the instance lies. If the prediction is correct, CDL simply remembers the new instance as an example of the hypothesis and no boundary movement is necessary. If the prediction is wrong, then the boundary should be moved towards the hypothesis in the prediction. For example, if the current hypothesis is $H = (x_2 \vee x_3)$ and the new instance is $i = 1100$, then the prediction $i \in H$ is wrong because $i \notin C$. In this case, the boundary should be moved towards H. That is, H should be "shrunk" and $\overline{\overline{H}}$ should be "expanded."

Since each hypothesis is associated with a list of previous examples that belong to the hypothesis, to find out how much that hypothesis should be shrunk (i.e., the second task) entails finding the differences between the new instance and all the previous examples of that hypothesis. The differences will be a list of conjunctions of features that are true for previous examples but false for the new instance. The list can be interpreted as a disjunctive Boolean formula of conjunctive features. To find the minimum amount of differences that distinguish the previous examples from the new instance, CDL uses the "minimum description" heuristic implemented in the procedure presented in Figure 4.13. Given a set of examples, this procedure first computes the set difference between each individual example and the new instance. It then orders these differences by their length in a list and returns the elements from the beginning of the list until all the previous examples are distinguished from the new instance. To illustrate this procedure, suppose that the previous examples of $H = (x_2 \vee x_3)$ are 0011, 0010, 1010, and 1111, and the new instance is 1100. Then the difference list is $(\overline{x_1 x_2} x_3 x_4, \overline{x_1 x_2} x_3, \overline{x_2} x_3, x_3 x_4)$. Ordering this list by length,

1   Let C be the target concept, H and $\overline{H}$ be the hypothesis boundary,
2   For each new instance i, do:
3   If $i \in H$, then set the prediction $P = H$, else $P = \overline{H}$,
4   If $i \in C$, then set the feedback $F = positive$, else $F = negative$,
5   If the prediction is correct, i.e., $(P = H) \wedge (F = positive)$ or
     $(P = \overline{H}) \wedge (F = negative)$,
6   Then store i as an example of P,
7   Else (this is a surprise)
8   Let $D = \text{DIFFERENCES}(\text{examplesOf}(P), i)$,
9   Use D to shrink P and expand the complement of P,
10   Store i as an example of the complement of P.

Figure 4.14   The basic CDL framework: *predict, surprise, identify*, and *revise*.

we have $(\overline{x_2}x_3, x_3x_4, \overline{x_1x_2}x_3, \overline{x_1x_2}x_3x_4)$. The first two elements, $\overline{x_2}x_3$ and x_3x_4, are returned as the differences because they are sufficient to distinguish all the previous examples from the new instance: $\overline{x_2}x_3$ distinguishes (0011, 0010, 1010) from 1100, and x_3x_4 distinguishes (1111) from 1100.

After the differences are found, the task of moving the boundary (i.e., the third task) is accomplished by shrinking the incorrect hypothesis and expanding its complement. The new instance is then remembered as an example of the expanded (complement) hypothesis. In some simple cases, such as learning propositional logic expressions, the shrinking can be done by conjoining the hypothesis with the differences. The expanding can be done by setting the complement to be the negation of the shrunken hypothesis. For example, to shrink the hypothesis $H = (x_2 \vee x_3)$ using the differences $(\overline{x_2}x_3 \vee x_3x_4)$ just found, one can set H and $\overline{H}$ to be

$$
\begin{aligned}
H &= (x_2 \vee x_3) \wedge (\overline{x_2}x_3 \vee x_3x_4) = x_3(\overline{x_2} \vee x_4) \\
\overline{H} &= \neg H = \overline{x_3} \vee x_2\overline{x_4}
\end{aligned}
$$

Notice that the new instance 1100 is no longer covered by the new hypothesis H but belongs to $\overline{H}$. It is remembered as an example of $\overline{H}$.

4.7.1   The Framework of Predict-Surprise-Identify-Revise

With the solutions for the three tasks in place, the CDL framework can be summarized as the *predict-surprise-identify-revise* procedure shown in Figure 4.14. Whenever a new instance is seen, CDL first predicts the classification of the instance based on the current hypothesis boundary (i.e., classifies the new instance). If the prediction is correct, then CDL remembers the instance as an example of the hypothesis in the prediction. Otherwise, CDL has a surprise (i.e., the prediction does not match the feedback). In this case, CDL first identifies the source of the surprise by comparing this new instance with all known good examples, then revises the current concepts by moving the hypothesis boundary in the proper direction. The new instance is remembered as an example of the complement of the prediction.

Although we have introduced CDL in the context of concept learning, the *predict-surprise-identify-revise* framework can be presented easily in the context of learning from the environment. In that case, as shown in Figure 4.15, every time CDL is about to do some action in the environment, it makes a prediction based on the current model that has been learned (e.g., a prediction rule of state-action-prediction). It then executes the action, observes the actual consequence of the action, and compares the consequence with the prediction. If it is a surprise, CDL identifies the reason for that surprise by finding the differences between the current state-action-prediction and some previous experience of that particular rule. The differences so found are then used to revise the current model (e.g., revise the state condition of the prediction rule).

We will shortly see that the CDL framework is general and powerful. In particular, it is used for learning Boolean concepts, decision lists, and prediction rules. In later chapters, we will find that CDL provides the basis for designing an extended framework for learning from translucent environments. Such an extended framework is used to learn translucent finite automata (Section 5.7), and it is at the heart of the LIVE system to abstract models from the environment (Chapter 10) and to discover hidden features in the environment (Chapter 11). But before all that discussion, let us walk through a complete example to see how CDL works.

Consider again the shape-size example in Section 4.5. Let the target concept be $(\bullet, circle) \vee (\bullet, square)$ and the examples be $((small, circle)\ +)$, $((large, triangle)\ -)$,

1   Let M be the current model,
2   Let c be the current observation,
3   Let t be the current model state ($t = c$ in transparent environments),
4   Select a sequence of actions b,
5   For each action $a \in b$, do:
6   Make a prediction P based on $M : (C, a) \rightarrow P$, where C matches c,
7   Execute a in the environment,
8   Observe the actual consequence (or feedback) o from the environment,
9   If the prediction is correct (i.e., P matches o),
10   Then record the experience (c, a, o) as an example of $(C, a) \rightarrow P$,
11   Else (this is a surprise) do:
12   Identify the differences D between c and the examples of $(C, a) \rightarrow P$,
13   Revise M using D so that c is distinguished from C
                 and (c, a) has a prediction that matches o,
14   Record (c, a, o) as an example of the proper entry of M.

Figure 4.15 The CDL framework for learning from transparent environments.

$((large, circle) +)$, and $((large, square) +)$. (Recall that version space fails to learn this concept when the concept space is biased as in Figure 4.4.) CDL learns this concept as follows. When the first example, $((small, circle) +)$, is given, the algorithm forms its initial hypothesis:

H_0: $(size = \bullet) \wedge (shape = \bullet)$; $[(small, circle)]$
$\overline{H_0}$: $\emptyset$; $[\ ]$

The symbol $\bullet$ means "don't care," and the square brackets contain the successful instances for the hypothesis. When the second instance, $(large, triangle)$, is presented, the algorithm predicts that the instance belongs to H_0 (because $(large, triangle)$ matches H_0), but the prediction is wrong. It then compares $(small, circle)$, the success, with $(large, triangle)$, the failure, and finds that the difference is $(size = small) \wedge (shape = circle)$, which is true for the success but false for the failure. Putting the difference in conjunction with H_0, the algorithm shrinks or specializes H_0 as follows:

H_1: $(size = small) \wedge (shape = circle)$; $[(small, circle)]$

By negating H_1, the algorithm constructs $\overline{H_1}$ as follows:

$\overline{H_1}$: $\neg((size = small) \wedge (shape = circle))$
      $\Rightarrow \neg(size = small) \vee \neg(shape = circle)$
      $\Rightarrow \neg(size = small) \vee (shape = square) \vee (shape = triangle)$;
      $[(large, triangle)]$

Note that $\neg(shape = circle)$ is written as $(shape = square) \vee (shape = triangle)$ because it is known that the shape attribute has only these three possible values.

When the third instance, $(large, circle)$, is given, the algorithm predicts that the instance is negative because it matches $\overline{H_1}$. After being surprised, the algorithm compares $(large, triangle)$, the success of $\overline{H_1}$, with $(large, circle)$, the failure of $\overline{H_1}$, and finds that the difference is $(shape = triangle)$. Therefore, the hypothesis $\overline{H_1}$ is shrunk to become $\overline{H_2}$ by a conjunction with the difference, and H_1 is expanded to become H_2 by negating $\overline{H_2}$:

$\overline{H_2}$: $\overline{H_1} \wedge (shape = triangle) \Rightarrow (shape = triangle)$; $[(large, triangle)]$
H_2: $\neg(shape = triangle) \Rightarrow (shape = circle) \vee (shape = square)$;
      $[(small, circle)(large, circle)]$

At this point, the algorithm has learned the target concept. When the fourth instance, $(large, square)$, is presented, the algorithm correctly predicts that it is a positive example.

It is interesting to see how the algorithm could go further if the target concept were $(shape = circle)$ instead of $(shape = circle) \vee (shape = square)$. The fourth instance, $(large, square)$, would be negative, and the algorithm's last prediction would fail. That would force the algorithm to discriminate the hypothesis H_2 further. In that case, the algorithm would compare the previous successful instances $(large, circle)$ and $(small, circle)$ with the failure $(large, square)$ and find that the difference is $(shape = circle)$. Thus, the hypothesis H_2 would be shrunk to H_3 and $\overline{H_2}$ expanded to become the negation of H_3:

H_3: $((shape = circle) \vee (shape = square)) \wedge (shape = circle)$
$\qquad \Rightarrow (shape = circle); \quad [(small, circle)(large, circle)]$
$\overline{H_3}$: $\neg(shape = circle); \quad [(large, triangle)(large, square)]$

As we can see from this example, the idea of CDL is very simple. However, the framework has profound implications for designing new and powerful learning algorithms. In the next few sections, we will see that the CDL framework can be used to learn concepts from both attribute-based and structured instances. Interestingly, in some applications, CDL-based algorithms can outperform the best known algorithms.

4.8   Using CDL to Learn Boolean Concepts

4.8.1   The CDL1 Algorithm

In this section, we describe an implementation of the CDL framework, called CDL1, for learning concepts that are represented as expressions in propositional logic. In this context, instances are represented as binary feature vectors $(x_1, x_2, \ldots, x_n)$, and concepts and hypotheses are represented as Boolean formulae of features. For example, the concept (or hypothesis) $x_1 \wedge x_2$ represents the set of instances whose first two features are 1. Similarly, $\overline{x_4} \vee x_6$ represents the set of instances whose fourth feature is 0 or whose sixth feature is 1. The complement of a concept is represented as the negation of the concept. For example, the complement of $(x_1 \vee x_2)(\overline{x_3})$ is $(\overline{x_1 x_2}) \vee (x_3)$. We say a concept C (or a hypothesis H) covers an instance i if $i \in C$ (or $i \in H$). As extremes, the concept (hypothesis) $true$ covers everything and the concept (hypothesis) $false$ covers nothing.

The algorithm CDL1, shown in Figure 4.16, is just a simple implementation of the CDL framework. It can be easily understood in terms of the three tasks discussed before. For the first two tasks, that is, making predictions and determining the direction of boundary movement, CDL1 uses the same solution outlined in Section 4.7. For the third task, that is, moving the hypothesis boundary, CDL1 uses a procedure called REVISE to implement tasks that are specifically required for the representation.

The procedure REVISE performs two functions: It keeps the shrunken hypothesis in a canonical form, either in disjunctive normal form (DNF) or conjunctive normal form (CNF), and it resolves contradictions that may be contained in some conjunctions of features. The reason for keeping hypotheses in a canonical form is

Procedure CDL1():

1   Let C be the target concept, and H and $\overline{H}$ be the hypothesis boundary,

2     $H \leftarrow true$, and $\overline{H} \leftarrow false$,

3   For each new instance i, do:

4   If $i \in H$, then set the prediction $P = H$, else $P = \overline{H}$,

5   If $i \in C$, then set the feedback $F = positive$, else $F = negative$,

6   If the prediction is correct, i.e., $(P = H) \wedge (F = positive)$

          or $(P = \overline{H}) \wedge (F = negative)$,

7   Then store i as an example of P,

8   Else store i as an example of the complement of P, and

9   Let $D = $ DIFFERENCES(examplesOf(P), i),

10   If $(P = H)$,

11   Then $H \leftarrow$ REVISE(H, D, examplesOf($\overline{H}$)), and $\overline{H} \leftarrow \neg H$,

12   Else $\overline{H} \leftarrow$ REVISE($\overline{H}$, D, examplesOf(H)), and $H \leftarrow \neg \overline{H}$.

Procedure REVISE(P, D, NEG):

1   If $(P = true)$, then return D,

2   If P is in CNF, then convert D to CNF and return $P \wedge D$,

3   Convert $\Phi = P \wedge D$ to DNF and for each conjunction $\phi \in \Phi$, do:

4   If ϕ is logically subsumed by some other conjunction in Φ,

5   Then delete ϕ from Φ,

6   If $\phi = \psi x \overline{x}$ (i.e., ϕ contains some contradictions),

7   Then let $S(\phi)$ be a predicate "ϕ covers no examples in NEG,"

8   If $S(\psi x)$ is true and $S(\psi \overline{x})$ is false,

9   Then replace ϕ in Φ by ψx,

10   If $S(\psi \overline{x})$ is true and $S(\psi x)$ is false,

11   Then replace ϕ in Φ by $\psi \overline{x}$,

12   Else delete ϕ from Φ,

13   Return Φ.

Figure 4.16   The CDL1 learning algorithm.

for computational efficiency. Since CDL1 needs to ensure that H and $\overline{H}$ are always complementary, the operation of complement is performed very frequently. The canonical form can make this operation more efficient. Notice that CDL1 maintains the fact that if a hypothesis is in DNF, then its complement must be in CNF, and vice versa.

When the shrunken hypothesis is in DNF, some of the conjunctions may be redundant and some may have contradictions that need to be resolved. For example, suppose $D = \overline{x_1} \vee x_2 \overline{x_4}$, $H = \overline{x_1} x_2 \vee x_3 x_4$, and the examples of $\overline{H}$ (i.e., the "opposite" examples of H) are 1110, 1100, and 1010. Then the shrunken hypothesis $\Phi = H \wedge D$ is $\overline{x_1} x_2 \vee \overline{x_1} x_3 x_4 \vee \overline{x_1} x_2 \overline{x_4} \vee x_2 x_3 x_4 \overline{x_4}$. Among these four conjunctions, $\overline{x_1} x_2 \overline{x_4}$ will be

Class	Description			Representation (abcd)
	Height	Hair	Eyes	
−	short	blond	brown	0010
−	tall	dark	brown	1000
+	tall	blond	blue	1011
−	tall	dark	blue	1001
−	short	dark	blue	0001
+	tall	red	blue	1101
−	tall	blond	brown	1010
+	short	blond	blue	0011

Table 4.1   A simple learning task.

deleted because it is subsumed by $\overline{x_1}x_2$; $x_2x_3x_4\overline{x_4}$ contains a contradiction and will be replaced by $x_2x_3x_4$, which does not cover any opposite examples, while $x_2x_3\overline{x_4}$ does. Therefore, the new shrunken hypothesis is $H = \overline{x_1}x_2 \vee \overline{x_1}x_3x_4 \vee x_2x_3x_4$.

Note that although CDL1 uses binary features to represent instances, it can easily be extended to deal with multiple-valued features using multiple binary feature variables. For example, if a feature x_i has values 1, 2, and 3, then two binary variables x_{i1} and x_{i2} can be used to represent this feature. In this case, $x_i{=}1$ is represented as $x_{i1}x_{i2} = 00$, $x_i = 2$ is represented as $x_{i1}x_{i2} = 01$, and $x_i = 3$ is represented as $x_{i1}x_{i2} = 10$.

To illustrate CDL1, let us consider a classical learning task [85]. Each instance is described by three nonbinary features: *height*, color of *hair*, and color of *eyes*. The instances and their representations in CDL1 are shown in Table 4.1. We use variable a to represent height (0 for short and 1 for tall), bc for color of hair (00 for dark, 01 for blond, and 10 for red), and d for color of eyes (0 for brown and 1 for blue).

The performance of CDL1 on this task is summarized in Table 4.2. When the first instance arrives, CDL1 predicts that the instance belongs to H, but the feedback says that is wrong. Since H has no previous example yet, the procedure DIFFERENCES returns NIL and the procedure REVISE sets H to *false* and $\overline{H}$ to *true*. The instance is remembered as an example of $\overline{H}$. On the second instance, CDL1 predicts that it belongs to $\overline{H}$. Since the prediction is correct, the hypotheses remain the same and the instance is remembered as another example of $\overline{H}$. On the third instance, CDL1's prediction is again wrong. Since $\overline{H}$ has two examples {0010, 1000}, their differences compared to the instance 1011 are found to be $\overline{a}\overline{d} \vee \overline{c}\overline{d}$. The procedure REVISE sets $\overline{H}$ to be $true \wedge (\overline{a}\overline{d} \vee \overline{c}\overline{d}) = \overline{a}\overline{d} \vee \overline{c}\overline{d}$, and CDL1 sets H to be $(a \vee d)(c \vee d)$. The instance is remembered as an example of H.

Based on the new hypotheses, CDL1 predicts that the fourth instance is in H but the prediction is wrong. This time, the instance 1001 is compared with H's

Instance	Prediction	Feedback	Difference	H	$\overline{H}$
0010	H	–	NIL	*true* *false*	*false* *true*
1000	$\overline{H}$	–			
1011	$\overline{H}$	+	$\overline{a}\overline{d} \vee \overline{c}\overline{d}$		$\overline{a}\overline{d} \vee \overline{c}\overline{d}$
1001	H	–	c	$(a \vee d)(c \vee d)$ $(a \vee d)(c)$	
0001	$\overline{H}$	–			$\overline{a}\overline{d} \vee \overline{c}$
1101	$\overline{H}$	+	$\overline{b}$		$\overline{a}\overline{b}\overline{d} \vee \overline{b}\overline{c}$
1010	H	–	d	$(a \vee b \vee d)(b \vee c)$ $(b \vee c)(d)$	
0011	H	+			$\overline{b}\overline{c} \vee \overline{d}$

Table 4.2   An example of CDL1 learning.

example set $\{1011\}$ and the difference found is (c). This difference is conjoined with H to form the new hypothesis $H = (a \vee d)(c)$, and $\overline{H}$ is set to be $\overline{a}\overline{d} \vee \overline{c}$. The instance is remembered as an example of $\overline{H}$.

CDL1's prediction on the fifth instance is correct, so hypotheses are not changed and the instance becomes an example of $\overline{H}$. When the sixth instance arrives, CDL1 predicts it is in $\overline{H}$. Upon noticing that the prediction is wrong, CDL1 finds the differences between 1101 and $\overline{H}$'s previous examples $\{0010, 1000, 1001, 0001\}$ to be $\overline{b}$. Thus, $\overline{H}$ is revised to be $\overline{a}\overline{b}\overline{d} \vee \overline{b}\overline{c}$ and H to be $(a \vee b \vee d)(b \vee c)$. The instance is remembered as an example of H. Using these new hypotheses, CDL1 predicts that the seventh instance is in H, but the prediction is again wrong. Comparing 1010 with H's previous examples $\{1011, 1101\}$, CDL1 finds the difference to be (d). So the hypothesis H is revised to be $(b \vee c)(d)$, and $\overline{H}$ is revised to be $\overline{b}\overline{c} \vee \overline{d}$. At this point, the learned hypotheses classify all the instances correctly.

From this example, we can see that CDL1 manages the search for the target concept by "jumping" to a new hypothesis in the hypothesis space whenever the current hypothesis causes a prediction failure. This jumping may seem quite arbitrary or rash, but it is guided by the principle of finding the simplest boundary between the positive and negative instances seen so far. The landing place is neither the most general (liberal) nor the most specific (conservative) concept with respect to the instances that are available, but a place between these two extremes where the syntax structure is the simplest. The preference for seeking the simplest differences is the backbone of CDL's hypothesis selection.

4.8.2   Experiments and Analysis

To illustrate more of CDL1's performance, we now give detailed descriptions of two typical concept formation experiments: learning a multiplexor [7, 126] and learning a noisy LED display [11]. The data in the first task, although noise-free, contains exceptional cases that often cause problems for noise-tolerant algorithms.

Notice that both tasks involve learning multiple concepts. To use CDL1, multiple concepts (or classes) are represented by class variables. For example, to learn multiple classes W, X, Y, and Z, we will use two class variables c_1 and c_2 so that W, X, Y, and Z will be $c_1 c_2 = 00$, $c_1 c_2 = 01$, $c_1 c_2 = 10$, and $c_1 c_2 = 11$, respectively. These class variables will be given as inputs to CDL1 as if they were some extra features of instances. Thus, instead of telling CDL1 that an instance i belongs to a class C, we will state that (i, C) is a positive instance, i.e., $(i, C) \in H$. For example, to say that an instance 1001 belongs to W, we will say that $1001\overline{c_1 c_2}$ is a positive instance; to say that an instance 1100 does not belong to Y, we will say $1100 c_1 \overline{c_2}$ is a negative instance, i.e., $1100 c_1 \overline{c_2} \in \overline{H}$. Using these class variables, CDL1 can learn multiple concepts even though syntactically it learns only a single concept. For example, W, X, Y, and Z will be learned as a compound target concept $(\cdots W) \vee (\cdots X) \vee (\cdots Y) \vee (\cdots Z)$.

In the first experiment, CDL1 is to learn a multiplexor, shown in Figure 4.17, based on the input/output behavior. The inputs a and b indicate which input among c, d, e, or f will be output at g. Since variables are binary valued, there are 64 possible instances in this experiment. The task is to predict the output value given an input vector. This task is difficult for noise-free learning algorithms because the relevance of each of the four data-bit attributes to the output is a function of the values of the two address-bit attributes [125]. It is also difficult for noise-tolerant learning algorithms because every training case is equally important [134].

The 64 instances are presented incrementally to CDL1 as a circular list. CDL1's performance on this task is reported in Table 4.3, along with the performances of the algorithms reported in [125] and IWN [121]. The algorithms with "hats" are

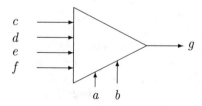

Figure 4.17   A multiplexor device.

Algorithm	Events	Running Time (sec.)	Accuracy (%)
ID3 †	53	630.4	100
$\widehat{\text{ID3}}$	61	92.3	100
ID4 ‡	384	327.7	63
$\widehat{\text{ID4}}$ ‡	384	258.1	50
ID5	57	184.3	100
$\widehat{\text{ID5}}$	74	83.5	100
IWN	320	(unknown)	97.6
CDL1	52	10.8	100

† Forced to run incrementally.
‡ Not stable.

Table 4.3   CDL1's performance in the multiplexor domain.

versions in which decision trees are updated only when the existing trees would misclassify a new training instance. One can see that CDL1 requires fewer training events (instances) to reach the 100% prediction rate. The time comparison is only a rough indicator because these algorithms are not tested on the same machine. Notice that ID3 is a nonincremental algorithm that was forced to run incrementally in this experiment.

It is interesting to note that the concept learned by CDL1 has a simple structure yet strong predictive power. For example, the concept of multiplexor learned by CDL1 is as follows:

$$\bar{a}\bar{b}c \vee \bar{a}bd \vee a\bar{b}e \vee abf \vee aef \vee bdf \vee \bar{a}cd \vee \bar{b}ce \vee cdef$$

This concept can be used to predict the output feature, even if the input features are not complete [25]. For instance, knowing only that features a, e, and f are true, one can conclude g even if the value of b, c, and d are unknown. The concept can also be used to predict other features when certain features are known. For instance, knowing that g is true and a is false, one can conclude that c or d must be true because the concept has three literals — $\bar{a}\bar{b}c$, $\bar{a}bd$, and $\bar{a}cd$ — that contain $\bar{a}$, and to make g true, one of $\bar{b}c$, bd, and cd must be true. This predictive ability is not easy to get if the concept is represented by a decision tree.

We now turn our attention to the second experiment of CDL1: learning a noisy LED display. The task is concerned with learning to predict decimal digits based on the displays of seven segments that are similar to those seen in the display on a normal calculator. To introduce noise, each display segment has a 10% chance of being inverted. The task is to recognize the correct digit despite the faulty

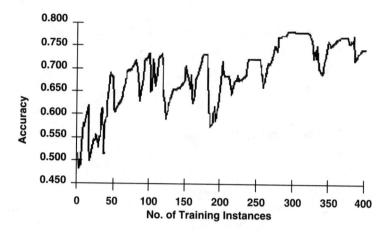

Figure 4.18   CDL's performance on noisy LED data.

display. Breiman [11] has shown that for a 10% noise rate, the upper bound for the performance of any system is 74%.

When the data are noisy, CDL1 must relax the criteria for finding differences. Instead of returning differences that distinguish *all* examples from the new instance, the procedure DIFFERENCES need only return differences that distinguish a sufficient number (say $M\%$) of previous examples from the new instance. In the following experiments, CDL1 is given $M = 90$ if the data are noisy. At the end of this section, we suggest a way to determine this parameter automatically.

We ran CDL1 incrementally on 400 randomly generated, 10% noise rate instances, uniformly distributed among the 10 digits. In this experiment, each instance had seven binary-valued attributes representing the seven segments, plus four class variables to represent the 10 digits (10 classes). Since CDL1 is incremental, we evaluated the performance whenever the concepts were revised. The test data were 500 instances that were randomly generated with the same noise rate. CDL1's performance curve is shown in Figure 4.18. The x-axis shows the number of training instances, and the y-axis shows the proportion of correct predictions on the 500 test instances. One can see that the prediction rate generally increased with the number of instances processed. After 350 instances, CDL1's performance oscillates around 74% (between 72.4% to 77%).[1] For comparison, the performance of the

---

[1]We think the reason that CDL1's performance is sometimes higher than 74% is that the testing data represent only a small subset of the sample space.

$$(U_l U_r \overline{M} B_l B_r B \bar{c}_1 \bar{c}_2 \bar{c}_3 \bar{c}_4) \vee (U U_l U_r \overline{M} B_l B \bar{c}_1 \bar{c}_2 \bar{c}_3 \bar{c}_4) \vee$$
$$(\overline{U M} B_l B_r \overline{B} \bar{c}_1 \bar{c}_2 \bar{c}_3 c_4) \vee$$
$$(\overline{U}_l U_r M \overline{B}_r B \bar{c}_1 \bar{c}_2 \bar{c}_4 c_3) \vee$$
$$(\overline{U}_l U_r \overline{B}_l B \bar{c}_1 \bar{c}_2 c_4 c_3)(U \overline{U}_l U_r \overline{M} B_l B \bar{c}_1 \bar{c}_2 c_4 c_3) \vee$$
$$(\overline{U} U_l \overline{B}_l \overline{B} \bar{c}_1 \bar{c}_3 \bar{c}_4 c_2) \vee$$
$$(\overline{U}_r \overline{B}_l \bar{c}_1 \bar{c}_3 c_4 c_2) \vee$$
$$(U_l \overline{U}_r M B_l \bar{c}_1 \bar{c}_4 c_3 c_2)(\overline{U}_r M B_l B_r \bar{c}_1 \bar{c}_4 c_3 c_2) \vee$$
$$(U \overline{U}_l \overline{M} B_l \bar{c}_1 c_3 c_2 c_4)(U \overline{U}_l \overline{U}_r \overline{M} \bar{c}_1 c_3 c_2 c_4) \vee$$
$$(U \overline{U}_l \overline{B}_l \overline{B} \bar{c}_1 c_3 c_2 c_4)(U \overline{U}_r \overline{M} B_l \overline{B} \bar{c}_1 c_3 c_2 c_4) \vee$$
$$(U_l U_r M B_l B \bar{c}_2 \bar{c}_3 \bar{c}_4 c_1)(U U_l U_r M B_l \bar{c}_2 \bar{c}_3 \bar{c}_4 c_1) \vee$$
$$(U_l U_r \overline{B}_l B \bar{c}_2 c_4 \bar{c}_3 c_1)(U U_l U_r \overline{B}_l \bar{c}_2 c_4 \bar{c}_3 c_1)$$

Figure 4.19 The LED concept learned from a noise-free display by CDL1. The variables $c_1 c_2 c_3 c_4$ represent the 10 digits. The variables U, U_l, U_r, M, B_l, B_r, and B represent the display of the *Upper*, *Up-Left*, *Up-Right*, *Middle*, *Bottom-Left*, *Bottom-Right*, and *Bottom* segment, respectively.

nonincremental algorithm IWN was 73.3% on 400 instances [121]; the performance of ID3 was 71.1% using 2000 training instances nonincrementally [88].

We also ran CDL1 on the LED data that were noise-free with $M = 100$. In that case, CDL1 learned the LED concept shown in Figure 4.19. It is interesting to note that each conjunction (a single line) in this concept can be viewed as a classification rule. Using these rules, one can infer the digit that is on display by matching the segments of the display to the description. For example, seeing that $U_l U_r \overline{M} B_l B_r B$ is displayed, one can infer a 0 (i.e., $\bar{c}_1 \bar{c}_2 \bar{c}_3 \bar{c}_4$) even if the upper segment is not lit.

It is important to note that when learning from noisy data there is always a trade-off between the simplicity of the learned concept and the accuracy of the concept on the given data. If this trade-off is not well managed, the learned concepts can "overfit" the data. Based on experiments in this domain, CDL1 seems to manage the trade-off well. For example, after processing 400 noisy instances in the LED domain, the concept learned by CDL1 is a DNF of 36 disjuncts. Running on additional instances does not jeopardize its simplicity or its predictive ability. We have also run CDL1 repeatedly on a database of 100 noisy LED instances; the number of disjuncts oscillates between 20 and 30, and the learned concept does not overfit the data.

Finally, as we pointed out earlier, CDL1 was given the parameter $M = 90$ for finding differences in this particular noisy domain. However, to learn from natural data, CDL1 must determine the value of M automatically. One way to achieve this is to initiate $M = 100$ and lower the value when evidence shows that the data are noisy. This can be done at the time of searching for the minimum number of differences using the following heuristic. When most of the differences distinguish only a single example from the new instance, the value of M should be lowered by some factor, say 0.05. With a lower M value, CDL1 can ignore some insignificant differences that are likely caused by noise.

We now turn our attention to analyze and estimate CDL1's complexity. Assuming that the data are noise-free, we first observe that if a new instance i is wrongly covered by a current hypothesis P, and the differences between the examples of P and i are D, then the shrunken hypothesis $P \wedge D$ will still cover the examples of P but exclude the examples of $\overline{P}$ and i. To see that this is true, let E be the examples of P, and $\overline{E}$ the examples of $\overline{P}$. Notice that the differences D are guaranteed to exclude i and cover E. Thus, $P \wedge D$ will still cover E because both P and D cover E; $P \wedge D$ will exclude $\overline{E}$ and i because P excludes $\overline{E}$ and D excludes i.

Now, let n be the number of instances seen so far and d the number of features of each instance. The procedure DIFFERENCES examines $O(dn \log n)$ attributes: $O(dn)$ for constructing D and $O(dn \log n)$ for sorting D and determining the minimum subset of D. The procedure REVISE examines $O(d|\Phi|n + |\Phi|^2)$ attributes because determining logical subsumption of each ϕ in Φ takes $|\Phi|^2$, and resolving contradictions takes at most $d|\Phi|n$.

To find a hypothesis that classifies all n instances correctly, CDL1 will loop no more than n times. Thus, the total number of attributes examined by CDL1 is

$$\sum_{i=1}^{n} O(di \log i + d|\Phi|i + |\Phi|^2) \approx O(dn^2 \log n)$$

Notice that this is just an estimate of complexity because we are ignoring the time for converting hypotheses into canonical forms.

4.9   Using CDL to Learn Decision Lists

As we saw in Section 4.8, the efficiency of the CDL framework depends on its implementation. In the case of CDL1, the hypothesis boundary is represented separately as H and $\overline{H}$. Consequently, one must make sure that H and $\overline{H}$ are complementary every time the boundary is moved. To save some computation, CDL1 keeps these two complements in canonical DNF and CNF forms. However, since the differences between a new instance and previous examples are always in DNF, it is computationally expensive to keep the concepts in these canonical forms. Moreover, CDL1 is awkward for multiple concepts. Since there is only one boundary to keep, the names of multiple concepts must be represented as artificial features of the instances so that CDL1 can learn them as if they were binary concepts.

Thus, in order to use the idea of CDL efficiently, a better representation for complementary concepts must be found. Decision lists seem to be an ideal choice. Decision lists have one nice property that is well suited to complementary discrimination learning: They are closed under complementation. This makes it possible to represent a concept and its complement in a single format, thus eliminating the burden of maintaining separate representations for complements. In the rest of this section, we will describe this idea in detail. The result is another implementation of the CDL framework, called CDL2, that represents concepts as decision lists. Since complementary discrimination is incremental, this implementation also represents the first incremental mechanism to learn decision lists.

The integration of complementary discrimination learning and decision lists gives some surprising results. The most salient one is efficiency. In the experiments we conducted, CDL2 outperforms some of the best incremental algorithms, including ID5r. When instances have a large number of attributes, CDL2 is even faster than some nonincremental algorithms such as ID3. Compared to back-propagation neural networks, CDL2 is much faster to train and has comparable results in recognizing handwritten numerals that are noisy and inconsistent. CDL2 also extends Rivest's definition of decision lists from binary concepts to multiple concepts. Such decision lists provide a compact representation for concepts. When applied to Quinlan's classic chess task [85], CDL2 has learned a decision list of 36 decisions, in contrast with the best decision tree of 58 decision nodes known in this domain [126].

4.9.1 The CDL2 Algorithm

A *decision list* is a representation schema proposed by Rivest for Boolean formulas [91]. He proves that k-DL (decision lists with functions that have at most k terms) are more expressive than k-CNF (conjunctive normal forms whose clauses contain at most k literals), k-DNF (disjunctive normal forms whose terms contain at most k literals), and decision trees. He also gives a polynomial-time algorithm for learning decision lists from instances. However, one of the open problems listed in his paper is that there is no known incremental algorithm for learning decision lists.

Following Rivest, a decision list is a list L of r pairs

$$L \equiv (f_1, v_1), \ldots, (f_r, v_r)$$

where each test function f_j is a conjunction of literals, each v_j is a value in $\{0, 1\}$, and the last function f_r is the constant function *true*. For convenience, a pair (f_j, v_j) is called the jth *decision*, f_j the jth *decision test*, and v_j the jth *decision value*. Here, we use an extended definition of decision lists in which v_j is a value from a finite set of concept names rather than from the binary set $\{0, 1\}$.

A decision list L defines a set of concepts as follows: For any instance x, the decision on x is defined to be $D_j = (f_j, v_j)$, where j is the least index such that $f_j(x) = 1$. The value v_j is the concept of x.

To see how decision lists represent concepts, consider the decision tree shown in Figure 4.20. The concept defined by this tree is equivalent to a Boolean formula in DNF:

$$\overline{x}_1 \overline{x}_3 \vee x_1 x_2 \vee x_1 \overline{x}_2 x_4$$

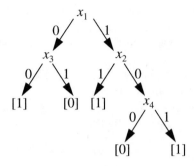

Figure 4.20 An example of a decision tree.

This can easily be translated into a decision list:

$$(\overline{x}_1\overline{x}_3, 1)(x_1x_2, 1)(x_1\overline{x}_2x_4, 1)(true, 0)$$

Since a decision list can have values other than 1s, the same concept can also be represented as either of the following two decision lists:

$$(\overline{x}_1\overline{x}_3, 1)(\overline{x}_1x_3, 0)(\overline{x}_2\overline{x}_4, 0)(true, 1)$$
$$(\overline{x}_1x_3, 0)(x_2, 1)(x_1\overline{x}_4, 0)(true, 1)$$

Decision lists make the movement of hypothesis boundaries easier. Let $|D|$ denote the domain of a decision $D = (f, v)$, which is a set of instances $\{x | f(x) = 1\}$. An interesting property of decision lists is that decisions with smaller indices block decisions with larger indices if their domains overlap. To discriminate a decision, one can simply shrink or break the domain of the decision so that instances that do not belong to this decision can "fall through" to later decisions that have the correct values.

Consider, for example, a decision list $((\overline{x}_3, 1)(true, 0))$. If evidence shows that the domain of $(\overline{x}_3, 1)$ is too large — that is, some part of that domain, say those that have $\overline{x}_1$, should have concept value 0 instead of 1 — then one can simply append $\overline{x}_1$ to $\overline{x}_3$ to shrink the decision $(\overline{x}_3, 1)$ and get a new decision list: $((\overline{x}_1\overline{x}_3, 1)(true, 0))$. This is actually the key concept of the new complementary discrimination learning algorithm CDL2.

Using decision lists, CDL2 accomplishes the three tasks of CDL differently from CDL1. For the first task, CDL2 does the following: When a new instance x (with a concept value v_x) arrives, the learner uses the current decision list to predict what concept the new instance belongs to. The prediction is the value v_j, where j is the least index such that $f_j(x) = 1$. If v_j is not equal to v_x, then the decision (f_j, v_j) is too general.

Since each decision in the decision list is associated with a list of previous examples that belong to the decision, to find out what part of f_j is overly general (i.e., how much to shrink the hypothesis) entails finding the difference between the new instance and all of the previous examples that belong to f_j. Again, the difference will be a list of terms that are true for previous examples but false for the new instance.

Let the differences so found be a list $\{\sigma_1, \ldots, \sigma_d\}$. To shrink or break the decision (f_j, v_j), we replace it with a list of new decisions $((f_j \wedge \sigma_1, v_j) \ldots (f_j \wedge \sigma_d, v_j))$. Clearly, none of the new decisions will capture the new instance again. The previous examples of the old decision are then distributed to these new decisions in the following manner: An example e is distributed to $f_j \wedge \sigma_i$ where i is the least index such that $[f_j \wedge \sigma_i](e) = 1$.

After the incorrect decision is replaced, the new instance continues to look for a decision in the remainder of the old decision list. Suppose the new prediction is from the decision D_k, where $k \geq j+d$. If $v_k = v_x$, then the instance is remembered as an example of D_k. Otherwise, D_k is shrunken or broken just as D_j was. This process continues until the instance finds a decision with the correct value. If the instance reaches the end of the list, i.e., $D_k = (true, v_k)$, then either $v_k = v_x$ and x can be added to D_k's example list, or D_k is shrunk and a new default decision $(true, v_x)$ is appended at the end of the list with x as its only example. The pseudocode of the CDL2 algorithm is listed in Figure 4.21.

It is interesting to note that Rivest's nonincremental learning algorithm constructs decision lists from the beginning to the end, while CDL2 constructs decision lists from the end to the beginning (roughly). This is because CDL's style of learning is based on discrimination, and decisions with greater indices are more general than those with smaller indices. The use of discrimination also sets CDL2 apart from "exemplar-based learning" mechanisms [97]. The main idea of those algorithms is to grow regions around seed instances, while the idea of CDL2 is to repartition regions based on surprising instances. Furthermore, the decision tests learned by CDL2 are very similar to the features used at the nodes of decision trees [81].

To illustrate the algorithm, let us go through an example to see how CDL2 learns the concept defined in Figure 4.20, $\overline{x}_1 \overline{x}_3 \vee x_1 x_2 \vee x_1 \overline{x}_2 x_4$. We assume that

---

Let x be the new instance and v_x be its concept value.
Loop: Let $D_j = (f_j, v_j)$ be the decision on x,
1   If the decision is correct, i.e., $v_x = v_j$,
2   Then store x as an example of D_j and return,
3   Let $(\sigma_1, \ldots, \sigma_d) = \text{DIFFERENCES}(\text{examplesOf}(D_j), x)$,
4   Replace (f_j, v_j) by $(f_j \wedge \sigma_1, v_j), \ldots, (f_j \wedge \sigma_d, v_j)$,
5   Distribute the examples of D_j to the new decisions,
6   If D_j was the last decision,
7   Then append $(true, v_x)$ at the end of the decision list.

Figure 4.21   The basic CDL2 learning algorithm.

the training instances are from 00000 to 11111 and will be given in that order. Each training instance has a concept value. For example, (11000 +) means the instance 11000 is in the concept, while (00111 −) means 00111 is not in the concept.

When the first training instance, (00000 +), arrives, CDL2 initiates a decision list with a single default decision:

$$((true, +))$$

The instance is stored as an example of this sole decision. Since the next three instances — 00001, 00010, and 00011 — are all predicted correctly, they also become examples of the default decision. The fifth instance is (00100 −), and CDL2's prediction + is wrong. Because the difference between (00000 00001 00010 00011) and 00100 is found to be $(\overline{x}_3)$, the decision is shrunk to be $(\overline{x}_3, +)$, and a new default $(true, −)$ (with the instance 00100 as its example) is appended at the end. The new decision list is now

$$((\overline{x}_3, +)(true, −))$$

With this decision list, the succeeding instances are predicted correctly until 10000. CDL2's decision is $(\overline{x}_3, +)$ but the instance belongs to −. Comparing the examples of the decision with the new instance, CDL2 finds the difference to be $\overline{x}_1$. The decision is then replaced by $(\overline{x}_1\overline{x}_3, +)$:

$$((\overline{x}_1\overline{x}_3, +)(true, −))$$

The troublesome instance then finds $(true, −)$ to be correct, and it becomes an example of the default decision. For succeeding instances, CDL2's prediction is correct on 10001 but wrong on 10010. The decision is $(true, −)$ but 10010 is a +. The differences found are $\{x_3\overline{x}_1, \overline{x}_4\}$, so the decision $(true, −)$ is replaced by $((x_3\overline{x}_1, −)(\overline{x}_4, −)(true, +))$, yielding

$$((\overline{x}_1\overline{x}_3, +)(x_3\overline{x}_1, −)(\overline{x}_4, −)(true, +))$$

With this decision list, CDL2 correctly predicts the next five instances — 10011, 10100, 10101, 10110, and 10111 – but fails on 11000. The decision is $(\overline{x}_4, −)$, but the instance is a +. The difference between $\overline{x}_4$'s examples (10101 10100 10001 10000) and the instance 11000 is found to be $(\overline{x}_2)$. The decision $(\overline{x}_4, −)$ is then shrunk into $(\overline{x}_4\overline{x}_2, −)$ and the new decision list now becomes

$$((\overline{x}_1\overline{x}_3, +)(x_3\overline{x}_1, −)(\overline{x}_4\overline{x}_2, −)(true, +))$$

This decision list is equivalent to the target concept, and it correctly predicts 11001 through 11111.

The basic CDL2 algorithm can be improved in several ways. The first is to construct shorter decision lists. CDL2 does not guarantee learning the shortest decision list, and the length of the final decision list depends on the order of the training instances. If the instances that are more representative (i.e., that represent the critical differences between complementary concepts) appear earlier, then the length of the decision list will be shorter. Although learning the shortest decision list is an NP-complete problem [91], there are some strategies for making the list as short as possible.

Every time a decision is replaced by a list of new decisions, we can check to see if any of these new decisions can be merged with any of the decisions with greater indices. A merger of two decisions (f_i, v) and (f_j, v) is defined to be (f_m, v), where f_m is the intersection of the literals of f_i and f_j. Two decisions $D_i = (f_i, v_i)$ and $D_j = (f_j, v_j)$, $i < j$, can be merged if the following conditions are met: (1) The two decisions have the same value, i.e., $v_i = v_j$; (2) none of the examples of D_i are captured by any decisions between i and j that have different decision values; and (3) the merged decision (f_m, v_j) does not block any examples of any decisions after j that have different values.

To illustrate the idea, consider the following example. Suppose the current decision list is $((\overline{x}_3, +)(x_1, -)(true, +))$, and examples of these three decisions are (010, 000), (111, 101), and (011), respectively. Suppose the current instance is (100 $-$), for which CDL2 has made the wrong decision $(\overline{x}_3, +)$. Since the difference between (010, 000) (the examples of D_1) and 100 is $(\overline{x}_1)$, the decision $(\overline{x}_3, +)$ should be replaced by $(\overline{x}_3 \overline{x}_1, +)$, which would result in a new decision list $((\overline{x}_3 \overline{x}_1, +)(x_1, -)(true, +))$. However, the new decision $(\overline{x}_3 \overline{x}_1, +)$ can be merged with $(true, +)$ because it has the same decision value, and none of its examples can be captured by $(x_1, -)$, and the merged decision, which is $(true, +)$, does not block any decisions that follow it. Thus, the decision list is shortened to $((x_1, -)(true, +))$.

The second improvement over the basic CDL2 algorithm concerns inconsistent data. When data are inconsistent, there are no differences between some instances that have different concept values. In other words, the same instance may belong to different concepts simultaneously. To handle such data, we relax the criterion for a correct decision to be the following:

A decision $D_j = (f_j, v_j)$ is *correct* on an instance x that has concept value v_x if either $v_j = v_x$ or x is already an example of D_j.

For example, suppose a decision $(x_1 x_2, +)$ currently has the example $((11\ +))$ and a new instance (11 $-$) arrives; then the decision $(x_1 x_2, +)$ will be considered correct because 11 is already in its example set. With this new criterion, a decision may have duplicate examples. Examples that belong to the same decision may have the same instance with different concept values, and the value of the decision may be inconsistent with some of its examples. To deal with this problem, we adopt a policy that the value of a decision is always the same as the concept value that is supported by the most examples. (When there is a tie, the current decision value is not changed.) If another example (11 $-$) is also in the decision above, then the value of the decision will be changed from + to $-$ because $-$ will be supported by two examples versus only one example for +.

4.9.2 Experiments and Analysis

To date, the improved CDL2 has been tested in four domains: 6-bit multiplexor, Quinlan's chess task [85], the noisy LED display data, and a handwritten character recognition task. The first two domains are noise-free, while the last two domains are noisy and contain inconsistent instances. In this section, we report CDL2's performance only on the two more difficult tasks: the chess task and the recognition of handwritten numerals. We also compare CDL2 with other learning algorithms.

In Quinlan's chess task, the instances are configurations of endgames in chess, each of which is represented as a binary feature vector of length 39. Each instance is labeled either "win" or "lose," and the task is to learn the concept of "win" (or "lose") from a given set of 551 endgames. We have compared CDL2 with two leading algorithms on this domain: the nonincremental ID3 and incremental ID5r. The results are listed in Table 4.4.

The first column in the table is the name of the algorithm. ID3 is a nonincremental algorithm that learns decision trees [86]. ID5$\hat{r}$ and ID5r are incremental algorithms that learn decision trees [126]. The difference between ID5$\hat{r}$ and ID5r is that when the decision tree is revised, ID5r ensures that all the previous instances are still correctly classified, while ID5$\hat{r}$ does not.

The second column is the number of passes that each algorithm made on the data set. This number is not meaningful for the nonincremental ID3 because it requires seeing all the instances at once (i.e., we did not force ID3 to run incrementally). The rest of the columns are the running times, the percentage of instances that are correctly classified after learning, and the size of the smallest concept that is learned, respectively. All algorithms are implemented in Allegro Common Lisp on Sun4, and the running time is an average for runs in which the instances are presented in different orders. As the table shows, with the same accuracy, CDL2 is about 200 times faster than ID5r and even faster than the nonincremental algorithm ID3. The size of the concept learned by CDL2 is also very competitive with that learned by the other algorithms. In this domain, the best-known decision tree has 58 decisions [126], while CDL2 has learned a decision list that has only 36

Algorithm	Passes	Running Time (sec.)	Accuracy (%)	No. of Decisions
ID3	N.A.	15.7	100.00	78
ID5$\hat{r}$	1	408.6	88.92	65
	8	1420.5	100.00	78
ID5r	1	2277.7	100.00	85
CDL2	1	11.4	100.00	36

Table 4.4 Comparison on classifying chess endgames.

decisions. (However, a fair comparison of sizes between decision trees and decision lists requires a very lengthy discussion.)

The second set of experiments performed is in the domain of recognizing hand-written numerals. The instances are 3301 numerals (from 0 to 9) written by humans, each of which is represented as an 8 by 8 binary bit map. The data are noisy and have inconsistent instances (i.e., two bit maps that look the same may represent different numerals). The task is to learn to recognize these numerals by training on some numerals (65% of the data), then testing the recognition on numerals that have not been seen before (35% of the data). Note that a random guess in this domain has only a 10% chance of being correct.

CDL2 is compared to some existing back-propagation neural networks and ID3. (This task is too complex for ID5$\hat{r}$ and CDL1.) The results are summarized in Table 4.5. Compared to ID3, CDL2 is slightly slower but more accurate on the test data. Compared to the neural network, CDL2 learns faster and is more accurate on the training data but does not perform as well on the test data. One reason is that the concepts in this domain are a set of arbitrary shapes (which can be handled by the neural net), while CDL2's current generalization is best suited for hyperrectangles in a high-dimensional space. Another reason is that CDL2 is overfitting. Yet another reason is that CDL2, unlike these networks, has no knowledge about this domain. If such knowledge were embedded in the algorithm, as it is in the choice of architecture for the networks, the performance of CDL2 might improve.

We now turn our attention to analyzing the complexity of the CDL2 algorithm. Let d be the number of attributes of instances, and let n be the number of training instances. We assume all the attributes are binary and analyze the complexity under the following three cases.

In the first case, which is extreme, we assume that every training instance will cause a prediction failure for CDL2, and the length of the decision list is always

Program	Passes	Running Time (min.)	Accuracy (%) (Training)	(Testing)	Size
ID3	N.A.	4.4	99.9	74.2	440 decisions
CDL2	1	13.1	99.9	77.9	360 decisions
Linked Local Neural Net	30 45 50	300 450 500	96.6 96.9 96.9	87.8 87.8 88.2	385 nodes 2860 weights

Table 4.5 Comparison on the numeral recognition task.

the longest possible (the number of decisions in the list is equal to the number of instances seen so far). When the ith instance arrives, the length of the decision list is $i - 1$, and each decision has only one example. Therefore, finding a decision for the instance takes at most $d(i - 1)$ bit comparisons, finding the difference takes at most d comparisons, and replacing the decision takes 1 deletion and 1 insertion. Since we assume each decision can only capture one instance, the decision must be at the end of the list and the new instance will find a correct decision after one loop. Thus the total number of comparisons to process the ith instance is $O(di)$. There are n training instances, so the total number of comparisons to process all the training instances is

$$\sum_{i=1}^{n} O(di) = O(dn^2)$$

In the second case, which is also extreme, we assume that there is only one decision, and it has all the previous $i - 1$ examples. In this case, finding a decision takes d comparisons, finding the differences takes $d(i - 1)$ comparisons, replacing the decision takes 1 deletion and at most $i-1$ insertions, and distributing examples takes at most $(i - 1)^2 d$ comparisons. This explosion of decisions can happen only once; after that the analysis is the same as in the first case. To be conservative, we assume that the explosion happens at the nth instance, so the total complexity is

$$dn^2 + \sum_{i=1}^{n} O(di) = O(dn^2)$$

In the third case, we assume the number of decisions is $\sqrt{i}$ and each of them has $\sqrt{i}$ examples. Then finding a decision takes $d\sqrt{i}$ comparisons, finding the difference takes $d\sqrt{i}$ comparisons, replacing decisions takes 1 deletion and at most $\sqrt{i}$ insertions, and distributing examples takes at most $d\sqrt{i}\sqrt{i}$ comparisons. We assume conservatively that in the worst case all the $\sqrt{i}$ decisions are broken (i.e., CDL2 loops $\sqrt{i}$ times for the ith instance), and the total time for processing all n instances is

$$\sum_{i=1}^{n} O(di^{\frac{3}{2}})$$

The above analysis is for the basic CDL2 algorithm. In the improved version, new decisions may be merged with the existing ones. Suppose there are $\sqrt{i}$ decisions in the list; then a merge may take $d\sqrt{i}\sqrt{i}$ comparisons (condition 1 takes at most $\sqrt{i}$, conditions 2 and 3 together take at most $d\sqrt{i}\sqrt{i}$). There are at most $\sqrt{i}$ new decisions, so revising a decision may require $di\sqrt{i}$ comparisons. We conservatively assume that all the $\sqrt{i}$ decisions are broken, and the total time becomes

$$\sum_{i=1}^{n} O(di^2) = O(dn(n + 1)(2n + 1)) = O(dn^3)$$

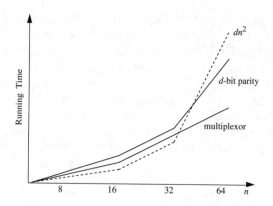

Figure 4.22   Comparison of CDL2 experiments with dn^2.

Intuitively it seems possible to tighten the above analysis considerably because CDL2's performance in practice is much better. To gain more information about the real complexity, we compared the improved CDL2's actual running time with the complexity dn^2. The result is in Figure 4.22. In these experiments, we ran the improved CDL2, whose complexity is conservatively estimated at $O(dn^3)$ in theory, on two tasks: learning the d-bit parity concept and learning the d-bit multiplexor. The first task is known to be the worst case for learning decision trees [126], and the length of its decision list is n (corresponding to the first case in our analysis above). The second task has concepts that have exceptional instances and the length of its decision list is roughly $\sqrt{n}$ (corresponding to our analysis in the third case). In all these experiments, CDL2 is presented with all 2^d instances.

As we can see in Figure 4.22, the improved CDL2's complexity is less than dn^2 in both tasks. These results suggest that our complexity analysis may indeed be too conservative. Nevertheless, the current complexity of CDL2 is at least comparable with that of ID3 and ID5r. ID3 takes $O(nd^2)$ additions and $O(2^d)$ multiplications, and ID5r takes $O(nd2^d)$ additions and $O(2^d)$ multiplications [126]. CDL2 uses only comparison operations, and its complexity has no exponential components.

4.10   Using CDL to Learn Concepts from Structured Instances

In this section, we discuss how to apply CDL to learning concepts from structured instances. We outline the basic idea of such applications and illustrate the ideas through examples. A more detailed discussion of the subject will be given in Chapter 10, where CDL is used by the LIVE system to learn models from structured observations.

To apply CDL to learning from structured instances, we need only to extend the CDL2 algorithm in two places: enhancing decision lists so that they can represent structured concepts and revising the procedure DIFFERENCES so that the differences between instances are not a list of attribute values but a conjunction of predicates or their negations with variables.

As we know, a decision list $L = ((f_1, v_1) \ldots (f_r, v_r))$ was originally defined so that each decision test f_j is a conjunction of literals of attribute values, and each decision value v_j is a constant representing the name of a concept. We now extend this definition so that each test function f_j is a conjunction of predicates or their negations with variables, and each v_j is a predicate or its negation that is to be learned. As before, we will call the jth pair in the list the jth *decision*. With this new definition, decision lists are at least as powerful as Horn clauses.

To illustrate the ideas, consider again the concept $CanReach(x, y)$ in the network shown in Figure 4.11, which is used in illustrating the FOIL algorithm. Using a decision list, such a concept can be represented as the following decision list:

$$((LinkedTo(x_1, x_2), CanReach(x_1, x_2))$$
$$(LinkedTo(x_1, x_3) \wedge CanReach(x_3, x_2), CanReach(x_1, x_2))$$
$$(true, \neg CanReach(x_1, x_2)))$$

Like the FOIL algorithm, the learner here is given a set of background predicates that are extensionally defined. In the above example, the predicates $CanReach$ and $LinkedTo$ are each defined by a set of object tuples that satisfy the relation. The meaning that an instance $\vec{x}$ satisfies a decision (f, v) is defined in the same way as $\vec{x}$ satisfying a Horn clause $v \leftarrow f$ in Section 4.6.

As before, a decision list L defines a set of relational concepts as follows: For any structured instance $\vec{x}$ (a tuple of objects), the decision on $\vec{x}$ is defined to be $D_j = (f_j, v_j)$, where j is the least index such that $\vec{x}$ satisfies (f_j, v_j). The value v_j is the relational concept to which $\vec{x}$ belongs.

Since instances are now tuples of objects instead of values of attributes, the differences between instances must be expressed in a different way. All differences are now expressed in terms of existing predicates and their negations. Therefore, the procedure of DIFFERENCES must be modified to take a set of structured instances and to return a conjunction of literals with variables.

Let us illustrate this new procedure through examples. Suppose the CDL is to find the difference between the new instance $i = [0, 0]$ and the set of examples $E = \{[0, 1]\}$ of a decision $(true, CanReach(x_1, x_2))$. The first step is to express the given instances in terms of the predicate. For example, using the background predicate $LinkedTo$, the instance i is expressed as $i' = \neg LinkedTo(x_1, x_2)$, and the set E is expressed as $E' = \{LinkedTo(x_1, x_2)\}$. Then i' is compared with E' and $E' \setminus \{i'\} = \{LinkedTo(x_1, x_2)\}$ is returned as the difference. Notice that differences are therefore the literals in E' but not in i'. In this example, the difference between $[0, 0]$ and $\{[0, 1]\}$ is found to be $\{LinkedTo(x_1, x_2)\}$.

There are several restrictions on what can be returned as differences. First, the returned expression must use all the variables that are used in the corresponding decision value (i.e., the predicate to be learned). For example, the difference $\{LinkedTo(x_1, x_2)\}$ found above must use the variables x_1 and x_2 because these are the variables used in the decision. Second, the returned expression must contain predicates other than the predicate in the decision value. This prevents useless recursive definitions. In the above example, $CanReach(x_1, x_2)$ can also be used to distinguish i from E, but we cannot return it as the final difference. Third, when there are more than one set of legal differences, CDL chooses the one that is satisfied by the most number of examples in E.

The situation is more complicated if there are no differences between i' and E'. In this case, we must introduce new variables as links to construct the conjunction of predicates to express the differences. For example, suppose that the new instance $i = [0, 6]$ and the examples of a decision $(true, \neg CanReach(x_1, x_2))$ are $E = \{[0, 0]\}$. Then after expressing them using $i' = \neg LinkedTo(x_1, x_2)$ and $E' = \{\neg LinkedTo(x_1, x_2)\}$, there are no differences between i' and E' (i.e., $E' \setminus \{i'\} = \emptyset$). In this case, we introduce a new variable x_3 and consider all combinations of two predicates using x_1, x_2, and x_3:

$$LinkedTo(x_1, x_2) \wedge LinkedTo(x_2, x_3)$$
$$LinkedTo(x_1, x_3) \wedge LinkedTo(x_3, x_2)$$
$$LinkedTo(x_2, x_1) \wedge LinkedTo(x_3, x_2)$$
$$LinkedTo(x_3, x_1) \wedge LinkedTo(x_3, x_2)$$

$$\vdots$$

$$LinkedTo(x_1, x_2) \wedge CanReach(x_3, x_2)$$
$$LinkedTo(x_1, x_3) \wedge CanReach(x_3, x_2)$$
$$LinkedTo(x_2, x_1) \wedge CanReach(x_3, x_2)$$
$$LinkedTo(x_3, x_1) \wedge CanReach(x_3, x_2)$$

Notice that the combination of $CanReach \wedge CanReach$ is not considered because it does not use any predicates other than the predicate to be learned. Among all these variablizations, only $LinkedTo(x_1, x_3) \wedge CanReach(x_3, x_2)$ can distinguish $[0, 6]$ from $[0, 0]$. In other words, it is satisfied by $[0, 6]$ but not $[0, 0]$. So the procedure returns the expression $\neg(LinkedTo(x_1, x_3) \wedge CanReach(x_3, x_2))$ as the final difference.

Thus, the new difference procedure DIFFERENCES$^+$ can be summarized as in Figure 4.23. Notice that the search space may be very large when the number of background predicates is large. However, there are effective heuristics for selecting promising combinations. That will be discussed in detail in Section 10.2.1.

With the new DIFFERENCES$^+$ procedure, CDL can be applied to learning from structured instances in a straightforward way. Figure 4.24 presents the CDL3 algorithm. This algorithm is the same as CDL2 except for some slight modifications. On line 3, the procedure DIFFERENCES$^+$ is called (instead of DIFFERENCES),

Inputs: A set of previous examples E, and a new instance i.
Outputs: The minimal differences to distinguish E from i.
Procedure DIFFERENCES$^+$(E,i):
1   For each individual background predicate P,
2   Express E as E', and i as i' using P,
3   Return $E' \setminus \{i'\}$ if it is not empty,
4   Introducing a new variable x_n,
5   For each combination ϕ of background predicates and variable assignment,
6   Express E as E', and i as i' using ϕ,
7   Return $E' \setminus \{i'\}$ if it is not empty.

Figure 4.23   Finding the relational differences between structured instances.

Let $\vec{x}$ be a new instance and $v_{\vec{x}}$ be its relational concept.
Loop: Let $D_j = (f_j, v_j)$ be the decision on $\vec{x}$,
1   If the decision is correct, i.e., $v_{\vec{x}} = v_j$,
2   Then store $\vec{x}$ as an example of D_j and return,
3   Let $\phi = $ DIFFERENCES$^+$(examplesOf(D_j),$\vec{x}$),
4   Replace (f_j, v_j) by $(f_j \wedge \phi, v_j)$,
5   If D_j was the last decision,
6   Then append $(true, v_{\vec{x}})$ at the end of the decision list.

Figure 4.24   The CDL3 algorithm for learning from structured instances.

which returns a conjunction of background predicates ϕ. On line 4, ϕ is directly conjoined with the existing decision test (instead of spreading ϕ into pieces as CDL2 does), and there is no need to redistribute the examples of this decision. Like CDL2, CDL3 is an incremental learning algorithm. (In contrast, the FOIL algorithm discussed in Section 4.6 is nonincremental.)

To further illustrate the CDL3 algorithm, let us go through an example of learning the relational concept $CanReach(x_1, x_2)$ in the context set up in Section 4.6. Since CDL3 is incremental, examples are given one at a time. Suppose the first example is $[0, 1]$. Since this is a positive example of $CanReach$ and the decision list is empty, the following decision list is created:

$$((true, CanReach(x_1, x_2)))$$

and $[0, 1]$ is remembered as an example of this decision. Now, suppose the second example is $[0, 0]$. Since it is a negative example (i.e., it belongs to the relational concept $\neg CanReach(x_1, x_2)$), CDL3's prediction is wrong. At this point, the

procedure DIFFERENCES$^+$({[0, 1]},[0, 0]) is called, and it returns the difference
$LinkedTo(x_1, x_2)$. Thus, the decision list is modified to become:

$$((LinkedTo(x_1, x_2), CanReach(x_1, x_2))(true, \neg CanReach(x_1, x_2)))$$

and $[0, 0]$ is remembered as an example of the last decision. Now, suppose the
third instance is $[0, 6]$. CDL3's decision is $\neg CanReach(x_1, x_2)$ but it is wrong.
So DIFFERENCES$^+$({[0, 0]},[0, 6]) is called and the difference is found to be
$\neg(LinkedTo(x_1, x_3) \wedge CanReach(x_3, x_2))$ as we described before. Thus, the new
decision list is:

$$((LinkedTo(x_1, x_2), CanReach(x_1, x_2))$$
$$(\neg(LinkedTo(x_1, x_3) \wedge CanReach(x_3, x_2)), \neg CanReach(x_1, x_2))$$
$$(true, CanReach(x_1, x_2)))$$

and $[0, 6]$ is remembered as an example of the last decision. At this point, the
reader might notice that the performance of CDL3 depends on the quality of the
training examples. If the third example was $[0, 2]$ instead of $[0, 6]$, then CDL3 would
learn a concept of $LinkedTo(x_1, x_3) \wedge LinkedTo(x_3, x_2)$. However, based on the
examples that CDL3 has seen so far, this concept is certainly a reasonable one.
As more informative examples appear later, CDL3 will eventually learn the correct
definition of $CanReach$.

4.11   Model Abstraction by Neural Networks

The concept languages we have used so far are more or less logical expressions of the
instances. In this section, we will see another type of concept/function language:
neural networks. We will very briefly discuss what neural networks are and illustrate
a commonly used learning method called back propagation [61].

A typical neural network can be thought as a black box that implements an
arbitrary mapping function from its inputs to its outputs [37]. What seems like
magic is that one does not need to go inside the box to twiddle the internal "nuts
and bolts" in order to have the box behave as desired; there exist learning algorithms
that do that for you if the box is given enough input/output pairs. Back propagation
is one of those learning methods.

A neural network consists of a set of *units*, each of which is a function itself that
maps its inputs to its output. Typically, the mapping is from many inputs to one
output. Units in a network are connected to each other through *links*. Each link
has a *weight* indicating how strong the link is. If a network has only links that
connect some units' outputs to other units' inputs, then the network is called a
feedforward network. Units in a feedforward network can be organized into *layers*.
The outputs of the units in one layer can only go to the inputs of the next layer.

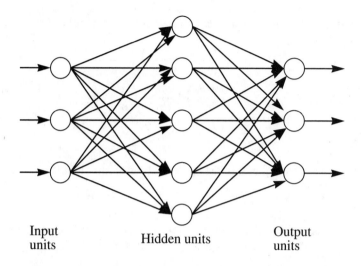

Input
units

Hidden units

Output
units

Figure 4.25   An example of a feedforward neural network.

A typical network has an input layer, an output layer, and several hidden layers in between. Figure 4.25 shows a three-layer feedforward network.

The output o_j of a unit j in a network depends on the unit's mapping function f_j, its inputs $o_{i_1}, o_{i_2}, \ldots, o_{i_m}$ (these are outputs of units that feed into unit j), and the weights associated with each input $w_{i_1 j}, w_{i_2 j}, \ldots, w_{i_m j}$. If we define the net input to the unit j to be

$$I_j = \sum_i o_i w_{ij}$$

then the output of unit j is given as

$$o_j = f_j(I_j)$$

The objective of a learning algorithm, such as back propagation, is to change the weights in a network to reduce the difference between the the actual output of the network and the desired output provided by the training examples.

Let t_j be the desired output of unit j and o_j the actual output of unit j. We define the difference to be

$$E = \frac{1}{2}(t_j - o_j)^2$$

Using the gradient descent method, how much a weight w_{ij} needs to be changed can be computed as

$$w_{ij} = w_{ij} - \eta \nabla E \qquad (4.3)$$

where η is a step size. The factor ∇E can be computed as follows:

$$\begin{aligned}
\nabla E &= \frac{\partial E}{\partial w_{ij}} = \left(\frac{\partial E}{\partial o_j}\right)\left(\frac{\partial o_j}{\partial w_{ij}}\right) \\
&= \left(\frac{\partial E}{\partial o_j}\right)\left(\frac{\partial o_j}{\partial I_j}\right)\left(\frac{\partial I_j}{\partial w_{ij}}\right) \\
&= \frac{\partial E}{\partial o_j} f'_j(I_j)o_i
\end{aligned}$$

When the unit j is an output unit, then according to the definition of E, we have $\frac{\partial E}{\partial o_j} = -(t_j - o_j)$, thus

$$\nabla E = -f'(I_j)o_i(t_j - o_j) \tag{4.4}$$

When the unit j is not an output unit, then the error of o_j depends on the units k that j outputs to. Thus, we can rewrite $\frac{\partial E}{\partial o_j}$ as

$$\frac{\partial E}{\partial o_j} = \sum_k \left(\frac{\partial E}{\partial I_k}\right)\left(\frac{\partial I_k}{\partial o_j}\right) = \sum_k \frac{\partial E}{\partial I_k} w_{jk}$$

where unit k is the unit from j through w_{jk} and I_k is net input of the unit k. Thus, we have

$$\nabla E = f'(I_j)o_i \sum_k \frac{\partial E}{\partial I_k} w_{jk} \tag{4.5}$$

Using equations 4.3, 4.4, and 4.5, we can update every weight in the network. These three equations represent the method of back propagation.

Since a model of the environment is essentially a function $\delta(x, a) \rightarrow y$, it is straightforward to apply neural networks to model abstraction tasks. Figure 4.26 illustrates such an application. One can set up a network whose input units represent the current state $x(n-1)$ and action $a(n-1)$, whose output units represent the predicted next state $x'(n)$, and whose hidden layers represent the transition function. To abstract a model from the environment, one can use the back-propagation method to train the network on pairs $(x(n-1), a(n-1))$ and the actual next state $x(n)$. Every time an action $a(n-1)$ is applied to the current state $x(n-1)$, we can use the difference between $x(n)$ and $x'(n)$ as the error to change the weights in the model. There are many existing systems that utilize this approach, and we will show one in Chapter 7. Interested readers can find more examples in [41, 73, 78].

Finally, we need to point out that although neural networks are powerful enough to simulate any function, they have some undesirable features in certain applications. For example, there is no known way to tell what has been learned. All we have is a black box that does the right thing. In some applications, for example, discovering regularities or errors in large databases, one often wishes to see the contents of the black box in order to find out what regularities or errors have been discovered.

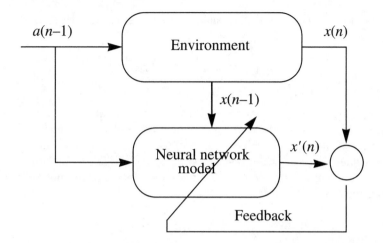

Figure 4.26   Learning a neural network model from the environment.

4.12   Bayesian Model Abstraction

This section introduces Bayesian probability theory and its application to model abstraction. We will present the basic ideas and computations and illustrate them through examples. For readers who want to learn more about this subject, we highly recommend the marvelous book by Jaynes [39] as well as the work by Jeffery [40] and Cox [17].

In Bayesian probability theory, a probability $P(A|B)$ is defined as the learner's *degree of belief* for a proposition A (such as a model, a transition, or a concept) given that the current available evidence and knowledge are B. For example, if A is the proposition "It was cloudy at 9:45 AM today," B is the evidence "It rained at 10:00 AM today," and C is the evidence "It was cloudy at 10:00 AM today." Then our belief of A is much more certain if B is given than if C is given. That is, $P(A|B) > P(A|C)$. Notice that this definition is different from the frequency definition normally taught in textbooks: A probability reflects the state of knowledge in the head of the learner, it is not some intrinsic property of the environment.

Bayesian probability theory has some distinctive properties that are very suitable for machine learning. First of all, it is very simple. The entire theory can be derived from the following two simple axioms:

Sum axiom: $P(A|C) + P(\overline{A}|C) = 1$

Product axiom: $P(AB|C) = P(A|C)P(B|AC) = P(B|C)P(A|BC)$

As one may guess, the famous Bayesian theorem can be directly derived from the product axiom

$$P(A|BC) = \frac{P(A|C)P(B|AC)}{P(B|C)}$$

The second important property of Bayesian probability theory is that it is a generalization of classic deductive logic. Since probabilities represent the learner's beliefs of propositions, the value of a proposition in Bayesian theory can have quantitative degrees other than just the simple "true," "false," or "unknown" that exist in classical logic. As for inference, Bayesian theory includes not only deductive reasoning, such as

If $A \to B$ and A, then B.
If $A \to B$ and $\neg B$, then $\neg A$.
If $A \to B$ and B, then "A becomes more plausible."

but also inductive inferences, such as

If $A \to B$ and $\neg A$, then "B becomes less plausible."
If $A \to$ "B becomes more plausible" and B, then "A becomes more plausible."

As an example of the last inference rule, let C stands for the background knowledge. Then the premise on the left-hand side takes the form $P(B|AC) > P(B|C)$, and the Bayesian theorem tells us immediately $P(A|BC) > P(A|C)$.

With such powerful built-in inference mechanisms for reasoning with incomplete knowledge, Bayesian theory seems to be a more natural and principled approach than many others, such as nonmonotonic reasoning and default logic. Furthermore, the ability to unify induction and deduction makes the theory a very promising candidate for analogical reasoning (if analogy can be placed in a position somewhere between deduction and induction).

The third important property of Bayesian probability theory is that it truthfully reflects the process of learning. Intuitively, learning is the process of changing your knowledge based on the evidence you observe. The Bayesian theorem tells us how to make this change. Let C be your current knowledge (accumulated from all of your previous experience), A be a new theory you are learning, and B a new experiment or observation result. Then the Bayesian theorem $P(A|BC) = P(A|C)P(B|AC)/P(B|C)$ simply says, "Given your background knowledge C, your new knowledge of the theory A after the experiment B is the product of what you know about A without knowing B, $P(A|C)$, and the possibility B if your current understanding of A were correct, $P(B|AC)$, divided by the possibility of knowing B anyway, $P(B|C)$." Notice that this process is recursive. The new understanding of A then becomes a part of C, which is used to make a newer understanding of A when a new experiment or observation becomes available.

It is interesting to note that the Bayesian definition of probability is the original definition of probability made by Bernoulli, Bayes, and Laplace. Although the theory has been known for 200 years, it is still the best framework known for inductive reasoning. As we will see in the following examples, the theory provides a measurement of a learner's knowledge, as well as a mechanism for reasoning and updating such knowledge as new evidence becomes available.

4.12.1 Concept Learning

Let us go through a very simple example that illustrates the application of Bayesian probability theory to concept learning. Suppose we are given a learning task X in which the instance space has three instances, $\{1, 2, 3\}$, and we consider the complete hypothesis space, which in this case has eight hypotheses:

$$C_0 \equiv \emptyset \quad C_2 \equiv \{2\} \quad C_4 \equiv \{1,2\} \quad C_6 \equiv \{2,3\}$$
$$C_1 \equiv \{1\} \quad C_3 \equiv \{3\} \quad C_5 \equiv \{1,3\} \quad C_7 \equiv \{1,2,3\}$$

Let the proposition A_i stands for "C_i is the unknown concept," and D_j for "the instance j is in the unknown concept." Note that given X, all possible data the learner might see is $D_1, \overline{D_1}, D_2, \overline{D_2}, D_3$, and $\overline{D_3}$. We assume there is a probability of 10^{-6} that a training example is in error. Since the learner has no knowledge to favor any particular concept at the offset, we set the initial probabilities $p(A_i|X) = \frac{1}{8}$, where $0 \leq i \leq 7$. From this simple learning task, we wish to see how each training example D_j is used to compute the probabilities $p(A_i|D_jX)$. The concept with the highest probability will then be the best guess for the target concept.

Now suppose the first training example is D_1, "instance 1 is in the unknown concept." By the Bayesian theorem, we can calculate $p(A_i|D_1X)$ as follows:

$$p(A_i|D_1X) = p(A_i|X)\frac{p(D_1|A_iX)}{p(D_1|X)}$$

The terms on the right-hand side are easy to compute. To compute $p(D_1|A_iX)$, notice the fact that C_0, C_2, C_3, and C_6 do not cover instance 1 unless the training example is incorrect. If A_0 were true (i.e., the concept C_0 was the target concept), then the probability of seeing D_1, D_2, or D_3 is 10^{-6}, and $p(D_1|A_0X) = \frac{1}{3}(10^{-6})$. This reasoning can also be applied to the cases of assuming A_2, A_3, and A_6. So we have

$$p(D_1|A_0X) = p(D_1|A_2X) = p(D_1|A_3X) = p(D_1|A_6X) = \frac{1}{3}(10^{-6})$$

If the target concept were one of C_1, C_4, C_5, and C_7, then D_1 is a correct training example. Since the probability of seeing a correct training example in these cases is $(1 - 10^{-6})$ and D_1 is one of the three possibly correct training examples, the probability of seeing D_1 is $\frac{1}{3}(1 - 10^{-6})$. So we have

$$p(D_1|A_1X) = p(D_1|A_4X) = p(D_1|A_5X) = p(D_1|A_7X) = \frac{1}{3}(1 - 10^{-6})$$

Finally, since given X there are six possible training examples, we have $p(D_1|X) = \frac{1}{6}$. (Another way to compute $p(D_1|X)$ is as follows. Since $D_1 = D_1A_0 + D_1A_1 + \cdots + D_1A_7$, we have $p(D_1|X) = p(D_1A_0|X) + p(D_1A_1|X) + \cdots + p(D_1A_7|X)$. The reader can verify that this is also $\frac{1}{6}$.) Putting them all together, we have

$$p(A_0|D_1X) = \frac{1}{4}(10^{-6}) \qquad p(A_4|D_1X) = \frac{1}{4}(1 - 10^{-6})$$
$$p(A_1|D_1X) = \frac{1}{4}(1 - 10^{-6}) \quad p(A_5|D_1X) = \frac{1}{4}(1 - 10^{-6})$$
$$p(A_2|D_1X) = \frac{1}{4}(10^{-6}) \qquad p(A_6|D_1X) = \frac{1}{4}(10^{-6})$$
$$p(A_3|D_1X) = \frac{1}{4}(10^{-6}) \qquad p(A_7|D_1X) = \frac{1}{4}(1 - 10^{-6})$$

Notice that $\sum_{i=0}^{7} p(A_i|D_1X) = 1$.

At this point, we can compare this probabilistic concept learning with the version space. We notice that, just as in version space, after seeing the first positive example D_1, the plausible concept space that contains the target concept is narrowed down to C_1, C_4, C_5, and C_7. But unlike version space, the other concepts are not completely dead, although their probability is very low.

To go further into the learning process, now suppose the second training example is $\overline{D_2}$: "Instance 2 is not in the unknown concept." To process this training example, the Bayesian theorem is used again:

$$p(A_i|\overline{D_2}X') = p(A_i|X')\frac{p(\overline{D_2}|A_iX')}{p(\overline{D_2}|X')}$$

Notice that at this point the background information is not X but $X' = XD_1$, for D_1 is now a part of the learner's experience. As before, the terms on the right-hand side are ready to be computed: The values for $p(A_i|X')$ were just computed above. The value of $p(\overline{D_2}|X') = p(\overline{D_2}|X) = \frac{1}{6}$ because the training examples are given to be independently chosen. The values of $p(\overline{D_2}|A_iX')$, which is equal to $p(\overline{D_2}|A_iX)$ because of the independence of D_1 and $\overline{D_2}$, can be computed as

$$p(\overline{D_2}|A_0X') = p(\overline{D_2}|A_1X') = p(\overline{D_2}|A_3X') = p(\overline{D_2}|A_5X') = \frac{1}{3}(1 - 10^{-6})$$

because $\overline{D_2}$ is a correct training example for C_0, C_1, C_3, and C_5, and

$$p(\overline{D_2}|A_2X') = p(\overline{D_2}|A_4X') = p(\overline{D_2}|A_6X') = p(\overline{D_2}|A_7X') = \frac{1}{3}(10^{-6})$$

because $\overline{D_2}$ is an incorrect training example for C_2, C_4, C_6, and C_7.

Putting them all together, we have

$$p(A_0|\overline{D_2}X') = \frac{1}{4}(10^{-6}) \cdot 6 \cdot \frac{1}{3}(1 - 10^{-6})$$

$$p(A_1|\overline{D_2}X') = \frac{1}{4}(1 - 10^{-6}) \cdot 6 \cdot \frac{1}{3}(1 - 10^{-6})$$

$$p(A_2|\overline{D_2}X') = \frac{1}{4}(10^{-6}) \cdot 6 \cdot \frac{1}{3}(10^{-6})$$

$$p(A_3|\overline{D_2}X') = \frac{1}{4}(10^{-6}) \cdot 6 \cdot \frac{1}{3}(1 - 10^{-6})$$

$$p(A_4|\overline{D_2}X') = \frac{1}{4}(1 - 10^{-6}) \cdot 6 \cdot \frac{1}{3}(10^{-6})$$

$$p(A_5|\overline{D_2}X') = \frac{1}{4}(1 - 10^{-6}) \cdot 6 \cdot \frac{1}{3}(1 - 10^{-6})$$

$$p(A_6|\overline{D_2}X') = \frac{1}{4}(10^{-6}) \cdot 6 \cdot \frac{1}{3}(10^{-6})$$

$$p(A_7|\overline{D_2}X') = \frac{1}{4}(1 - 10^{-6}) \cdot 6 \cdot \frac{1}{3}(10^{-6})$$

Notice again that $\sum_{i=0}^{7} p(A_i|\overline{D_2}X') = 1$.

We can see that after two training examples, the possible target concepts have been narrowed down to C_1 and C_5, each with probability about $\frac{1}{2}$. Other concepts have such small possibilities that they can be ignored. In general, as more and more training examples become available, the probability distribution of concepts become more and more concentrated around the target concept.

4.12.2   Automatic Data Classification

Bayesian probability theory is a very general framework for inductive inference. Given different definitions of hypotheses to be inferred, the theory will take care of the rest. To elaborate this point, let us look at another application of this theory: automatic data classification. This is the same task addressed in the AUTOCLASS program [15], but the derivation here shows how clear and straightforward this application can be.

The task of automatic data classification is as follows: Given a set of objects, divide the objects into classes that best reflect the information manifested by the objects. For example, given a boat of freshly caught fishes, you may classify them by their species, for example, salmon versus cod, or by their size (when their species are very diverse), for example, big versus small. Of course, we assume that there are a set of fish attributes that you can perceive.

Formally, let the symbol X denote the fact that we are given a K-dimensional data space $\mathcal{D}$, where each point D_i in this space is an object with K attributes: $D_i = (d_{i1}, \ldots, d_{ik}, \ldots, d_{iK})$ (the value of an attribute may be continuous or discrete). Let $D \equiv D_1, D_2, \ldots, D_I$, be a set of I data points that have been observed. Our task is to divide the space $\mathcal{D}$ into a set of regions that best reflect the information contained in D. Let H_J be the proposition that "the data space $\mathcal{D}$ is covered by J classes: $\mathcal{D} = C_1 + \cdots + C_j + \cdots + C_J$, where each C_j is defined as a set of K probability distribution functions (pdf's): $f_{j1}, \ldots, f_{jk}, \ldots, f_{jK}$, one for each attribute." Then our task can be formalized as finding an H_J such that the probability of H_J given D and X is the highest.

Using the Bayesian theorem, the probability of H_J given D and X is

$$P(H_J|DX) = P(H_J|X)\frac{P(D|H_JX)}{P(D|X)} \tag{4.6}$$

So our task is simply computing the terms on the right-hand side of this equation for every possible H_J.

Let us first consider $P(D|H_JX)$. Assuming that the data points D_i are independent, we have

$$P(D|H_JX) = \prod_{i=1}^{I} P(D_i|H_JX) \tag{4.7}$$

Furthermore, since each data point D_i must belong to some class, we have

$$D_i = D_i(C_1 + \cdots + C_j + \cdots + C_J)$$

and, by the sum and product axioms,

$$P(D_i|H_JX) = \sum_{j=1}^{J} P(D_iC_j|H_JX) = \sum_{j=1}^{J} P(C_j|H_JX)P(D_i|C_jH_JX) \tag{4.8}$$

By the definition of classes, we also have

$$P(D_i|C_jH_JX) = P(d_{i1}, \ldots, d_{ik}, \ldots, d_{iK}|f_{j1}, \ldots, f_{jk}, \ldots, f_{jK}, H_J, X) \tag{4.9}$$

If attributes can be assumed independent, then we have

$$P(D_i|C_jH_JX) = \prod_{k=1}^{K} P(d_{ik}|f_{jk}, H_J, X) \tag{4.10}$$

(When attributes are not independent, as we will see in Section 5.10, we must use the product axiom to compute this term.)

For an attribute k that is continuous, we assume that the corresponding pdf f_{jk} is a Gaussian function $\mathcal{N}(\mu_{jk}, \sigma_{jk}^2)$, where μ_{jk} and σ_{jk}^2 are the mean and variance of f_{jk}, respectively. In this case, the corresponding term in equation 4.10 is computed as

$$P(d_{ik}|f_{jk}, H_J, X) = \mathcal{N}(d_{ik}, \sigma_{jk}^2) \cdot \Delta d_{ik}$$

where Δ is the error in measuring d_{ik}.

For an attribute k that has a set of discrete values $v_1, \ldots, v_m$, the corresponding pdf f_{jk} is assumed to be a set of probabilities $p_1, \ldots, p_m$, where p_m is the probability of the attribute having the value v_m. In this case, the corresponding term in equation 4.10 is computed as

$$P(d_{ik}|f_{jk}, H_J, X) = d_{ik}p_i$$

To compute the term $P(H_J|X)$ in equation 4.6, we assume that we have no prior knowledge about the number of classes, and so J can be any index from 1 to I:

$$P(H_J|X) = \frac{1}{I}$$

To compute the denominator of equation 4.6, $P(D|X)$, we notice that the number of classes cannot be more than the number of data points I, and $D = D(H_1 + \cdots + H_i + \cdots + H_I)$, thus,

$$P(D|X) = \sum_{i=1}^{I} P(DH_i|X) = \sum_{i=1}^{I} P(H_i|X)P(D|H_iX)$$

where both $P(H_i|X)$ and $P(D|H_iX)$ on the right-hand side are as computed above.

Putting all this information together, we can now compute the probability $P(H_J|DX)$ as follows, which is derived from the right-hand side of equation 4.6:

$$\frac{P(H_J|X) \cdot \prod_{i=1}^{I} \sum_{j=1}^{J} P(C_j|H_JX) \prod_{k=1}^{K} P(d_{ik}|f_{jk}, H_J, X)}{\sum_{h=1}^{I} P(H_h|X) \cdot \prod_{i=1}^{I} \sum_{j=1}^{h} P(C_j|H_hX) \prod_{k=1}^{K} P(d_{ik}|f_{jk}, H_h, X)} \qquad (4.11)$$

To illustrate the use of equation 4.11, let us consider a simple example. Suppose we are given four data points, $D = \{1.0, 3.0, 101.0, 103.0\}$, in a 1-dimensional space. What is the best way to classify them? Should they all belong to a single class? Or should they be placed in two, three, or four classes? Intuition tells us that there are two classes in this data, but what will the Bayesian theorem say?

In this example, we have $K = 1$ and $I = 4$. Since we have no initial knowledge to prefer any choice for $J = 1, 2, 3,$ or 4, we also have $P(H_J|D) = \frac{1}{4}$. Furthermore, since the the denominator of equation 4.11 is the same for all choices, we need only compute $P(D|H_JX)$ to determine the best choice for H_J.

In the following computation, we assume that, for each J, all classes C_j, $j = 1, \ldots, J$, are equally likely; thus $P(C_j|H_J) = \frac{1}{J}$, and every class is represented as a Gaussian distribution

$$N(\mu_j, 1) = \frac{1}{\sqrt{2\pi}} e^{-\frac{(x_i - \mu_j)^2}{2}}$$

where the x_i are data points and μ_j is assumed to be the best choice for class C_j with respect to $P(H_J|DX)$. We can use the Bayesian theorem to prove that the optimal value of μ_j for a class C_j is the mean of all the data points that are in C_j

[56]. In general, however, there is no known efficient way to determine which points should be included in C_j other than by searching among all possible combinations or using heuristics like Monte Carlo methods.

Under these conditions, the probability of $P(D|H_JX)$ can be computed as follows (see equation 4.7 and equation 4.8):

$$P(D|H_JX) = \prod_{i=1}^{4}\sum_{j=1}^{J} P(C_j|H_JX)P(D_i|C_jH_JX)$$

$$= \left(\frac{1}{J\sqrt{2\pi}}\right)^4 \prod_{i=1}^{4}\sum_{j=1}^{J} e^{-\frac{(x_i-\mu_j)^2}{2}}$$

where $J, \mu_1, \ldots, \mu_J$ are given. Thus, when $J = 1$ and $\mu_1 = 52$, we have

$$P(D|H_1X) = \left(\frac{1}{\sqrt{2\pi}}\right)^4 [e^{\frac{-(1-52)^2}{2}}][e^{\frac{-(3-52)^2}{2}}][e^{\frac{-(101-52)^2}{2}}][e^{\frac{-(103-52)^2}{2}}]$$

$$= \frac{e^{-[51^2+49^2]}}{(2\pi)^2}$$

When $J = 2$, $\mu_1 = 2$, and $\mu_2 = 102$, we have

$$P(D|H_2X) = \left(\frac{1}{\sqrt{2\pi}}\right)^4 [e^{-\frac{(1-2)^2}{2}} + e^{\frac{(1-102)^2}{2}}][e^{-\frac{(3-2)^2}{2}} + e^{\frac{(3-102)^2}{2}}]$$

$$[e^{-\frac{(101-2)^2}{2}} + e^{\frac{(101-102)^2}{2}}][e^{-\frac{(103-2)^2}{2}} + e^{\frac{(103-102)^2}{2}}]$$

$$= \frac{e^{-2}}{(8\pi)^2}$$

When $J = 4$ (we skip the case $J = 3$), $\mu_1 = 1$, $\mu_2 = 3$, $\mu_3 = 101$, and $\mu_4 = 103$, we have

$$P(D|H_4X) = \frac{(1 + e^{-2})^4}{(32\pi)^2}$$

Since $P(D|H_2X) > P(D|H_3X) > P(D|H_4X) > P(D|H_1X)$, the Bayesian theorem tells us that H_2 is the best choice, which matches our intuition perfectly. Furthermore, it is interesting to note that the Bayesian theorem solves the overfitting problem automatically. The choice that each data point should be a class by itself, H_4 in our example, is not always the best. In other words, the theory seems to prefer simpler models unless more complex models give much better performance: It has a built-in Occam's razor.

4.12.3   Certainty Grids

As another application of Bayesian theory, let us consider the task of learning space maps using *certainty grids* [71]. A certainty grid is a regular finite element model of space. Each cell x of the grid contains a probability $P(o_x|B)$, where o_x is the proposition "x has property o" and B is the background knowledge including all the previous perceptions from different perception devices. Here, we are primarily concerned with the property of occupation, so o_x means "x is occupied" and $\overline{o_x}$ means the negation of o_x. When it is clear what x is, we simply refer to the probability $P(o_x|B)$ as $P(o|B)$.

By the definition of probability, we know that $P(o_x|B)$ reflects the robot's current knowledge about whether x is occupied or not. Notice that the truth value of o_x is determined by the environment and may not be known by the robot at the beginning. To gain more knowledge about o_x, the robot must make perceptions. The question then becomes "How does the robot compute its new knowlege $P(o|MB)$ when a new measurement M becomes available?"

For simplicity, we compute $Odds(o|MB)$ instead of $P(o|MB)$. By definition, probability $P(X|Y)$ and odds $Odds(X|Y)$ are interchangable, for they have the relations

$$Odds(X|Y) \quad = \quad \frac{P(X|Y)}{P(\overline{X}|Y)} = \frac{P(X|Y)}{1 - P(X|Y)}$$

$$P(X|Y) \quad = \quad \frac{Odds(X|Y)}{1 + Odds(X|Y)}$$

So when $Odds(o|MB)$ is known, we can compute $P(o|MB)$ easily.

To compute $P(o|MB)$ using the Bayesian theorem, notice that

$$P(o|MB) \quad = \quad \frac{P(o|B)P(M|oB)}{P(M|B)}$$

$$P(\overline{o}|MB) \quad = \quad \frac{P(\overline{o}|B)P(M|\overline{o}B)}{P(M|B)}$$

and

$$Odds(o|MB) = \frac{P(o|MB)}{P(\overline{o}|MB)} = \left[\frac{P(o|B)}{P(\overline{o}|B)}\right]\left[\frac{P(M|oB)}{P(M|\overline{o}B)}\right]$$

The term $P(o|B)/P(\overline{o}|B)$ is known because of the current certainty grid. To compute $P(M|oB)/P(M|\overline{o}B)$, we have two choices, depending on what is assumed to be known. In the first case, we assume $P(o|M)$ is known, and the dependence between M and B can be factored out. That is, $M = M'D$ and $B = B'D$ in such a way that M is independent from B' and B is independent from M'. Thus,

$$\frac{P(M|oB)}{P(M|\overline{o}B)} = \frac{P(M|oB'D)}{P(M|\overline{o}B'D)} = \frac{P(M|oD)}{P(M|\overline{o}D)} = \frac{P(o|MD)P(\overline{o}|D)}{P(\overline{o}|MD)P(o|D)}$$

and

$$Odds(o|MB) = \left[\frac{P(o|B)}{P(\overline{o}|B)}\right]\left[\frac{P(o|M)}{P(\overline{o}|M)}\right]\left[\frac{P(\overline{o}|D)}{P(o|D)}\right]$$

As Moravec suggested [72], the values $P(o|M)$ and $P(o|D)$ can be either learned or supplied as prior knowledge. To learn $P(o|M)$, one can accumulate actual occupancy statistics in known environments for each spatial location around a sensor for each possible reading. Although we assume $P(o|M)$ is a reading from a sensor, in principle it can also be interpreted as another map. Thus, the above computation can also be used to fuse two existing maps togaher.

In the second case of computing $P(M|oB)/P(M|\bar{o}B)$, we assume that $P(M|o)$ and $P(M|\bar{o})$ are known and M and B are independent. Thus,

$$\frac{P(M|oB)}{P(M|\bar{o}B)} = \frac{P(M|o)}{P(M|\bar{o})}$$

and

$$Odds(o|MB) = \left[\frac{P(o|B)}{P(\bar{o}|B)}\right]\left[\frac{P(M|o)}{P(M|\bar{o})}\right] \tag{4.12}$$

The terms $P(M|\bar{o})$ and $P(M|o)$ reflect the reliability of the device that perceives M. Their values are fixed for each device and independent from the current map. The term $P(M|\bar{o})$ is the probability of the device giving a "false alarm." A false alarm is when a cell x is empty in the real world but M says it is occupied. The term $P(M|o)$ is the probability of "confirmation" of the device. A confirmation is when a cell x is occupied in the real world and M says it is occupied.

Equation 4.12 tells us that $Odds(o|MB)$ is computed based on the prior probability $P(o|B)$ and the reliability of the device that perceives M. It is interesting to note that if the device has a very low rate of false alarm, i.e., $P(M|\bar{o})$ is close to 0, then the perception of M causes $Odds(o|MB)$ to be very high. On the other hand, if the device is very uncertain, e.g., $P(M|\bar{o}) = P(M|o) = 0.5$, then the perception of M would not change the robot's knowledge, since $Odds(o|MB) = Odds(o|B)$.

Moravec refers to the first case of computing $P(M|oB)/P(M|\bar{o}B)$ as *context-free*, and the second as *context-sensitive*. According to his experiments, context-free works better than context-sensitive since it relies less heavily on the assumption that M and B are independent.

4.13   Summary

Model abstraction from a transparent environment is a problem of search in model spaces. We have seen different approaches to the problem from symbolic concept learning, neural networks, and probability theory. For each of these approaches, there is always a struggle between what we can do in theory and what we can perform in experiments.

Consider our discussion of symbolic concept learning. We have seen that inductive bias, correctness criteria, and efficiency are the three major factors in measuring concept learning algorithms. With these measures, in what kind of environments can we effectively abstract reasonable models?

According to the theoretical results we have amassed so far, the situation is really gloomy. For passive learning — that is, the learner is given a set of examples randomly drawn from the instance space according to some fixed but unknown distribution — effective algorithms (those requiring only polynomial computational resources) exist only for a few less complex concept languages, such as pure conjunctive, k-CNF, or k-DNF. Most interesting problems, such as learning relational concepts, Turing machines, and natural languages, are beyond our computational power.

Maybe we can do better if the learner is active. Unfortunately, the theoretical answers obtained so far are also pessimistic. By allowing learners to make membership queries, equivalence queries, subset queries, or any combination, we still cannot effectively learn anything more than deterministic finite state machines.

With all these negative theoretical results, there hardly seems any hope for model abstraction, because any real environment and any useful model will almost certainly be more complex than a finite state automaton. However, I personally believe that there is still hope for model abstraction for the following three reasons.

First, there are existing systems, such as humans and intelligent animals, that do learn more complex things, such as learning natural languages and how to drive a boat, than do k-CNF, k-DNF, or deterministic finite state machines.

Second, the conditions in theoretical analysis may not match what are important in natural learning systems. Our notation of queries may be too restrictive (membership queries assume that the learner has only one percept, yes or no). We may put too much emphasis on the worst-case scenario. For example, in the proof that equivalence queries are not sufficient for learning deterministic finite automata (state machines) [2], it is assumed that the teacher always gives you the examples that contain the least information, the so-called fingerprint, for your learning. Furthermore, the correctness criteria currently in use may be too demanding. For example, a learning algorithm is considered PAC correct only when it can learn all concepts in a class with all possible distributions of examples.

Finally, there are existing computational systems that do useful things. For example, some model abstraction techniques have been successfully applied to real-time predicting and controlling of production processes in chemical factories [32], analyzing astronomical data [15], classifying genetic data [31], and learning maps for robot navigation [47]. Therefore, I believe that as new technologies become available, nature will one day reveal the mystery of autonomous learning.

CHAPTER 5

MODEL ABSTRACTION IN TRANSLUCENT ENVIRONMENTS

The model abstraction methods described in Chapter 4 are best suited for transparent environments, where the learner's current observation can completely determine the current state of the environment. This is not the case, however, in the translucent environment. Because of the hidden states of the environment, the learner must look back into the history of observations in order to determine the current environmental state. For example, when the little prince of Chapter 2 sees nothing, he can be either at the north pole or at the south pole, depending on what he has done and seen previously. In this chapter, we will discuss learning methods that deal with such problems. However, the reader should be aware that most of the methods in this chapter are for model construction (i.e., they construct models that have the same size as the environment). At present, very little effort (see Section 5.8) has been directed to the problem of model abstraction in translucent environments (i.e., creating learning models that are more compact than the environment containing hidden states).

Technically, the model to be abstracted from the translucent environment is no longer in the form

$$M = \begin{cases} (O_0^1, a_0^1) \rightarrow P^1 \\ \quad \vdots \\ (O_0^n, a_0^n) \rightarrow P^n \end{cases}$$

where n is the number of prediction rules, but in the form

$$M = \begin{cases} (O^1_{-m}, a^1_{-m}, \ldots, O^1_{-1}, a^1_{-1}, O^1_0, a^1_0) \rightarrow P^1 \\ \qquad\qquad\qquad \vdots \\ (O^n_{-m}, a^n_{-m}, \ldots, O^n_{-1}, a^n_{-1}, O^n_0, a^n_0) \rightarrow P^n \end{cases}$$

where $m > 0$. Each prediction rule now involves mapping a sequence of observations and actions (rather than mapping a single pair of observation and action) to a prediction. The extra work the learner must do is to decide how far back into the history it needs to look (i.e., the value of m), and how to represent such historical conditions in the model.

5.1   The Problems of Construction and Synchronization

To study learning in translucent environments formally, we shall first confine ourselves to a special case of translucent environments, namely translucent deterministic finite state machines. Although such machines do not solve all the problems of translucent environments, they do illustrate the two fundamental problems in learning from translucent environments: the construction problem and the synchronization problem. But first let us define some terms.

Just as in Section 4.2, we define an environment $\mathcal{E}$ to be a Moore machine $(A, P, Q, \delta, \rho, r)$. However, we restrict $\mathcal{E}$ to be translucent by insisting that $|Q| > |P|$ (as defined below) and that ρ be a many-to-one mapping:

- A is a finite set of input actions.

- P is a finite set of output symbols.

- Q is a finite set of environmental states where $|Q| > |P|$.

- δ, a function from $Q \times A$ to Q, is the transition function of the environment.

- ρ, a many-to-one function from Q to P, is the appearance function of the environment.

- r is the current state of $\mathcal{E}$. When an action a is received by $\mathcal{E}$, r is updated to be $\delta(r, a)$. Initially r can be any state in Q.

We represent a model M of the environment $\mathcal{E}$ as a machine $(A, P, S, \phi, \theta, t)$, where

- A is a set of actions, which is the same as the set of input actions into $\mathcal{E}$,

- P is a set of percepts, which is the same as the set of output symbols of $\mathcal{E}$,

- S is a set of model states,

- ϕ, a function from $S \times A$ to S, is the transition function of M,

- θ, a function from S to P, is the appearance function of M, and

- t is the current model state of M. When a basic action a is applied to M, t is updated to be $\phi(t, a)$.

Clearly, in order to model the environment successfully, the size of S must be greater than the size of P, and θ must be a many-to-one function.

We denote the set of all finite action sequences by $B = A^*$ and extend the domain of the function $\delta(q, \cdot)$ to B in the following way: $\delta(q, \lambda) = q$, and $\delta(q, ba) = \delta(\delta(q, b), a)$ for all $q \in Q, a \in A$, and $b \in B$. Here λ denotes the empty (null) string. Thus, $\delta(q, b)$ denotes the environmental state reached by executing sequence b from environmental state q. We note that all these extensions and notations on δ also apply to M's transition function ϕ.

We assume that the learner can apply any basic action $a \in A$ to the environment (and to the model as well) and observe the current output $p = \rho(r)$ $(p \in P)$ from the environment. We say that a model state s is *visibly equivalent* to an environmental state q if $\rho(q) = \theta(s)$, where $q \in Q$ and $s \in S$. Furthermore, we say that M is *perfect* and *synchronized* with respect to $\mathcal{E}$ if the current model state t is visibly equivalent to the current environmental state r, and for all sequences of actions $b \in B$, the model state $\phi(t, b)$ is also visibly equivalent to the environmental state $\delta(r, b)$. Our objective here is to abstract a perfect and synchronized model from the environment.

With all definitions in place, we now discuss the two basic problems in learning from translucent environments: the *construction problem* of when and how to construct new model states and the *synchronization problem* of how to determine in what model state the learner currently is.

These two problems are trivial if the environment is transparent, as we have seen in the D algorithm in Section 4.2. Since the number of states in the model is equal to the number of difference percepts, a new model state is created whenever a new environmental state is observed. Since what you see is where you are, there is no ambiguity in the current model state; thus the model is always synchronized with the environment.

When the environment is translucent, however, the problems become substantial. Because the appearance function ρ is many-to-one, two or more environmental (and model) states may have the same output, and the learner's current observation cannot uniquely determine what the current environmental (and model) state is. In this case, the construction problem is real, because the number of necessary model states is greater than the number of percepts, and the learner does not known ahead of time how many model states are necessary. The synchronization problem is also complex because the learner's current observation is not sufficient to determine uniquely the current model state (i.e., two different model states may look the same).

In the following sections, we will describe several methods for dealing with these two problems. In particular, the L^* algorithm provides a solution for the construction problem, and Rivest–Schapire's algorithm gives a solution for synchronizing L^* with the environment. The CDL+ framework, a natural extension of the CDL framework discussed in Chapter 4, provides a single mechanism for solving both problems. CDL+ also integrates concept learning with model construction so that compact models, instead of direct models, can be learned from a translucent environment. Finally, we will review stochastic automaton models and hidden Markov models. Both types are suitable for model abstraction from stochastic environments.

5.2   The L^* Algorithm for Learning Finite Automata

Angluin's algorithm L^* [1] was developed for learning regular sets (which are equivalent to finite deterministic automata). The algorithm shows how to infer the structure of any finite state automaton efficiently in the presence of a *minimally adequate teacher*. Such a teacher can answer two kinds of queries: In a *membership query*, the learner asks whether a given input string w is in the unknown language U, that is, whether the string is accepted by the unknown machine. The teacher then answers the query. In an *equivalence query*, the learner conjectures that the unknown automaton is isomorphic to one it has constructed. Again, the teacher answers the query; if there is no isomorphism between the machine and the model, the teacher provides a counterexample w, a string accepted by one automaton but not the other. Angluin later proved that these two types of queries are necessary for learning deterministic finite state machines in polynomial time [2]. The L^* algorithm also incorporates a reset button to solve the synchronization problem. By pressing this button, the learner can force the environment to jump back to a fixed environmental state.

The main idea of the algorithm is that two states in the unknown automaton are different (even though they may appear the same to the learner, e.g., they are all accepting states) if and only if there exists a string e (analogous to a sequence of actions) that leads from these two states to two states that are visibly different (e.g., one resulting state is an accepting state and the other is not). Angluin calls the string e an *experiment*.

Let the unknown regular set be denoted by U, and assume that it is over a fixed, known, finite alphabet A. At any given time, the algorithm L^* has information about a finite collection of strings over A, classifying them as members or nonmembers of the unknown regular set U. This information is organized into an *observation table* (S, E, T). Here, S is a nonempty, finite, prefix-closed set of strings, and E is an nonempty, finite, suffix-closed set of strings. (A set S of strings is suffix-closed provided that if $s_1 s_2$ is in S, then s_2 is in S; a set S of strings is prefix-closed provided that if $s_1 s_2$ is in S, then s_1 is in S.) We can think of S as a set of strings that lead from the initial state to the states of the unknown automaton, and E as the set of experiments that are executed from these states. The result of these experiments are recorded in the 2-dimensional table T whose rows are given by $S \cup S \cdot A$ and whose columns are given by E. Each entry $T(se)$, where $s \in S \cup S \cdot A$ and $e \in E$, records whether the string se is in the unknown language. Initially $S = E = \{\lambda\}$ (the empty string), so the table T contains only one row and one column. As learning continues, more elements are added to S and E and the table T is augmented accordingly.

To illustrate the representation of the observation table, consider U as the set of all strings over $A = \{0, 1\}$ with an even number of 0s and an even number of 1s. An observation table with $S = \{\lambda, 0, 1, 11\}$ and $E = \{\lambda, 0\}$ is shown in Table 5.1. As we can see, the entry $T(00, 0)$ is "reject" because the string 000 has an odd number of 0s. The entry $T(11, \lambda)$ is "accept" because the string 11 has even number of 0s and 1s.

Given an observation table (S, E, T), it is straightforward to build a corresponding finite state automaton M_T that accepts the language and is consistent with the information in the table. Observe that the elements in S are strings that lead from the initial state to states of the unknown automaton (environment), so the states of M_T are the set of different states that the strings in S can lead to. This is equal to the set of different rows in the upper part of Table 5.1 that is labeled by S. Two rows are different only when the results of the same experiment are different. So $row(\lambda)$ is different from $row(0)$, but it is not different from $row(11)$ (note that the experimental results of $row(\lambda)$ and $row(11)$ are both ["accept" "reject"]). Thus, the

T_0		E	
		λ	0
S	λ	accept	reject
	0	reject	accept
	1	reject	reject
	11	accept	reject
$S \cdot A$	00	accept	reject
	01	reject	reject
	10	reject	reject
	110	reject	accept
	111	reject	reject

Table 5.1   An example of observation table T_0.

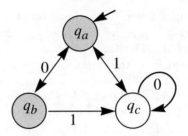

Figure 5.1 The automaton built from the observation table T_0.

corresponding machine of this table has three states: the state q_a includes $row(\lambda)$ and $row(11)$, the state q_b includes $row(0)$, and the state q_c includes $row(1)$.

The initial state of M_T is $row(\lambda)$ because this is where all strings in S start execution. The final states are those rows labeled by S that contain "accept" because these are the states where strings can be accepted.

The transition function of M_T is built based on the rows labeled $S \cdot A$. Each $row(sa)$, where $s \in S$ and $a \in A$, is interpreted as the state reached by the character (or action) a from the state $rwo(s)$, where $s \in S$. To ensure that the state after transition is one of the states that have been defined, the observation table must be *closed*. That is, for each sa in $S \cdot A$, there exists an s' in S such that $row(sa) = row(s')$. To ensure that the transition function is deterministic, the observation table must be *consistent*. That is, whenever s_1 and s_2 are elements of S such that $row(s_1) = row(s_2)$, for all a in A, $row(s_1a) = row(s_2a)$. In other words, executing the same action from the same state will lead to the same result state.

Thus, given a closed and consistent observation table (S, E, T), a corresponding automaton M_T with state set Q, initial state q_0, accepting states F, and transition function δ can be built as follows:

Model states:	$\{row(s) : s \in S\}$
Initial state:	$row(\lambda)$
Final states:	$\{row(s) : s \in S$ and $T(s) =$ "accept"$\}$
Transitions:	$\phi(row(s), a) = row(sa)$

From the observation table in Table 5.1, the automaton built according to these rules is shown in Figure 5.1.

Angluin has shown that M_T is consistent with the finite function T defined by the closed and consistent observation table (S, E, T). Any other acceptor consistent with T but not equivalent to M_T must have more states.

The L^* algorithm is shown in Figure 5.2. The main loop of the algorithm uses membership queries to construct a closed and consistent observation table and then asks whether the constructed automaton is correct through equivalence

1   Initialize S and E to $\{\lambda\}$,
2   Ask membership queries for λ and each $a \in A$,
3   Construct the initial observations table (S, E, T),
4   Repeat:
5   While (S, E, T) is not closed or not consistent:
6   If (S, E, T) is not consistent, then
7   Find s_1 and s_2 in S, $a \in A$, and $e \in E$ such that $row(s_1) = row(s_2)$
                 but $T(s_1 \cdot a \cdot e) \neq T(s_2 \cdot a \cdot e)$,
8   Add $a \cdot e$ to E,
9   Extend T to $(S \cup S \cdot A) \cdot E$ using membership queries,
10   If (S, E, T) is not closed, then
11   Find $s_1 \in S$ and $a \in A$ such that $row(s_1 \cdot a)$ is different from $row(s)$
12   for all $s \in S$,
13   Add $s_1 \cdot a$ to S,
14   Extend T to $(S \cup S \cdot A) \cdot E$ using membership queries,
15   Construct M_T and ask an equivalence query for M_T,
16   If the teacher replies with a counterexample w, then
17   Add w and all its prefixes to S,
18   Extend T to $(S \cup S \cdot A) \cdot E$ using membership queries,
19   Until the teacher replies *yes* to the conjecture M_T,
20   Halt and output M_T.

Figure 5.2   The L^* learning algorithm.

queries. If the automaton is correct, the algorithm terminates; otherwise, it uses the counterexample obtained from the equivalence queries to increase the size of S (so that more states are defined) and makes the observation table closed and consistent again before asking another equivalence query.

If an observation table (S, E, T) is not consistent (lines 6–9), then there must exist a state q_x denoted by two equivalent rows $row(s_1) = row(s_2)$ such that the same transition from q_x, say applying a, results in two different states, i.e., $T(s_1 \cdot a \cdot e) \neq T(s_2 \cdot a \cdot e)$. To fix this inconsistency, we need to distinguish $row(s_1)$ and $row(s_2)$ so that they will represent two different states instead of the single state q_x. This can be accomplished by introducing a new experiment, $a \cdot e$ in this case, whose results ensure that $row(s_1)$ and $row(s_2)$ are different in the extended observation table.

When an observation table (S, E, T) is not closed (lines 10–13), that means there exists a state transition, denoted by $row(s_1 \cdot a)$, that leads into a state that has not yet been defined (i.e., $row(s_1 \cdot a)$ is different from all $row(s)$ for $s \in S$.) To fix this problem, new states must be defined. This is accomplished by introducing the string $s_1 \cdot a$ into S, so that in the extended observation table this string denotes the missing state.

When an observation table is both closed and consistent (line 14), the learner constructs a state machine M_T and makes an equivalence query. If a counterexample w is provided by the teacher (line 15), then the algorithm knows that there are states in the unknown automaton that have not been visited yet. Since w can lead to such a new state, one can simply put w and all its prefixes into S so that the new state will be defined in the extended table (lines 16 and 17).

Angluin has proven that given any minimally adequate teacher presenting an unknown regular set U, the learner L^* eventually terminates and outputs an acceptor isomorphic to the minimum deterministic finite automata (DFA) accepting U. Moreover, if n is the number of states of the minimum DFA accepting U and m is an upper bound on the length of any counterexample provided by the teacher, then the total running time of L^* is bounded by a polynomial in m and n, namely, $O(m^2n^2 + mn^3)$. If the teacher always presents counterexamples of minimal length, then they will be at most n in length and L^* will run in time polynomial in n, namely, $O(n^4)$.

Although L^* is developed for learning regular sets, a learner can use it to construct a model of a finite state automaton environment if (1) the learner is given a means for resetting the environment to a fixed start state, and (2) there is a teacher who can provide counterexamples when the model constructed is different from the environment. In this context, the alphabet is the set of actions of the learner, and the "accept" and "reject" are the percepts of the learner. Notice that the percepts need not be binary; they can be any finite set. In this case, the entries in an observation table will be observations (i.e., a set of percepts) as defined in Chapter 2. To make a membership query on w, the learner resets the environment, executes the actions of w, then makes an observation in the last state reached. To perform an equivalence query, the learner resets the environment and then asks the teacher for a counterexample. The learning terminates when there are no more counterexamples.

Let us go through a complete example to see how L^* can be used by the little prince to construct a model of his world. Let us assume that in the fixed initial state in this environment the little prince sees the volcano and faces clockwise. Furthermore, the little prince has a magic action, say, pushing a reset button, that can bring him back to the starting state any time he wants.

Initially the little prince is at the initial state and the S set has only the action λ (doing nothing). He then performs membership queries for the actions $f(orward)$, $b(ackward)$, and $t(urn\text{-}around)$ (obtained by appending each possible action to λ) and contructs the observation table T_1 shown in Table 5.2.

This table is consistent but not closed, since $row(f)$ and $row(b)$ are different from all $row(s)$. So L^* moves $row(f)$ from the SA set to the S set and then performs membership queries for actions ff, fb, and ft (obtained by appending each possible action to f) and constructs the observation table T_2 shown in Table 5.3.

This observation table is consistent but not closed, since the $row(ff)$ is different from all the rows of S. L^* now moves ff to the set S and performs membership

T_1		E
		λ
S	λ	$v(olcano)$
SA	f	$n(othing)$
	b	$n(othing)$
	t	$v(olcano)$

Table 5.2   The initial observation table T_1.

T_2		E
		λ
S	λ	v
	f	n
SA	b	n
	t	v
	ff	$r(ose)$
	fb	v
	ft	n

Table 5.3   The observation table T_2.

queries for action sequences *fff*, *ffb*, and *fft* (obtained by appending each possible action to ff). The new observation table T_3 is shown in Table 5.4.

This table is closed and consistent, so L^* makes a conjecture of the model M_3 shown in Figure 5.3. However, M_3 is not a correct model of the environment, so the teacher replies with a counterexample. In this case, we will assume the counterexample is *ftf*. According to M_3, the predicted observation at the end of *ftf* will be *rose*, but the actual observation is *volcano*.

To process the counterexample, L^* adds *ftf* and its prefixes, *ft* and *f*, to the S set (*f* is already in S) and performs membership queries of *ftf*, *ftb*, *ftt*, *ftff*, *ftfb*, and *ftft* (obtained by appending each possible action to *ft* and *ftf*). It then constructs the observation table T_4 shown in Table 5.5.

This table is closed but not consistent, since $row(f) = row(ft)$ but $row(ff) \neq row(ftf)$. Thus, L^* adds f to E, and queries the action sequence *bf*, *tf*, *fbf*, *ffff*, *ffbf*, *fftf*, *ftbf*, *fttf*, *ftfff*, *ftfbf*, and *ftftf* (obtained by appending f to each element in SA) to construct the table T_5, shown in Table 5.6.

T_3		E
		λ
S	λ	v
	f	n
	ff	r
SA	b	n
	t	v
	fb	v
	ft	n
	fff	n
	ffb	n
	fft	r

Table 5.4   The observation table T_3.

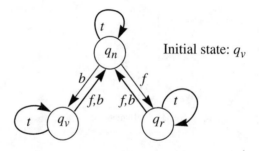

Initial state: q_v

Figure 5.3 M_3, the first conjecture made by L^*.

This table is both closed and consistent, so L^* makes a conjecture that the model of the environment M_5 is as shown in Figure 5.4. Since this model is correct, the teacher returns no counterexample, and the learning terminates. The whole process has made 2 equivalence queries and 34 membership queries or observations, and has taken 101 actions.

5.3   Synchronizing L^* by Homing Sequences

A serious limitation of Angluin's L^* algorithm is its critical dependence on a means of resetting the environment to a fixed start state. Thus, a L^* learner can never really get lost or lose track of its current state since it can always reset the environment to a fixed state. Clearly, this is not always possible in practice. Rivest

T_4		E
		λ
S	λ	v
	f	n
	ff	r
	ft	n
	ftf	v
SA	b	n
	t	v
	fb	v
	fff	n
	ffb	r
	fft	r
	ftf	v
	ftb	r
	ftt	n
	$ftff$	n
	$ftfb$	n
	$ftft$	v

Table 5.5   The observation table T_4.

and Schapire [93] have developed an extension of L^* that uses homing sequences to eliminate the need for a reset.

A homing sequence exists for every finite state automaton. Informally, a *homing sequence* is a sequence of actions that, when applied to the automaton, is guaranteed to orient the learner: The observation sequence produced by a homing sequence uniquely determines the state reached by the automaton at the end of the homing sequence.

Formally, let $h = a_1 a_2 \cdots a_r$ be a sequence of actions, and let Q be the set of states of the environment. Then the observation sequence produced by h from a state $q \in Q$ is defined as

$$q\langle h\rangle = \langle \rho(q), \rho(qa_1), \rho(qa_1a_2), \ldots, \rho(qa_1a_2\cdots a_r)\rangle$$

where $qa_1 \cdots a_i$ is the state reached by executing actions $a_1 \cdots a_i$ from the state q, and $\rho(x)$ is the observation made at the state x. A sequence of actions h is a homing sequence if and only if

$$(\forall q_1 \in Q)(\forall q_2 \in Q)q_1\langle h\rangle = q_2\langle h\rangle \Rightarrow q_1 h = q_2 h$$

T_5		E	
		λ	f
S	λ	v	n
	f	n	r
	ff	r	n
	ft	n	v
	ftf	v	n
SA	b	n	v
	t	v	n
	fb	v	n
	fff	n	v
	ffb	r	r
	fft	r	n
	ftf	v	n
	ftb	r	n
	ftt	n	r
	$ftff$	n	r
	$ftfb$	n	n
	$ftft$	v	n

Table 5.6 The observation table T_5.

In words, if the two observation sequences that are produced by executing the same homing sequence from any two states are the same, then these two executions must reach the same state. (For a complete discussion of homing sequences, see Kohavi [42].)

As a simple example, the action sequence f is a homing sequence for the little prince environment. From any state q of that environment (see Figure 5.4), if the observation of $q\langle f \rangle$ is "{nothing}, {rose}," then the learner must have reached the state q_r; if $q\langle f \rangle$ is "{rose}, {nothing}," then the learner must have reached the state q_{nv}; if $q\langle f \rangle$ is "{volcano}, {nothing}," then the learner must have reached the state q_{nr}, and if $q\langle f \rangle$ is "{nothing}, {volcano}," then the learner must have reached the state q_v.

Given full knowledge of the structure of a finite state automaton environment, it is easy to construct a homing sequence h, as shown in Figure 5.5. Initially, we have $h = \lambda$. On each iteration of the loop, a new sequence of actions x is appended to the end of h so that h now distinguishes two states not previously distinguished. Thus, $|Q\langle h \rangle| < |Q\langle hx \rangle| \leq n$, where $n = |Q|$, and therefore the program will terminate

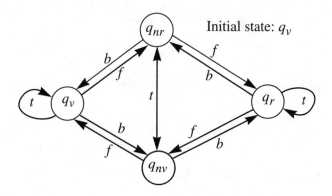

Figure 5.4 M_5, the second conjecture made by L^*.

Input: A finite state automaton.
Output: A homing sequence h.
Procedure:
1    $h \leftarrow \lambda$,
2   While $(\exists q_1, q_2 \in Q)q_1\langle h \rangle = q_2\langle h \rangle$ but $q_1 h \neq q_2 h$ do:
3   Let $x \in A^*$ distinguish $q_1 h$ and $q_2 h$,
4        $h \leftarrow hx$,
5   End.

Figure 5.5 Constructing a homing sequence.

after at most n iterations. Further, since each extension need only have length n, a homing sequence constructed this way has length at most n^2.

We note that the homing sequences constructed by the preceding algorithm are the best possible in the sense that there exist environments whose shortest homing sequence has length $\Omega(n^2)$. However, given a finite state automaton, it is NP-complete to find the shortest homing sequence for the automaton.

In many respects, a homing sequence behaves like a reset: By executing the homing sequence, the learner discovers where it is — which state it is at in the environment. However, unlike a reset, the final state is not fixed, and the learner does not know beforehand what state it will end up in.

To see how the learner can use homing sequences to construct a model of the environment, let us first assume the learner is given a correct homing sequence h. Later, we will show how to remove this assumption.

Suppose the learner executes h from the current state q, producing a sequence of observations $\sigma = q\langle h \rangle$. If the learner should repeat this experiment from state q' and find $q'\langle h \rangle = \sigma$, then, because h is a homing sequence, the states where it

Input: Actions, percepts, and a homing sequence h.
Output: A perfect model of the environment.
Procedure:

1 Repeat:
2   Execute h, producing a sequence of observations σ,
3   If it doesn't exist, create L_σ^*, a new copy of L^*,
4   Simulate the next query of L_σ^*,
5   If L_σ^* queries the membership of action sequence b,
6   Then execute b and supply L_σ^* with the observation of the final state
         reached,
7   If L_σ^* queries an equivalence query,
8   Then if the conjectured model is correct,
9   Then stop and return the model,
10   Else obtain a counterexample and supply it to L_σ^*.

Figure 5.6   Model construction with a given homing sequence.

finished must be the same in both cases: $qh = q'h$. If the learner can guarantee
that the output of h comes up σ with regularity, then the learner simply infers the
model of the environment by simulating the L^* algorithm, treating qh as the initial
state. When L^* demands a reset, the learner executes h: If the output comes up σ,
then the learner must be at qh, and the reset is successful; otherwise, the learner
tries again. Unfortunately, in the general case, it may be very difficult to make h
produce σ regularly.

Instead, Rivest and Shapire simulate an independent copy L_σ^* of L^* for each
possible output σ of executing h, as shown in Figure 5.6. Since $|Q\langle h\rangle| < n$ (i.e.,
the number of possible outputs of h is less than n), no more than n copies of L^*
will be created and simulated. Furthermore, on each iteration of the loop, at least
one copy makes one query and so makes progress towards inference of the correct
model of the environment. Thus, this algorithm will succeed in inferring the model
after no more than n times the time required by each individual L^*.

The algorithms in Figure 5.5 and Figure 5.6 can be combined to learn the homing
sequence and to infer the model at the same time, as shown in Figure 5.7. The main
idea is to maintain a sequence h that is presumed to be a true homing sequence.
Using this h, the algorithm constructs a table $(S_\sigma, E_\sigma, T_\sigma)$ for each output σ of h
in the same way as shown in Figure 5.6. When evidence indicates that h is not a
homing sequence, h is extended and improved, using the algorithm in Figure 5.5.
Eventually a correct homing sequence is constructed. Initially we use the sequence
$h = \lambda$.

When h is incorrect, we may discover *inconsistent behavior* in the course of
simulating some copy of L^*: Suppose on two different iterations of the loop in
Figure 5.6, we begin in states q_1 and q_2, execute h, produce output $q_1\langle h\rangle = q_2\langle h\rangle =
\sigma$, and, as part of the simulation of L_σ^*, execute action sequence x. If h were a

Inputs: Actions, percepts, and n environmental states.
Output: A perfect model of the environment.
Procedure:

1   $h \leftarrow \lambda$,
2   Repeat:
3   Execute h, producing a sequence of observations σ,
4   If it doesn't already exist, create L^*_σ, a new copy of L^*,
5   If $|\{row(s) : s \in S_\sigma\}| \le n$,
6   Then simulate the next query of L^*_σ as in Figure 5.6 (and check for
7   inconsistency),
8   Else
9   Let $\{s_1, \ldots, s_{n+1}\} \subset S_\sigma$ be such that $row(s_i) \ne row(s_j)$,
10   Randomly choose a pair s_i, s_j from this set,
11   Let $e \in E_\sigma$ be such that $T_\sigma(s_i e) \ne T_\sigma(s_j e)$,
12   With equal probability, re-execute either $s_i e$ or $s_j e$
13   (and check for inconsistency),
14   If inconsistency found executing some string x,
15   Then $h \leftarrow hx$ and discard all existing copies of L^*,
16 Until a correct conjecture is made.

Figure 5.7 Model construction by learning a homing sequence.

homing sequence, then x's output would have to be the same on both iterations since $q_1\langle h\rangle$ and $q_2\langle h\rangle$ must be equal.

If h is not a homing sequence, then it may happen that $q_1 h\langle x\rangle \ne q_2 h\langle x\rangle$. That is, we have discovered that x distinguishes $q_1 h$ and $q_2 h$, and so, just as was done in Figure 5.5, we replace h with hx, producing in a sense a better approximation. At this point, the existing copies of L^* are discarded, and the algorithm begins from scratch but with a better approximation of a homing sequence. Since h can be extended in this fashion only n times, this means a slowdown by at most a factor of n, compared to the algorithm in Figure 5.6.

Notice that the algorithm uses a probabilistic strategy to find an inconsistency quickly when h is known to be incorrect. For the moment, we assume n, the number of global states, has been given to the learner. We will later prove that this assumption can be removed without increasing the worst-case runtime by more than a small constant factor. Suppose we execute h from state q, which produces observation sequence σ and puts the learner in the initial state of L^*_σ, and find that for L^*_σ there are more than n distinct rows (this indicates that there are more states in L^*_σ than n). Then let $s_1, \ldots, s_{n+1}$ be as in Figure 5.7. By the pigeonhole principle, there is at least one pair of distinct rows s_i, s_j such that $qhs_i = qhs_j$ (i.e., they are actually the same environmental state). Further, since $row(s_i) \ne row(s_j)$, there is some $e \in E_\sigma$ for which $T_\sigma(s_i e) \ne T_\sigma(s_j e)$. However,

$\rho(qhs_ie) = \rho(qhs_je)$, because they are the same environmental state. Therefore, either $\rho(qhs_ie) \neq T_\sigma(s_ie)$ or $\rho(qhs_je) \neq T_\sigma(s_je)$, and so re-executing s_ie (or s_je, respectively) to form the current state qh will produce the desired inconsistency.

So the chance of choosing the correct pair s_i, s_j as above is at least $\binom{n+1}{2}^{-1}$, and the chance of then choosing the correct experiment to rerun s_ie or s_je is at least 0.5. Thus, it can be verified that the probability of finding an inconsistency using the technique outlined above is at least $1/n(n+1)$. Also, since the number of distinct possible outputs of h is at most n (there are only n states) and L^* starts over from scratch at most n times, no more than n^2 copies of L^* are ever created, and $|h|$ does not exceed $O(n^2 + nm)$, where $m = |A|$.

Using all these facts, Rivest and Schapire prove the following theorem (the result is simplified here by assuming that no counterexample has length greater than n):

THEOREM 5.3.1 (Rivest–Shapire) Given δ, $0 < \delta \leq 1$, the algorithm described in Figure 5.7 will correctly infer the model of the environment with probability at least $1 - \delta$ after executing

$$O(n^6 \log(n/\delta))$$

actions.

This result increases only by a small constant factor when the learner is not given the number of environmental states n. The algorithm can be modified as follows: Let n_b be the estimate of n. Initially we have $n_b = 1$. If the estimate of n is too small, then the learning procedure will fail to find a correct model within the known worst-case time bound. If this happens, then we stop the current execution of the algorithm and start over from scratch, increase the estimate to n_b by a factor of 2. Once n_b exceeds n, the algorithm will finish (since at this point n_b will actually be an upper bound on n).

Let $T(n)$ be the known worst-case time complexity of the algorithm in Figure 5.7. The total time spent by this modified algorithm is at most

$$U = T(1) + T(2) + T(4) + \cdots + T(n^*)$$

where n^* is the value of n_b the first time it exceeds n. Clearly, $n^* \geq n$ and n^* is a power of 2, say $n^* = 2^r$ for some r. Since $T(n)$ is a polynomial, say cn^k for some constants c and k, then using a standard formula for geometric series, we have

$$U = \sum_{i=0}^{r}(c2^{ik}) = c\left(\frac{2^{k(r+1)} - 1}{2^k - 1}\right) = O(2^{kr}) = O((n^*)^k) = O(n^k) = O(T(n))$$

As an example, we apply the algorithm to the environment of the little prince. This time, the little prince does not have the reset button that magically enables him to go back to a fixed state. However, we assume that the number of global states $n = 4$ is given to the learner.

The little prince can start from any state, say the state where the volcano is seen. At the beginning, $h = \lambda$. According to the algorithm, the learner executes h to go home and observes v. Since this observation is new, a copy L_v^*, whose home state is v, is created, and its observation table T_1 is shown in Table 5.7.

To gain more information for this table, the learner chooses to query f and observes $n(othing)$. This information is used to augment the table of L_v^*. After that, the learner executes h to go home. The output of h is n. Since this is a new output of h, a new copy L_n^*, whose home state is n, is created. Now there are two observation tables, shown in Figure 5.8.

The learner is now at the home state of L_n^*. It chooses to query f and uses the result, $r(ose)$, to augment the table for L_n^*. It then executes h to go home. Since

$$L_v^*$$

T_1		E
		λ
S	λ	v
	f	?
SA	b	?
	t	?

Table 5.7   The observation table T_1 using a homing sequence.

$$L_v^* \qquad\qquad L_n^*$$

T_1		E
		λ
S	λ	v
	f	n
SA	b	?
	t	?

T_2		E
		λ
S	λ	n
	f	?
SA	b	?
	t	?

Figure 5.8   Observation tables of two L^*s.

h's output r is new, a new copy L_r^*, whose home state is r, is created. Figure 5.9 shows the observation tables of three L^*s.

The learner then queries f for L_r^* and observes n. The result of this query is used to augment the table of L_r^*. After that, it executes h to go home. Since the output of h is n, the learner is now at the home state of L_n^*.

The learner chooses to query b and augments the table for L_n^*. It then executes h and goes to the home state of L_r^* (because the output of h is r). It queries b for L_r^* and the result of executing h puts it back to the home state of L_n^*. Now the learner queries t for L_n^*, and the resulting tables are shown in Figure 5.10.

Now the learner queries ff for L_n^*. Here, it discovers an inconsistent behavior: According to the current table of L_n^*, executing f from the home state should result in r; however, the actual outcome is v. At this point, the homing sequence $h = \lambda$ is revised to $h = f$, and all the tables are discarded.

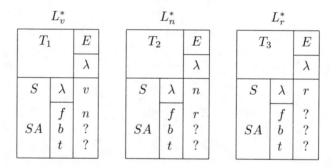

Figure 5.9 Observation tables of three L^*s.

Figure 5.10 Updated observation tables of three L^*s.

Since the homing sequence $h = f$ is correct, the learner will now successfully build a correct model of the environment. In the new run, four copies of L^* will be created, since the homing sequence has four possible outputs: vn, nr, rn, nv. We omit the details of the trace; the reader should be able to continue the example easily.

So far, both L^* and its extensions require that a teacher supply counterexamples. However, this requirement can be replaced by a random walk by the learner. To find a counterexample, the learner randomly chooses a sequence of actions. The actions are then executed, and the consequence of each step is compared with the entries in the observation table. If an inconsistent behavior is discovered, the actions that have been executed so far constitute the counterexample.

5.4   The CDL+ Framework

In this section, we apply the CDL framework to learning from translucent environments. The objective is to integrate concept learning, as discussed in Chapter 4, with translucent model abstraction. In other words, we would like to extend CDL from *history-insensitive* concept learning to *history-sensitive* concept learning.

It turns out that there is a natural place in the CDL framework for such an extension. Recall that CDL is a framework of predict-surprise-identify-revise (see Figure 4.15), where the identify process is to find the differences between the current observation and the relevant previous experience. If the environment is transparent and noise-free, this identify process can always find differences. However, if the environment is translucent, then there is no such guarantee. We need to do something extra when the identify process fails to find any differences between the current observation and the relevant past observations.

Such a situation arises when two states look exactly the same yet yield different consequences when the same action is applied. To apply CDL to this situation, we must revise the identify process so that the current observation is compared not only with the relevant experience but also its ancestors, that is, the history of the current observation and the history of that relevant experience. By doing so, we again ensure that some differences will be found by the identify process.

Clearly, when differences must be found in the history, the process of model revision must also be extended. It now must use these historical differences to distinguish the different behaviors of two environmental states in the model that seem to be the same. There are many ways to accomplish this. One can increase the length of "lookback" when making predictions, or one can create hidden state variables to differentiate the seemingly identical environmental states by two or more model states.

Finally, since the model is translucent, the synchronization problem becomes substantial and CDL must be extended to synchronize the model with the environment.

1   Let M be the current model,
2   Let c be the current observation,
3   Let t be the current model state synchronized with the environment,
4   Select a sequence b of actions,
5   For each action $a \in b$, do:
6   Make a prediction P based on M: $(C, a) \to P$, where C matches c,
7   Execute a in the environment,
8   Observe the actual consequence o from the environment,
9   If the prediction is correct (i.e., P matches o),
10   Then record the experience (c, a, o) as an example of $(C, a) \to P$,
11   Else (this is a *surprise*) do:
12   Identify the differences between c and the examples of $(C, a) \to P$,
13   If differences are found,
14   Then revise M as in CDL,
15   Else search for differences in the history of c and c',
16   Revise M using the historical differences so that the predictions on
                       (c, a) and (c', a) are history sensitive,
17   Record (c, a, o) as an example of the proper entry of M.

Figure 5.11   The CDL+ framework for learning from translucent environments.

The CDL+ framework presented in Figure 5.11 incorporates the necessary extensions to CDL just described. Notice that it is the same as the basic CDL framework except for lines 3, 15, and 16. Line 3 solves the synchronization problem where the learner synchronizes itself with the environment. An example of such a synchronization solution is the homing sequence technique presented in Section 5.3. Line 15 is the extension of the identify process. It deals with the case where c and c' look the same but produce different consequences for the same action. This line is where the learner must search for differences in the histories of the observations c and c'. The search may have to use different criteria and strategies for different representations of observations and model states. For example, if observations are numerical vectors, then the differences may be the distance between two vectors. If observations are structured instance graphs, as used in the LIVE system (see Chapter 10), then the difference may be a list of predicates and the strategy to find them may involve a search. After the historical differences are found, line 16 is where the model is revised. Many techniques can be used to accomplish this task. We will see examples of such techniques in the following sections as well as in later chapters on the LIVE system.

To illustrate the CDL+ framework, we will describe two applications in the following sections. The first application is learning from environments that are translucent finite state machines. The result is an algorithm called CDL+1, which solves the construction problem and the synchronization problem using a single mechanism. The second one is an algorithm for learning structured prediction rules and discovering hidden features in the environment. This algorithm is used in the LIVE system and will be discussed at length in Chapter 10 and Chapter 11.

5.5   Local Distinguishing Experiments (LDEs)

As we have seen in Section 5.2 and Section 5.3, learning from deterministic finite machines involves both the construction problem and the synchronization problem. The L^* algorithm is primarily a solution for the construction problem, while Rivest–Schapire's algorithm is mainly for solving the synchronization problem. However, can these two problems be solved using a single mechanism? In this section, we define a simple mechanism called "local distinguishing experiments," which will enable us to use CDL+ to solve both problems.

As before, we define an environment $\mathcal{E}$ to be a Moore machine $(A, P, Q, \delta, \rho, r)$ with the restrictions that $|Q| > |P|$ and ρ is a many-to-one function. However, we define the model of the environment $M \equiv (A, P, S, \phi, t)$ slightly differently, as follows:

- A is a set of actions, the same as the set of input actions into $\mathcal{E}$.

- P is a set of percepts, the same as the set of output symbols from $\mathcal{E}$.

- S is a set of model states represented as $P\{0, 1\}^i$, where $\{0, 1\}^i$ is a finite sequence of binary symbols constructed by the learner.

- ϕ, a function from $S \times A$ to S, is the transition function of M.

- t is the current model state of M. When a basic action b is applied to M, t is updated to be $\phi(t, b)$.

Notice that model states S are now defined to be concatenations of P and some constructed binary symbols. With $i > 0$, the number of model states $|S|$ is clearly greater than the number of percepts $|P|$ and the model is translucent.

Model states are described by expressions $s = p\{0, 1\}^*$, where $p \in P$. A description s represents a set of model states whose prefix is s. For example, $p1$ represents all the model states whose prefixes are $p1$, and $p10$ represents all the model states whose prefixes are $p10$. Clearly, $p10$ is a subset of $p1$. Notice that the symbol s is used to denote both a set of model states and a single model state (when the set is a singleton). From the context, this uniform representation of model state(s) should not cause any confusion.

As before, we assume that the learner can apply any basic action $a \in A$ to the environment (and to the model as well) and can observe the current output $p = \rho(r)$ $(p \in P)$ from the environment. We denote the set of all finite action sequences by $B = A^*$ and extend the domain of the function $\delta(q, \cdot)$ to B in the following way: $\delta(q, \lambda) = q$ and $\delta(q, ba) = \delta(\delta(q, b), a)$ for all $q \in Q, a \in A, b \in B$. Here, λ denotes the empty (or null) string. Thus, $\delta(q, b)$ denotes the environmental state reached by executing sequence b from an environmental state q. We note that all these extensions and notations on δ also applies to M's transition function ϕ.

In the process of learning, we allow the function $\phi(s, b)$ to be nondeterministic. That is, the value $s' = \phi(s, b)$ may represent a set of model states whose prefix is s'. In that case, $\phi(s, b)$ denotes the set of model states s' reachable by executing the actions b from the model state s. As a special case, if $\phi(s, b)$ does not exist, we write $\phi(s, b) =?$. The symbol ? represents the entire set of model states. In other words, if the learner executes b from s, it could be anywhere in the model.

Given a description $s = p\{0, 1\}^*$, we use $\alpha(s)$ to denote the observed part of s, and $\beta(s)$ for the constructed part of s. For example, if $s = p0110$, then $\alpha(s) = p$ and $\beta(s) = 0110$.

We say that a single model state s is visibly equivalent to an environmental state q if $\rho(q) = \alpha(s)$. Furthermore, we say that M is perfect and synchronized with respect to E if the current model state t is visibly equivalent to the current environmental state r and, for all sequences of actions $b \in B$, the model state $\phi(t, b)$ is also visibly equivalent to the environmental state $\delta(r, b)$. Our objective is to learn a perfect and synchronized model of the environment.

Let r be the current environmental state. We refer to the sequence of percepts observed in the environmental states visited by executing $b = a_0 a_1 \cdots a_e$ from r as the *observation sequence OS of b from r*:

$$OS(r, b) \equiv [\rho(r), \rho(\delta(r, a_0)), \rho(\delta(r, a_0 a_1)), \ldots, \rho(\delta(r, a_0 a_1 \cdots a_e))]$$

We assume that the environment is reduced; that is, for every pair of unequal environmental states q_1 and q_2, there is an action sequence b such that $OS(q_1, b) \neq OS(q_2, b)$.

Somewhat parallel to an observation sequence of b from r, we define the *prediction sequence PS of b at t* to be the sequence of model states visited by executing actions $b = a_0 a_1 \ldots a_e$ from the current model state t:

$$PS(t, b) \equiv [t, \phi(t, a_0), \phi(t, a_0 a_1), \ldots, \phi(t, a_0 a_1 \cdots a_e)]$$

When ϕ is nondeterministic (this is possible during learning), then $\phi(t, a_1, \ldots, a_i)$ may represent a set of model states.

As we mentioned earlier, model states are represented by both the learner's percepts and hidden symbols that are constructed during learning. These hidden symbols are created to reflect the different behaviors of look-alike model states. These behaviors are represented as local distinguishing experiments (LDEs), and these LDEs are created when the learner encounters a surprise and differences must be found in the history of the current observation.

Before we formally define local distinguishing experiments, let us first consider an example. Suppose you are to predict whether you can lift some boxes before actually doing so. These boxes look identical from the outside. However, if you open the lid, you can see whether a box is empty or contains some weight that is too heavy for you to lift. In order to make a correct prediction, all you need to do is open the lid and look inside. The sequence of open-lid and look-inside comprises a local distinguishing experiment. It uses your actions and percepts to reveal more information about a particular environmental state.

Formally, let $p = \rho(r)$ be the current observation from the environment (seeing a box), and $s = pc$, where c is a binary string, be a set of model states (the box is either empty or too heavy) that contains the current model state t (the true status of the box). Notice that the necessary condition for s to contain t is that $\alpha(s) = \alpha(t)$. We refer to a set of relations that can reduce the set pc to either $pc0$ or $pc1$, whichever contains t, as a *local distinguishing experiment of pc*, denoted as $LDE(pc?)$:

$$LDE(pc?) = (b;\ pc0,\ [x];\ pc1,\ [y])$$

where b is a sequence of actions, $[x] = OS(q_1, b)$ and $[y] = OS(q_2, b)$ are two different previous observation sequences of b from some environmental states q_1 and q_2 whose appearance are p (i.e., $\rho(q_1) = \rho(q_2) = p$), and $b, [x], [y]$, and the current environmental state r satisfy the relation

$$pc? = \begin{cases} pc0 & \text{if } OS(r, b) = [x] \\ pc1 & \text{if } OS(r, b) = [y] \end{cases}$$

Thus, if it is known that the current model state t is in pc (e.g., a box is either empty or too heavy), then one can determine if t is in $pc0$ or $pc1$ by executing b (e.g., opening the lid) in the current environmental state r, comparing the actual observation sequence (e.g., what you see inside the box) with $[x]$ and $[y]$, and concluding either t was in $pc0$ or t was in $pc1$. We define the length of $LDE(pc?)$ to be the length of its actions b.

5.6 Model Construction with LDEs

To solve the construction problem, we shall instantiate CDL+'s predict-surprise-identify-revise framework to this particular model representation. As we mentioned earlier, if the environment is transparent, then the direct recording D algorithm (see Section 4.2) can be used to solve the construction problem. However, in translucent environments this simple D algorithm will not work because the learner's current observation cannot determine the current environmental state. For example, in the SHAPE environment shown in Figure 5.12 [93], there are two actions, x and y, and four environmental states, I, II, III, and IV. A learner (a little robot), however, can only see the two shapes of the nodes, □ and ◇. When □ is seen, the learner (at state I) does not have enough information to determine whether the current environmental state is I or II.

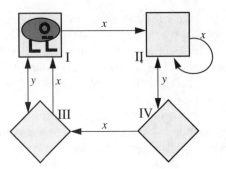

Figure 5.12   The SHAPE environment.

To model a translucent environment, model states must consist of both observed symbols and constructed symbols in order to distinguish different environmental states that appear alike. For example, one way to model the states in the SHAPE environment is to use one hidden binary symbol for the model states. So, one can use $\square 0$ for state I, $\square 1$ for state II, $\diamond 0$ for state III, and $\diamond 1$ for state IV.

Because of the hidden symbols in the model states, both the construction problem and the synchronization problem are substantial. In particular, since the number of model states is greater than the number of percepts, the learner must determine when and how to construct new model states. Since there is more than one model state whose observed part matches the current observation, the learner must also determine which model state is current. Clearly, the simple D algorithm must be extended to deal with these problems.

To make this extension possible, we apply the CDL+ framework to the D algorithm. At the beginning, the learner treats the environment as if it were transparent and uses the D algorithm to construct a simple and direct model. Unlike the D algorithm, however, the learner always predicts the consequence of its action based on the model that is learned. Whenever the actual consequence does not match the predicted consequence (a surprise), the learner identifies, by searching through the history, a faulty state in the model that is responsible for the surprise and splits that state into two by appending to it a newly created binary symbol. The action sequence that causes the surprise, along with the prediction sequence and the observation sequence at that time, is defined as a new LDE for distinguishing the two new states in the future. Let us now go through the steps in the surprise-identify-revise paradigm carefully.

5.6.1   Surprise

Let r be the current environmental state (which is unknown to the learner), $p_0 = \rho(r)$ the current observation, and s_0 the current model state, where $\alpha(s_0) = p_0$.

After executing a sequence of actions $b = a_0 a_1 \cdots a_e$, we have a prediction sequence and observation sequence as follows:

$$PS(s_0, b) = [s_0, s_1, \ldots, s_e, s_{e+1}] \tag{5.1}$$
$$OS(r, b) = [p_0, p_1, \ldots, p_e, p_{e+1}] \tag{5.2}$$

We say that there is a surprise if the latest prediction is visibly different from the latest observation: $p_{e+1} \neq \alpha(s_{e+1})$.

To illustrate the idea, suppose a learner in the SHAPE environment has learned, using the D algorithm, the following model:

$$M_0 = \begin{bmatrix} \phi(\diamond, x) &=& \diamond \\ \phi(\square, x) &=& \square \\ \phi(\diamond, y) &=& \square \\ \phi(\square, y) &=& \diamond \end{bmatrix}$$

Now suppose that the current environmental state is III (which is unknown to the learner), and the learner's current observation is $\diamond$. Since the learner thinks that the current model state is $\diamond$, the prediction sequence and the observation sequence of executing the action x are

$$PS(\diamond, x) = [\diamond, \diamond]$$
$$OS(\text{III}, x) = [\diamond, \square]$$

There is a surprise in the above prediction and observation sequences because their last elements are visibly different: $\diamond \neq \square$.

5.6.2 Identify and Split

Since the learner's predictions are based on previous observations, a surprise means that some model state is mistakenly representing more than one environmental state. The learner must identify this faulty model state and split it into two new model states, one representing the prediction and the other representing the surprising observation.

The process of identify and split is simple when the surprise is the first one the learner encounters (i.e., there are no previously defined LDEs). In this case, the state s_e in $PS(s_0, b)$ (see equation 5.1) is the faulty state. This is because s_e is the state to which the same action, a_e, causes different consequences, s_{e+1} and p_{e+1}. Thus, s_e is split into $s_e 0$ and $s_e 1$, and a local distinguishing experiment for s_e is defined, namely,

$$LDE(s_e?) = (a_e;\ s_e 0, [\alpha(s_e), \alpha(s_{e+1})];\ s_e 1, [p_e, p_{e+1}]) \tag{5.3}$$

For example, in the above surprise between $PS(\diamond, x)$ and $OS(\text{III}, x)$, the faulty model state is $\diamond$. It is thus split into $\diamond 0$ and $\diamond 1$, and a new LDE is defined as follows:

$$LDE(\diamond?) = (x;\ \diamond 0, [\diamond, \diamond];\ \diamond 1, [\diamond, \square]) \tag{5.4}$$

When the surprise is not the first one, then the process of identify and split is more complex. In this case, since there exist previously defined LDEs, the elements in $PS(s_0, b)$ (see equation 5.1) and $OS(r, b)$ (see equation 5.2) may represent sets of model states. Before the faulty state can be identified, these elements must be refined (i.e., the number of model states each element represents must be reduced) using the existing LDEs. In fact, such a refinement is conducted every time the prediction and observation sequences are extended (i.e., a new pair of action and observation becomes available).

The refinement of the prediction sequence is accomplished as follows. Let

$$\widehat{PS}(s_0, b) = [u_0, u_1, \ldots, u_e, u_{e+1}]$$

be the refined sequence of $PS(s_0, b)$. By definition, the relation between $PS(s_0, b)$ and $\widehat{PS}(s_0, b)$ is that $u_i \subseteq s_i$ for all $0 \leq i \leq e + 1$. Initially each u_i is copied from the correspondent s_i in the prediction sequence $PS(s_0, b)$ except when $s_i = ?$ (i.e., there is no prediction for step i), in which case u_i is copied from p_i in the observation sequence $OS(r, b)$. Then, for each u_i in $\widehat{PS}(s_0, b)$ from the end to the beginning, we check to see if it can be shrunk by some existing LDEs. In other words, for each u_i, we check to see if there exists an $LDE(u_i?) = (l; u_i 0, [x]; u_i 1, [y])$ such that l is equal to a subsequence of b that begins with a_i, say $l = a_i \cdots a_j$, and $[x]$ (or $[y]$) is equal to the subsequence $u_i, \ldots, u_{j+1}$ in $OS(r, b)$. If so, u_i is set to be $u_i 0$ (or $u_i 1$). The same procedure is also used to refine the observation sequence $OS(r, b)$ to get

$$\widehat{OS}(r, b) = [o_0, o_1, \ldots, o_e, o_{e+1}]$$

where $o_i \subseteq p_i$ for all $0 \leq i \leq e + 1$. The entire refinement procedure is summarized in Figure 5.13.

Inputs: $PS(s_0, b) = [s_0, s_1, \ldots, s_e, s_{e+1}]$ and $OS(r, b) = [p_0, p_1, \ldots, p_e, p_{e+1}]$
Output: $\widehat{PS}(s_0, b) = [u_0, u_1, \ldots, u_e, u_{e+1}]$ and $\widehat{OS}(r, b) = [o_0, o_1, \ldots, o_e, o_{e+1}]$
Procedure:

1   For $(i = e + 1; i \geq 0; i - -)$ do:
2       $o_i = p_i$,
3   If $s_i = ?$, then $u_i = p_i$, else $u_i = s_i$,
4   For $(i = e; i \geq 0; i - -)$ do:
5   While exists $LDE(u_i?) = (a_i \cdots a_j; u_i 0, [x]; u_i 1, [y])$ such that $i \leq j \leq e$,
6   Set $u_i = \begin{cases} u_i 0 & \text{if } [u_i, \ldots, u_{j+1}] = [x] \\ u_i 1 & \text{if } [u_i, \ldots, u_{j+1}] = [y] \end{cases}$
7   While exists $LDE(o_i?) = (a_i \cdots a_j; o_i 0, [x]; o_i 1, [y])$ such that $i \leq j \leq e$,
8   Set $o_i = \begin{cases} o_i 0 & \text{if } [o_i, \ldots, o_{j+1}] = [x] \\ o_i 1 & \text{if } [o_i, \ldots, o_{j+1}] = [y] \end{cases}$

Figure 5.13   Refining the prediction and observation sequences using LDEs.

To illustrate the refinement procedure, suppose that the learner's current model of the SHAPE environment is M_1 (we will show how M_1 is built from M_0 shortly):

$$M_1 = \begin{bmatrix} \phi(\Diamond 0, x) & = & \Diamond? \\ \phi(\Diamond 1, x) & = & \Box \\ \phi(\Box, y) & = & \Diamond? \\ \phi(\Box, x) & = & \Box \end{bmatrix}$$

and the current prediction sequence and observation sequence are

$$PS(\Box, yx) = [\Box, \Diamond, ?]$$
$$OS(\mathrm{II}, yx) = [\Box, \Diamond, \Diamond]$$

After the first loop in Figure 5.13 (lines 1–3), we have $\widehat{PS}(\Box, yx) = [\Box, \Diamond, \Diamond]$ and $\widehat{OS}(\mathrm{II}, yx) = [\Box, \Diamond, \Diamond]$. Notice that the third element of $\widehat{PS}(\Box, yx)$ is copied from $OS(\mathrm{II}, yx)$ because the corresponding prediction in $PS(\Box, yx)$ is a ?. After the second loop (lines 4–8), we have

$$\widehat{PS}(\Box, yx) = [\Box, \Diamond 0, \Diamond]$$
$$\widehat{OS}(II, yx) = [\Box, \Diamond 1, \Diamond]$$

Notice that the second elements in $\widehat{PS}(\Box, yx)$ and $\widehat{OS}(\mathrm{II}, yx)$ are inferred by the existing $LDE(\Diamond?) = (x; \Diamond 0, [\Diamond \Diamond]; \Diamond 1, [\Diamond \Box])$, defined in equation 5.4, respectively.

Once PS and OS are refined to be $\widehat{PS}$ and $\widehat{OS}$, we are ready to identify the faulty state. The faulty state is the state u_k in $\widehat{PS}(s_0, b)$, where k is the greatest index such that $u_k \subseteq o_k$ and $u_{k+1} \not\subseteq o_{k+1}$. The motivation is that u_k is the state to which applying the same action yields different next states. It can be proven that such a u_k always exists when a surprise occurs. However, whether u_k is always the optimal faulty state to split is still a open question. When u_k is not optimal, the states created by splitting u_k may become wasted: They eventually become unreachable.

After u_k is identified, it is split into $u_k 0$ and $u_k 1$, and a new local distinguishing experiment for u_k is defined as follows:

$$LDE(u_k?) = (a_k \cdots a_e; \ u_k 0, [\alpha(u_k), \ldots, \alpha(u_{e+1})]; \ u_k 1, [p_k, \ldots, p_{e+1}]) \qquad (5.5)$$

Notice that equation 5.5 is a generalized version of equation 5.3. Notice also that the length of the new LDE (because of the way u_k is identified) is at most 1 plus the maximum length of the existing LDEs.

In the SHAPE environment example, after $\widehat{PS}(\Box, yx)$ and $\widehat{OS}(\mathrm{II}, yx)$ are computed, the state $\Box$ is identified as faulty, and it is split into $\Box 0$ and $\Box 1$. A new local distinguishing experiment $LDE(\Box)$ is then defined as

$$LDE(\Box?) = (yx; \ \Box 0, [\Box, \Diamond, \Diamond]; \ \Box 1, [\Box, \Diamond, \Box]) \qquad (5.6)$$

5.6.3   Model Revision

Models are revised on two occasions: When the refined prediction sequence is more deterministic than the model, and when a new LDE is defined after a surprise (i.e., a model state is split).

In the first case, since a refined prediction sequence incorporates the most recent observations from the environment, it may contain information that is not in the current model. Such information can be used to update the model accordingly. For example, from $\widehat{PS}(\Box, yx)$ we can upgrade the nondeterministic transition $\phi(\Box, y) = \Diamond?$ in M_1 to $\phi(\Box, y) = \Diamond 0$, and the updated M_1, which we shall call M_1', becomes

$$
M_1' = \begin{bmatrix}
\phi(\Diamond 0, x) & = & \Diamond? \\
\phi(\Diamond 1, x) & = & \Box \\
\phi(\Box, y) & = & \Diamond 0 \\
\phi(\Box, x) & = & \Box
\end{bmatrix}
$$

In general, the transition function is updated according to $\widehat{PS}$ as follows. If there exist u_i, a_i, and u_{i+1} such that u_i is a single model state and u_{i+1} is a subset of $\phi(u_i, a_i)$, then $\phi(u_i, a_i)$ is assigned to be u_{i+1}.

In the second case, after the model state u_k is split, the transition function ϕ is modified as follows: (1) Delete the obsolete transitions $\phi(u_k, \cdot)$ from ϕ since u_k is no longer a single model state; (2) insert two new transitions $\phi(u_k 0, a_k) = u_{j+1}$ and $\phi(u_k 1, a_k) = o_{j+1}$ into ϕ. Notice that all the transitions that go into u_i, namely, $\phi(\cdot, \cdot) = u_i$, now become nondeterministic (since u_k now represents two model states, $u_i 0$ and $u_i 1$). Such nondeterminism will be resolved in future explorations by model revision as we described above.

An example of model revision after a surprise is how M_1 is built from M_0. When the state $\Diamond$ is split in model M_0 after the first surprise (see equation 5.4), we get model M_1 according to the above revision steps. (The reader can verify this fact.) Similarly, when the state $\Box$ is split after the second surprise (see equation 5.6), the model M_1' becomes a new model:

$$
M_2 = \begin{bmatrix}
\phi(\Diamond 0, x) & = & \Diamond 1 \\
\phi(\Diamond 1, x) & = & \Box? \\
\phi(\Box 0, y) & = & \Diamond 0 \\
\phi(\Box 1, y) & = & \Diamond 1
\end{bmatrix}
$$

5.7   The CDL+1 Learning Algorithm

With each step in the predict-surprise-identify-revise in place, we now present the CDL+1 algorithm in Figure 5.14. For the moment, we assume that a procedure GOTO-A-M-STATE, which tells the learner what the current model state is, solves the synchronization problem.

It is interesting to see that the CDL+1 algorithm is an extension of the D algorithm (see Figure 4.1), which learns only from transparent environments. Line 3

Procedure CDL+1():
1 Initialize $S = P$, $\phi = \{\}$, and $t =?$,
2 Repeat:
3   While t is not a single model state, $t \leftarrow$ GOTO-A-M-STATE(),
4   Let r be the unknown current environmental state,
5   Select actions $b = b'a$ such that $\phi(\phi(t, b'), a) = p$ and p is not
            a single model state (i.e., either $LDE(p?)$ exists or $p =?$),
6   If $b = \lambda$,
7   Then $b =$ random action sequence,
8   Else $b = b \cdot l$ where l is the actions in $LDE(p?)$,
9   For each action a_j in $b = a_0, a_1, \ldots, a_j, \ldots, a_{|a|}$, do:
10   Execute a_j,
11   Construct $PS(t, a_0 \cdots a_j) = [s_0, \ldots, s_j, s_{j+1}]$ and $OS(r, a_0 \cdots a_j) =$
                $[p_0, \ldots, p_j, p_{j+1}]$,
12   Compute $\widehat{PS}(t, a_0 \cdots a_j) = [u_0, \ldots, u_j, u_{j+1}]$ and $\widehat{OS}(r, a_0 \cdots a_j) =$
                $[o_0, \ldots, o_j, o_{j+1}]$,
13   For $(i = 0; i \leq j; i + +)$, if $u_i \in S$ and $u_{i+1} \subset \phi(u_i, a_i)$, then set
                $\phi(u_i, a_i) = u_{i+1}$,
14   If $\alpha(s_{j+1}) \neq p_{j+1}$ (a surprise), then
15   Call IDENTIFY-SPLIT($\widehat{PS}(t, a_0 \cdots a_j)$, $\widehat{OS}(r, a_0 \cdots a_j)$),
16   Goto 1,
17   Until no surprises for at least Ω actions,
18   Return ϕ and $t = u_{|b|+1}$.

Procedure IDENTIFY-SPLIT($\widehat{PS}(t, b), \widehat{OS}(r, b)$):
1 Let k be the greatest index in $\widehat{PS}(t, b)$ such that $u_k \subseteq o_k$, $u_{k+1} \not\subseteq o_{k+1}$,
2 Replace u_k in S by $u_k 0$ and $u_k 1$,
3 Define $LDE(u_k?) = (a_k \ldots a_{|b|}, [\alpha(u_k), \ldots, \alpha(u_{|b|+1})], [\alpha(o_k), \ldots, \alpha(o_{|b|+1})])$,
4 Delete $\phi(u_k, \cdot)$ and set $\phi(u_k 0, a_k) = u_{k+1}$ and $\phi(u_k 1, a_k) = o_{k+1}$.

Figure 5.14 The CDL+1 algorithm for learning from translucent finite state machines.

determines the current model state t using the assumed procedure GOTO-A-M-STATE. Lines 5 to 8 select actions. As in the D algorithm, where actions are selected for constructing nonexisting transitions, here actions are selected to reduce the nondeterminism of existing transitions. (A nonexisting transition is a nondeterministic transition that goes to the entire set of model states.) To reduce the nondeterminism of $\phi(\phi(t, a'), b) = p$, we use $LDE(p?)$ and run its actions l after $a'b$ (line 8). If the current transition ϕ is already both complete (i.e., $\phi(s, b)$ exists for all $s \in S$ and $b \in B$) and deterministic (i.e., $\phi(s, b) \in S$ for all $s \in S$ and $b \in B$), then a sequence of random actions is selected at line 7. The purpose of the random actions is to look for surprises (or counterexamples). If an oracle were available to provide such counterexamples, line 7 will be the place to call the oracle.

For each action that is selected, line 11 constructs the prediction and observation sequence; line 12 computes the refined prediction and observation sequence (see Figure 5.13 for details); and line 13 uses the refined prediction sequence to tighten up some nondeterministic transitions in ϕ (see case 1 in Section 5.6.3). Lines 14 and 15 check for surprises and call the procedure IDENTIFY-SPLIT, which implements the identify-split-revise procedure discussed in Sections 5.6.2 and 5.6.3.

The termination for CDL+1 is different from that for the D algorithm. In a translucent environment without an oracle, the learner cannot be absolutely certain that it has learned the perfect and synchronized model of the environment. Therefore, the learner must continue to wander in the environment even though its current model is already complete and deterministic. How long such wandering goes on depends on the degree of confidence desired in the model. For the moment, we assume that the wandering time before termination is a constant Ω.

Finally, one should also notice that the CDL+1 algorithm is just an instantiation of the CDL+ framework. The correspondence between CDL+ and CDL+1 are quite obvious. They both select actions, make predictions, and get surprises. However, the identify process in CDL+1 is somewhat simpler (CDL+1 does not contain lines corresponding to lines 12–14 in CDL+). When prediction s_{j+1} does not match the feedback p_{j+1}, CDL+1 does not try, as CDL+ does, to find the differences between the current instance p_j and the relevant previous example s_j. This is because in the representation of finite automata, different observations imply different environmental states (i.e., the number of environmental states is no less than the number of different observations), and we know there is no difference between p_j and s_j. In concept learning, however, this is not the case, because one concept may cover many instances (observations), as we have seen in Chapter 4.

5.7.1   Synchronization by LDEs

We now describe the solution for the synchronization problem implemented in the procedure GOTO-A-M-STATE. The main idea is to use the concatenation of the actions in the existing LDEs as a homing sequence of the current model and to construct a homing function for identifying the model states that are reached at the end of executing the homing sequence.

The concept of the homing sequence is well known in automata theory [42], but only recently has it been used in learning [93]. A homing sequence for an environment $E = (A, P, Q, \delta, \rho, r)$ is a sequence of actions h such that the state reached by executing h from any state $q \in Q$ is uniquely determined by the observation sequence $OS(q, h)$. That is, h is a homing sequence if and only if

$$(\forall q_1, q_2 \in Q)[OS(q_1, h) = OS(q_2, h)] \implies [\delta(q_1, h) = \delta(q_2, h)]$$

It is known that every finite automaton has a homing sequence. So a model $M = (A, P, S, \phi, t)$ must have a homing sequence, too. We say that h is a homing sequence for M if and only if

$$(\forall s_1, s_2 \in S)[\alpha(PS(s_1, h)) = \alpha(PS(s_2, h))] \implies [\phi(s_1, h) = \phi(s_2, h)]$$

where $\alpha(PS(s, h))$ is the visible part of $PS(s, h)$.

Interestingly, the concatenation of the actions in the existing LDEs, in the order of their creation, is always a homing sequence for the current model. This can be proven by induction on the number of existing LDEs as follows: Let i be the number of existing LDEs, M_i the current model, and S_i the set of model states in M_i. When $i = 0$, $S_0 = P$ and all model states are visibly different, so $h_0 = \lambda$ is a homing sequence of M_0. Now assume that for M_i, $h_i = \hbar_1 \cdots \hbar_i$ is a homing sequence, where $\hbar_i$ denotes the actions in LDE_i (LDE_i denotes the ith LDE in the order of their creation). To see that $h_{i+1} = h_i \hbar_{i+1}$ is a homing sequence for M_{i+1}, we notice that the only difference between S_i and S_{i+1} is that a state $s_x \in S_i$ is replaced by $s_x 0$ and $s_x 1$ in S_{i+1}. Furthermore, $s_x 0$ and $s_x 1$ are the only two states in S_{i+1} that cannot be distinguished by h_i; that is, $s_x 0$ and $s_x 1$ can be reached from some states s_0 and s_1 in S_{i+1} by h_i and $OS(s_0, h_i) = OS(s_1, h_i)$. However, LDE_{i+1} is defined to distinguish $s_x 0$ and $s_x 1$, and $\hbar_{i+1}$ has the property that $OS(s_x 0, \hbar_{i+1}) \neq OS(s_x 1, \hbar_{i+1})$. Therefore, $OS(s_0, h_{i+1}) \neq OS(s_1, h_{i+1})$, and h_{i+1} is a homing sequence for M_{i+1}. Notice that since the length of LDE_i is at most $i + 1$, the length of h_i is at most $\sum_{j=1}^{i} |\hbar_j| = i(1 + i)/2$.

Once we know the homing sequence h_i for the current model M_i, the synchronization problem can be solved by constructing a *homing function* H. The function H is a mapping from $P^{|h_i|+1}$ to S_i, where $P^{|h_i|+1}$ are observation sequences of length $|h_i| + 1$. Given an observation sequence $OS(q, h_i)$, $H(OS(q, h_i))$ is the model state that is reached at the end of h_i, regardless of what q is.

Thus, the task for GOTO-A-M-STATE is to construct the function H for the current model M_i until H is good enough to return a single model state immediately after executing h_i. Figure 5.15 presents the details of the implementation. Notice that every time GOTO-A-M-STATE is called, either the current model is updated due to a surprise, or the function H becomes more deterministic. In the first case, the procedure resets H and returns a ?. (A new H will be constructed for the new model when the procedure is called again.) In the second case, the execution of $LDE(s)$ at line 8 gains more information for the model state s, and that information is used to make $H(OS(r, h_i))$ more certain at line 11. For a model M_i, the number of actions to construct a complete H is at most $i(i + |P|)(i^2 + i + 1)$: There are $i + |P|$ possible entries in H, each of them takes at most i updates to complete, and each update takes at most $i^2 + i + 1$ actions (a homing sequence plus an LDE). Once H is complete for M_i, the procedure GOTO-A-M-STATE takes only h_i actions to execute for M_i and always returns a single model state.

1   Let r be the unknown current environmental state, and $s_0 = \rho(r)$,
2   Execute h_i and construct $PS(s_0, h_i)$, $OS(r, h_i)$, $\widehat{PS}(s_0, h_i)$, and $\widehat{OS}(r, h_i)$,
3   If a surprise occurs in step 1,
4   Then call IDENTIFY-SPLIT($\widehat{PS}, \widehat{OS}$); set $H = $ NULL; return ?,
5   Let $s \leftarrow H(OS(r, h_i))$ (when $h_i = \lambda$, $H(s_0) = s_0$),
6   If $s = ?$, then set both s and $H(OS(r, h_i))$ to be the last element in $\widehat{PS}(s_0, h_i)$,
7   If s is a single model state, then return s,
8   Execute the actions $\hbar_s$ in $LDE(s)$ and extend $PS, OS, \widehat{PS}$, and $\widehat{OS}$
        to $PS(s_0, h_i\hbar_s)$, $OS(r, h_i\hbar_s)$, $\widehat{PS}(s_0, h_i\hbar_s)$, and $\widehat{OS}(r, h_i\hbar_s)$,
9   If a surprise occurs in step 8,
10   Then call IDENTIFY-SPLIT($\widehat{PS}, \widehat{OS}$); set $H = $ NULL; return ?,
11   Set $H(OS(r, h_i))$ to be the lth element in $\widehat{PS}(s_0, h_i\hbar_s)$, where $l = |h_i|$,
12   Return the last element in $\widehat{PS}(s_0, h_i\hbar_s)$.

Figure 5.15   The procedure GOTO-A-M-STATE.

5.7.2 Examples and Analysis

To further understand the algorithm CDL+1, we first present a complete example of CDL+1 learning from the little prince environment and then analyze the complexity of CDL+1.

Assume the prince is initially at a state where he can see the volcano, and the learner explores its actions in the order of (turn-around (t), forward (f), and backward (b)). From the initial state, the learner does an action t and observes a volcano (v). So it builds a transition $\phi(v, t) = v$. It then does an action f, which leads to a state where it can see nothing; it builds another transition $\phi(v, f) = n$. At that state, the learner does t and sees nothing again, so $\phi(n, t) = n$ is built. It then does f and sees a volcano, from which $\phi(n, f) = v$ is built. In this state, since actions t and f have already been explored, the learner does a b and sees nothing. So $\phi(v, b) = n$ is built. After 10 exploration actions, the learner has developed the following model:

$$
M_0 = \begin{bmatrix}
\phi(r, b) & = & n \\
\phi(r, f) & = & n \\
\phi(r, t) & = & r \\
\phi(n, b) & = & r \\
\phi(v, b) & = & n \\
\phi(n, f) & = & v \\
\phi(n, t) & = & n \\
\phi(v, f) & = & n \\
\phi(v, t) & = & v
\end{bmatrix}
$$

At this moment, the learner is at the state n, where nothing can be seen. The underlying environmental state is se, where the little prince is at the south pole and facing east. Since M_0 is now both complete and deterministic, the learner decides to do a random action b and predicts that the next state is r. However, the actual consequence state is v, and a surprise occurs. At this moment, the prediction sequence and the observation sequence are the following:

$$PS(r, bb) = [r, n, r]$$
$$OS(se, bb) = [r, n, v]$$

From this surprise, the state n is split into $n0$ and $n1$, and $LDE(n?)$ is defined as

$$LDE(n?) = (b; n0, [n, r]; n1, [n, v])$$

The model M_0 is updated to become M_1 as follows:

$$M_1 = \begin{bmatrix} \phi(n1, b) & = & v \\ \phi(n0, b) & = & r \\ \phi(r, b) & = & n \\ \phi(r, f) & = & n \\ \phi(r, t) & = & r \\ \phi(v, b) & = & n \\ \phi(v, f) & = & n \\ \phi(v, t) & = & v \end{bmatrix}$$

Based on this new model, the learner continues to explore the environment to fill in the missing and nondeterministic transitions in M_1. Since the current state is v and $\phi(v, b) = n$ is nondeterministic, the learner does the action b and observes $n?$. Since b is the homing sequence for M_1, a new entry for the homing function is inserted: $H_1([v, n]) = n?$. In order to find out whether $n? = n0$ or $n? = n1$, the action b in $LDE(n?)$ is executed. The resulting state is r, so the learner concludes that $n? = n0$. Based on this conclusion, $\phi(v, b) = n$ is updated to $\phi(v, b) = n0$ and $H_1([v, n]) = n?$ is updated to $H_1([v, n]) = n0$. A new entry $H_1([n, r]) = r$ is also created. Such exploration and discrimination continues for another 15 actions, at which point the learner has the following model:

$$M_1 = \begin{bmatrix} \phi(n1, f) & = & r \\ \phi(n1, t) & = & n0 \\ \phi(n0, f) & = & v \\ \phi(n0, t) & = & n1 \\ \phi(n1, b) & = & v \\ \phi(n0, b) & = & r \\ \phi(r, b) & = & n1 \\ \phi(r, f) & = & n0 \\ \phi(r, t) & = & r \\ \phi(v, b) & = & n0 \\ \phi(v, f) & = & n1 \\ \phi(v, t) & = & v \end{bmatrix}$$

Thus, if started from the state where the volcano is seen, CDL+1 takes 29 steps to learn a perfect and synchronized model of the little prince environment.

To analyze the complexity of CDL+1, let us first consider how many actions are executed between the creation of M_i and the creation of M_{i+1}. During this period, actions are executed for three purposes: to build up H, to revise M_i, and to look for counterexamples. We already know that building up H takes at most $O((i + p)^4)$ actions, where $p = |P|$. Revising M_i takes at most $O(m(i + p)^3)$ actions, where $m = |A|$. This is because there are $p + i$ model states in M_i, each state needs to be visited at most $O(mi)$ times to build up transitions for all actions, and each visit takes at most $O(i + p)$ actions. Finally, looking for counterexamples takes at most Ω actions. Thus, the total number of actions during this period is at most

$$\max(O((i + p)^4), O(m(i + p)^3), \Omega)$$

which we take roughly as $\max(O(i^4), \Omega)$ when m and p are small relative to i.

If there is an oracle to supply counterexamples for each M_i, then the constant Ω is irrelevant and the construction of models $M_0, M_1, \ldots, M_i$ stops when $i = n - p$, where $n = |Q|$. There are no more surprises after M_{n-p} is completed, and M_{n-p} has exactly n model states, which have a one-to-one correspondence to the environmental states. In this case, the total number of actions to learn a perfect and synchronized model of the environment is at most

$$\sum_{i=0}^{n-p} O(i^4) = O(n^5)$$

When there is no oracle, the value of Ω can be estimated by stochastic approximation using the technique proposed in [127] and used in [1]. Let us assume that there is some probability distribution P_r on the set of all sequences over the action set A and that P_r is unknown to the learner. In addition, we assume that the learner, at the start of the computation, is given two positive numbers between 0 and 1: the accuracy ϵ and the confidence ξ.

Let $\mathcal{E} = (A, P, Q, \delta, \rho, r)$ be the environment, and $M_i = (A, P, S_i, \phi_i, t)$ be a model of $\mathcal{E}$. When M_i is complete and deterministic, there is a mapping γ from S_i to Q. We say that M_i is an ϵ-approximation of $\mathcal{E}$ provided that, at any state $s \in S_i$,

$$\sum_{b \in A^*} P_r(b) \leq \epsilon \quad \text{where} \quad \alpha(\phi(s, b)) \neq \rho(\delta(\gamma(s), b))$$

Thus, if M_i is an ϵ-approximation of $\mathcal{E}$, then the probability of CDL+1 finding a prediction failure after a random sequence of actions is at most ϵ. Using this definition, we have the following proposition: If CDL+1 terminates after

$$\Omega \geq \frac{1}{\epsilon} \left(\log \frac{1}{\xi} \right)$$

consecutive actions without surprises, then the probability that the learned model M_i is an ϵ-approximation of $\mathcal{E}$ is at least $1 - \xi$.

To see that this holds, notice that according to the definition of ϵ-approximation, the probability of having a single successful prediction is at least $1 - \epsilon$. If Ω actions are tested, the probability that all predictions are correct is at least $(1-\epsilon)^\Omega$. Under this condition, the probability that M_i is not an ϵ-approximation of $\mathcal{E}$ is at most $(1-\epsilon)^\Omega$. We wish $(1-\epsilon)^\Omega \leq \xi$ so that we can have at least $1 - \xi$ confidence that M_i is an ϵ-approximation of $\mathcal{E}$. Thus, $(1-\epsilon)^\Omega \leq \xi$, and therefore $\Omega \log(1-\epsilon) \leq \log \xi$, $\Omega(-\epsilon) \leq -\log \frac{1}{\xi}$ (because $-\epsilon \leq \log(1-\epsilon)$ when $0 \leq \epsilon \leq 1$), and $\Omega \geq \frac{1}{\epsilon} \log \frac{1}{\xi}$.

Finally, the reader should be cautioned that there are unresolved problems when no oracle is available. For example, in learning randomly generated directed graphs with 25 states, 3 basic actions, and 2 percepts, the best performance of the algorithm is about 1500 actions. But there are times when it generates over 50 states and uses more than 30,000 actions. The final model is correct but contains many garbage states that are not reachable; the upper bound of the number of wasted states is still unknown. One possible solution is to learn and utilize an *adaptive* homing sequence. Interested readers are referred to [94] for details.

5.8 Discovering Hidden Features When Learning Prediction Rules

This section outlines the second application of the CDL+ framework, namely, combining learning prediction rules with discovering hidden features in the environment. Since this application is at the heart of the LIVE system to be discussed in later chapters (in particular Chapter 11), our description here will be brief.

In essence, LIVE is a system that actively abstracts models from environments for solving problems. Unlike building a state machine model that has the same size as the environment, LIVE learns a model that is much smaller than the environment. The compact model is represented as a set of prediction rules. These rules are transition functions like *concept* $\times$ *action* $\rightarrow$ *prediction*, where *concept* is a set of states that share some properties, and *prediction* is a set of features of states.

Due to this objective, LIVE simultaneously faces two problems of opposite nature. On the one hand, it tries to shrink the environment into a compact model. On the other hand, it must expand the definition of internal states when the environment is translucent. To apply the CDL+ framework to this situation, LIVE uses the CDL proper part (lines 12–14 in Figure 5.11) to learn the prediction rules. However, LIVE does not literally compare two examples to find differences. Instead, LIVE first generalizes the examples by replacing some of their constants with the variables that are bounded in the applications of the prediction rules. In doing so, two examples may be considered exactly the same even if they are literally different.

With this generalized criteria for finding differences, LIVE uses the extended part of the CDL+ framework (lines 15 and 16 in Figure 5.11) for discovering hidden features. Whenever two applications of the same prediction rule yield a surprise where no differences can be found, LIVE will search into the history of these two applications to find historical differences. Hidden features are defined according to the differences so found, just as we saw in the case of learning from translucent finite state machines (Section 5.7).

Although there is no existing theoretical analysis for such applications of CDL+, the paradigm is empirically applied in several cases. In Chapter 11 LIVE uses CDL+ to discover the concept of genes in an environment simulating Mendel's experiments on breeding garden peas [62]. In Chapter 12 LIVE applies the algorithm to the translucent environment of the "Plates of Hanoi," a variation of the Tower of Hanoi, and discovers two hidden concepts, PUTable and PICKable, in the process of learning prediction rules.

Finally, if a learner's given percepts and actions can be viewed as biases of its learning abilities, then the CDL+ framework is a constructive approach that largely overcomes such biases by defining new terms.

5.9   Stochastic Learning Automata

All the environments and automata we have studied so far are deterministic in nature. In this section, we will briefly discuss a case of nondeterminism: learning stochastic automata from a random environment [75].

A *random environment* $\mathcal{E}$ is defined as a tuple (B, Z, ρ) with parameters defined as follows:

- $B = \{b_1, b_2, \ldots, b_r\}$ is a finite set of input symbols.

- $Z = \{z_1, z_2, \ldots, z_r\}$ is a set of output symbols where $0 \leq z_i \leq 1$ for $1 \leq i \leq r$. Frequently these symbols have binary values $\{0, 1\}$, with 0 being called the "nonpenalty response" and 1 the "penalty response."

- $\rho = (\rho_1, \rho_2, \ldots, \rho_r)$ is a set of probabilistic mappings from B to Z. That is, if the environment receives an input b_i, $1 \leq i \leq r$, then the probability of the output being 1 is ρ_i. We say an environment $\mathcal{E}$ is stationary if ρ does not change with time. Otherwise, the environment is nonstationary.

A stochastic automaton model M of the environment $\mathcal{E}$ is defined as $\{B, Z, P, A\}$, where

- B is a set of basic actions and is the same as the set of input symbols of $\mathcal{E}$,

- Z is a set of percepts and is the same as the set of output symbols of $\mathcal{E}$,

- P is the action probability vector governing the choice of actions at each discrete time point n; that is, at each time n, $P(n) = (p_1(n), p_2(n), \ldots, p_r(n))$ and $\sum_{i=1}^{r} p_i(n) = 1$, and

- A is an algorithm (also called an "updating scheme" or "reinforcement scheme") that generates $P(n+1)$ from $P(n)$.

The objective of this type of learning is to search for an (optimal) action probability vector such that the actions chosen according to this vector will minimize the penalties from the environment (e.g., seeing the smallest elements in Z as often as possible).

To quantify this objective, we define the average penalty received by the learner. At a certain stage n, if the action b_i is selected with probability $p_i(n)$, then this average penalty, $M(n)$, conditioned on $P(n)$ is

$$M(n) = E[z(n)|P(n)] = \sum_{i=1}^{r} p_i(n)\rho_i$$

Clearly the best a learner can do is to reach the optimal

$$\lim_{n\to\infty} E[M(n)] = \rho_l = \min_{1\le i\le r}\{\rho_i\}$$

In the optimal behavior, the learner chooses with probability 1 the action l that is the least likely to evoke a penalty response. Thus,

$$p_i = \begin{cases} 1 & \text{if } i = l \\ 0 & \text{if } i \neq l \end{cases}$$

Since the environment's response function ρ is unknown to the learner, the learner must learn the function $p(n)$ based on the feedback of each action. Formally, we have

$$p(n+1) = A[p(n), b(n), z(n)]$$

where A is the reinforcement scheme, and $b(n)$ and $z(n)$, respectively, represent the action and its response from the environment at instant n.

The basic idea behind any reinforcement scheme is rather simple. If the learning automaton selects an action b_i at instant n and a nonpenalty response is received, the action probability $p_i(n)$ is increased, and all the other components of $p(n)$ are decreased (to meet the constraint $\sum_{i=1}^{r} p_i(n) = 1$). Similarly, if the action receives a penalty response, then $p_i(n)$ is decreased and other components of $p(n)$ are increased. In general, when the action at n is b_i,

$$p_{j\neq i}(n+1) = \begin{cases} p_j(n) - f_j(p(n)) & \text{if } z_i(n) = 0 \\ p_j(n) + g_j(p(n)) & \text{if } z_i(n) = 1 \end{cases}$$

$$p_i(n+1) = \begin{cases} p_i(n) + \sum_{j\neq i} f_j(p(n)) & \text{if } z_i(n) = 0 \\ p_i(n) - \sum_{j\neq i} g_j(p(n)) & \text{if } z_i(n) = 1 \end{cases}$$

where $f_j(\cdot)$ and $g_j(\cdot)$ are nonnegative continuous functions. Much research has been done on the behavior and convergence of different (e.g., linear and nonlinear) functions for f_j and g_j [75]. We will not go into any details here.

5.10   Hidden Markov Models

Another example of a stochastic model is the hidden Markov model. (This section involves many applications of Bayesian probability theory. See Section 4.12 for more background information.) Here we extend the normal definition of a hidden Markov model [90] to include actions as well. In particular, an action-driven hidden Markov model M is a stochastic process $(B, Z, S, P, \theta, \pi)$ with the components defined as follows:

- B is a set of basic actions. As before, the actions can be applied to both the environment and the model.

- Z is a set of percepts and represents the output symbols of the environment that can be observed by the learner.

- S is a finite set of (internal) model states. We assume that at any single instant t, the current environmental state q_t corresponds to exactly one model state s_t, and the identity of s_t is sufficient to stochastically determine the effects of action in the environment. This is the *Markov assumption*.

- $P = \{P_{ij}[b]\}$ is a set of probabilities concerning model state transitions. For each basic action $b \in B$ and a pair of model states s_i and $s_j \in S$, the quantity $P_{ij}[b]$ specifies the probability that executing action b when the current model state is s_i will move the environment to an environmental state that corresponds to the model state s_j.

- $\theta = \{\theta_i(k)\}$, where $\theta_i(k) = p(z_k|s_i)$, $z_k \in Z$, and $s_i \in S$, is a set of probability distributions of observation symbols in each model state. (This corresponds to the appearance function for the deterministic models defined at the beginning of this chapter.) For each observation symbol z_k, the quantity $\theta_i(k)$ specifies the probability of observing z_k if the current model state is s_i.

- $\pi(t) = \{\pi_i(t)\}$ is the probability distribution of the current model state at time t. That is, $\pi_i(t) = p(i_t = s_i)$, where i_t denotes the current model state and $s_i \in S$ specifies the probability of s_i being the current model state at time t.

It is worth noting that all the specifications above are with respect to the models, not the environment. As in Chapter 2, the nature of the environment is unknown to the learner. However, since hidden Markov models can simulate the behavior of hidden states, such models are suitable for both transparent and translucent environments. Furthermore, since the models are stochastic in nature, they can also learn from noisy environments.

For the moment, we assume the number of states in the environment is known; thus the size of S is known (the problem of learning S will be considered in Chapter 7). The problem is the following: We are given a model

$$M = (B, Z, S, P, \theta, \pi)$$

and an experience

$$E \equiv \{z_1, b_1, z_2, b_2, \ldots, z_{T-1}, b_{T-1}, z_T\}$$

where the subscripts $1, 2, \ldots, T$ are discrete moments in time, $\{b_1, b_2, \ldots, b_{T-1}\}$ is a sequence of actions (denoted as A), and $\{z_1, z_2, \ldots, z_{T-1}, z_T\}$ is a sequence of percepts (denoted as O) observed from the environment $\mathcal{E}$ as actions A are executed in $\mathcal{E}$. Our goal is to adjust P, θ, and π so that M can best predict the behavior of $\mathcal{E}$. Here, *best* means the highest probability of making correct predictions in the stochastic sense.

In Bayesian probability theory, the above objective is to find a model M^* such that $p(M^*|EC)$ is the maximum among all possible models in the model space. (See Sections 4.1 and 4.4.2 for the definition of model space.) The variable C here represents all the relevant background knowledge. Such knowledge may include the physical properties of the learner, the size of the model space, and so on.

According to Bayesian probability theory, for each model M and given experience E, the quantity $p(M|EC)$ can be calculated as follows:

$$p(M|EC) = p(M|C) \left[\frac{p(E|MC)}{p(E|C)} \right] \tag{5.7}$$

This equation tells us that our "after experience," or *posterior probability* of M, is obtained by multiplying our "before experience," or *prior probability* of M, $p(M|C)$, by the probability of the experience assuming the truth of the model M, $p(E|MC)$, and dividing the result by the probability that we would have seen the experience anyway, $p(E|C)$.

Since the prior probability $p(M|C)$ reflects all the background information and previous experience about M, equation 5.7 can be viewed as a loop of learning: The posterior probability $p(M|EC)$ calculated after the last experience E is used as the prior probability $p(M|C')$ for a new experience E' to calculate the new posterior probability $p(M|E'C')$. The initial (i.e., before any experience) prior probability should be determined based on existing knowledge about the world. If no knowledge exists, then an equal value should be assigned to every model in the model space. That is, $p(M|C) = 1/|\mathcal{H}|$ where $\mathcal{H}$ is the model space.

Since the experience E is a combination of A and O, that is, $E = OA$, equation 5.7 can be written in other forms to reflect the fact that A can be chosen *independently* of M. In that case, we have

$$p(M|EC) = p(M|OAC) = p(M|C) \left[\frac{p(O|AMC)}{p(O|AC)} \right] \tag{5.8}$$

The proof of equation 5.8 is as follows:

$$
\begin{aligned}
p(M|OAC) &= p(M|C)\left[\frac{p(OA|MC)}{p(OA|C)}\right] \\
&= p(M|C)\left[\frac{p(A|MC)p(O|AMC)}{p(A|C)p(O|AC)}\right] \\
&= p(M|C)\left[\frac{p(O|AMC)}{p(O|AC)}\right]
\end{aligned}
$$

where the last step holds because M and A are independent. It is interesting to note that equation 5.7 is more general than equation 5.8. When actions must be chosen according to the current model (see model applications in Chapter 6), the term $p(A|MC)/p(A|C)$ reflects that fact. In the following discussion, however, only equation 5.8 is used.

5.10.1   The Forward and Backward Procedures

One important term in equation 5.8 is $p(O|AMC)$. It represents how likely it is that O will be seen given that M is true and A is executed. In this section, we will investigate how it is computed.

The most straightforward way to compute $p(O|AMC)$ is to think about every possible internal model state sequence $I = i_1 i_2 \cdots i_T$ that M must go through because of A in order to produce O. Thus, $p(O|AMC)$ can be expanded to be the sum of all possible I. That is,

$$
p(O|AMC) = \sum_I p(O, I|AMC) = \sum_I p(I|AMC)p(O|IAMC)
$$

In this equation, the second step is an application of the product rule in Bayesian theory. The last two terms can be computed as follows:

$$
\begin{aligned}
p(I|AMC) &= \pi_{i_1}(1)P_{i_1 i_2}[b_1]P_{i_2 i_3}[b_2]\cdots P_{i_{T-1} i_T}[b_{T-1}] \\
p(O|IAMC) &= \theta_{i_1}(z_1)\theta_{i_2}(z_2)\cdots\theta_{i_{T-1}}(z_{T-1})\theta_{i_T}(z_T)
\end{aligned}
$$

Therefore, we have

$$
p(O|AMC) = \sum_{I=i_1 i_2 \ldots i_T} \pi_{i_1}(1)\theta_{i_1}(z_1)P_{i_1 i_2}[b_1]\cdots\theta_{i_{T-1}}(z_{T-1})P_{i_{T-1} i_T}[b_{T-1}]\theta_{i_T}(z_T)
$$

However, this straightforward way of computing $p(O|AMC)$ is very expensive. It requires on the order of $2TN^T$ calculations, since at every time $t = 1, 2, \ldots, T$, there are N possible states to go through and for each summand about $2T$ calculations are required. Clearly a more efficient procedure is required. One such procedure is the combination of the forward and backward procedures.

The idea of the forward procedure is simple. Instead of expanding $p(O|AMC)$ to include every possible internal model state sequence, we expand it to every step of E. In other words, we calculate $p(O|AMC)$ incrementally on the time $t = 1, 2, \ldots, T$ as follows:

$$
\begin{aligned}
\alpha_1(i) &= p(z_1, i_1 = s_i | AMC) \\
\alpha_2(i) &= p(z_1, z_2, i_2 = s_i | AMC) \\
&\;\;\vdots \\
\alpha_t(i) &= p(z_1, z_2, \ldots, z_t, i_t = s_i | AMC) \\
&\;\;\vdots \\
\alpha_{T-1}(i) &= p(z_1, z_2, \ldots, z_{T-1}, i_{T-1} = s_i | AMC) \\
\alpha_T(i) &= p(z_1, z_2, \ldots, z_{T-1}, z_T, i_T = s_i | AMC)
\end{aligned}
$$

The term $\alpha_1(i)$ represents the probability of being in state s_i and seeing z_1 at time $t = 1$. The term $\alpha_t(i)$ represents the probability of seeing $\{z_1, \ldots, z_t\}$ and ending in state s_i at time t.

The computation of $\alpha_t(i)$ is straightforward. When $t = 1$, the probability of $\alpha_1(i)$ depends only on θ and π:

$$\alpha_1(i) = \pi_i \theta_i(z_1) \tag{5.9}$$

Furthermore, the value of $\alpha_{t+1}(j)$ can be computed recursively based on the values of $\alpha_t(i)$. In other words, in order to be in state s_j at time $t + 1$, the system must have been in any previous state s_i at time t (with probability $\alpha_t(i)$) and then made a transition to state s_j with probability $P_{ij}[b_t]$. Thus the probability of reaching state s_j at time $t + 1$ is the sum, for all $i \in S$, of the product of three probabilities: $\alpha_t(i)$, the probability of being at state s_i at time t; $P_{ij}[b_t]$, the probability of taking the transition from s_i to s_j under action b_t; and $\theta_j(z_{t+1})$, the probability of seeing z_{t+1} at state s_j. That is,

$$\alpha_{t+1}(j) = \sum_{i \in S} \alpha_t(i) P_{ij}[b_t] \theta_j(z_{t+1}) \tag{5.10}$$

Finally, when $\alpha_T(i)$ is known for all i, we can calculate the value of $p(O|AMC)$ by summing up $\alpha_T(i)$ on all model states. That is,

$$p(O|AMC) = \sum_{s_i \in S} \alpha_T(i) \tag{5.11}$$

Thus equations 5.9, 5.10, and 5.11 constitute the forward procedure. The complexity of this procedure is $O(TN^T)$. Compared to expanding to state sequences, this procedure saves many orders of magnitude of computation and makes the calculation of $P(O|AMC)$ computationally feasible.

The backward procedure is symmetric to the forward procedure. Instead of incrementing E from the beginning to the end, it increments from the end to the beginning. In particular, we have

$$\beta_{T-1}(i) = p(z_T|AMC, i_{T-1} = s_i)$$
$$\beta_{T-2}(i) = p(z_{T-1}, z_T|AMC, i_{T-2} = s_i)$$
$$\vdots$$
$$\beta_t(i) = p(z_{t+1}, \ldots, z_{T-1}, z_T|AMC, i_t = s_i)$$
$$\vdots$$
$$\beta_2(i) = p(z_3, \cdots, z_{T-1}, z_T|AMC, i_2 = s_i)$$
$$\beta_1(i) = p(z_2, z_3, \cdots, z_{T-1}, z_T|AMC, i_1 = s_i)$$

Each quantity $\beta_t(i)$ specifies the probability of seeing the sequence $z_{t+1}, \ldots, z_T$ if the state at time t is s_i.

As in the forward procedure, the value of $\beta_{t-1}(i)$ can be easily computed. When $t = T$, we define

$$\beta_T(i) = 1 \text{ for all states } s_i \qquad (5.12)$$

Furthermore, the value of $\beta_{t-1}(i)$ can be computed based on the values of $\beta_t(j)$. In other words, in order to be in state s_i at time $t - 1$, the system would have to be (with probability $\beta_t(i)$) in some next state s_j at time t with observation z_t, having made a transition from s_i to s_j with probability $P_{ij}[b_{t-1}]$. Thus, the probability of being at state i at time $t - 1$ is the sum of the product of the following three probabilities: $P_{ij}[b_{t-1}]$, the probability of taking the transition from s_i to s_j under action b_{t-1}; $\theta_j(z_t)$, the probability of seeing z_t at s_j; and $\beta_t(j)$, the probability of seeing the rest of the observations after time t given state j at time t. Thus, our equation is

$$\beta_{t-1}(i) = \sum_{j \in S} P_{ij}[b_{t-1}]\theta_j(z_t)\beta_t(j) \qquad (5.13)$$

Finally, when all $\beta_1(i)$ are known, $p(O|AMC)$ can be computed by summing up $\beta_1(i)$ on all model states. That is,

$$p(O|AMC) = \sum_{s_i \in S} \pi_i(1)\theta_i(z_1)\beta_1(i) \qquad (5.14)$$

Thus, equations 5.12, 5.13, and 5.14 constitute the backward procedure.

5.10.2   Optimizing Model Parameters

With the value of $p(O|AMC)$ computed, we can now use equation 5.8 to calculate $p(M|EC)$, the likelihood of a model M given experience E. The question now is how to use these values to find the best (most probable) model.

Intuitively it seems that we can first calculate $p(M|EC)$ for every model M and then choose the model that has the maximal $p(M|EC)$ value. However, this straightforward approach is computationally infeasible; there are simply too many models to consider. In fact, there are infinitely many models because each model $M = (B, Z, S, P, \theta, \pi)$ has $|B||S|^2 \cdot |S||Z| \cdot |S| = |B||Z||S|^4$ parameters, and each parameter assumes a value ranging from 0 to 1. (The situation is even worse if S is also considered as a parameter.)

Nevertheless, this problem is an optimization problem. The task is to search in the multidimensional parameter space for a point (i.e., a set of values for a model) that gives the maximal $p(M|EC)$ value. Although there is no known way to solve the optimization problem analytically, there exist gradient techniques (see, for example, Section 4.11) and iterative procedures for estimating the best values. Here we will introduce the Baum–Welch iterative procedure, which can be easily visualized.

The main idea of Baum–Welch's procedure can be summarized in the following three formulae for (re)estimating the new values of $\pi_i(1)$, $P_{ij}[b]$, and $\theta_i(z)$:

$\overline{\pi}_i(1) \quad \Longleftarrow \quad$ the probability of being in state s_i at time $t = 1$ given M and E

$\overline{P}_{ij}[b] \quad \Longleftarrow \quad$ the ratio of the expected number of transitions from state s_i to s_j under action b divided by the expected number of transitions out of state s_i under action b, given M and E

$\overline{\theta}_i(k) \quad \Longleftarrow \quad$ the ratio of the expected number of times of being in state s_i and observing symbol z_k divided by the expected number of times of being in state s_i, given M and E

To calculate these expected numbers, we first need to define two important variables. The first variable, $\gamma_t(i)$, is defined as the probability of being at state s_i at time t, given M, $E = OA$, and C. By the Bayesian rule, the product rule, and the values of $\alpha_t(i)$ and $\beta_t(i)$ calculated by the forward and backward procedures, the value of $\gamma_t(i)$ can be calculated as follows:

$$
\begin{aligned}
\gamma_t(i) &= p(i_t = s_i | EMC) \\
&= \frac{p(i_t = s_i | AMC)p(O|i_t = s_i, AMC)}{p(O|AMC)} \\
&= \frac{p(O, i_t = s_i | AMC)}{p(O|AMC)} \\
&= \frac{\alpha_t(i)\beta_t(i)}{p(O|AMC)}
\end{aligned}
$$

where $\alpha_t(i)$ accounts for having seen $\{z_1, \ldots, z_t\}$ ending in s_i at time t, and $\beta_t(i)$ accounts for seeing $\{z_{t+1}, \ldots, z_T\}$ after time t given state s_i at time t.

The second variable, $\xi_t(i, j)$, is defined as the probability of making the transition from state s_i to state s_j at time t, given M, E, and C. As in the above computation, the value of $\xi_t(i,j)$ can be calculated as follows:

$$
\begin{aligned}
\xi_t(i,j) &= p(i_t = s_i, i_{t+1} = s_j | EMC) \\
&= \frac{p(i_t = s_i, i_{t+1} = s_j | AMC)p(O|AMC, i_t = s_i, i_{t+1} = s_j)}{p(O|AMC)} \\
&= \frac{p(O, i_t = s_i, i_{t+1} = s_j | AMC)}{p(O|AMC)} \\
&= \frac{\alpha_t(i) \cdot P_{ij}[b_t] \cdot \theta_j(z_{t+1}) \cdot \beta_{t+1}(j)}{p(E|MC)}
\end{aligned}
$$

where $\alpha_t(i)$ accounts for having seen $\{z_1, b_1, \ldots, z_t\}$ ending in state s_i at time t, $P_{ij}[b_t] \cdot \theta_{t+1}(z_{t+1})$ accounts for the transition from s_i to s_j under action b_t and then seeing z_{t+1} at time $t+1$, and $\beta_{t+1}(j)$ accounts for seeing $\{z_{t+2}, \ldots, z_T\}$ after time $t+1$ given state s_j at time $t+1$.

With $\gamma_t(i)$ and $\xi_t(i,j)$ so defined, we can compute the expected numbers in the Baum–Welch formulae easily. In particular, the probability of being in state s_i at time $t = 1$ given M and E is simply $\gamma_1(i)$. The expected number of transitions from state s_i to s_j under action b given M and E is the sum of $\xi_t(i,j)$ for all t such that $b_t = b$, and the expected number of transitions out of state s_i under action b given M and E is the sum of $\gamma_t(i)$ for all t such that $b_t = b$. The expected number of times of being in state s_i and observing symbol z_k given M and E is the sum of $\gamma_t(i)$ for all t such that z_k is observed, and the expected number of times of being in state s_i given M and E is the sum of $\gamma_t(i)$ for $t = 1$ to $t = T$. Thus the Baum–Welch formulae can be computed as follows:

$$
\begin{aligned}
\overline{\pi}_i(1) &= \gamma_1(i) \qquad \text{for all } s_i \in S \\
\overline{P}_{ij}[b] &= \frac{\sum_{t=1, b_t=b}^{T} \xi_t(i,j)}{\sum_{t=1, b_t=b}^{T} \gamma_t(i)} \\
\overline{\theta}_i(k) &= \frac{\sum_{t=1, z_t=z_k}^{T} \gamma_t(i)}{\sum_{t=1}^{T} \gamma_t(i)}
\end{aligned}
$$

If we define the initial model as M and the reestimation model as $\overline{M}$, consisting of the above $\overline{\pi}_i(1), \overline{P}_{ij}[b]$, and $\overline{\theta}_i(k)$, then it can be proven [8] that either

1. the initial model M defines a critical point of the likelihood function, in which case $\overline{M} = M$, or

2. model $\overline{M}$ is more likely in the sense that $p(O|A\overline{M}C) > p(O|AMC)$; that is, we have found another model $\overline{M}$ in which O is more likely to be observed when A is executed.

Therefore, if we iteratively use $\overline{M}$ in place of M and repeat the above reestimation calculation, we can improve the model until some limiting point is reached. The result is the estimated model.

Finally, it is interesting to note that $\gamma_t(i)$ can be used to update the distribution of the current model state $\pi_i(t)$ in a stepwise fashion, that is, $t = 1$ and $t + 1 = T$. In particular, when an action b_t is executed at time t and a new observation z_{t+1} is obtained at time $t+1$, $\pi_j(t+1)$ can be computed based on $\pi_i(t)$ using the following equation:

$$\pi_j(t+1) = \frac{\theta_j(z_{t+1}) \sum_i \pi_i(t) \theta_i(z_t) P_{ij}[b_t]}{p(z_t, z_{t+1} | M, C, b_t)}$$

This can be easily proved as follows:

$$
\begin{aligned}
\pi_j(t+1) &= \gamma_j(T) \\
&= \frac{\alpha_T(j) \beta_T(j)}{p(O|AMC)} \\
&= \frac{\alpha_T(j)}{p(O|AMC)} \\
&= \frac{\sum_i \alpha_1(i) P_{ij}[b_t] \theta_j(z_{t+1})}{p(O|AMC)} \\
&= \frac{\sum_i \pi_i(t) \theta_i(z_t) P_{ij}[b_t] \theta_j(z_{t+1})}{p(z_t, z_{t+1} | M, C, b_t)} \\
&= \frac{\theta_j(z_{t+1}) \sum_i \pi_i(t) \theta_i(z_t) P_{ij}[b_t]}{p(z_t, z_{t+1} | M, C, b_t)}
\end{aligned}
$$

5.11 Summary

In this chapter, we have addressed the problem of learning from translucent environments. In particular, we have seen that the learner must deal with both the construction problem and the synchronization problem in order to abstract a perfect and synchronized model from a translucent environment. We have illustrated several methods — the L^*, Rivest–Schapire, and CDL+ algorithms, and hidden Markov methods — for learning from translucent finite state machines. However, most known methods can only construct a model that has the same size as the translucent environment. There is no satisfactory solution to combine and balance the trade-off between constructing hidden states and model abstraction (i.e., learning models that are more compact than the environment). The methods for learning prediction rules (Section 5.8) provide some special-case solutions for the problem, but more general solutions are needed.

CHAPTER 6

MODEL APPLICATION

Models are used to solve problems. As we pointed out in Chapter 3, this process involves two subtasks: (1) searching for a solution that leads the learner from an initial state to a goal state and (2) generating new, short-term goals. In this chapter we discuss some methods for performing these subtasks.

6.1 Searching for Optimal Solutions

Seeking goal states by using a given model can be formalized as a search problem [77]. All that is required is a set of states, a set of transitions that map states to states through actions, an initial state, and a set of goal states. These requirements are met when the model and the goal are given, and the current state is considered as the initial state. A solution (or a plan) is a sequence of actions that leads the learner from the initial state to one of the goal states. A solution (plan) is optimal if its reward is maximal (or its cost is minimal). A solution (plan) is "satisficing" if it can be found within given constraints (such as computational time or space) [115]. We will first discuss methods of searching for optimal solutions and then consider methods that find satisficing solutions.

6.1.1 Dynamic Programming

Assume that in addition to the ability to recognize a goal state, we are also given a *reward* function, $R(s, a)$, where s is a state and a is an action, that tells us how each pair of state and action, (s, a), pertains to reaching goal states. For example, in a Tower of Hanoi environment, let s be the state where the target peg is empty and

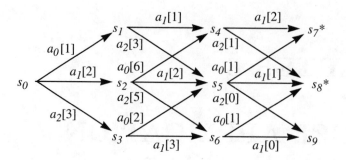

Figure 6.1 An example state machine. Asterisks indicate goal states, and numbers in brackets are rewards.

a be the action that puts the largest disk on the target peg. Then $R(s,a)$ should have a high reward value because (s,a) here is essential to reaching the goal state.

Our objective is to find an optimal solution that leads from the initial state to a goal state. Let s_0 be the initial state and s_g a goal state. A *solution* (or a *plan*) is a sequence of states and actions, $s_0, a_0, \dots, s_i, a_i, \dots, s_g$, where the s_i are states and the a_i are actions. We say a solution is *optimal* if the accumulated value of $R(s,a)$ associated with a solution is no less than the accumulated value associated with any other solution. Each step in a solution is also called a *decision*, which is a mapping $\pi(s_i) \to a_i$. The set of all possible decisions is called a *policy*, because it determines for any state which action to take.

To illustrate the idea, consider the finite state machine in Figure 6.1. This machine has 10 states, s_0 through s_9, and 3 actions, $a_0, a_1,$ and a_2. The figure illustrates both the state transition function $\delta(s,a)$ and the reward value of $R(s,a)$ for each transition (they are the numbers in brackets). For example, $\delta(s_0, a_1) = s_2$ and $R(s_0, a_1) = 2$. If s_0 is the initial state and s_7 and s_8 are the goal states (indicated by asterisks), then there are 12 solutions:

$$(s_0, a_0, s_1, a_1, s_4, a_1, s_7)$$
$$(s_0, a_0, s_1, a_1, s_4, a_2, s_8)$$
$$\vdots$$
$$(s_0, a_1, s_2, a_0, s_4, a_1, s_7)$$
$$\vdots$$
$$(s_0, a_2, s_3, a_1, s_6, a_0, s_8)$$

Among these, $(s_0, a_1, s_2, a_0, s_4, a_1, s_7)$ is the optimal solution, because its accumulated value, 10, is greater than that of any other solution.

Given the state transition function and the reward function, a naive way of developing an optimal policy from a given initial state is to calculate the accumulated value of $R(s, a)$ for every possible path of length n (assuming every goal is reached by n actions) and then choose the path with the maximal value. This approach is clearly exponential, because there are $O(m^n)$ such paths, where m is the number of actions.

Dynamic programming is a much more efficient way to find an optimal solution [9, 96]. Instead of evaluating solutions path by path, this technique calculates the accumulated value stage by stage. First, it finds the value of all paths of length i and then, using these results, it finds the value of all paths of length $i + 1$. In the backward application, the paths are extended from the goal states step by step toward the initial state. In the forward application, the paths are extended from the initial state step by step toward the goal states. We will describe the backward version, but the argument for the forward version is completely analogous.

In Figure 6.1, since the paths of length $i = 1$ that can reach the goals can only start from state s_4, s_5, or s_6, the best values for paths from these states are recorded. For example, the best value one can get from state s_4 to a goal state is 2, denoted as $V(s_4) = 2$. Similarly, $V(s_5) = 1$ and $V(s_6) = 1$. These values are then used to calculate the best values for paths that reach a goal in two steps, that is, $i = 2$. Since all such paths must start from state s_1, s_2, or s_3, we record the best values of all paths from these states. For example,

$$\begin{aligned}
V(s_1) &= \max\{R(s_1, a_1) + V(s_4), R(s_1, a_2) + V(s_5)\} = \max\{1 + 2, 3 + 1\} = 4 \\
V(s_2) &= \max\{R(s_2, a_0) + V(s_4), R(s_2, a_1) + V(s_5), R(s_2, a_2) + V(s_6)\} \\
&= \max\{6 + 2, 2 + 1, 5 + 1\} = 8 \\
V(s_3) &= \max\{R(s_3, a_0) + V(s_5), R(s_3, a_1) + V(s_6)\} = \max\{2 + 1, 3 + 1\} = 4
\end{aligned}$$

Finally, we can calculate the best values for paths that reach the goal states in three steps. Since all these paths start from state s_0, we have

$$\begin{aligned}
V(s_0) &= \max\{R(s_0, a_0) + V(s_1), R(s_0, a_1) + V(s_2), R(s_0, a_2) + V(s_3)\} \\
&= \max\{1 + 4, 2 + 8, 3 + 4\} = 10
\end{aligned}$$

The values of all states calculated in this fashion are shown in Figure 6.2.

In general, the value of a state s_i can be calculated as follows:

$$V(s_i) = \max_a\{R(s_i, a) + V(s_j)\} \text{ where } s_i \xrightarrow{a} s_j \tag{6.1}$$

Equation 6.1 is called *backward recursion* since the values are calculated from the goal states to the initial state. *Forward recursion* can be expressed by the following equation:

$$U(s_j) = \max_a\{U(s_i) + R(s_i, a)\} \text{ where } s_i \xrightarrow{a} s_j \tag{6.2}$$

The state values computed using forward recursion are shown in Figure 6.3.

It is worth noting that equations 6.1 and 6.2 can each be extended to deal with stochastic environments. In a stochastic environment, executing action a in

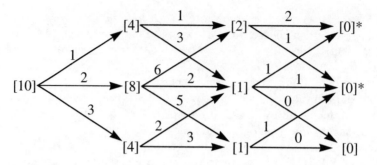

Figure 6.2 State values $V(s)$ computed by backward recursion. Asterisks indicate goal states.

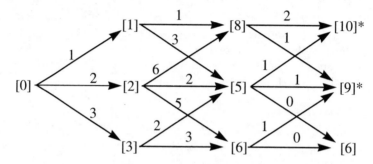

Figure 6.3 State values $U(s)$ computed by forward recursion. Asterisks indicate goal states.

state x may go to any environmental state y. The probability of the transition is given as $P_{xy}[a]$. To generalize equation 6.1, we need only to replace $V(s_j)$ by $\sum_j P_{s_i s_j}(a)V(s_j)$. Likewise, to generalize equation 6.2, we need only to replace $U(s_i)$ by $\sum_i P_{s_i s_j}(a)U(s_i)$.

With the values of the states so calculated, it is straightforward to construct the optimal policy π^* for any state s. If the values are calculated by backward recursion, then the optimal decision at a state s is to choose the action a leading to the next state that has the maximal value. That is, $\pi^*(s) = a^*$ such that

$$R(s, a^*) + V(\delta(s, a^*)) = \max_{a \in A}\{R(s, a) + V(\delta(s, a))\}$$

where A is the set of actions. In our example, if you are at state s_2, then your decision will be action a_0 because $\delta(s_2, a_0) = s_4$ and $V(s_4)$ is greater than $V(s_5)$ or $V(s_6)$.

Dynamic programming is an efficient procedure. (Note that dynamic programming is not a single algorithm. It is a methodology that can be used to design an

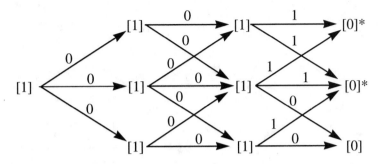

Figure 6.4   State values computed when there are no intermediate rewards. Asterisks indicate goal states.

efficient algorithm for each problem.) The values for each stage are calculated only once, and they are used to calculate the values for the next stage. Because of this efficiency, dynamic programming can find an optimal solution in a polynomial time of the number of states.

However, dynamic programming poses two problems that make it unsuitable for learning from the environment. One problem is that the value $V(s_j)$ in equation 6.1 often cannot be computed exactly because one does not know a priori where the goal states are in the search space. To avoid this problem, forward recursion can be used. But that requires a breadth-first search, which is often impractical when the search space is large.

The second problem is that the value of $R(s, a)$ must be known before the action a is executed in state s. Furthermore, the value of r must be available for all the intermediate states in such a way that the accumulated values on the way to a goal can be set up to be greater than along nongoal paths. In other words, dynamic programming cannot take advantage of *delayed* rewards. If all intermediate states have zero reward, then calculating the state values will not be helpful in deciding the optimal policy because states near the initial state cannot be discriminated. For example, if we let

$$R(s, a) = \begin{cases} 1 & \text{when } \delta(s, a) \text{ is a goal} \\ 0 & \text{otherwise} \end{cases}$$

then the state values calculated by backward recursion in our example are those shown in Figure 6.4. One can see that these values will not help to determine the optimal action for the initial state.

6.1.2   The A^* Algorithms

The A^* algorithms [80] address the first problem of dynamic programming (not knowing the values of backward recursion) by combining the forward recursion

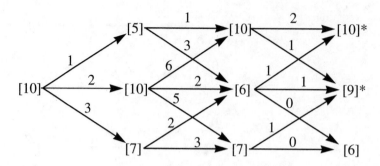

Figure 6.5 States with the combined value $V(s) + U(s)$. Asterisks indicate goal states.

with a domain-specific function $h(s)$ to estimate $V(s)$ (see equation 6.1) for the states ahead. The estimation function $h(s)$ requires little or no "look-ahead" (i.e., mental execution of actions), yet it can still guide the search for an optimal solution. An example of such an estimation function in the eight-puzzle game is to count the number of misplaced tiles on the current board [80]. (An eight-puzzle game is to move eight numbered pieces, 1 through 8, to their numbered positions, 1 through 9, on a tic-tac-toe like board.) It is known that the necessary condition for A^* to find an optimal solution is that $h(s) \geq V(s)$ for $\forall s$. That is, $h(s)$ never underestimates the value of $V(s)$. Interested readers can find a proof by Nilsson [80]. (Note that the proof there uses the minimum as optimal, while we have been using the maximum as optimal.)

To motivate the idea of A^*, consider state values that are computed as $U(s) + V(s)$ (see equations 6.1 and 6.2). In our current example, the state values so computed are shown in Figure 6.5. As we can see, the states along the optimal solution all have the same value, 10, which is the maximal value that is obtained for states. Clearly, if $U(s)$ and $V(s)$ are available for every state, we can easily construct an optimal solution.

The idea behind A^* is exactly the same as using $U(s) + V(s)$ except that $V(s)$ is replaced by an estimation $h(s)$. Starting from the initial state s_0, A^* selects the action that leads to the next state whose value for $V(s) + h(s)$ is maximal. The search continues until a goal state is reached. (We assume the ability to recognize a goal state.) Since $h(s)$ is only an estimate of $V(s)$, an A^* algorithm must also keep a list of states that are still open so that it can backtrack to earlier alternatives.

Figure 6.6 presents the A^* algorithm. The list $OPEN$ contains states that are to be expanded (to go outward), and $CLOSED$ stores states that have already been expanded. At any time, we always choose to expand the open state that has the maximal W-value (i.e., the most promising state). If it is a goal, then we have found the best solution. Otherwise, it is expanded. To ensure the optimal solution, if a state s' is revisited, then we have to make sure that its W-value is the best it can be (line 10).

1   Let s_0 be the initial state, $OPEN = \{s_0\}$, and $CLOSED = \{\}$,

2   Loop:

3   Select s from $OPEN$ such that $W(s) = U(s) + h(s)$ is maximal,

4   If s is a goal state,

5   Then return the path from s_0 to s,

6   Move s to $CLOSED$,

7   For each s' that is reachable from s by a single action, do:

8   If s' is not in $OPEN$ or $CLOSED$,

9   Then add s' to $OPEN$,

10   Else update $W(s')$ and its path.

Figure 6.6 The A^* algorithm.

The algorithm can be illustrated using our example. The $U(s)$ values of our example are listed in Figure 6.3. Figure 6.7 shows an example estimation function $h(s)$ of the same machine. Note that the relation $h(s) \geq V(s)$ holds for all states s.

At the beginning, the list $OPEN$ contains the state s_0 only. After expanding s_0, $OPEN$ contains states s_1, s_2, and s_3 because these are the states that can be reached from s_0 via a single action. For convenience, we record $OPEN$ as the following:

$$OPEN = \{s_1^{\{s_0\}}(11), s_2^{\{s_0\}}(11), s_3^{\{s_0\}}(9)\}$$

The superscript indicates the path to the state, and the number in parentheses is the state's W-value. For example, $s_2^{\{s_0\}}(11)$ means that the state s_2 is reached from s_0, and its W-value is 11 (because $U(s_2) = 2$ and $h(s_2) = 9$). Now suppose that at line 3 the state s_1 is selected from $OPEN$. Expanding s_1, the new $OPEN$ list is

$$OPEN = \{s_2^{\{s_0\}}(11), s_3^{\{s_0\}}(9), s_4^{\{s_0 s_1\}}(7), s_5^{\{s_0 s_1\}}(7)\}$$

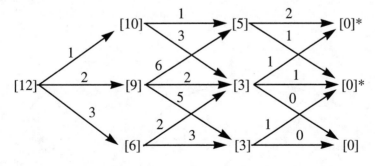

Figure 6.7 The values of $h(s)$ for estimating $V(s)$.

This time the state s_2 will be chosen because it has the maximal W-value. Expanding state s_2, the $OPEN$ list now becomes:

$$OPEN = \{s_4^{\{s_0 s_2\}}(13), s_5^{\{s_0 s_2\}}(7), s_6^{\{s_0 s_2\}}(10), s_3^{\{s_0\}}(9), s_5^{\{s_0 s_1\}}(7)\}$$

Note that s_4 is reachable via $s_0 s_1$ and $s_0 s_2$. However, $s_4^{\{s_0 s_1\}}(7)$ is not in the $OPEN$ list because reaching s_4 via $s_0 s_2$ has a higher value $s_4^{\{s_0 s_2\}}(13)$.

Next, the state s_4 is chosen and expanded. Thus, we get the following $OPEN$ list:

$$OPEN = \{s_7^{\{s_0 s_2 s_4\}}(10), s_8^{\{s_0 s_2 s_4\}}(9), s_5^{\{s_0 s_2\}}(7), s_6^{\{s_0 s_2\}}(10), s_3^{\{s_0\}}(9), s_5^{\{s_0 s_1\}}(7)\}$$

At this point, state s_7 will be chosen and the algorithm will stop because s_7 is a goal state. The path $s_0 s_2 s_4 s_7$ is returned as an optimal solution.

6.1.3 Q-Learning

Q-learning is a technique for learning from delayed rewards [132, 133]. The main idea behind Q-learning is to constantly adjust the estimate of $V(s)$ while back-propagating later rewards to the earlier stage. Furthermore, Q-learning does not need to know the environment model $P_{xy}[a]$ (the probability of $x \xrightarrow{a} y$) or the reward function $R(x, a)$. All it requires is to receive a reward and transit to a next state step by step. Strictly speaking, Q-learning is not part of model application because it does not require a model per se. However, since the technique is closely related to dynamic programming and in fact provides a solution for learning from delayed rewards (such as those shown in Figure 6.4), we introduce the technology here.

To illustrate the idea, consider the simple environment shown in Figure 6.8. In this environment, there are n states s_1 through s_n. Each state has two actions: a_1 moves to the next state, and a_2 moves back to the initial state s_1. Furthermore, the reward for all state-action pairs is 0, that is, $R(s_i, a_j) = 0$, except the move into the goal state s_n, which has a reward of 100; that is, $R(s_{n-1}, a_1) = 100$. In this environment, a Q-learner first explores all the actions in all states indiscriminately until it has executed a_1 in state s_{n-1}. Then the reward obtained from $R(x_{n-1}, a_1)$

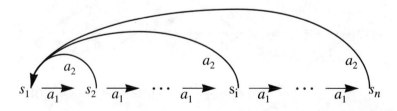

Figure 6.8   A simple environment for Q-learning.

is gradually back-propagated into other state–action pairs until for every state s_i the Q-value for (s_i, a_1) is always higher than the Q-value for (s_i, a_2). Naturally, a learner with such a Q-value distribution will always go to the goal state s_n.

Formally, the environment in Q-learning is a controlled Markov process with a set of states X. At step n, the learner observes the current state of the environment $x_n \in X$, and selects an action a from its finite action set A as defined above. The learner receives a probabilistic reward r_n, whose mean value $R(x_n, a_n)$ depends only on the state and action. This reward can be thought of as an embedded goal; it tells the learner how good it is with respect to the goal states to act in the current state in the chosen way. Upon receiving a_n in state x_n, the state of the environment changes to y_n according to a probabilistic transition function $P_{x_n y_n}[a_n]$ (think of the environment as a stochastic process).

The objective of the learner is to collect as much reward as it can, which in turn implicitly means to get as close as possible to the goal states. To do so, all the learner needs to know is which action to choose in every state x. This is determined by a policy function, $\pi(x) \rightarrow a$. Thus, the task facing the learner is to determine an optimal policy, one that maximizes the total discounted expected reward. By *discounted reward*, we mean that rewards received m steps later are worth less than rewards received now by a factor of $\gamma^m (0 < \gamma < 1)$. Under a policy π, the value of state x (again with respect to $R(x, a)$) is

$$V^\pi(x) \equiv R(x, \pi(x)) + \gamma \sum_y P_{xy}[\pi(x)]V^\pi(y)$$

because the learner expects to receive $R(x, \pi(x))$ immediately for performing the action $\pi(x)$ recommended by π and then moves to a state that is worth $V^\pi(y)$ to it with a probability $P_{xy}[\pi(x)]$. According to the theory of dynamic programming, there is at least one optimal stationary policy π^* such that

$$V^*(x) \equiv V^{\pi^*}(x) = \max_a \left\{ R(x, a) + \gamma \sum_y P_{xy}[a]V^{\pi^*}(y) \right\}$$

is the best that a learner can do from state x. Although this formula might look circular, it is actually well defined. Dynamic programming provides a number of methods for calculating V^* and one π^*, assuming that $R(x, a)$ and $P_{xy}[a]$ are known. However, the task facing a Q-learner is that of determining a π^* *without* initially knowing the values of $R(x, a)$ and $P_{xy}[a]$. There are traditional methods for learning these values while concurrently performing dynamic programming, but any assumption of certainty equivalence (i.e., calculating actions as if the current model of the environment were accurate) costs dearly in the early stages of learning. Watkins [132] classifies Q-learning as incremental dynamic programming because of the step-by-step manner in which it determines the optimal policy.

For a policy π, we define Q-values as

$$Q^\pi(x, a) = R(x, a) + \gamma \sum_y P_{xy}[\pi(x)]V^\pi(y)$$

In other words, the Q-value is the expected discounted reward for executing action a at state x and following policy π thereafter. The object in Q-learning is to estimate the Q-values for an optimal policy. For convenience, define these as $Q^*(x,a) \equiv Q^{\pi^*}(x,a)$, for all x and a. It is straightforward to show that $V^*(x) = \max_a Q^*(x,a)$ and that if a^* is an action at which the maximum is attained, then an optimal policy can be formed as $\pi^*(x) \equiv a^*$. Herein lies the utility of the Q-values: If a learner can learn them, it can easily decide which choices are optimal. Although there may be more than one optimal policy or a^*, the Q^*-values are unique.

In Q-learning, the learner's experience consists of a sequence of distinct stages, or *episodes*. In the nth episode, the learner

- observes its current state x_n,

- selects and performs an action a_n,

- observes the subsequent state y_n,

- receives an immediate payoff r_n, and

- adjusts its Q_{n-1}-values using a learning factor α_n according to the formula

$$Q_n(x,a) = \begin{cases} (1-\alpha_n)Q_{n-1}(x,a) + \alpha_n[r_n + \gamma V_{n-1}(y_n)] & \text{if } x = x_n, a = a_n \\ Q_{n-1}(x,a) & \text{otherwise} \end{cases}$$

where

$$V_{n-1}(y) \equiv \max_a \{Q_{n-1}(y,a)\}$$

The value $V_{n-1}(y)$ is the best the learner thinks it can do from state y. Of course, in the early stages of learning, the Q-values may not accurately reflect the policy they implicitly define. The initial Q-values, $Q_0(x,a)$, for all states and actions are assumed to be given.

Note that the description here assumes a lookup table representation for the $Q_n(x,a)$. Watkins [132] shows that Q-learning may not converge correctly for other representations.

The convergence of Q-learning is guaranteed by the following theorem:

THEOREM 6.1.1 (Watkins) Given bounded rewards $|r_n| \leq R$, learning rates $0 < \alpha_n < 1$, and

$$\sum_{i=1}^{\infty} \alpha_{n^i(x,a)} = \infty, \qquad \sum_{i=1}^{\infty} [\alpha_{n^i(x,a)}]^2 < \infty, \qquad \forall x, \forall b$$

where $n^i(x,a)$ is the index of the ith time that action a is tried in state x, we have $Q_n(x,a) \to Q^*(x,a)$ as $n \to \infty$ with probability 1 for all x and b.

The most important condition implicit in the convergence theorem is that the sequence of episodes that forms the basis of learning must include an infinite number of episodes for each starting state and action. This may be considered a strong condition on how states and actions are selected. However, under the stochastic conditions of the theorem, no method can be guaranteed to find an optimal policy under weaker conditions. Note, however, that the episodes need not form a continuous sequence; that is, the y of one episode need not be the x of the next episode.

It is interesting to notice that Q-learning does not need to know the functions of $R(x, a)$ and $P_{xy}[a]$. It is only required that, for each action performed in every state, the learner receives a reward and is told what the next state is. In other words, the Q-values can tell you which action is the best to do, but it cannot tell you what state the action will lead to. It learns the optimal way to solve a problem (with a plan) from any initial state, but it does not learn the model of the environment. This can be quite costly if the environment or the goals are changing. For example, consider an agent in a maze looking for food. When the food is at one corner, Q-learning can build an optimal policy to go to the food. However, if the food is moved to another corner, the Q-values must be relearned. We will have more to say about this in Section 7.1.1.

Q-learning assumes that all the states in the environment can be distinguished. This has two implications. First, the task of Q-learning is different from the tasks addressed in Chapter 5. For environments in which states cannot be distinguished, Q-learning must be performed concurrently with some mechanisms that generate hidden states. The most recent results along this line can be found in [16]. Second, treating all states distinctly is impractical when the number of the states in the environment is very large. In that case, Q-learning must work with other mechanisms that do the work of generalization, that is, of clustering states into classes according to their function. Some of the mechanisms will be discussed in Chapter 7.

6.2 Searching for Satisficing Solutions

Optimal solutions can only be found at dear prices. All the algorithms in Section 6.1 require space and time that are at least exponential in the number of states. However, as observed by Simon and Kadane [116], it is relatively rare that optimal solutions are actually required; near-optimal, or "satisficing," solutions are perfectly acceptable for most real-world problems. In this section, we describe several algorithms that can find a solution efficiently. In this type of search, the objective is to reach a goal state. We care about the length of the search but not about the length of solution.

6.2.1 The Real-Time A^* Algorithm

The real-time A^* (RTA*) algorithm [44] is a modification of the A^* algorithm. It can find a satisficing solution in time or space that is linear in the size of the environment. Furthermore, like Q-learning, this algorithm can improve its performance by successively solving multiple problem instances in the same search space with the same set of goals.

As we saw in Section 6.1.2, in order to find an optimal solution, A^* does not commit to any actual move in the environment until it searches all the way to an optimal solution. The reason is that an optimal first move cannot be guaranteed until the entire solution has been found and shown to be at least as good as any other solution.

As we saw in Section 6.1.1, the optimality of a solution is reflected in the state value $V(s)$. This value tells you the minimal (or maximal) cost from the initial state s to a goal state. (Although in our previous discussion $V(s)$ maximized the reward, it can be applied to minimizing costs as well. Costs can be thought of as the negatives of rewards.) If the function $V(s)$ is known, then a move can be made immediately to a neighbor state $s' = \delta(s, a)$, where s is the current state and a is the action such that $R(s, a) + V(\delta(s, a))$ is the minimum among all possible actions. Here the value $R(s, a)$ is the cost of moving from state s to s' through the action a. Such a move is guaranteed to be optimal. However, the exact value of $V(s)$ cannot be known unless it works recursively backward from all the goals. Otherwise, $V(s)$ can only be estimated by a heuristic function $h(s)$. If one makes any move based on $h(s)$, then two problems must be dealt with to find a solution:

- The values of neighbor states must be estimated as accurately as possible.

- One must be able to backtrack to the previous state if the current search path is not promising.

For the first problem, we know that for any given state s, the least we can do is to take the value $h(s)$ and the most we can do is to look ahead far enough to all the goals and then use backward recursion to compute the exact value $V(s)$. With limited resources, we cannot compute the exact value of $V(s)$, but we can still do better than $h(s)$ by looking ahead some steps. In fact, the RTA* algorithm uses exactly this technique to compute the values of the neighbors of the current state.

Let s be the current state, s' be its neighbors, and n be the depth of the lookahead (also called the *search horizon*). The lookahead estimation $h^+(s')$ can be computed by the following backward recursion equation (see Section 6.1.1 for details):

$$h^+(s_i) = \min_a \{R(s_i, a) + h^+(s_{i-1})\} \text{ where } s_i \xrightarrow{b} s_{i-1} \text{ and } h^+(s_0) \doteq h(s_0)$$

Note that states s_0 are the states at the search horizon, and their values are estimated by the heuristic function h.

After the h^+-values are computed for all the neighbors, RTA* actually moves to the best neighbor state $s^* = \delta(s, a)$ such that the value of $R(s, a) + h^+(s^*)$ is minimal among all neighbors. The state s^* then becomes the current state.

The second problem is solved by recording the values of those states that are actually visited (i.e., states that were current at some time in the past). These states are kept in a list called $PATH$. Every time the current state is moved from s to s', the state s is put on the $PATH$ list, and its value is set to $p(s) = R(s, a) + h^+(s')$. Since $h^+(s')$ is computed by an n-step lookahead, $p(s)$ is the value of an $(n+1)$-step lookahead.

Note that backtracking is possible because some of the neighbors of the current state may already be in the $PATH$ list. However, they compete just like all the other neighbors. If the best neighbor happens to be in $PATH$, then the algorithm will visit it again. Note also that such backtracking will not result in an infinite loop. To see this, suppose two states x and y have some local-minimum h^+-values, and the algorithm bounces back and forth between them via an action a. At the beginning, $p_0(x) = h^+(x)$ and $p_0(y) = h^+(y)$. After the first bounce between x and y, we have

$$
\begin{aligned}
p_1(x) &= R(x, a) + p_0(y) \\
p_1(y) &= R(y, a) + p_1(x) = R(y, a) + R(x, a) + p_0(y)
\end{aligned}
$$

If the cost function is positive, we have $p_1(y) > p_0(y)$ and in general $p_{i+1}(s) > p_i(s)$. Therefore, even if the initial estimates of h for x and y are mistakenly low, their p-values will eventually fill up and the algorithm will escape the loop.

The RTA* algorithm shown in Figure 6.9 puts the two solutions together. Let s be the current state, and $PATH$ be a list of previously visited states with p-values. RTA* computes the h^+-values for all the neighbors of s that are not in $PATH$. For the neighbors of s that are in $PATH$, their p-values are used instead. RTA* then moves to the best neighbor state $s' = \delta(s, a)$ such that the value of $R(s, a) + h^+(s')$ is a minimum. The state s' now becomes the current state. The state s is then put into $PATH$, and its value is set to be $R(s, a) + h^+(s')$. This process repeats until a goal state is found.

1   Let the current state s be the initial state, and $PATH = \{\}$,

2   Loop:

3   Compute values of $h^+(s')$ using lookahead backward recursion for all neighbors s' of s (if $s' \in PATH$, let $h^+(s') = p(s')$),

4   Move to the best neighbor $s^* = \delta(s, a)$ such that the value of $R(s, a) + h^+(s^*)$ is minimal among all neighbors s',

5   If s^* is a goal state, return success,

6   Insert s into $PATH$, set $p(s) = R(s, a) + h^+(s^*)$ and $s = s^*$.

Figure 6.9 The real-time A^* algorithm.

To illustrate the algorithm, consider the example in Figure 6.7 and assume that the lookahead $n = 1$. At state s_0, the h^+-values of states s_1, s_2, and s_3 are computed:

$$\begin{aligned}
h^+(s_1) &= R(s_1, a_1) + h(s_4) = 1 + 5 = 6 \\
h^+(s_2) &= R(s_2, a_0) + h(s_4) = 6 + 5 = 11 \\
h^+(s_3) &= R(s_3, a_1) + h(s_6) = 3 + 3 = 6
\end{aligned}$$

Since s_2 has the highest value, we move from s_0 to s_2 and the $PATH$ list is updated to be $\{p(s_0) = 2 + 11 = 13\}$. From state s_2, we compute the h^+-values for its neighbors s_4, s_5, and s_6: $h^+(s_4) = 2, h^+(s_5) = 1$, and $h^+(s_6) = 1$, and move to state s_4. The p-value of s_2 is $p(s_2) = R(s_2, a_0) + h^+(s_4) = 6 + 2 = 8$. The $PATH$ list is now $\{p(s_0) = 13, p(s_2) = 8\}$. From state s_4, we compute the h^+-value for states s_7, s_8, and s_9. Since s_7 is a goal state, a satisficing solution $s_0 s_2 s_4 s_7$ is found.

The RTA* algorithm guarantees making a move in a constant time. This is because the depth of the lookahead is fixed and does not vary with the size of the environment. (The lookahead search can be more efficient with alpha pruning, see [43] for details.) The space requirement of the algorithm is only linear in the length of a solution, because the list $PATH$ contains only those states that are actually visited. The conditions under which RTA* actually finds a solution are summarized in the following theorem (interested readers can find its proof in [43]):

THEOREM 6.2.1 (Korf) In a finite problem space in which the edge costs are positive, the heuristic state values are finite, and a goal state is reachable from every state, RTA* will find a solution.

The RTA* algorithm can learn to improve its performance over several trials on the same problem. This is accomplished by using the p-values learned in the previous runs as the h-values in the new attempt. As we can see, by doing this the p-values in the new run are computed much more accurately, and so the algorithm finds the solution faster.

It is interesting to compare RTA* with Q-learning. They both can act in a constant time in the environment and improve their performance by experience. The difference is that Q-learning attempts to find the optimal solution while RTA* searches for a satisficing solution. In addition, RTA* uses a model of the environment (for looking ahead) while Q-learning does not.

6.2.2   Means–Ends Analysis

In the above discussion, we did not pay any attention to the internal structure of the states. The only way to talk about them is by their names. However, in many applications, states are not the most basic elements of the environment; instead, they are composed of more fundamental elements, such as objects, properties, and relations. In fact, this is what we had in mind when we defined learning from the environment in Chapter 2.

When states consist of more basic elements, the transition function can be more abstract. Actions are not just a means to transfer a single state to another single state but a way to change the elements of states. Thus, each transition specifies how a set of states changes to another set of states. In this context, a transition is a rule that has three components: the preconditions, the action, and the effects. The relation among these components can be stated in a number of ways. One way is that the preconditions specify the conditions under which applying an action will achieve certain effects. Another way is that in order to obtain the effects, the action must be applied to a state that satisfies the preconditions. Clearly, the use of a rule includes applying it to a particular situation and a particular action.

State structures also provide a natural way to speak about the evaluation of a state with respect to a goal. The distance between two states can be defined as the number of differences between the two states. The method of means–ends analysis employs this intrinsic property of states in finding a satisficing solution.

Means–ends analysis was first identified as a search control technique by Simon and Newell in the late 1950s [77]. Here we will discuss the main idea and then describe its first implementation program, called General Problem Solver (GPS), and its descendent STRIPS [23].

Means–ends analysis is a recursive procedure. Given the current state and a desired state, the procedure first finds the differences between the two states. Then it identifies some rules whose effects can eliminate these differences. If a relevant rule's preconditions are satisfied in the current state, then its action is applied. Otherwise, the preconditions of the desired rule become a new desired state, and the procedure continues to find relevant rules until a rule that can be immediately applied is found. A pseudocode of this procedure is given in Figure 6.10.

Notice that means–ends analysis controls its search by regressing the goal state towards the current state. Also notice that the procedure stops as soon as a solution is found. The quality of the solution (i.e., the length or the costs) depends on the order in which the difference d is selected from D (line 3) and the order in which the rule r is selected from all applicable rules (line 4). The order in which d is selected is important when the elements in D depend on each other in a certain

Means-ends-analysis(S, T):
1   While $S \neq T$, do:
2   Find the differences D between S and T,
3   For each $d \in D$, do:
4   For each rule r that can be instantiated to eliminate d, do:
5                $P \leftarrow$ the instantiated precondition of r,
6   Call Means-ends-analysis(S, P),
7                $S \leftarrow$ applying the instantiated action of r to S.

Figure 6.10 The basic idea of means–ends analysis.

way. For example, in the Tower of Hanoi problem, if D contains two differences $d1 = ON(disk1, pegA)$ and $d2 = ON(disk2, pegA)$, where the size of $disk2$ is greater than that of $disk1$, then it is better to select $d2$ first.

Means–ends analysis can be implemented in a number of different ways. Each method depends on how the rules are represented and how the rules are accessed through differences. Here we describe two representative implementations: GPS and STRIPS.

GPS (General Problem Solver) was the first implementation of the means–ends analysis. In GPS, transition rules are represented as pairs of (*precondition action*). The access from differences to a rule is implemented in a difference table, which is a mapping:

$$differences \rightarrow (precondition\ action)$$

It is interesting to note that the differences, which are essentially effects of actions, are implemented separately from the transition rules themselves.

The STRIPS implementation differs from GPS in the representation of the transition rules. In STRIPS, each rule contains all three components: precondition, action, and effects. The effects are represented as an *ADD* list and a *DELETE* list. The former contains the elements that are not in the condition state but will be added to the result state by the action, and the latter contains the elements that are in the condition state but will be removed by the action. So a rule in STRIPS is in the form of

$$(precondition\ action) \rightarrow ADD/DELETE$$

Because of this representation, one can identify relevant rules from differences by directly comparing the differences with the *ADD/DELETE* lists of a rule. Thus, there is no need for a difference table in the STRIPS implementation.

6.2.3 Distal Supervised Learning

For a particular set of goal states G, neural networks can be trained to approximate a policy function, $h(G, x) \rightarrow a$, that can choose the correct action a in any state x such that the action is best or good for reaching the goal states in G. Such a function can be learned with or without knowledge of the model of the environment. Since we are interested in model application, we will focus our attention on methods that use models, and we will assume that a correct (or approximated) model is available.

One method that utilizes a model of the environment in training h is *distal supervised learning* [41]. The basic idea is illustrated in Figure 6.11. In this figure, x represents the states of the environment, g is a goal, and a is an action. The relationships between these quantities are as follows:

$$
\begin{aligned}
x_n &= \alpha(\phi(x_{n-1}, a_{n-1})) \\
a_n &= h(g, x_n)
\end{aligned}
$$

where subscripts are the indices of discrete moments of time. The model functions — the transition function ϕ and the output function α — are given. The objective

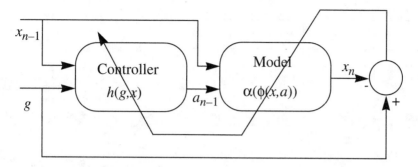

Figure 6.11 Block diagram of distal learning.

is to learn the function $h(g, x)$. The distinct characteristic of distal learning is that h is not learned in isolation but in conjunction with a model of the environment. The feedback for learning does not come directly from the values for h (i.e., the action a) but from x_n, the effect of a on the model. As we can see, the reason this is called distal learning is that the target function is learned not on the basis of its "proximal" (direct) output but on the "distal" outcome through the model.

Since $x_n = g$ when the goal state is reached, the function h must be trained to minimize the error $x_n - g$. Furthermore, since learning occurs in the context of a model of the environment, this error must be propagated *through* the fixed function $\phi \circ \alpha$ to the h network to adjust the weights. To solve this any supervised learning algorithm can be used. In the following discussion, however, we will only describe the back-propagation algorithm.

Let us define the error J of the entire network at time n as the following:

$$J_n = \frac{1}{2}(g - x_n)^T(g - x_n)$$

As we know from Section 4.11, the network changes its weights w at each time step based on the gradient of J on w:

$$w_{n+1} = w_n - \eta\nabla_w(J_n)$$

where η is a step size. Since x is a function of action a and a is a function of w, the gradient $\nabla_w(J_n)$ can be computed by the chain rule as follows:

$$\nabla_w(J_n) = -\left(\frac{\partial a}{\partial w}\right)\left(\frac{\partial x}{\partial a}\right)(g - x_n) \qquad (6.3)$$

where $\partial x/\partial a$ and $\partial a/\partial w$ are evaluated at time $n - 1$.

The factors in this expression can be understood as follows. The factor $\partial x/\partial a$ describes the propagation of derivatives from the predicted next states to the actions. The factor $\partial a/\partial w$ describes the propagation of derivatives from the h network's

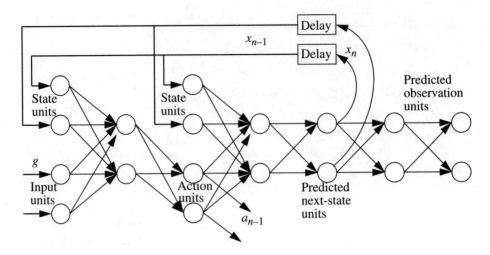

Figure 6.12   A network architecture for distal learning.

output (i.e., actions) to the weights of the network, and the factor $g - x_n$ is the distal error. Note that the factor $\partial x/\partial a$ should ideally be computed using the environment itself. However, here we assume the model is adequate enough for that purpose. In summary, equation 6.3 describes the back propagation of the distal error $g - x_n$ through the model and down into the controller where the weights are changed. The network architecture in which these computations take place is shown in Figure 6.12. This network is a straightforward realization of the block diagram in Figure 6.11.

Finally, we point out that the function h can also be learned without using a model. However, experiments show that these direct learning methods do not perform as well as distal learning methods [41]. This fact can be regarded as further evidence that a model is indeed a useful and necessary part of learning from the environment.

6.3   Applying Models to Predictions and Control

Applying models to prediction and control is perhaps the most straightforward way to use models, yet it can give autonomous systems sufficient power to perform complex tasks. In this section, we describe one such application: dynamic vision and real-time control.

Following Dickmanns and Graefe [19], the problem of dynamic vision is to detect in real time a set of critical features from a sequence of perceived images in order to control a system so that it is in some desirable state. One instance of such a problem is the control of autonomous road vehicles. To keep such a vehicle driving on the road safely, the control system must keep an eye on the edges of the road, other vehicles on the road, traffic lights, and so on. The task is difficult because real-time images are perceived at very high rates and contain a tremendous amount of information (a typical image contains 10^6 pixels), yet they must be processed quickly (a typical control cycle is 100 milliseconds). Traditional image-processing techniques cannot perform such tasks.

Dickmanns and Graefe [19] describe a system that uses models of the environment to accomplish the dynamic vision task. The power of the model comes in two ways: specifying *which* features the system should pay attention to and predicting *where* in the next image the system should search for these features.

For each control task, the images have a relevant set of features. These features should be abstracted into the model. (The abstraction in Dickmanns's system is done by human designers.) The number of such features for a given task is usually small (less than 10). For example, in balancing a vertical rod whose base is hinged on an electric cart (the movement of the cart can be controlled), it is sufficient to know the coordinates of two points on the rod as a function of time. In docking vehicles, it is sufficient to know the corners of the docking place. In driving autonomous road vehicles, the necessary features are the edges of the road and obstacles on the road.

These features are represented in the vision system as *masks*, which are a set of expected pixel values. For example, an edge mask and a corner mask are shown in Figure 6.13. The masks are kept small. For example, to detect edges, different masks are used for different orientations. The system uses these masks to find patterns in a given image based on a common technique called *correlation*.

Given a mask $M_{-K} \cdots M_K, M_{-L} \cdots M_L$, and a point (i, j) in an image I and its surrounding pixels, the correlation function C_{ij} is defined as

$$C_{ij} = \sum_{k=-K}^{K} \sum_{l=-L}^{L} I_{i+k,j+l} M_{kl}$$

If the pixels surrounding (i, j) are indeed the feature that is represented by the mask, then the value C_{ij} will be high. Thus the objective of correlation is to find a point in I such that C_{ij} has a peak value. This approach, although simple, is very robust and works well in noisy situations. However, it is very expensive to search

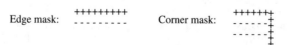

Figure 6.13   An edge mask and a corner mask.

the whole image. Let n be the number of pixels in I ($n \approx 10^6$) and m the pixels in a mask M ($m \ll n$); then the entire operation requires mn operations, which is very large.

However, with predictions from a well-specified model, the search space can be reduced by several orders of magnitude. In most natural environments, scenes do not change suddenly but are governed by some regularities. If a feature's location in the current image is known, then its location in the next image should be nearby and so can be predicted by the model. Thus, to search for a feature that had been located in the previous image, one does not need to search the entire new image but just a small region near the previous location. The model can predict this small region. Furthermore, such predictions need not be exact. They simply provide a restricted space so that a feature can be found quickly, say in one cycle of time. In most cases, zero-order prediction (i.e., "the object will at the same place") is sufficient. For very fast moving objects, first order prediction that takes the velocity of the object into account will be enough.

The entire system can be summarized as in Figure 6.14. The 4-dimensional world model is a set of differential equations as follows:

$$X_{t+T}^* = A_t X_t + B_t u_t$$

where A is an $n \times n$ state transition matrix over one sampling period, X is the state vector of n variables, T is the sampling period (0.1 second for this application), and B is the $n \times q$ control effectiveness matrix for the q components of the control vector u, which is the action of the system and assumed to be constant over T. All coefficients are assumed to be constant over T. Thus the predicted state value X^* is the system's prediction of the location of the pertinent features in the next image.

This approach works remarkably well in many applications (e.g., balancing an inverted pendulum, aircraft landing, and vehicle docking) compared with some sophisticated methods, such as anisotropic nonlinear filters. Most remarkably, Dick-

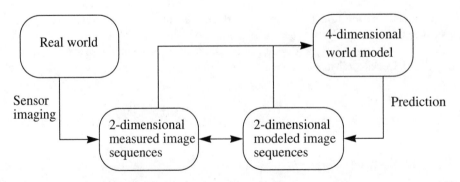

Figure 6.14   4-dimensional dynamic scene analysis by a spatiotemporal world model.

manns and his group have constructed an autonomous road vehicle that can go at a maximum speed of 96 kilometers per hour for 20 kilometers. Although the model in their system is not learned, they remark in their paper that "in the long run, the system should be able to learn from statistics it accumulates during each mission."

6.4 Designing and Learning from Experiments

What we have studied so far is applying models to searching solutions. As we pointed out earlier, models can also be used to generate new goals. In this section, we describe how to use models to design experiments — a special type of goal that improves the learned model.

Learning from experiments, or actively choosing training instances, is very helpful in learning a target concept. In Section 3.4.1, we saw that in approximating functions by polynomials, whether the instances are drawn randomly (from a uniform distribution) or selected by using the Čebyšev formula

$$x_n = \cos \frac{2k+1}{2(n+1)} \pi \quad (k = 0, 1, \ldots, n)$$

determines whether the approximation converges to the actual function. In addition, we can see from this example that a model plays an essential role in choosing instances: the current approximation (model) of degree $n-1$ is used to choose the next point in order to construct the approximation formula of degree n. Thus, in addition to solving problems or reaching goals, models are also used to design experiments.

Learning from experiments is a new but promising area of research. There have been several investigations in this topic in many fields of learning. For example, Gross studied how to choose instances for concept learning [30], Carbonell and Gil investigated the role of experiments in problem solving [13, 28], and MacKay used a Bayesian method to select instances for training neural networks [58]. This section outlines a simple description of experiments to prepare for the material in Chapters 8 and 10.

Given a learned model and a deficiency in the model, an *experiment* is an apparatus to gain more information from the environment for the purpose of rectifying the deficiency. An experiment consists of three parts: the condition state, a sequence of actions that should be applied to the condition state, and a result expected by the current model after the experiment is conducted. An experiment is *confirmed* if the result observed from the environment matches the expected result; it is *rebuffed* otherwise. When an experiment is rebuffed, it is treated as a surprise and appropriate actions are taken to refine the model. Clearly, the condition state is a goal state for the learner to reach before the experiment can be carried out.

This notion of an experiment is a generalization of many forms of active learning queries. For example, the membership query (see Section 5.2) is a special case of an experiment. In a membership query, the question is whether a string (which can be thought of as the concatenation of the [condition] state, actions, and result) belongs to a particular concept or language. The query can be thought of as an experiment in which the string is executed with a null prediction. On the other hand, an equivalence query is not an experiment according to this definition because a query does not propose any actions or instances. Rather, the teacher provides the counterexample.

Exploration is another special case of experimentation. An exploration is an experiment with an unknown result. It is an experiment in which anything may happen, and anything that does happen is treated as a surprise. Thus, a mechanism that can learn from experiments can also learn from exploration.

6.5 Summary

In this chapter, we have discussed various applications of models. As we have seen, models can be used to find optimal or satisficing solutions, make predictions, or design experiments and learn from them. Such applications are not limited to any particular computational paradigm; they appear in symbolic logic, neural networks, and control theories.

One assumption made throughout this chapter is that a perfect model is being used. This is, however, not always the case when learning from the environment. To relax this assumption and allow the learner to use imperfect models, all methods for model application must be integrated with model abstraction. The next chapter focuses on the issues related to this integration.

CHAPTER 7

INTEGRATION

How can we integrate a system that learns from the environment? We have seen that the actions of an autonomous agent has two purposes: to build a model of the environment (model abstraction) and to achieve some goals (model application). Integration of the system refers to the ability to switch between these two functions so that one function can help the other.

The simplest integration is just to perform these activities in sequence: No model application before a model has been built, and no model construction or abstraction after the model has been applied. This approach is not practical for at least two reasons. First, in a realistic environment, it is impossible to tell whether a model has been adequately built. Therefore, it is difficult to know when to stop model abstraction. Furthermore, once model abstraction has ended, there is no guarantee that the model will be sufficient to achieve the desired goals. Second, nature seems to reject this sequential approach to integration. In observing how humans solve unfamiliar problems that are written as instructions, researchers have noticed that humans alternate between model building and model application [35]. They start to solve the problem (i.e., model application) with only partial understanding of the instructions (i.e., an inadequate model) and later come back and read the instructions when they make mistakes or have trouble finding the solution.

To combine model abstraction and model application, many integration architectures have been proposed. In this chapter, we will detail several approaches and make references to others. We will consider two types of integration: model construction with model application and model abstraction with model application. (Recall that model construction refers to situations where the learned model is the same size as the environment, while model abstraction refers to situations where the learned model is more compact than the environment). In each of these discussions, we will classify an approach according to the type of environment (transparent or translucent) in which it functions.

7.1 Integrating Model Construction and Model Application

7.1.1 Transparent Environments

Sutton presents a system that integrates Q-learning with constructing and applying models in transparent environments [120]. Q-learning by itself, as we have seen in Section 6.1.3, requires no model to function. Although this is a desirable feature in some cases, it makes it difficult for a system to adapt to changing situations after the optimal Q-values have been learned. In this section, it is assumed that the system is interested only in optimal solutions.

There are two types of changes in the environment that can make optimal Q-values become suboptimal. The first type is called "blocking," in which the optimal solution cannot be executed. In this case, of course, one knows that the solution no longer works. The second type is called a "shortcut," in which a new and better solution is introduced without disturbing the original optimal solution. In this case, there is no indication that the original solution is no longer optimal.

These two types of changes also apply to changes in the goals. Blocking in this context means that the optimal goal has moved within the search space, so it seems to the learner that the goal has disappeared. The shortcut change means that a new and less costly goal has been placed in the search space.

Q-learning can be modified to deal with these problems to some extent. Instead of choosing the action b^* at state x such that $Q(x, b^*)$ is the best among all possible actions, one chooses the action according to the Boltzmann distribution

$$P(b|x) = \frac{e^{tQ(x,b)}}{\sum_j e^{tQ(x,j)}} \tag{7.1}$$

where t is the temperature that controls the degree of randomness of the action that is chosen. This approach could solve the blocking and the shortcut problems when t is high. However, when t is low, which is always the case after an optimal solution has been found, the system is very reluctant to deviate from the current solution to find new solutions.

Sutton's integration is based on two ideas. First, the model of the world is constructed so that the learned Q-values are propagated to more states without actually moving in the real environment. Second, the rule for updating the Q-values is slightly modified so that those states that have not been visited for some time (as well as those states that lead to them) are assigned higher Q-values so that the system will tend to move to those states and thus experience the changes.

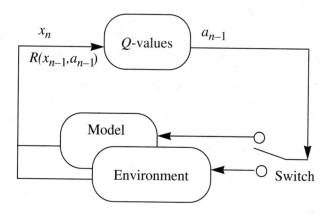

Figure 7.1   Integrating Q-learning with model application.

The first idea is implemented as follows. As the learner acts in the real environment, it records each transition and its reward in the model. Because the environment is transparent, this simple recording is sufficient to construct a model (see Section 4.2). In addition to the moves in the real environment, state–action pairs are also sampled in the model to propagate the Q-values that are learned from the real environment to more states in the model. The interleaving of the acting in the environment and the sampling is accomplished by a switch that controls whether to run the Q-learning in the real environment or in the model. The architecture is shown in Figure 7.1.

The integration algorithm is shown in Figure 7.2. Steps 1 and 2 decide whether the next action will be performed in the environment or in the model. Step 3 chooses the action according to the current Q-values. Steps 4 and 5 execute the action, receive the information from the environment (when RealExperience = 1) or

Repeat forever:
1   Decide RealExperience = 1 or 0 (for a hypothetical experience),
2   If RealExperience = 1, then $x \leftarrow$ the current state,
       Else $x \leftarrow$ select a state at random uniformly over the states in the model,
3   Choose an action a such that $Q(x, a)$ is the maximum,
4   Do action a and receive next state y and reward r from the environment
          or the model,
5      $Q(x, a) \leftarrow (1 - \alpha)Q(x, a) + \alpha(r + \gamma V(y))$ where $V(y) = \max_b Q(y, b)$,
6   If RealExperience = 1, update the model from x, a, y, and r.

Figure 7.2   Sutton's integration algorithm for Q-learning.

the model, and update the Q-value accordingly. Step 6 does the model construction if the experience was in the environment. Compared to standard Q-learning, this algorithm builds up the Q-values much faster (since updating is not limited to the current state) and solves problems much more efficiently, as demonstrated in [120].

To address the shortcut problem, the second key idea of this integration is to modify the rule for updating Q-values so that state–action pairs that have not been experienced recently get higher values. This encourages the system to explore alternatives. Technically, for each state–action pair (x, a), a record n_{xa} is kept of the number of time steps since a was tried in x in a real experience. The square root $\sqrt{n_{xa}}$ is used as a measure of the uncertainty about $Q(x, a)$. To encourage exploration, step 5 in the algorithm is modified as

$$Q(x, a) \leftarrow (1 - \alpha)Q(x, a) + \alpha(r + \epsilon\sqrt{n_{xa}} + \gamma V(y))$$

where ϵ is a small positive parameter.

The key to this integration of learning and planning is the unique functionality of Q-values. As we saw in Section 6.1.3, Q-values can be used to implement a policy as well as to calculate state values with respect to the goals. If one learns the Q-values, then one solves the problem (i.e., finds the best solution). The utility of running Q-learning in the model is that the system can select *any* state for which it wishes to propagate the Q-values, while in the real environment one has to stick with the current state.

In light of this, the algorithm can be improved by modifying the selection criterion at step 2. Instead of treating all states in the model uniformly, the selection should favor state–action pairs that can reach states that already have high values. In that way, the Q-values can quickly be propagated to other states.

7.1.2   Translucent Environments

When the environment is translucent, there is another element involved in integrating model construction and model application, namely, dynamically creating hidden states in the model. As we know, model construction in such an environment is not just simply recording what is observed; the learner must also create new model states when its perception cannot distinguish two environmental states.

Chrisman proposed an integration of model construction and model application in the translucent environment [16]. In his integration, shown in Figure 7.3, a model is represented as an action-driven hidden Markov model, upon which a Q-learner is trained to select the optimal actions. The hidden Markov model and the Q-learner together can be viewed as a partially observable Markov decision process [57, 60].

As we discussed in Section 5.10, a hidden Markov model, such as the one in Figure 7.3, is a model of six parameters, $(B, Z, S, P, \theta, \pi)$, where B is a set of basic actions, Z is a set of percepts, S are the internal model states (also known as *classes*), P is the probabilistic state transition function, θ is the probability

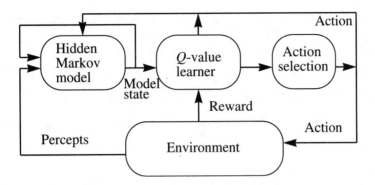

Figure 7.3 Integrating a hidden Markov model with Q-learning in a translucent environment.

distribution of percept symbols for each state, and π is the probability distribution of the current state.

The integration of model construction and Q-learning is accomplished as follows. Initially, the model may be set to be some known model or it may simply start with two classes and randomly generated values for P, θ, and π. The agent executes a prespecified number of actions in the environment, recording each action–observation pair and continuously performing Q-learning. This collected experience, denoted as E, is then fed to the model construction process to produce a better model. The entire process is then repeated.

Model construction here involves two activities: adjusting P, θ, and π to make better predictions while assuming that S is correct, and adjusting S when necessary. Since the first activity was discussed in Section 5.10, we will concentrate on the second here.

As in the D^* algorithm, the adjustment S consists mainly of splitting some existing class into two. To detect which class to split and when, Chrisman's system also looks for surprises. In this context, a surprise is a statistically significant difference in the system's behavior. By the Markov assumption, if the current system has the correct number of classes, then the expected number of transitions from class i to j by action b should not change significantly in two very similar experiences. If any significant change is detected under this circumstance, then the class i should be split.

To detect whether such a change exists, the experience E is partitioned into two groups, E_1 and E_2, with E_1 in the earlier half of E and E_2 in the latter half. Recall from Section 5.10 that the expected number of transitions from i to j by action b in the experience E_1 can be calculated as $\Xi_1 = \sum_{t=1, b_t=b}^{|E_1|} \xi_t(i,j)$, and the expected number of transitions from i to j by action b in the experience E_2 can be calculated as $\Xi_2 = \sum_{t=|E_1|, b_t=b}^{|E|} \xi_t(i,j)$. The values Ξ_1 and Ξ_2 are then compared, say by the chi-square test, to see if they are significantly different. If so, the class i is split (i.e., the number of states in S is increased by one). Whenever a class is split, the complete model learning algorithm is reinvoked recursively.

7.2   Integrating Model Abstraction and Model Application

In Chapters 4 and 5, we described several methods for model abstraction, including symbolic concept learning, neural networks, and statistical procedures. Here we will describe how these mechanisms can be integrated with model application in both tranparent and translucent environments.

7.2.1   Transparent Environments

7.2.1.1   Distal Learning with Neural Networks

In Section 4.11 we saw that neural networks can be used to abstract a model from the environment. In Section 6.2.3, we saw that distal learning networks can be trained, when an approximately correct model is available, to select appropriate actions to achieve goals. The question here is whether these two activities can be interleaved.

The answer is yes. The reason is that distal learning requires only an approximate model to train its controller. Because of this property, the integration is surprisingly simple [41]. One can simply run the model learning and the controller learning simultaneously with hardly any degradation in performance.

The integration is shown in Figure 7.4. As we can see, there are two learning activities occurring simultaneously. One is the learning of the model driven by the

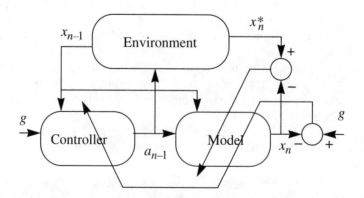

Figure 7.4   Integrating distal learning with model learning.

prediction error $\frac{1}{2}(x_n^* - x_n)^2$ (see Section 4.11). The other is the learning of the controller, through the current model, driven by the error $\frac{1}{2}(x_n - g)^2$ (see Section 6.2.3). The procedure is straightforward. At the current environmental state x_{n-1}, the learner chooses the action a_{n-1} recommended by the current controller and makes a prediction x_n based on the current model. Then, the learner applies the action to the environment and observes the next state x_n^*. Based on the difference between x_n^* and x_n, we use back propagation to update the weights in the model. Based on the difference between g and x_n, we use distal learning to update the weights in the controller. This process repeats until the controller can choose the correct action for the goal in all the states.

7.2.1.2   Integrating Q-Learning with Generalization

In Section 6.1.3, we saw that Q-learning can learn Q-values for all the state–action pairs such that the values determine an optimal solution for a goal. We also saw that the method itself does not do any generalization on the states. When the environment is large, the requirement of visiting all the state–action pairs is sometimes unrealistic.

However, Q-learning can be integrated nicely with other generalization methods. For example, Lin integrates Q-learning with neural networks [55]. In his system, the Q-values are implemented in a neural network, and the network is trained on the basis of the difference between the predicted Q-value and the actual Q-value received from the environment. The architecture of Lin's implementation is presented in Figure 7.5, and the algorithm is presented in Figure 7.6.

The algorithm is easy to understand in light of the discussions in Sections 6.1.3 and 4.11. At the current state x (strictly speaking, x is not an environmental state but the observation from the current environmental state), an action b^*, with its predicted Q-value Q_{xb^*}, is chosen stochastically according to the Q-values stored in the current network and the current temperature t (see equation 7.1). This action

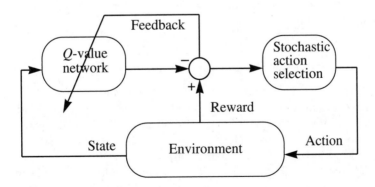

Figure 7.5   Integrating Q-learning with neural networks.

Repeat ($b \in B$ are basic actions):

1     $x \leftarrow$ current (observation) state,

2   Let Q_{xb} be the Q-value for state x and action b obtained from the current
        network,

3   Select an action b^* by equation 7.1 using the current temperature t
        and Q_{xb},

4   Perform action b^*,

5   Obtain new state y and reinforcement r,

6   Compute the actual Q-value $Q^+_{xb*} \leftarrow r + \gamma \cdot \max_b\{Q_{yb}\}$,

7   Adjust Q-value network by back-propagating error:

$$\Delta Q_{xb} = \left\{ \begin{array}{ll} Q^+_{xb} - Q_{xb} & \text{if } b = b^* \\ 0 & \text{otherwise} \end{array} \right.$$

Figure 7.6 Q-learning with back propagation.

is then executed and the next state y and reward r are obtained. Based on y and
r, the actual Q-value Q^+_{xb} is then calculated at line 6. The network is trained on
the basis of the error that is defined at line 5.

Compared to the table representation of Q-values, the neural network does the
generalization automatically (i.e., similar states x and actions b will have similar
Q-values). Because of this generalization ability, the system can still function in
a translucent environment. In fact, Lin tests the system in an environment where
the agent cannot perceive the entire environmental state. In such an environment,
the results of an agent's action may appear nondeterministic.

Finally, notice that actions are selected at line 3 not only according to their
Q-value but also according to the current temperature t (see Section 7.1.1). In
this way, an action with suboptimal Q-values may be chosen, giving the system a
built-in factor for exploring the environment.

In addition to neural networks, Q-learning can also be integrated with other
generalization methods, for example, statistical clustering. Interested readers can
find more examples in [14] and [59].

7.2.1.3   Integration via Prediction Sequence

This section describes a symbolic approach to the integration problem. Recall that
the objective of integration is to combine model application with model abstraction.
However, model application is a diverse notion in itself. A model can be used to
solve problems (planning), to gather new information (exploration), or to find out
why the model is incorrect (experimentation).

Regardless of their differences, however, planning, exploration, and experimentation are all sequences of actions with predictions. Recall that a prediction, relative
to a condition and an action, is a statement that describes the expected observa-

tion from the result state. In learning from the environment, predictions can be sequenced as follows:

$$(S_0, a_1, P_1, a_2, P_2, \ldots, a_n, P_n)$$

where S_0 is the observation from the current state, a_i is an action, and P_i is a prediction.

As the actions in this sequence are executed, observations from the environmental states S_i are perceived in a sequence: $S_0, a_1, S_1, a_2, S_2, \cdots, a_n, S_n$. A prediction failure occurs as soon as a prediction P_i is not confirmed by the corresponding observation S_i. Notice that a prediction failure is different from a failure to achieve a goal. With respect to a goal, an action can be successful by accident (i.e., the result state is the goal) even though the prediction is wrong (i.e., the result state does not satisfy the prediction). Thus, learning from prediction failures means both learning from failures and learning from successes.

With a prediction sequence so defined, planning, exploration, and experimentation are all special cases:

- A *plan* is a prediction sequence whose accumulated prediction, $\sqcup_{i=1}^n P_i$, satisfies the goal G (recall that a goal is a set of percepts). (The operator $\sqcup$ is a set union with undos. For example, if $P_i = \{\neg b\}$ and $P_{i+1} = \{b\}$, then $P_i \sqcup P_{i+1} = \{b\}$ because b undoes $\neg b$.) A plan may or may not produce prediction failures, and it succeeds only if there is no prediction failure.

- An *exploration* is a prediction sequence in which some of the predictions are "false." Since a false prediction cannot be satisfied by any observation, an exploration is guaranteed to produce prediction failures and thus improve the model. The motivation for this approach is that when you don't know what might happen after an action (i.e., when you explore an action), whatever happens will be valuable information for improving the model.

- An *experiment* is a prediction sequence whose final prediction is expected to fail. This is an effective way to seek counterexamples (prediction failures) when the current model is known to have particular errors. For example, if the model says $(P_{n-1}, a) \rightarrow P_n$ but there is a strong reason to believe this is false, then experiments of $(\ldots, P_{n-1}, a, P_n)$ will be very useful for revising the model because it may produce a prediction failure.

Using the notion of a prediction sequence, model application and model abstraction can be easily integrated by the loops in Figure 7.7. This integration contains two loops. The outer loop is responsible for generating new goals and new experiments. (Here we treat experiments as a special type of goal.) The inner loop is responsible for model application and abstraction. In the inner loop, the learner's default activity is model application (lines 3, 4, and 5), and it switches to model abstraction only when there is a prediction failure (line 6). The inner loop repeats until the current goal or experiment is successfully accomplished.

Repeat:
1   Generate a new goal or a new experiment (based on the current model),
2   While the goal or experiment is not accomplished:
3   Generate a prediction sequence for achieving the goals/experiment,
4   Execute the actions in the prediction sequence,
5   Perceive information from the environment,
6   If there is a prediction failure,
7   Then call model abstraction (e.g., CDL) to refine the model.

Figure 7.7   Integration by prediction sequences in a transparent environment.

Notice that this loop links together all the tasks of the learner. Problem solving, exploration, and experimentation are all used in making prediction sequences. Model application and model abstraction are linked by prediction failures. That is, model abstraction is invoked whenever there is a prediction failure, regardless of whether the failure is in a plan, an exploration, or an experimentation. When the model is revised, the loop uses it again to generate new prediction sequences until the current goals are reached. After that, new goals are generated in the outer loop based on the lifetime innate goals and what the learner knows so far about the current world.

This integration can be viewed as search in two spaces. One space is the space of observations and actions, and the other is the model space. The search in the former space is to find instances that provide information for the search in the model space. The model found in the model space provides guidance in selecting the next action for achieving the goals.

In light of this, the integration here can be seen as a special case of the two-space search theory first proposed by Simon and Lea for unifying rule induction with problem solving [117]. Our model space is a special case of their rule space, and our experience space is a special case of their problem space.

7.2.2   Translucent Environments

Integrating model abstraction and model application in a translucent environment is a challenging task. On the one hand, there are too many states in the environment, and the agent must generalize what it sees. On the other hand, the agent's percepts may be limited and unable to see the hidden states of the environment; it must therefore introduce new internal states (see Chapter 5).

7.2.2.1   Integration Using the CDL+ Framework

The CDL+ framework can be considered as a candidate for the task. In particular, we have seen that this framework combines solutions to two problems into one.

Repeat:
1   Generate a new goal or a new experiment (based on the current model),
2   While the goal or experiment is not accomplished:
3   Generate a prediction sequence for achieving the goals or experiment,
4   Execute the actions in the prediction sequence,
5   Perceive information from the environment,
6   If there is a prediction failure,
7   Then find the difference between a success and the failure,
8   If some difference is found,
9   Then call CDL to improve the current model,
10   Else call CDL+1-like algorithms to create new features or variables.

Figure 7.8   Integration in translucent environments using the CDL framework.

It contains CDL for generalization, and it also contains the extension of searching historical differences for defining hidden states (as used in CDL+1). The switch between these two activities is accomplished naturally. When a prediction failure occurs, the successful situation and the failed situation are compared. If the agent's perception ability allows it to find differences between these two situations, then CDL is used to do the generalization task. If no differences can be detected between the two situations, then new features of the environment are defined to reflect the differences found in the history.

Therefore, the integration loop in Figure 7.7 needs only slight modification in order to function in translucent environments. When a prediction failure occurs, the learner first tries to find the differences between a success and a failure. If differences are found, the learner calls CDL to modify the model. If no difference is found, the learner calls some mechanism of the CDL+1 algorithm to create new features for the model. The new integration loop is illustrated in Figure 7.8. Since this loop will be discussed extensively in Chapter 8 and Chapter 11, we will not go into details at this point.

7.3   Summary

In this chapter, we have described several approaches for the third major task of learning from the environment: integrating model abstraction with model application. For models that have the same size as the environment (i.e., model construction), we have seen that both Q-learning and hidden Markov learning can be integrated with planning. For models that are more compact than the environment, we have seen the examples of distal learning with neural networks and Q-learning in conjunction with generalization. Finally, we have outlined the CDL+ style of integration that uses prediction sequences as the glue for unifying learning and problem solving. Readers may have noticed that most integration techniques are driven by model application. That is, the system uses the model whenever it can and fixes the model only when it runs into problems. This seems consistent with how humans solve complex, novel problems.

CHAPTER 8

THE LIVE SYSTEM

In previous chapters, we defined the problem of learning from the environment and its three main tasks: model abstraction, model application, and integration. For each of these tasks, we also discussed many existing solutions and their scopes.

In the rest of the book, we will not talk about methods in general but focus our attention on a particular system called LIVE. LIVE was developed as part of my doctoral dissertation. It is included in this book not because it is the best system available but because it can show how the ideas that have been presented are actually implemented and how such a system performs.

We will first introduce the architecture of the LIVE system, which includes different components and the relations between them. Then we will focus on LIVE's internal model representation and its problem-solver component. Other components of the system will be covered in detail in the chapters that follow.

8.1 System Architecture

LIVE is an implementation of the integration idea presented in Section 7.2.2. Its structure is presented in Figure 8.1. Corresponding to the integration loop presented in Figure 7.8, LIVE has three main modules: the prediction sequence generator (corresponding to step 3 in the integration loop), the executor/perceiver (steps 4–6), and the model builder/reviser (steps 7–10). The system is implemented in a general way that can be used by any learner. That is, the LIVE system can be instantiated in different learners by giving it different percepts, actions, and mental languages.

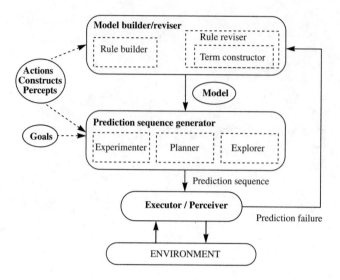

Figure 8.1 The LIVE architecture.

As the name implies, the prediction sequence generator is responsible for generating a prediction sequence, both for revising the model and for achieving the goals. It has three submodules: the planner, the explorer, and the experimenter. The submodules are coordinated as follows. The planner, which uses means–ends analysis, is called first to construct a path to the goals using the current model. If it fails, then either the explorer or the experimenter is called. The explorer is called if the failure of plan construction is due to a lack of prediction rules in the model (i.e., given the current set of rules, there is no path between the current state and the goals.) The experimenter is called when prediction rules cause errors during planning. Two common types of planning errors are a regression deadlock and a regression loop. A *regression deadlock* (or *goal contradiction*) means that subgoals proposed by the rules conflict with each other no matter how the subgoals are ordered. A *regression loop* (or *subgoal looping*) means that the same subgoal is repeatedly proposed forever. How the explorer and the experimenter generate their prediction sequences will be described later.

The executor/perceiver module executes the generated prediction sequence in the environment. This module compares the result of each action with the corresponding prediction. If there is a prediction failure, it calls the model builder/reviser module. At this point, the executor/perceiver normally relinquishes its control and waits for a new prediction sequence. However, if the current prediction sequence is an exploration, it will resume execution after the model is revised. In this case, it does not relinquish control until the whole exploration sequence has been completed.

The model builder/reviser module has two submodules. If the failed prediction is equal to "false" (i.e., the action is an exploration), the submodule rule builder is called to create a new prediction rule. Otherwise, the submodule rule reviser is called to change the rule that made the incorrect prediction. In the revising process, if no differences can be found to explain the prediction failure, then the submodule term constructor (corresponding to CDL$^+$ style learning) is called to define new relations and terms. All functions and relations of the modules and their components are summarized in Figure 8.2.

1. Planner (Problem Solver):
   Find the differences between the goal/experiment and the current state;
   Find a rule for each difference;
   If no rule can be found, then call explorer;
   Order the differences by their rules;
   If goal contradiction is detected, call experimenter;
   Select the first difference and its rule;
   If the rule is executable in the current state,
   then call executor/perceiver   .
   else if subgoal looping is detected
        then call experimenter
        else call planner;

2. Explorer:
   Propose an explorative plan;
   Call executor/perceiver to execute the explorative plan;

3. Experimenter:
        Design an experiment for the planning error;
        Call executor/perceiver to execute the experiment;

4. Executor/Perceiver:
        If all the given goals are accomplished, then exit;
        Execute each action in the prediction sequence;
        If there is a prediction failure
        then call model builder/reviser to create/revise a rule;

5. Model Builder/Reviser:
        If the prediction is nil,
        then create a new prediction rule
        else if differences can be found to explain the failure
             then revise the faulty rule
             else call term constructor.

Figure 8.2 An outline of LIVE's control.

8.2   Prediction Rules: The Model Representation

As we can see from the architecture, the internal model is LIVE's knowledge base. It reflects how much the system knows about the environment and provides the backbone for all the other components in the system. For instance, the planner (problem solver) uses it to plan solutions for achieving the goals, the explorer uses it to propose explorative plans, the experimenter uses it to design experiments, and the rule reviser accesses it to detect knowledge errors and rectify them. Therefore, the representation of the internal model must serve several purposes.

Given these constraints, LIVE's knowledge representation consists of a set of prediction rules with three components: conditions, actions, and predictions. The actions in the prediction rules are those given to the learner at the outset. The conditions and predictions of the prediction rules are well-formed formulae in LIVE's description language $\mathcal{L}$ (see Section 8.3). The action contained in a rule can be executed whenever the conditions of that rule are satisfied, and the prediction of the rule forecasts the effects of the action. The prediction rules are very much like STRIPS operators but have one important difference: The postconditions of STRIPS operators modify the perceived world by deleting and adding elements, while the predictions of prediction rules serve only as templates for checking and matching the perceived world. Thus, a prediction rule does not change states as the add/delete list would in STRIPS's case. A prediction can fail, while add/delete lists, as they are used in STRIPS, cannot. The prediction rules are also like the operators used in Carbonell and Gil's learning from experimentation [13]. However, LIVE represents the inference rules and the operators uniformly and appears more natural. For example, since only ALUMINIZE(obj), among others actions in Carbonell and Gil's program, can be the last action for making a mirror, their Operator-3 and Inference-Rule-1 can be combined into one prediction rule in a LIVE representation.

As an example, let us take a close look at some of the prediction rules learned by the LOGIC1 learner (see Section 2.4), which is an instantiation of LIVE in the Tower of Hanoi environment. (In these rules, and for all rules henceforth, the constants and predicates are shown in uppercase and variables in italics. Elements in a list are conjuncts, and negations are represented by the symbol ¬. Objects and their features are represented as a list with square brackets. Variables are quantified as described in Section 8.3.)

RuleID:	RuleX
Condition:	$\text{INHAND}(x) \wedge \neg\text{ON}(y\ p)$
Action:	$\text{Put}(x\ p)$
Prediction:	$\text{ON}(x\ p) \wedge \neg\text{INHAND}(x)$

RuleID:	RuleY
Condition:	INHAND(x) $\land$ ON$(y\ p)$
Action:	Put$(x\ p)$
Prediction:	INHAND(x)

RuleX says that if there is a disk x in hand and no disk y on peg p, then the action Put$(x\ p)$ will place disk x on peg p and disk x will not be in hand any more. Similarly, RuleY says that if disk x is in hand and there is a disk y on peg p, the action will have no effect on disk x; that is, disk x will be still in hand.

In addition to relational predicates like ON and INHAND, the conditions and the predictions of prediction rules can also contain the feature vectors of objects represented as square bracket lists. For example, [OBJ3 DISK RED 10] represents a red disk with a diameter of 10 centimeters. Sometimes certain features of an object are unimportant to a rule; such features are represented as a "don't care" symbol, •, which can be matched to any value. If object feature vectors are also included, then RuleX might look like the following:

RuleID:	RuleX'
Condition:	INHAND(x) $\land$ $\neg$ON$(y\ p)$ $\land$ [x DISK RED 10] $\land$ [y DISK • •] $\land$ [p PEG • •]
Action:	Put$(x\ p)$
Prediction:	ON$(x\ p)$ $\land$ $\neg$INHAND(x) $\land$ [x DISK RED 10] $\land$ [y DISK • •] $\land$ [p PEG • •]

The prediction rules have some interesting and useful characteristics. Like productions, prediction rules have a simple and uniform structure. This makes learning easier than modifying programs (as demonstrated in many adaptive production systems [131]). In particular, since prediction rules make predictions, it is straightforward to detect incorrect rules. After a rule's action is applied, the actual outcome is compared to the rule's prediction; if the comparison detects some differences, then the rule is wrong and must be revised. For example, if RuleY is applied when disk x is smaller than disk y, then the prediction INHAND(x) will be wrong because disk x will be put on peg p and so not be in hand.

The prediction rules can also be used as problem reduction rules when applied backwards. Given some goals to reach, the actions of the rule whose predictions match the goals become the means to achieve the goals, and the conditions of that rule, if not true already, are the subgoals that must be achieved beforehand. For example, in order to put a disk x on a peg p, RuleX tells us that action Put must be performed and INHAND(x) and $\neg$ON$(y\ p)$ must be satisfied before the action can apply.

Finally, and most interestingly, prediction rules have sibling rules. This is because whenever a rule is found to be incorrect, LIVE's learning method, like the CDL algorithm, will split the rule into two rules with a discriminating condition (see Chapter 10). Sibling rules share the same action but have some opposite conditions and different predictions. For instance, RuleX and RuleY are sibling rules; they have the same action, Put(x p), but their predictions are different and their conditions differ at ON(y p). As we will see later, sibling rules play an important role in designing experiments.

8.3   LIVE's Model Description Language

As we pointed out in the last section, the conditions and predictions of prediction rules are expressions in LIVE's description language. In fact, the same language also describes the state of the environment (a state is perceived as a set of ground atomic formulae in this language). In this section, we will describe the language's syntax and semantics and give details of how a rule's conditions and predictions are matched to the states perceived from the environment.

8.3.1   The Syntax

The description language $\mathcal{L}$ has the following alphabet of symbols once the percepts and constructors are given:

- Variables $x_1, x_2, \ldots$, including the "don't care" symbol $\bullet$,

- Individual constants $a_1, a_2, \ldots$, such as DISK, RED, and SPHERE,

- Predicates A_i^n, such as ON, SIZE>, =, and >,

- Identifiers of objects O_i, such as OBJ3,

- Functions f_i^n, such as + and ×,

- The grouping symbols (and),

- The logical connectives ∧ (represented as lists) and ¬, and

- The existential quantifier ∃ (wherever there are free variables).

Note that for different environments, $\mathcal{L}$ may have different alphabets depending on the percepts. Also, the number of relational predicates is not fixed, because LIVE can define new ones during the learning process. For example, if the relational predicate = is given as a constructor, then new predicates such as DISTANCE= and WEIGHT= might be defined. Although the alphabet does not include the logical connective OR (∨), LIVE can still learn disjunctive conditions and predictions of the form $P_1 \vee P_2$ by using the logically equivalent expression $\neg(\neg P_1 \wedge \neg P_2)$.

To define well-formed formulae in $\mathcal{L}$, we first define a *term* in $\mathcal{L}$ as follows (terms are those expressions in $\mathcal{L}$ that will be interpreted as objects or features of objects):

1. Variables and individual constants are terms.

2. If f_i^n is a function and $t_1, \ldots, t_n$ are terms in $\mathcal{L}$, then $f_i^n(t_1, \ldots, t_n)$ is a term in $\mathcal{L}$.

3. The set of all terms generated by the previous two definitions.

An *atomic formula* in $\mathcal{L}$ is defined as follows: If X is a predicate or an identifier in $\mathcal{L}$ and $t_1, \cdots, t_n$ are terms in $\mathcal{L}$, then $(X\ t_1 \ldots t_n)$ is an atomic formula of L. An atomic formula is *ground* if all $t_1, \ldots, t_n$ are constants. Atomic formulae are the simplest expressions in $\mathcal{L}$. They are to be interpreted as relationships among objects or as individual objects with features. For example, $\text{ON}(x\ y)$ means object x is on y, and [OBJ3 DISK RED] means the object OBJ3 is a red disk.

Based on atomic formulae, the *well-formed formulas* (wfs) of $\mathcal{L}$ are defined as follows:

1. Every atomic formula of $\mathcal{L}$ is a wf of $\mathcal{L}$.

2. If A and B are wfs of $\mathcal{L}$, so are $(\neg A)$, $(A \wedge B)$ and $(\exists_{x_i})(A)$, where x_i is a variable.

3. All the wfs of $\mathcal{L}$ generated by the previous two definitions.

8.3.2 The Interpretation

The learner applies the expressions of $\mathcal{L}$ to the objects and perceives relations between objects from the external world. For instance, the predicate symbols A_i^k are interpreted as relations among objects, the object identifiers O_i are the names assigned to the external objects, and the function symbols f_i^n are interpreted as functions. Variables in $\mathcal{L}$, if they appear in a relational atomic formula, are interpreted as objects. If they appear in an object's feature vector, they are interpreted as the object's features.

The following defines what it means for an expression in $\mathcal{L}$ to be *true*, or *matched*, in a state perceived from the external world:

1. An atomic formula is true if and only if there is a ground relation or an object feature list in the state that corresponds with the formula.

2. A conjunctive expression is true if and only if all of its conjuncts match the state.

3. The negation of an expression is true if and only if the expression does not match the state.

4. An existentially quantified expression is true if and only if there exists an assignment of values to each of the variables such that the substituted expression is true in the state. For example, $\exists_x(\text{ON}(x\ \text{PEG1}) \wedge \text{SIZE} > (x\ \text{DISK1}))$ is true if and only if there is a disk on PEG1 and its size is greater than DISK1.

Since all variables are interpreted as being existentially quantified, we will omit the symbol ∃ in future expressions; instead, we will use the following convention (note that this may restrict the set of logical relations that can be expressed):

$$
\begin{aligned}
P(x) &\implies \exists_x P(x) \\
\neg P(x) &\implies \neg\exists_x P(x) \\
\neg(P(x) \wedge Q(x)) &\implies \neg\exists_x(P(x) \wedge Q(x)) \\
\neg(P(x) \wedge \neg Q(x)) &\implies \exists_x(\neg P(x) \vee Q(x)) \\
\neg(\neg P(x) \wedge Q(x)) &\implies \exists_x(P(x) \vee \neg Q(x)) \\
\neg(\neg P(x) \wedge \neg Q(x)) &\implies \exists_x(P(x) \vee Q(x)) \\
(P(x) \wedge Q(x\ y)) &\implies \exists_x(P(x) \wedge (Q(x\ y)))
\end{aligned}
$$

Therefore, the expression

INHAND(x) $\wedge$ $\neg$(ON(y PEG3) $\wedge$ SIZE>(x y)) $\wedge$
[x DISK *color size*] $\wedge$ [PEG3 PEG • •]

is equivalent to

$\exists_x\exists_{color}\exists_{size}$(INHAND($x$) $\wedge$ $\neg\exists_y$(ON(y PEG3) $\wedge$ SIZE>(x y)) $\wedge$
[x DISK *color size*] $\wedge$ [PEG3 PEG • •])

8.3.3 Matching an Expression to a State

In order to understand LIVE's description language, it is necessary to know how the system matches conditions and predictions to a state that is perceived from the external environment.

When an expression is given, LIVE matches all the positive relational predicates to the state before matching any negative relations, and it matches all the negative relations before matching object feature lists. Matching is done from left to right in each of these three matching processes. Every time a subexpression is successfully matched, the bindings from that match are immediately used to substitute all occurrences of the bound variables in the whole expression. If all the subexpressions are true, the match succeeds. If any of the subexpressions are false, the matching process will backtrack and continue searching for a new match in a depth-first fashion. The final result of a successful match is the set of bindings established in the process.

To illustrate the matching process, let us look at an example of how the matcher works on the following expression and state:

Expression: INHAND(x) $\wedge$ $\neg$(ON(y PEG3) $\wedge$ SIZE>(x y)) $\wedge$
[x DISK   *color size*] $\wedge$ [PEG3 PEG • •]

> State: ON(DISK3 PEG3) ON(DISK2 PEG3) SIZE>(DISK3 DISK1)
> SIZE>(DISK2 DISK1) SIZE>(DISK3 DISK2) INHAND(DISK1)
> [PEG1 PEG BLUE 5] [PEG2 PEG BLUE 5] [PEG3 PEG BLUE 5]
> [DISK1 DISK RED 1] [DISK2 DISK RED 2] [DISK3 DISK RED 3]

The first positive relational predicate $INHAND(x)$ in the expression matches INHAND(DISK1) because there is only one INHAND relation in the state. Thus x is bound to DISK1, and all instances of x in the expression are substituted by DISK1. Since $INHAND(x)$ is the only positive relation in the expression, the negative relation

$$\neg(ON(y\ PEG3) \wedge SIZE>(DISK1\ y))$$

is now taken under consideration. (Note that x in this negative expression has been replaced by DISK1.) There is a free variable y in this negative expression, so we have to make sure all possible values are tried. First, y is bound to DISK3 because the state contains ON(DISK3 PEG3), which matches $ON(y\ PEG3)$. The matcher cannot find SIZE>(DISK1 DISK3) so this binding fails. Next y is bound to DISK2 since there is a relation ON(DISK2 PEG3) in the state, but this binding also fails because there is no SIZE>(DISK1 DISK2). After these two failures, the negative expression returns "true" (because the matcher cannot find any other value in the state that can be bound to y) and the match continues. The last two subexpressions are true in the state, x is already bound to DISK1, so [x DISK *color size*] will be matched to [DISK1 DISK RED 1], and [PEG3 PEG • •] will be matched to [PEG3 PEG BLUE 5]. Thus the expression is true in the state, and the matcher returns the set of bindings that have been made, (x/DISK1, *color*/RED, *size*/1), where the variable to the left of the slash is bound by the constant on the right.

To see how the matcher backtracks, suppose the state also contains the following facts: INHAND(DISK4), SIZE>(DISK4 DISK3), SIZE>(DISK4 DISK2), SIZE>(DISK4 DISK1), and [DISK4 DISK RED 4]. In other words, the state contains a fourth and largest disk, and this disk is in hand. Suppose LIVE first matches $INHAND(x)$ to INHAND(DISK4) instead of INHAND(DISK1). The match will eventually fail because there exist DISK2 and DISK3 that are on PEG3, and they are smaller than DISK4. After the failure, the matcher will look for the next possible value for x and will match $INHAND(x)$ to INHAND(DISK1). Then the match will succeed as before.

8.4 LIVE's Model Application

8.4.1 Functionality

LIVE's planner plans solutions for the goals that are given; the plan is then passed to the executor/perceiver to execute in the environment. During execution, the executor/perceiver continues to detect prediction failures.

The planner uses means–ends analysis. It first finds the differences between the goals and the current state; then, for each difference, it selects from the current internal model a rule whose prediction indicates that the difference would be eliminated. If more than one such rule is found, a set of heuristics is used to select the best one. After the differences are associated with rules, a plan is constructed by ordering these differences according to the conditions of their rules. The ordering criteria are similar to the methods used in HACKER [119] and goal regression [129]. The rules whose conditions interfere with the other differences in the plan are executed later, while the rules whose conditions cause little or no interference with the other differences are executed earlier.

Once a plan is constructed, the executor/perceiver executes the actions in the plan in order. To monitor the execution, whenever an action is taken, the actual outcome in the environment is compared to the prediction made by the rule that specified the action. If all the predictions in the plan are fulfilled and all the given goals are achieved, LIVE then terminates.

Error detection occurs during both planning and execution. During planning, two kinds of errors are possible. The *No-Rule* error happens when there is no rule to achieve the given goals. In this case, the explorer is called to gather more information from the environment. The *Goal Contradiction* error occurs when the goals always conflict with each other (according to some rules) no matter how they are ordered. In this case, the experimenter is called to find out how to revise the rules causing the contradictions. An error is also possible during execution if a rule's prediction fails to match the actual outcome of its action. In this case, the error is a surprise, and the rule reviser is called to analyze the error and rectify the faulty rule.

The most important feature of LIVE's problem solver is that the execution of a plan is interleaved with learning. Here, one cannot assume that the results of actions will always be what is expected. Executing a planned solution is not the end of problem solving; instead, it is an experiment for testing the correctness of the knowledge that has been learned so far. In LIVE, the coordination of learning and problem solving is made possible by associating actions with predictions, which is one of the important advantages of using prediction rules to represent the model.

8.4.2   An Example of Problem Solving

To illustrate the problem solver, let us go through an example. Suppose the learner LOGIC1 is currently in the environmental state shown in Figure 8.3. Suppose also that the following goals are given (note that goals are written in the language $\mathcal{L}$ described in Section 8.3):

$$ON(DISK1\ PEG3) \wedge ON(DISK2\ PEG3) \wedge ON(DISK3\ PEG3)$$

LIVE first perceives the environment and constructs the internal state shown in Figure 8.3. Then the planner compares the state with the given goals and finds

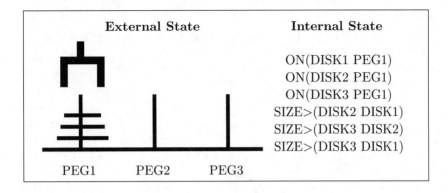

Figure 8.3 The initial state of a problem.

the differences: ON(DISK1 PEG3), ON(DISK2 PEG3), and ON(DISK3 PEG3). Since the internal model is empty at the beginning, the problem solver fails to find any rule to eliminate these differences, hence a *No-Rule* error is detected, and the explorer is called. After exploring the environment (the details will be discussed in Chapter 9), two rules are created:

RuleID:	Rule0
Condition:	ON(x p) $\wedge$ ¬INHAND(x)
Action:	Pick(x p)
Prediction:	INHAND(x) $\wedge$ ¬ON(x p)

RuleID:	Rule1
Condition:	INHAND(x)
Action:	Put(x p)
Prediction:	ON(x p) $\wedge$ ¬INHAND(x)

Rule0 is a general rule about the Pick action; it says that the action can pick up a disk from a peg if the disk is on that peg. Rule1 is a rule about the Put action; it says that the action can move the hand to a peg and put a disk on that peg if the disk is in hand. With these two rules, the problem solver can now plan its actions for the goals because Rule1 has a prediction, ON(x p), that can be matched to each of the given goals. A new plan is then constructed as shown in Table 8.1.

This plan is constructed by associating with each of the goals a rule that predicts achieving that goal. For example, the goal ON(DISK1 PEG3) is associated with Rule1 because Rule1's prediction ON(x p) can reach the goal. This association is done by searching all the rules in the model and finding the rules whose prediction matches the goal. Sometimes more than one rule will be found. In this

Goal	Rule	Prediction and Bindings	Condition
ON(DISK1 PEG3)	Rule1	ON(x p), (x/DISK1, p/PEG3)	INHAND(x)
ON(DISK2 PEG3)	Rule1	ON(x p), (x/DISK2, p/PEG3)	INHAND(x)
ON(DISK3 PEG3)	Rule1	ON(x p), (x/DISK3, p/PEG3)	INHAND(x)

Table 8.1 A plan to achieve a set of goals.

case, a set of heuristics (see Section 8.4.3) is used to decide which one to use. After all the goals are associated with rules, the problem solver reorders the goals according to the conditions of the rules. In our example, since none of the conditions INHAND(x) interferes with any of the goals ON(DISK1 PEG3), ON(DISK2 PEG3), or ON(DISK3 PEG3), the reordering does not change the order of the goals.

Given this plan, LIVE now starts executing the rules one by one using means–ends analysis. Working on the first goal ON(DISK1 PEG3), the problem solver realizes that Rule1 has a condition, INHAND(x), which must be satisfied in order to apply its action. Here the solver proposes a subgoal INHAND(DISK1) by substituting the variable using the bindings of the rule. (If the subgoals contain free variables that are not bound by the bindings of the rule, then the set of heuristics in Section 8.4.3 is used to bind them to concrete objects.)

As before, to reach the new goal INHAND(DISK1), LIVE searches all the rules in the model and finds that Rule0 predicts the goal. So Rule0 is associated with INHAND(DISK1), and a new entry is pushed on top of the plan as shown in Table 8.2.

LIVE continues to execute the plan. This time Rule0's action Pick(DISK1 p) can be executed because Rule0's condition ON(DISK1 p) is satisfied in the current state. ON(DISK1 p) is matched to ON(DISK1 PEG1), and p is bound to PEG1. LIVE then executes Pick(DISK1 PEG1) and predicts that INHAND(DISK1). After the action is taken, LIVE senses the external world and builds a new internal state shown in Figure 8.4.

LIVE compares the prediction INHAND(DISK1) with the state and finds it is fulfilled, so the plan execution continues. Now, Rule1's action Put(DISK1 PEG3)

Goal	Rule	Prediction and Bindings	Condition
INHAND(DISK1)	Rule0	INHAND(x) (x/DISK1)	ON(DISK1 p)
ON(DISK1 PEG3)	Rule1	ON(x p), (x/DISK1, p/PEG3)	INHAND(x)
ON(DISK2 PEG3)	Rule1	ON(x p), (x/DISK2, p/PEG3)	INHAND(x)
ON(DISK3 PEG3)	Rule1	ON(x p), (x/DISK3, p/PEG3)	INHAND(x)

Table 8.2 A new step to achieve INHAND(DISK1).

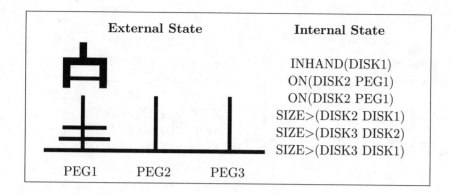

Figure 8.4   The external and internal states after Pick(DISK1 PEG1).

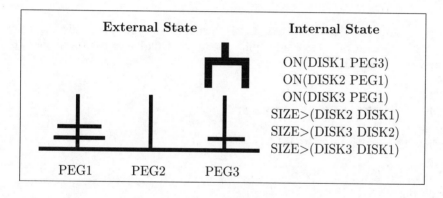

Figure 8.5   The external and internal state after Put(DISK1 PEG3).

can be executed because the condition INHAND(DISK1) is true in the current state. The action Put(DISK1 PEG3) is taken, and LIVE senses the external world shown in Figure 8.5.

The prediction of Rule1, ON(DISK1 PEG3), is fulfilled, and LIVE now works on the next goal in the plan, ON(DISK2 PEG3). As before, INHAND(DISK2) is proposed as a subgoal and Rule0 is chosen to achieve it. After the action Pick(DISK2 PEG1) is executed successfully, the state is as shown in Figure 8.6.

Since Rule1's condition INHAND(DISK2) is now satisfied, LIVE executes the action Put(DISK2 PEG3) and expects ON(DISK2 PEG3). After sensing the external world, it finds that the prediction is false: DISK2 is not on PEG3 but still in hand (because DISK1 is on PEG3 and DISK1 is smaller than DISK2).

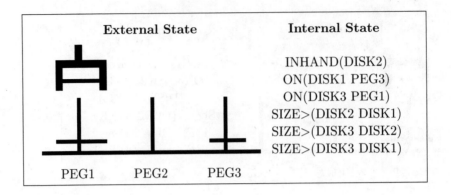

Figure 8.6   The external and internal state after Pick(DISK2 PEG1).

This is a surprise. At this point, LIVE suspends its plan and calls the rule reviser, which analyzes the error and splits the faulty Rule1 into the following two new rules (details are in Chapter 10):

RuleID:	Rule1
Condition:	INHAND$(x) \land \neg$ON$(y\ p)$
Action:	Put$(x\ p)$
Prediction:	ON$(x\ p) \land \neg$INHAND(x)

RuleID:	Rule2
Condition:	INHAND$(x) \land$ ON$(y\ p)$
Action:	Put$(x\ p)$
Prediction:	INHAND(x)

The new Rule1 says that in order to successfully put a disk on a peg, the peg must be empty (no y is on the peg); otherwise, as Rule2 predicts, the disk will still be in hand. With these new rules, a new plan is constructed as shown in Table 8.3. Note that ON(DISK1 PEG3) is already satisfied in the current state, so it does not appear in the new plan.

Unfortunately, when reordering these two goals, LIVE finds that no matter which goal is to be achieved first, it will always be destroyed by the later goals. For example, if ON(DISK2 PEG3) is achieved first, it will be destroyed by the condition of Rule1, $\neg$ON(y, p), for achieving the goal ON(DISK3 PEG3). Here, a *Goal Contradiction* error is found, and Rule1 is the troublesome rule. The problem solver stops its planning and calls the experimenter to gather information for revising Rule1 (the details are in Chapter 10).

Goal	Rule	Prediction and Bindings	Condition
ON(DISK2 PEG3)	Rule1	ON(x p) (x/DISK2, p/PEG3)	INHAND(x) ¬ON(y p)
ON(DISK3 PEG3)	Rule1	ON(x p) (x/DISK3, p/PEG3)	INHAND(x) ¬ON(y p)

Table 8.3 A new plan after a rule revision.

Goal	Rule	Prediction and Bindings	Condition
ON(DISK3 PEG3)	Rule3	ON(x p) (x/DISK3, p/PEG3)	INHAND(x) ¬(ON(y p) ∧ SIZE>(x y))
ON(DISK2 PEG3)	Rule3	ON(x p) (x/DISK2, p/PEG3)	INHAND(x) ¬(ON(y p) ∧ SIZE>(x y))

Table 8.4 LIVE's plan after a set of correct rules are learned.

Up to this point, we have illustrated all the basic activities of LIVE's problem solver. The alternation of planning, execution, and learning is repeated until a set of correct rules is finally learned. To complete this example, one of the final rules is the following:

RuleID:	Rule3
Condition:	INHAND(x) ∧ ¬(ON(y p) ∧ SIZE>(x y))
Action:	Put(x p)
Prediction:	ON(x p) ∧ ¬INHAND(x)

and LIVE's final plan is as shown in Table 8.4.

Note that this time DISK3 is forced to be put on PEG3 before DISK2, because if DISK2 were put on PEG3 first, ON(DISK2 PEG3) would violate the condition ¬(ON(y PEG3) ∧ SIZE>(DISK3 y)) for putting DISK3 on PEG3. With this new plan, LIVE first moves DISK1 away from PEG3 and then successfully puts all the disks on PEG3 and solves all the given goals.

8.4.3   Some Built-in Knowledge for Controlling the Search

At present, LIVE cannot learn all the necessary knowledge for controlling the search [5, 66]. For example, when LIVE wants to put down a disk to empty its hand, it cannot learn that the "other" peg (in this example, PEG2) is a good place on which to place the disk. (The other peg concept is a part of the sophisticated perceptual strategy outlined in [114].) Thus, whenever faced with this situation, LIVE will simply make a random choice.

Since learning search control knowledge is not our main emphasis, we have given LIVE two sets of domain-dependent heuristics to guide some of the decision making in model application (planning and subgoal proposing). It should be noticed that without these heuristics, LIVE can still learn the correct rules from the environment; it just takes longer for the problem-solving component to reach the final goal state.

The first set of heuristics is for binding free variables in a rule when the rule is selected to propose subgoals. These heuristics implement exactly the other peg concept. For example, in order to move DISK3 from PEG1 to PEG3 when DISK2 is currently in hand, LIVE must first achieve the subgoal ¬INHAND(DISK2). Rule3 will be selected because its prediction contains ¬INHAND(x) (so x is bound to DISK2). However, when applying Rule3's action, Put(x p), LIVE will notice that p is still a free variable. In this case, the heuristics will bind p to PEG2, because PEG2 is the other peg when DISK3 is to be moved from PEG1 to PEG3.

The second set of heuristics is for selecting which rule to use when more than one rule predicts the same goal. The heuristics are necessary for the HAND-EYE learner (see Chapter 2 for the definition) because the number of rules is larger. For example, in order to pick up DISK2 when DISK1 is on the top, LIVE will generate a subgoal to move DISK1 away. This goal can be accomplished by picking up DISK1 and turning the hand away from DISK2. However, to turn the hand back to DISK2, two rules can be used. One rule turns the hand back whenever the hand is empty, and the other turns the hand back when the hand is full. Although the latter can be applied immediately (because DISK1 is in hand), it is the former rule that is needed. At present, the heuristics for the HAND-EYE environment are designed to help LIVE choose the right rule in this situation.

8.5 Summary

This chapter has described the LIVE system at a high level. In particular, we have seen the system's architecture, model representation, and model application. The architecture is designed to reflect the philosophy of integrating model abstraction and model application. The model is represented as a set of prediction rules, which we think is a better candidate for abstraction than many other formats, such as finite state machines, differential equations, or Markov models. Finally, LIVE's model application utilizes the standard general problem solver paradigm, which we have illustrated through simple examples.

CHAPTER 9

MODEL CONSTRUCTION THROUGH EXPLORATION

In Chapter 8, we outlined LIVE's architecture and introduced its model representation and application. In particular, we described in detail the functions of the
planner and the executor/perceiver and indicated that other modules are involved
when planning or execution confronts errors. In this chapter, we will take a closer
look at LIVE's model construction mechanism, the rule builder and the explorer
modules, and explain how rules like Rule0 and Rule1 in Chapter 8 were created
and how LIVE explores its environment.

9.1 How LIVE Creates Rules from Objects' Relations

Since LIVE does not know the consequences of its actions at the outset, it has
no idea how to achieve the given goals in a new environment. For example, if the
learner has never moved a disk before, it will not know which actions to use to move
one. Thus, when the current knowledge is insufficient for constructing any plans
to achieve certain goals, it is necessary for the learner to explore the environment
and create new rules to correlate its actions and its percepts. This is the main task
of the rule builder module. In this section, we will focus our attention on creating
new rules from objects' relations, while leaving the more complex case, creating
new rules from objects' features, to the next section.

Before the Action

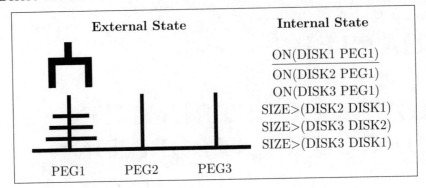

Action: Pick(DISK1 PEG1)
After the Action

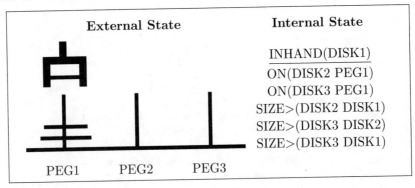

Figure 9.1 Creating new rules from the relations that have been changed.

To illustrate the idea, let us first consider an explorative scenario for learners like LOGIC1. Suppose that LIVE has decided to explore the action Pick(DISK1 PEG1) in the state shown in Figure 9.1 and observed the outcome from the environment after the action is taken. What rule should LIVE create from this scenario?

Since our intention here is to create a new prediction rule and the action part is already known as Pick(DISK1 PEG1), we need to construct the conditions and the predictions under the following three constraints: First, since we cannot take the whole state as the conditions or the predictions (the resulting rule would be useless), we must decide which relations from the initial state should be used as conditions and which from the final state should be used as predictions. Second, since the new rule is to correlate percepts and actions, the conditions and predictions must be related to the action. Third, since the rule should be useful in the future to predict similar events, it must be generalized from this particular scenario.

1. Compare the condition observation (before the action) with the result observation (after the action). Let the "vanished" percepts be those that are in the condition observation but not in the result observation, and the "emerged" percepts be those that are in the result but not in the condition.

2. Relate the condition and prediction with the action that is taken.

3. Create a new prediction rule as follows:

Condition:	the vanished percepts in conjunction with the negations of the emerged percepts
Action:	the executed action with parameters specified in terms of objects that were acted upon
Prediction:	the emerged percepts in conjunction with the negations of the vanished percepts

   and generalize all objects in the rule except those belonging to the learner (such as the hand and arm) into variables.

Figure 9.2   Creating prediction rules based on changes in relations.

To decide what must be included in the conditions and in the predictions, LIVE's strategy is to focus on changes in the relations. In this particular scenario, LIVE will select the relation ON(DISK1 PEG1) from the initial state and select IN-HAND(DISK1) from the final state because the former was true in the initial state but not in the final state, while the latter emerges in the final state but was not true in the initial state. Thus the condition will be ON(DISK1 PEG1) and ¬INHAND(DISK1); the prediction will be INHAND(DISK1) and ¬ON(DISK1-PEG1). Note that the negations of the relations are also included in the condition and the prediction. These inclusions reflect the changes of the relations in the rule and make the rule more useful in problem solving. Since both the conditions and the predictions already contain the elements mentioned in the action, namely, DISK1 and PEG1, the second constraint is satisfied automatically. Finally, to generalize the new rule, LIVE will replace DISK1 with a variable x and PEG1 with a variable p, so that they can be matched to any disk or peg in the future. Thus, a new rule (Rule0 in Chapter 8) is created as follows:

RuleID:	Rule0
Condition:	ON(x p) $\land$ ¬INHAND(x)
Action:	Pick(x p)
Prediction:	INHAND(x) $\land$ ¬ON(x p)

This simple example illustrates how LIVE creates new prediction rules in general. Roughly speaking, it is a three-step process as shown in Figure 9.2.

One important criterion is the usefulness of the newly created rule, that is, whether it can be applied to many similar cases to predict the outcomes of LIVE's actions. To ensure this, the method just outlined emphasizes that a new rule should be as general as possible. For example, if the set of percepts is more realistic, then there are many relations, such as shadow locations and hand altitude, that could be changed by the action. In that case, we ignore these relations in the new rule. If any of them is proven to be relevant in the future, it will be brought into the rule by our learning algorithm (see Chapter 10). In the process of creating rules, we prefer to keep a new rule overly general rather than overly specific. Thus, we will not only change the constants to variables but also put as few elements as possible in the condition. In the example above, the rule is indeed most general because the action happens to make one and only one change in relations. Now the question is, How do we choose conditions and predictions when an explorative action either does not change any relations or changes many relations?

When no relations are changed, consider the scenario in Figure 9.3, where LIVE explores the action Put(DISK1 PEG2) instead of Pick(DISK1 PEG1). Since there is nothing in LIVE's hand to be put down, nothing will be changed by Put(DISK1 PEG2), and comparing states will return no relation changes at all. In this case, a new rule will still be created except that its condition and prediction will be the same. To make the new rule as general as possible, LIVE will select only those relations that are relevant: those that share relations with the given goals and those that share objects with the taken action. In Figure 9.3, LIVE will use ON(DISK1 PEG1) as both condition and prediction because ON is a relation type mentioned in the given goals (see the goal specifications in Section 8.4.2) and DISK1 is in the action Put(DISK1 PEG2). (PEG2 is in the action too, but it does not have any ON relation in the current state.) Thus, LIVE creates a new rule as follows:

RuleID:	Rule$i$
Condition:	ON(x p)
Action:	Put(x p)
Prediction:	ON(x p)

If an explorative action causes many relation changes in the environment, then LIVE will select as few of them as possible so long as the selected ones describe the action adequately. In addition to the relevance criterion outlined above, this is accomplished by detecting overlaps among relation changes. Consider the scenario in Figure 9.4, where LIVE is given an additional relational percept ABOVE(x y).

Thus, in addition to the state information previously perceived, LIVE also finds that two ABOVE relations, ABOVE(DISK1 DISK2) and ABOVE(DISK1 DISK3), have vanished after the action Pick(DISK1 PEG1). In this case, before the vanished relations are used as conditions, LIVE detects that these two ABOVE relations are overlapping, thus only one of them will be chosen. At present, a simple technique

Before the Action

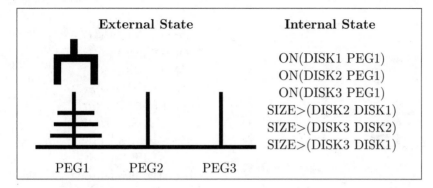

Action: Put(DISK1 PEG2)
After the Action

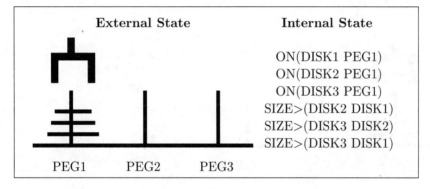

Figure 9.3 Explorative action causes no change in relations.

seems sufficient to detect overlapping relations: Two relations have the same relational predicate and at least one common parameter.[1] Thus the new rule that will be created is the following:

RuleID: Rule$j$
Condition: ON$(x\ p)$ ∧ ABOVE$(x\ y)$ ∧ ¬INHAND(x)
Action: Pick$(x\ p)$
Prediction: INHAND(x) ∧ ¬ABOVE$(x\ y)$ ∧ ¬ON$(x\ p)$

---

[1] An extreme but possible solution for making new rules as general as possible is to set the new rule's condition as a "don't care" symbol and later revise the rule by pulling in relevant conditions when the rule makes mistakes. The method for revising rules is described in Chapter 10.

Before the Action

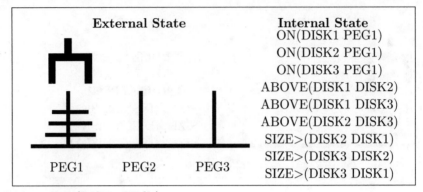

Action: Pick(DISK1 PEG1)

After the Action

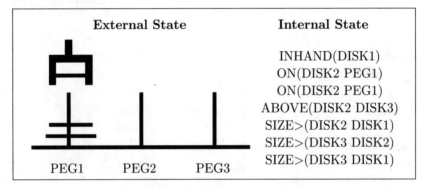

Vanished Relations: ON(DISK1 PEG1), ABOVE(DISK1 DISK2),
                        ABOVE(DISK1 DISK3)
Emerged Relation: INHAND(DISK1)

Figure 9.4 Explorative action with overlapping relation changes.

In real life, actions always make changes in the world. The reason we divide
the case into both "no change" and "many changes" is that the learner's scope
of attention is limited and sometimes to say that an action causes no change is
reasonable, even though there might be changes on a larger scale. For example,
tapping your fingers on a stable desk can be characterized as no change, but if
you look carefully there may be some changes on the surface of the desk and your
fingers may not be in the same positions as before.

One possible difficulty in LIVE's method for creating rules is that comparing
two states may be impossible in the real world because there may be an infinite
number of relations that can be perceived. (This is a version of the frame problem

[63].) For example, when comparing the two states in Figure 9.1, there may be many other irrelevant relations, such as "today is Friday" and "the moon is full." When the action Pick(DISK1 PEG1) is taken, the moon may become nonfull (it may become covered by clouds). How do we know whether the full moon relation should be included in our new rule?

To respond to this challenge, we have to back up a little to see how LIVE actually makes its comparisons. When information is perceived from the external world, it is represented in the system as a graphlike structure, where nodes are objects and edges are relations. After an action is taken, the comparison begins from a small set of nodes corresponding to the objects that are mentioned in the action. For example, the comparison begins from DISK1 and PEG1 in Figure 9.1. (If an action does not have any parameter, the comparison begins from the nodes corresponding to the learner's hand or body.) To look for changes in relations, LIVE does incremental checking on the subgraph that is currently under consideration. For example, in Figure 9.1 LIVE compares the relations involving DISK1 and PEG1 first. If any relation differences are found, no other objects or relations will be considered. Therefore, when hundreds or thousands of objects are given, LIVE will not spread its attention if relational differences can be found among the objects involved in the current action.

Of course, this does not mean LIVE has overcome this difficulty completely. (After all, this is the famous frame problem in AI.) In particular, "changes" and "no change" depend on all the objects and relations that can be perceived by LIVE in the world. This is why we have to assume that LIVE uses all the percepts that are given and that it is possible to check all the information that has been perceived.

9.2 How LIVE Creates Rules from Objects' Features

In the last section, we described LIVE's methods for creating new rules from observed relational changes. However, when the environment becomes more realistic, the high-level relations, such as ON and SIZE>, may not be available to the learner. What if the environment does not provide these relational percepts but provides features of objects instead? Can LIVE's methods still create useful rules without any given relational percepts?

9.2.1 Constructing Relations from Features

The answer to the above question is yes, provided that the system is given a set of m-constructors that includes the necessary primitive relations, such as = and >. In addition to the three steps outlined above, LIVE must construct new relational predicates (using the given constructors) when a comparison of states does not yield any relational changes. Let us take a close look at this problem through the HAND-EYE version of the Tower of Hanoi.

The environment of the HAND-EYE learner, outlined in Section 2.4, is shown in Figure 9.5. It consists of a symbolic robot with a rotatable arm along which a hand can slide back and forth. The location of objects in this environment is represented by three elements, the degree of rotation from the arm's zero position, the distance from the base of the robot, and the altitude from the ground. For example, in Figure 9.5, peg B's location is 70.0, 38.0, and 0.0; peg C's location is 30.0, 43.3, and 0.0; the hand's location is 45.0, 35.0, and 23.0; and the location of the smallest disk, disk 1, is 0.0, 30.0, and 6.0. (The other two disks and peg A are at the same direction and distance as disk 1 but with different altitudes.)

The robot, or the LIVE system, has been given percepts to sense object shape, size, direction, distance, and altitude, so that in this environment each object is represented as a feature vector [*objID shape size direction distance altitude*]. The unique identifier *objID* is assigned to each object by the learning system when an object is first seen. (Features of objects are assumed to be independent.) For example, the hand is represented as [OBJ1 HAND 10.0 45.0 35.0 23.0]; the three disks, from the smaller to the larger, are [OBJ2 DISK 5.0 0.0 30.0 6.0], [OBJ3 DISK 7.0 0.0 30.0 3.0], and [OBJ4 DISK 9.0 0.0 30.0 0.0], respectively; peg A is [OBJ5 PEG 12.0 0.0 30.0 0.0], where 12.0 is the height of the peg.

Although no relational predicates are given as percepts in this environment, LIVE has three primitive relations and functions, $=$, $>$, and $-$, as m-constructors. The relational constructors are used to construct relational predicates in the process of learning.

The robot can rotate the arm from -180.0° to 180.0° and slide the hand from 0.0 to 70.0 units of distance, and it can pick up or drop objects. Thus there are four kinds of actions that LIVE can perform: Rotate(θ), Slide(d), Pick() and Put(), where θ and d are real numbers within the range of the environment. For example,

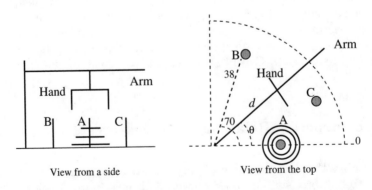

View from a side   View from the top

Figure 9.5   The HAND-EYE learner in the Tower of Hanoi environment.

in the configuration of Figure 9.5, if Rotate(−45.0) is executed, then the arm will be at 0.0 degrees. That means that the hand will be perceived in the new state as [OBJ1 HAND 10.0 0.0 35.0 23.0], where the underscore indicates an altered feature.

The robot is given the following goals to achieve:

([GOAL-OBJ2 DISK 5.0 70.0 38.0 (< 23.0)]
  [GOAL-OBJ3 DISK 7.0 70.0 38.0 (< 23.0)]
  [GOAL-OBJ4 DISK 9.0 70.0 38.0 (< 23.0)])

In words, all the disks must be located at direction 70.0 and distance 38.0 (this is where peg B is located), and the altitude of all these disks must be lower than 23.0, the altitude of the hand. In short, LIVE's goal is to move all three disks from peg A to peg B.

Since no relational percepts are given in this environment, to create new rules as before, LIVE must construct new relational predicates after comparing two states. For example, suppose LIVE decided to explore the action Rotate(25.0) in Figure 9.5. Executing the action will give LIVE the information on internal states listed in Table 9.1. Note that all that LIVE can perceive from the external environment are individual objects with features. How do we proceed from there?

Comparing these two states, LIVE finds no changes in relations but some changes in the features of the hand (specifically, the feature with index 3 changes from 45.0 to 70.0.) With the given primitive relations = and >, LIVE begins to examine the changed feature. It computes the = and > relations between this particular feature and the same feature of other objects and then compares those relations before and after the action (Table 9.2). For example, the relation = between the third feature of the hand and the third feature of peg B has changed from "no" (70.0 ≠ 45.0) to "yes" (70.0 = 70.0). Similarly, the relation > has also changed on the third feature of the hand and peg B.

Object	Action: Rotate(25.0)	
	State before Action	State after Action
Hand	[OBJ1 HAND 10.0 45.0 35.0 23.0]	[OBJ1 HAND 10.0 70.0 35.0 23.0]
Disk 1	[OBJ2 DISK 5.0 0.0 30.0 6.0]	[OBJ2 DISK 5.0 0.0 30.0 6.0]
Disk 2	[OBJ3 DISK 7.0 0.0 30.0 3.0]	[OBJ3 DISK 7.0 0.0 30.0 3.0]
Disk 3	[OBJ4 DISK 9.0 0.0 30.0 0.0]	[OBJ4 DISK 9.0 0.0 30.0 0.0]
Peg A	[OBJ5 PEG 12.0 0.0 30.0 0.0]	[OBJ5 PEG 12.0 0.0 30.0 0.0]
Peg B	[OBJ6 PEG 12.0 70.0 38.0 0.0]	[OBJ6 PEG 12.0 70.0 38.0 0.0]
Peg C	[OBJ7 PEG 12.0 30.0 43.3 0.0]	[OBJ7 PEG 12.0 30.0 43.3 0.0]

Table 9.1 The states before and after Rotate(25.0). An underscore indicates an altered feature.

Object	Before Action			After Action		
	Index 3	= 45.0	> 45.0	Index 3	= 70.0	> 70.0
Hand	45.0			70.0		
Disk 1	0.0	no	no	0.0	no	no
Disk 2	0.0	no	no	0.0	no	no
Disk 3	0.0	no	no	0.0	no	no
Peg A	0.0	no	no	0.0	no	no
Peg B	70.0	no	yes	70.0	yes	no
Peg C	0.0	no	no	0.0	no	no

Table 9.2   Identifying relational changes with constructors.

Upon finding these relational changes, LIVE concludes that the action Rotate(θ) can change the relationships = and > among objects on the feature of index 3. Since these relational changes must be built into the new rule, LIVE will construct two new relational predicates as follows ("elt" is a LISP function that fetches the value of an indexed element in a vector):

$$\text{REL234}(objx\ objy)\colon \text{TRUE} \iff (\text{elt } objx\ 3) = (\text{elt } objy\ 3)$$
$$\text{REL235}(objx\ objy)\colon \text{TRUE} \iff (\text{elt } objx\ 3) > (\text{elt } objy\ 3)$$

With these two new relational predicates, LIVE now has the vocabulary to express the changes in relation caused by the action. (This is one place where new terms are constructed for the language $\mathcal{L}$; see Section 8.3.) From now on, every time LIVE perceives an external state, it will compute these newly constructed relational predicates on the objects that have been perceived. Thus, LIVE's internal state will contain not only the individual objects but also some of their relations. For example, after the internal states in Table 9.1 are perceived, LIVE will compute REL234 and REL235 for the objects to get the new internal states shown in Table 9.3.

Another interesting and useful benefit of constructing new relational predicates is that the goals of the system are viewed differently. To see this, consider again our goals:

([GOAL-OBJ2 DISK 5.0 70.0 38.0 (< 23.0)]
  [GOAL-OBJ3 DISK 7.0 70.0 38.0 (< 23.0)]
  [GOAL-OBJ4 DISK 9.0 70.0 38.0 (< 23.0)])

Since the goal objects are virtual objects (in contrast to the real objects in the current state), once REL234 and REL235 are defined, we can view the goal objects

Action: Rotate(25.0)	
State before Action	State after Action
REL234(OBJ2 OBJ3), REL234(OBJ2 OBJ4) REL234(OBJ2 OBJ5), REL234(OBJ3 OBJ4) REL234(OBJ3 OBJ5), REL234(OBJ4 OBJ5)	REL234(OBJ2 OBJ3), REL234(OBJ2 OBJ4) REL234(OBJ2 OBJ5), REL234(OBJ3 OBJ4) REL234(OBJ3 OBJ5), REL234(OBJ4 OBJ5) REL234(OBJ6 OBJ1)
REL235(OBJ7 OBJ2), REL235(OBJ7 OBJ3) REL235(OBJ7 OBJ4), REL235(OBJ7 OBJ5) REL235(OBJ1 OBJ2), REL235(OBJ1 OBJ3) REL235(OBJ1 OBJ4), REL235(OBJ1 OBJ5) REL235(OBJ1 OBJ7), REL235(OBJ6 OBJ7) REL235(OBJ6 OBJ2), REL235(OBJ6 OBJ3) REL235(OBJ6 OBJ4), REL235(OBJ6 OBJ5) REL235(OBJ6 OBJ1)	REL235(OBJ7 OBJ2), REL235(OBJ7 OBJ3) REL235(OBJ7 OBJ4), REL235(OBJ7 OBJ5) REL235(OBJ1 OBJ2), REL235(OBJ1 OBJ3) REL235(OBJ1 OBJ4), REL235(OBJ1 OBJ5) REL235(OBJ1 OBJ7), REL235(OBJ6 OBJ7) REL235(OBJ6 OBJ2), REL235(OBJ6 OBJ3) REL235(OBJ6 OBJ4), REL235(OBJ6 OBJ5)
Hand: [OBJ1 HAND 10.0 45.0 35.0 23.0] Disk 1: [OBJ2 DISK 5.0 0.0 30.0 6.0] Disk 2: [OBJ3 DISK 7.0 0.0 30.0 3.0] Disk 3: [OBJ4 DISK 9.0 0.0 30.0 0.0] Peg A: [OBJ5 PEG 12.0 0.0 30.0 0.0] Peg B: [OBJ6 PEG 12.0 70.0 38.0 0.0] Peg C: [OBJ7 PEG 12.0 30.0 43.3 0.0]	[OBJ1 HAND 10.0 70.0 35.0 23.0] [OBJ2 DISK 5.0 0.0 30.0 6.0] [OBJ3 DISK 7.0 0.0 30.0 3.0] [OBJ4 DISK 9.0 0.0 30.0 0.0] [OBJ5 PEG 12.0 0.0 30.0 0.0] [OBJ6 PEG 12.0 70.0 38.0 0.0] [OBJ7 PEG 12.0 30.0 43.3 0.0]

Table 9.3   The states before and after Rotate(25.0), including relations.

through the relations to see how they are related to the real objects. In order to accomplish the goals, the real objects and the goal objects must correspond. In this case, the above goals will be augmented to give the following more useful goal expressions:

(REL234(GOAL-OBJ2 OBJ2) [GOAL-OBJ2 DISK 5.0 70.0 38.0 (< 23.0)]
  REL234(GOAL-OBJ3 OBJ3) [GOAL-OBJ3 DISK 7.0 70.0 38.0 (< 23.0)]
  REL234(GOAL-OBJ4 OBJ4) [GOAL-OBJ4 DISK 9.0 70.0 38.0 (< 23.0)])

As more relations are constructed, it will become more and more explicit how to achieve these goals (namely, by achieving the relations one by one as the LOGIC1 learner).

With the states expressed in terms of both relations and object feature vectors, it is now straightforward to find the relational differences between the state before the action and the state after the action. For example, in Table 9.3, it is easy to see that the relation REL235(OBJ6 OBJ1) has vanished, while the relation REL234(OBJ6 OBJ1) has emerged.

Just as for LOGIC1, comparing two states here can result in the situations of "no change" and "too many changes," but the solutions we gave earlier also work here. For example, if in Figure 9.5 LIVE did Rotate(5.0) instead of Rotate(25.0), then no relational change would be detected (or even constructed). As before, when no change is detected, we will use only the relations or the objects that are mentioned in the action or physically part of the learner. Thus the rule to be created will use only the feature vector for the hand as the condition and the prediction.

If an action causes many changes in the environment, for example, if LIVE did Rotate(−45.0) instead of Rotate(25.0), then many relational differences would be found after REL234 and REL235 were constructed. (For example, all the relations REL234 between the hand and the disks would become true because the disks all have 0.0 as their third feature.) In this case, LIVE would not use all the disks in the rule; instead, it would delete those overlapped relations and choose any one of the following relations to be included in the rule:

REL234(OBJ1 OBJ2)
REL234(OBJ1 OBJ3)
REL234(OBJ1 OBJ4)
REL234(OBJ1 OBJ5)

9.2.2   Correlating Actions with Features

Once relations are included in the internal states, new rules can be created as before. In particular, LIVE will first compare the states in Table 9.3 to find the relational differences caused by the action, which yields REL235(OBJ6 OBJ1) as a vanished relation and REL234(OBJ6 OBJ1) as an emerged relation. Then, LIVE will correlate these relations with the action Rotate(25.0) before it puts all the information together to form a new prediction rule.

However, in this environment, actions and percepts are not automatically correlated because Rotate(25.0) does not mention any particular objects as Pick(DISK1-PEG1) did in the LOGIC1's environment. In order to correlate the action with the percepts, LIVE must find a relation between the number 25.0 and the changes of features in the states, namely, 70.0 and 45.0, which are the values of the third feature of the hand before and after the action.

To find the relation between 25.0 and (70.0 45.0), LIVE again depends on its constructors. It will search through all the given m-constructors and find one that can fit in this example. The search is simple in this case because among all the given m-constructors ($=$, $>$, and $-$), only $-$ can fit in, that is, $25.0 = 70.0 - 45.0$. (Of course, LIVE could make a mistake here if some other constructor, say f, also fit in this single example, say $25.0 = f(70.0, 45.0)$. But LIVE's learning is incremental. If f is not the right correlation between Rotate's parameter and the feature changes of the hand, it will make a wrong prediction in the future and eventually $-$ will replace f.)

Since the action's parameter is related to the third feature of the hand, the condition and the prediction of the new rule will have to include the hand object and the values of its third feature before and after the action. In particular, the correlation will look like this:

[• HAND • 45.0 • •]
Rotate((70.0 − 45.0))
[• HAND • 70.0 • •]

After finding the relational differences and correlation between the action and the features that have been changed, a new prediction rule is ready to be created. LIVE will use the vanished relation and the negations of the emerged relations as the condition, use the emerged relations and the negations of the vanished relations as the prediction, and then generalize all the constants to variables (different constants will be generalized to different variables). In addition, since individual objects can be perceived in the HAND-EYE environment, they will also be included in the rule if their identifiers are mentioned in the relevant relations. For example, we will include both the hand and peg B because they are involved in the relations. (The hand is also involved in the correlation between the action and the percepts.) Moreover, since the hand is physically a part of the learner itself and future applications of this rule will always refer to the hand as a special object, it will not be generalized into a variable but will keep its identity. Thus, a new rule is finally created as follows:

Condition: $REL235(objx\ OBJ1) \land \neg REL234(objx\ OBJ1) \land$
               $[OBJ1\ HAND \bullet x_1 \bullet \bullet] \land [objx \bullet \bullet x_2 \bullet \bullet]$
Action: $Rotate(x_2 - x_1)$
Prediction: $REL234(objx\ OBJ1) \land \neg REL235(objx\ OBJ1) \land$
               $[OBJ1\ HAND \bullet x_2 \bullet \bullet] \land [objx \bullet \bullet x_2 \bullet \bullet]$

So far we have given some long and detailed examples of LIVE's method for creating rules based on the changes in features of objects. To complete the description, we summarize the procedure of creating prediction rules in Figure 9.6. This procedure is a generalization of the procedure specified in Figure 9.2, where rules are created based on changes in relations. When no changes in relations can be found, LIVE uses m-constructors to construct relations based on changes in features of objects and then builds new rules based on these new relations.

9.3 How LIVE Explores the Environment

In the description of rule creation, we have assumed that LIVE always chooses the right action to explore, which of course is not always the case in reality. When exploring an unfamiliar environment, there are many things you can do; choosing the relevant explorative action among a large number of possibilities is not an easy task. For example, when the LOGIC1 learner explores its environment in Figure 9.1, LIVE has many actions to choose from. Why should it explore Pick(DISK1 PEG1) rather than Pick(DISK2 PEG1) or Put(DISK3 PEG2)? For the HAND-EYE learner shown in Figure 9.5, the situation is even worse because some actions contain real numbers as parameters, like θ in Rotate(θ) and d in Slide(d), and in principle these parameters can have an infinite number of values.

This section describes the explorer module, which is designed to deal with the exploration problem. In particular, we will describe how the explorer generates

1. Compare the states before and after the action and find the vanished and emerged relations.

2. If no differences in relations are found but features of objects are changed, then use the given m-constructors to construct new relational predicates and find the relational changes in terms of these new relational predicates.

3. Correlate the changes of the state with the action that is taken.

4. Create a prediction rule as follows:

Condition: the vanished relations, plus the negations of the emerged relations, plus the objects involved in these relations or in the action

Action: the action that is taken with parameters expressed in terms of objects' identities or in terms of changed features with a proper m-constructor

Prediction: the emerged relations, plus the negations of the vanished relations, plus the objects that are involved in these relations or in the action

and then generalize all objects in the rule into variables except objects belonging to the learner itself, such as its hand, arm, or body.

Figure 9.6   Creating prediction rules in LIVE.

explorative plans and executes them to provoke and observe novel phenomena from which new rules can be created.

9.3.1   The Explorative Plan

An *explorative plan* is a sequence of actions with some empty predictions. For example, when you step into a complex building for the first time, you might take a walk without knowing for sure what you will see after turning a corner. As you can imagine, an explorative plan is different from a solution plan because any one of its steps may not be associated with any particular prediction. However, LIVE executes an explorative plan in the same manner as it executes a solution plan. Given an explorative plan, LIVE executes the actions in the plan from the beginning to the end. Whenever it is about to take an action, LIVE searches its internal model to see if any existing rules can be used to make any predictions about the consequences of this action. If predictions are made, LIVE executes the action and compares the prediction to the actual outcome of the action. (In this case, before LIVE executes the next explorative action, the learning module might be called if the prediction does not match the actual outcome, as we described in Chapter 8.)

If no prediction is found, LIVE simply executes the action, observes the outcome, and uses the observation to create a new rule (see Sections 9.1 and 9.2.)

Although explorative plans depend somewhat on chance, they are far from random actions. For example, a random action for the learner LOGIC1 can be any one of the following actions:

Pick(DISK1 PEG1), Pick(DISK2 PEG1), Pick(DISK3 PEG1)
Pick(DISK1 PEG2), Pick(DISK2 PEG2), Pick(DISK3 PEG2)
Pick(DISK1 PEG3), Pick(DISK2 PEG3), Pick(DISK3 PEG3)
Put(DISK1 PEG1), Put(DISK2 PEG1), Put(DISK3 PEG1)
Put(DISK1 PEG2), Put(DISK2 PEG2), Put(DISK3 PEG2)
Put(DISK1 PEG3), Put(DISK2 PEG3), Put(DISK3 PEG3)

However, a good explorative plan is Pick(DISK1 PEG1) followed by Put(DISK1 p) because all we want to know is how to move a disk from one peg to another. (Pick(DISK1 PEG1) is the only action that can make changes in the environmental state shown in Figure 9.1.)

Similarly, if the HAND-EYE learner explores its environment randomly, it might spend a very long time in that environment without learning anything interesting. A successful learner should certainly do better than random explorations.

9.3.2 Heuristics for Generating Explorative Plans

LIVE generates its explorative plan in an unfamiliar environment with the set of domain-independent heuristics shown in Figure 9.7. These heuristics are executed in the order listed. The general idea is that exploration should be guided by the existing knowledge and the desired goal. Thus, all these heuristics have access to LIVE's internal model and are intended to suggest more concise and productive explorative plans.

Let us illustrate these heuristics through a set of examples. To see how the first heuristic works, suppose the explorer module is called by the HAND-EYE learner in Figure 9.5 when LIVE's internal model is empty. The following explorative plan is an example proposed by the heuristics:

Rotate(−30.0), Slide(10.0), Pick(), Put()

Because the model is empty, these four actions are suggested by heuristic 3; heuristics 1 and 2 are not applicable at this point. The four actions are all that are available to LIVE and −30.0 and 10.0 are random values for action Rotate (whose parameters range from −180.0 to 180.0) and Slide (whose parameters range from 0.0 to 70.0), respectively.

With this explorative plan, four rules will be learned. Two of them are about Rotate and Slide, which indicate that these actions will change the arm's rotating degree and hand's distance, respectively. The other two learned rules are about Pick and Put, although they indicate no change at all in the current environment

- *Heuristic 1 (Goal Seeking): If an action B is known to change the feature F of objects, then explore B to change the value of F of the learner to be equal (or in some other relation) to the value of F of some goal object.* For example, if the action Rotate is known to change the direction of an arm, then the arm should be rotated to the direction of a goal disk.

- *Heuristic 2 (Anomalous Behavior Resolution): Explore actions that have no apparent effect in the environment.* For example, Pick has no effect when the disk to be picked is not the smallest on its peg, and Put has no effect when there is no disk in hand. Such actions need to be explored until effects are observed. The philosophy behind this heuristic is that all actions ought to have some effect on the environment.

- *Heuristic 3 (Curiosity): Once in a while, randomly explore some not-yet-explored actions with random parameters.*

Figure 9.7   Heuristics for generating explorative plans.

because there is no object under or in the hand at this moment. In this particular explorative plan, the order of these four actions does not make any difference.

After these four rules are learned, heuristics 1 and 2 will be useful. If the current active goal is [GOAL-OBJ2 DISK 5.0 70.0 38.0 (<23.0)], then the following explorative plan will be generated by these two heuristics:

Rotate(−15.0), Slide(−15.0), Put(), Pick()

In this explorative plan, the first two actions are proposed by heuristic 1 because LIVE has learned rules that can change objects' direction and distance, and the hand, whose current location is [15.0 45.0 23.0], should be manipulated to have the same direction and distance values as the goal for DISK1, whose current location is [0.0 30.0 •]. The actions Put() and Pick() are proposed by heuristic 2 because these two actions do not produce any observed changes in the environment. As we know from LIVE's method for creating rules, these four actions will give the system opportunities to construct new relational predicates and learn rules that move its hand to a desired location and pick up and put down objects.

For LOGIC1, these heuristics can also direct the exploration into a more productive path. When learning has just begun (no rule has been learned), heuristic 3 will force LIVE to try repeatedly the two actions with randomly generated values for the disk and the peg parameters until Pick(DISK1 PEG1) is selected (which might take a long time). This is because in the initial state (Figure 9.1), where all three disks are on PEG1, Pick(DISK1 PEG1) is the only action that can lead to changes. Once DISK1 is picked up, LIVE will repeatedly explore the action

Put(x p), as suggested by heuristic 2, until this action has made some changes in the environment; that is, DISK1 is put down on some peg.

The design of the heuristics is governed by two principles. First, exploration should provoke and observe new phenomena. The heuristics encourage the learner to interact with the objects that are relevant to the goals and try the actions that are more familiar. For example, to solve the goal ON(DISK1 PEG1), we should interact with DISK1 or PEG1. To learn how to swim, one should interact with water; to get the toy (see Figure 2.9), the child should play with the lever instead of waving his or her hands in the air or stamping on the floor. The second principle is that exploration should depend on existing knowledge; that is why all the heuristics have access to LIVE's internal model. We should point out that these heuristics represent only the beginning of research on the exploration issue; they are by no means complete.

9.4   Discussion

What are the pros and cons of LIVE's method for creating rules? First, this method correlates actions with percepts, which is very important in learning from the environment. Unless actions and percepts are correlated, one cannot act purposefully in an environment. Next, the method looks for the conditions and effects of an action around the action itself, which focuses the learner's attention when the environment is vast. Although it is not a complete solution for the frame problem, the LIVE rule creation method works well in some cases. Finally, this method somewhat overcomes the incompleteness of the concept description language. When new relational predicates are necessary to describe the environment, it constructs them in the process of learning. In doing so, the method abstracts a continuous environment into discrete relations, which are essential for solving problems.

Compared to some existing rule-learning mechanisms, such as Carbonell and Gil's learning from experimentation in the domain of making telescopes [13], our method shows that some problems in their program can be addressed at rule creation time. For example, the initial operator for ALUMINIZE in their program was assumed to have a missing prediction ¬IS-CLEAN(obj). In fact, such a prediction would be included here at rule creation time because IS-CLEAN(obj) would be changed when the action ALUMINIZE was applied.

As the reader may have already noticed, there are several drawbacks to the LIVE method for creating rules. First, the method cannot use objects' properties alone as building blocks; everything must be stated in terms of relations. As a consequence, the result always requires a reference to express the values of features. For example, LIVE cannot learn the rule that says, "If an x is red, then do this." Instead, it creates a rule that says, "If THE-SAME-COLOR(x OBJ5), then do this," which requires the existence of a red object (in this case, OBJ5). Second, as we pointed out earlier, in order to conclude that an action does not cause any changes in the environment, this method must check all the relations in the environment, which can be quite expensive. For example, if there are n objects and m binary relational predicates, then there will be $mn(n-1)$ potential relation links because each of the m predicates could have any one of $n(n-1)$ links. Finally, in order to construct useful relational predicates, the system must be given correct m-constructors. For example, if $=$ is not given, REL234 cannot be learned. Although this is a drawback, it also has some good points. We can provide our knowledge to the system through these m-constructors to focus its learning.

In closing, we ask this question: Will this approach be feasible if lower-level percepts and actions, like those used on a mobile robot, are given? Can the method really scale up? We have already shown that rules can be constructed from relational percepts and macro actions, and from features of objects and movements of a robot arm and a set of primitive relational m-constructors. But if the aim of this approach is to construct a real mobile robot that learns from the environment, this question must eventually be answered. In the literature of qualitative reasoning, there is already some positive evidence that complexity may not explode if one keeps in mind that most reasoning is at the qualitative level. Kuipers's work on learning qualitative maps is one example of such evidence [47].

Although it is still too early to predict the outcome, we think the LIVE approach is promising because it contains some viable ingredients. First of all, the target is fixed. No matter how you implement it, the final product should be the same: knowledge that can help the robot reason about its actions and solve problems. The prediction is only one implementation (though it is a convenient one). Second, the studies so far have revealed a hierarchy of percepts and actions. From the top down, this hierarchy contains the prediction rules, the relations of objects, and the features of objects. Going further down in this hierarchy, it is clear that the next building blocks must be some kind of spatial representation from which features of objects can be constructed. Finally, since this approach constructs new terms when necessary, the learner's initial description language does not have to be complete. We think this is a very important point in machine learning in general, because we believe that, in a very primitive sense, all the knowledge we have is constructed from what we can see and what we can do.

CHAPTER 10

MODEL ABSTRACTION WITH EXPERIMENTATION

In this chapter, we describe how LIVE abstracts and revises its prediction rules using the complementary discrimination learning (CDL) framework. We also explain how experiments are designed in the process of learning to rectify faulty rules detected during planning. At the end of the chapter, we compare LIVE's learning method with some existing techniques and argue that the method provides a new approach for incrementally learning both conjunctive and disjunctive rules from environments with considerably less representational bias than other methods.

10.1 The Challenges

In previous chapters, we defined learning from the environment as a problem of inferring rules from the environment (model abstraction) and argued that such learning must be interleaved with problem solving (model application). Although the area of rule learning has advanced considerably in the last two decades [12], in the context of learning from the environment it seems to face substantial challenges.

First, since learning from the environment may start with no a priori knowledge, techniques that rely on a heavily biased model (concept) space may have difficulty in determining a suitable initial search space. Without such initial biases, some algorithms either fail to converge or require exponential computational resources.

Second, learning from the environment must be incremental. Every time new evidence is available, we want to modify the existing model rather than build a new model from scratch. Thus, nonincremental algorithms (e.g., ID3 [87]), even though they are quite efficient, may not be suitable here (see Chapter 4 for details). Although there is no lack of incremental learning algorithms (e.g., [69, 98, 135]), only a few of them have been integrated with problem solving [70] and can learn disjunctive rules [128].

Finally, the most fundamental challenge is how to overcome the innate biases (i.e., the percepts and actions inherent in the learner) and construct new terms and relations when necessary. In fact, this is a crucial step in discovering new concepts from the environment (see Chapter 11 for some examples). In those cases, the learner must infer and construct hidden features and their relations using both its percepts and its actions; neither set alone is sufficient.

Faced with these challenges, it seems that learning by discrimination is the most feasible choice [10, 21, 22, 51, 76]. It does not require that any particular subset (or bias) of the model space be chosen (it works fine with the complete model space). It is incremental so that the learner does not need to rebuild the model every time new evidence comes along. Furthermore, most discrimination methods learn from mistakes. They seem very useful for learning from the environment because the models that support the learner's predictions are normally not perfect.

However, pure discrimination itself does not guarantee finding a consistent model in the model space. As we know from Chapter 4, model abstraction is a search in the model space (which is a lattice of models). Pure discrimination searches the space one way from general to specific; it is difficult to recover from errors and to learn from positive examples. Moreover, to learn disjunctive rules by discrimination, all the existing methods rely on getting what Bundy [12] called a *far miss* (i.e., more than one difference must be found between two instances), an event that depends very much on the order of the instances and is not always obtainable. Because of these problems, previous methods of learning by discrimination have not been satisfactory. This may be why such a powerful and well-known method (first discussed by John Stuart Mill, see [74]) has not gained much popularity in the literature on machine learning.

As we will shortly see, LIVE's learning method (an application of CDL to rule learning) is an advanced discrimination method. It solves the above problems by learning not only the concept itself but also its complement. This method performs both generalization and discrimination because generalizing a concept is equivalent to discriminating its complement, and vice versa. Moreover, the result that a concept and its complement go hand in hand during the learning process provides a convenient way for both designing experiments to recover from discrimination errors and discovering hidden features when necessary.

10.2   How LIVE Revises Its Rules

Complementary discrimination can easily be applied to revising incorrect rules. Let us first go through an example. As we saw in the last chapter, the rules created by LIVE during exploration are often too general and incomplete. For example, the following rule (the same as Rule0 in Chapter 9), which is created in the state in Figure 10.1 where LIVE successfully picked up DISK1 from PEG1, is clearly incomplete:

RuleID:	Rule0
Condition:	$ON(x\ p) \wedge \neg INHAND(x)$
Action:	$Pick(x\ p)$
Prediction:	$INHAND(x) \wedge \neg ON(x\ p)$

One point lacking in Rule0 is that if the hand is not empty then the rule's prediction will fail (because x will not be in hand but still on the p). Clearly, in using these kinds of rules to solve problems, LIVE will inevitably make mistakes.

However, no matter how incomplete new rules may be, they provide a springboard for further learning from the environment. It is because of the generality and incompleteness of rules that LIVE has the chance to be surprised, to learn from mistakes, and hence to increase its knowledge about the environment. The question is how LIVE detects these incomplete rules and corrects them after mistakes are made.

Detecting an incomplete rule is straightforward because every rule makes predictions, and LIVE compares a rule's prediction with the actual outcome in the environment whenever an action is taken. If a rule's prediction does not match the

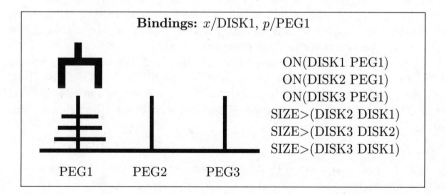

Figure 10.1   A successful application of Rule0.

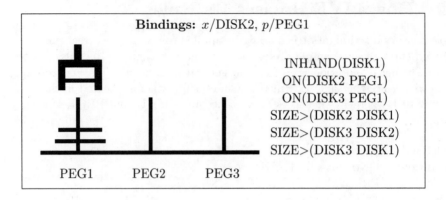

Figure 10.2   A failed application of Rule0.

actual outcome of the rule's action, then the rule is faulty. In that case, we say LIVE has encountered a surprise.

As an example of a surprise, suppose that Rule0 is applied in the state shown in Figure 10.2, where LIVE is trying to pick up DISK2 even though its hand is not empty. To get the desired result INHAND(DISK2), x must be bound to DISK2 and p bound to PEG1 (because DISK2 is on PEG1). Unfortunately, after the action Pick(DISK2 PEG1), LIVE is surprised to see that DISK2 is not in hand but still on PEG1 (because the environment allows only one disk to be picked up at a time). At this point, LIVE realizes that Rule0 is faulty.

In general, to revise an incomplete rule, LIVE discriminates the failed application from a successful application and finds out why it is surprised. It brings up a remembered success, such as in Figure 10.1, and compares it to the failure (Figure 10.2). (LIVE remembers the latest successful application for each existing rule, and the memorized information contains the rule ID, the state, and the set of variable bindings.) The differences found in the comparison are the explanations for the surprise and are used to split the faulty rule into two more specific and more complete rules. The two new rules are known as *siblings*.

In this example, comparing Figure 10.1 with Figure 10.2 results in the difference ¬INHAND(y). In other words, the reason Rule0 succeeded before is because there was nothing in its hand. (Why this reason is found but not others will be explained in Section 10.2.2.) With this explanation, Rule0 is then split into the following two new rules:

RuleID:	Rule3
Condition:	ON(x p) $\wedge$ ¬INHAND(x) $\wedge$ ¬INHAND(y)
Action:	Pick(x p)
Prediction:	INHAND(x) $\wedge$ ¬ON(x p)
Sibling:	Rule5

RuleID:	Rule5
Condition:	$ON(x\ p) \wedge \neg INHAND(x) \wedge INHAND(y)$
Action:	$Pick(x\ p)$
Prediction:	$ON(x\ p)$
Sibling:	Rule3

Note that Rule3 is a variant of Rule0 with the condition augmented by the difference; Rule5 is a new rule whose condition is the conjunction of the old condition and the negation of the difference ($INHAND(y)$ is a replacement of $\neg\neg INHAND(y)$) and whose prediction (constructed by the same method used in the rule creation) is the observed consequence of the current application.

10.2.1 Applying CDL to Rule Revision

From this simple example, we can now state LIVE's rule revision method as the following three-step procedure:

1. Detect an erroneous rule by noticing a surprise. A surprise occurs when a rule's prediction does not match the outcome of the rule's action. Because a prediction is an expression in LIVE's description language and an outcome is an internal state perceived from the external environment, a surprise is formally defined as follows:

$$\text{surprise} \iff \neg\text{matched}(\textit{prediction internalState})$$

   where "matched" is defined in Section 8.3.2.

2. Explain the surprise by finding the differences between the rule's previous success and its current failure. Given the state from a success and the state from a failure, along with the rule's variable bindings in both cases, LIVE conducts a comparison from the inner circles of the states to the outer circles of the states (which are defined below). The result of this step is a set of differences: $D_1, D_2, \ldots, D_j$, where each D_i is either a conjunction of relations or a negation of conjunctive relations that is true in the successful state but false in the surprising state.

3. If the erroneous rule m does not have any siblings, then it is split into two new sibling rules as follows (the initial condition I is constructed at the rule creation time):

$$
\begin{bmatrix}
\text{RuleID:} & m \\
\text{Condition:} & I \\
\text{Action:} & \alpha \\
\text{Prediction:} & \beta
\end{bmatrix}
\implies
\begin{cases}
\begin{aligned}
&\text{RuleID:} && m \\
&\text{Condition:} && I \wedge D_1 \wedge D_2 \cdots \wedge D_j \\
&\text{Action:} && \alpha \\
&\text{Prediction:} && \beta \\
&\text{Sibling:} && n \\
\\
&\text{RuleID:} && n \\
&\text{Condition:} && I \wedge \neg(D_1 \wedge D_2 \cdots \wedge D_j) \\
&\text{Action:} && \alpha \\
&\text{Prediction:} && \text{Observed effects} \\
&\text{Sibling:} && m
\end{aligned}
\end{cases}
$$

The first rule is a variant of the old rule, whose condition is conjuncted with the differences found in step 2; the second rule is a new rule, whose condition is a conjunction of the old condition with the negation of the differences, and whose prediction (constructed by the same method used in the rule creation) is the observed consequences in the current application.

If the erroneous rule m already has a sibling, then modify both of them as follows:

RuleID: m
Condition: $I \wedge C_1 \wedge C_2 \cdots \wedge C_i$
Action: α $\implies$
Prediction: β
Sibling: n

RuleID: m
Condition: $I \wedge C_1 \wedge \cdots \wedge C_i \wedge D_1 \wedge \cdots \wedge D_j$
Action: α
Prediction: β
Sibling: n

RuleID: n
Condition: $I \wedge O_1 \wedge O_2 \cdots \wedge O_i$
Action: α $\implies$
Prediction: γ
Sibling: m

RuleID: n
Condition: $I \wedge \neg(C_1 \wedge \cdots \wedge C_i \wedge D_1 \wedge \cdots \wedge D_j)$
Action: α
Prediction: γ
Sibling: m

Conditions $C_1, C_2, \ldots, C_i$ and $O_1, O_2, \ldots, O_i$ are the conditions that are learned after the rule is created. For example, $\neg\text{INHAND}(y)$ in Rule3 and $\text{INHAND}(y)$ in Rule5 are such conditions. Notice that the learned conditions of the sibling rules are always complements of each other, and that is why the method is called *complementary discrimination*.

In this rule revision method, the second step is the most crucial because it determines why the rule's prediction fails. In order to find the most relevant reasons for the surprise, LIVE uses an approach called *incremental enlargement*. The idea is to focus on changes that are related to the learner and to use as few changes as possible in the new rule. Technically, LIVE divides each state into inner and outer circles according to the rule's variable bindings in that state. The *inner circle* of a state includes the objects that are bound to variables, the learner itself, and all the relations among these objects. For example, in Figure 10.1, the inner circle includes one relation, ON(DISK1 PEG1), because this is the only relation among the bound objects DISK1 and PEG1. In Figure 10.2, the inner circle includes two relations, ON(DISK2 PEG1) and INHAND(DISK1), because DISK2 and PEG1 are bound objects and INHAND is a part of the learner itself. The *outer circle* of a state includes the inner circle as well as those objects that are related to the inner circle objects through some relations. For example, in Figure 10.1, the outer circle includes ON(DISK1 PEG1), ON(DISK2 PEG1), ON(DISK3 PEG1), SIZE > (DISK2 DISK1), and SIZE > (DISK3 DISK1) because they all contain either DISK1 or PEG1. In Figure 10.2, the outer circle includes INHAND(DISK1), ON(DISK2 PEG1), ON(DISK3 PEG1), SIZE > (DISK3 DISK2), and SIZE > (DISK2 DISK1) because they all contain DISK2, PEG1, or INHAND, all of which are in the inner circle. When two states are compared, LIVE finds the differences in the inner circles before considering the outer circles, as we will see in the next two subsections.

10.2.2 Explaining Surprises in the Inner Circles

In this section, we explain how LIVE finds differences in the inner circles. (Similar methods for finding differences can be found in Langley's SAGE program [49, 50, 51].) Continuing our example of revising Rule0 to create Rule3 and Rule5, let us see how ¬INHAND(y) is found by comparing Figure 10.1 and Figure 10.2.

For convenience, we reprint the states and the bindings from both figures and their inner circles in Table 10.1. The inner circle of the failed state includes the relation ON(DISK2 PEG1) because both DISK2 and PEG1 are bound objects and this is the only relation between them. It also includes INHAND(DISK1) because INHAND is a part of the learner itself. In the successful state, the inner circle includes only ON(DISK1 PEG1).

To find the differences between these two inner circles, LIVE first replaces the objects by the original variables specified in the bindings. The resulting inner circles are shown in Table 10.2.

Comparing these two sets, it is clear that INHAND(DISK1) is in the failed state but not in the successful state. Since DISK1 is not bound in the bindings of the failed application, it is generalized as y. Thus the comparison returns ¬INHAND(y), which is true in the successful application but false in the failed application.

Characteristic	Success (Fig. 10.1)	Failure (Fig. 10.2)
States	ON(DISK1 PEG1)	INHAND(DISK1)
	ON(DISK2 PEG1)	ON(DISK2 PEG1)
	ON(DISK3 PEG1)	ON(DISK3 PEG1)
	SIZE>(DISK2 DISK1)	SIZE>(DISK2 DISK1)
	SIZE>(DISK3 DISK2)	SIZE>(DISK3 DISK2)
	SIZE>(DISK3 DISK1)	SIZE>(DISK3 DISK1)
Bindings	x/DISK1, p/PEG1	x/DISK2, p/PEG1
Inner Circle	ON(DISK1 PEG1)	ON(DISK2 PEG1)
		INHAND(DISK1)

Table 10.1   The inner circles of states.

Characteristic	Success	Failure
Inner Circle	ON(x p)	ON(x p)
		INHAND(DISK1)

Table 10.2   Inner circles with variables.

10.2.3   Explaining Surprises in the Outer Circles

Differences between two states are not always found in the inner circles. When outer circle objects must be considered, LIVE uses a chaining method similar to the one used in [51] to find a set of relations that are true in one state but false in the other.

Let us consider the rule Rule3, which was just learned:

RuleID: Rule3
Condition: ON(x p) $\wedge$ ¬INHAND(x) $\wedge$ ¬INHAND(y)
Action: Pick(x p)
Prediction: INHAND(x) $\wedge$ ¬ON(x p)

Now suppose that LIVE is trying to pick up DISK3 in the state shown in Figure 10.3. The bindings are x/DISK3 and p/PEG1, and LIVE executes Pick(DISK3 PEG1) to get INHAND(DISK3). The outcome surprises LIVE because DISK3 is not in hand but still on PEG1.

Comparing this to the rule's last successful application, which is in Figure 10.1, LIVE constructs the inner and outer circles of the two states, as shown in Table 10.3.

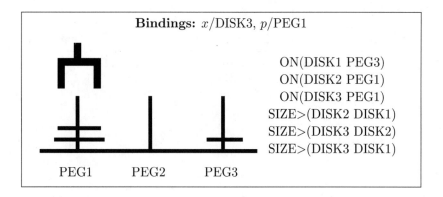

Bindings: x/DISK3, p/PEG1

ON(DISK1 PEG3)
ON(DISK2 PEG1)
ON(DISK3 PEG1)
SIZE>(DISK2 DISK1)
SIZE>(DISK3 DISK2)
SIZE>(DISK3 DISK1)

PEG1   PEG2   PEG3

Figure 10.3 Finding differences in the outer circles.

Characteristic	Success (Fig. 10.1)	Failure (Fig. 10.3)
States	ON(DISK1 PEG1) ON(DISK2 PEG1) ON(DISK3 PEG1) SIZE>(DISK2 DISK1) SIZE>(DISK3 DISK2) SIZE>(DISK3 DISK1)	ON(DISK1 PEG3) ON(DISK2 PEG1) ON(DISK3 PEG1) SIZE>(DISK2 DISK1) SIZE>(DISK3 DISK2) SIZE>(DISK3 DISK1)
Bindings	x/DISK1, p/PEG1	x/DISK3, p/PEG1
Inner Circle	ON(DISK1 PEG1)	ON(DISK3 PEG1)
Outer Circle	ON(DISK2 PEG1) ON(DISK3 PEG1) SIZE>(DISK3 DISK1) SIZE>(DISK2 DISK1)	ON(DISK2 PEG1) SIZE>(DISK3 DISK2) SIZE>(DISK3 DISK1)

Table 10.3 The inner and outer circles of states.

As before, LIVE first substitutes the variables for the objects and attempts to find differences in the relations of the inner circle. Unfortunately, no differences can be found there because ON(DISK3 PEG1) and ON(DISK1 PEG1) are the same after the variable substitutions (see Table 10.4).

Characteristic	Success	Failure
Inner Circle	ON(x p)	ON(x p)
Outer Circle	ON(DISK2 p) ON(DISK3 p) SIZE>(DISK3 x) SIZE>(DISK2 x)	ON(DISK2 p) SIZE>(x DISK2) SIZE>(x DISK1)

Table 10.4   The inner and outer circles after variable substitution.

LIVE is now forced to consider the objects in the outer circles. In order to find the differences in the outer circles, LIVE searches for a chain of relations that is false in the failed application but true in the successful application. The search starts with the variables. From p, LIVE finds a common element, ON(DISK2 p), that is true in both states, thus finding the first relation in the chain. Next, LIVE uses DISK2 as the new leading object and continues the search. SIZE $>$ (x DISK2) is then found in the failed state, but nothing similar can be found in the successful state. At this point LIVE concludes that a differential chain (ON(DISK2 p) $\wedge$ SIZE $>$ (x DISK2)) has been found. Since the learning algorithm requires the final result to be true in the successful application and false in the failed application, LIVE returns $\neg$(ON(y p) $\wedge$ SIZE $>$ (x y)), where y is a generalization of DISK2.

With this differential chain, Rule3 and its sibling rule, Rule5, are modified into the following two new rules (we will call them Rule7 and Rule9 for convenience):

RuleID:	Rule7
Condition:	ON(x p) $\wedge$ $\neg$INHAND(x) $\wedge$ $\neg$INHAND(y) $\wedge$ $\neg$(ON(y p)$\wedge$ SIZE$>$ (x y))
Action:	Pick(x p)
Prediction:	INHAND(x) $\wedge$ $\neg$ON(x p)
Sibling:	Rule9

RuleID:	Rule9
Condition:	ON(x p) $\wedge$ $\neg$INHAND(x) $\wedge$ $\neg$($\neg$INHAND(y) $\wedge$ $\neg$(ON(y p)$\wedge$ SIZE$>$ (x y)))
Action:	Pick(x p)
Prediction:	ON(x p)
Sibling:	Rule7

Rule7 says that in order to pick up a disk from a peg, the hand must be empty, as the condition $\neg$INHAND(y) indicates, and there must be no smaller disks on the peg, as the condition $\neg$(ON(y p) $\wedge$ SIZE $>$ (x y)) represents. Otherwise, as Rule9 predicts, the disk will remain on the peg.

Characteristic	Success	Failure
Outer Circle	ON(DISK3 p)	ON(DISK2 p)
	SIZE > (x DISK1)	SIZE > (x DISK2)
	SIZE > (DISK3 x)	SIZE > (x DISK1)

Table 10.5   An example of finding differental chains in outer circles.

In general, search for a differential chain of relations consists of pairing relations common to both states, starting with the variables. Such pairing stops when a relation in the failed state cannot be paired with any relation in the successful state; relations found in the failed state are then returned. The word *common* here does not necessarily mean equal. Two relations are common as long as they have the same relational predicate and the same position for the leading object. For example, if x is the lead, SIZE > (DISK3 x) and SIZE > (DISK2 x) are common, but SIZE > (x DISK1) and SIZE > (DISK3 x) are not. To search for a differential chain in Table 10.5, LIVE will start with p (because in this example starting with x fails to find any differential chain). LIVE will find that ON(DISK2 p) and ON(DISK3 p) are common (p is the leading object). In searching for the next relation, DISK2 becomes the leading object in the failed state, and DISK3 becomes the leading object in the successful state. However, no more pairs can be found because SIZE > (x DISK2) and SIZE > (DISK3 x) are not considered to be common. Thus, (ON(DISK2 p)$\wedge$ SIZE > (x DISK2)) is the differential chain, and as before it will be returned as $\neg$(ON(y p)$\wedge$ SIZE > (x y)).

10.2.4   Defining New Relations for Explanations

Sometimes, when the relations perceived from two states are the same but the objects' features are different, new relational predicates may be defined in order to discriminate the two states. For example, suppose objects are perceived as vectors of four features, [$objID$ f_1 f_2 f_3 f_4], and LIVE is given > as an m-constructor. Assume that LIVE has defined the following predicates in its previous learning:

$$F1(x \ y) \Longleftrightarrow (\text{elt } x \ 1) > (\text{elt } y \ 1)$$
$$F2(x \ y) \Longleftrightarrow (\text{elt } x \ 2) > (\text{elt } y \ 2)$$
$$F3(x \ y) \Longleftrightarrow (\text{elt } x \ 3) > (\text{elt } y \ 3)$$

Suppose LIVE is now to compare the two states for two objects A and B in Table 10.6 in order to revise some faulty rule. No relational differences are perceived between the success and the failure. However, object A's features are different in these two states. In the state of the success, object A's fourth feature is greater than object B's fourth feature (6 > 4), while in the state of the failure, no such relation

Characteristic	Success	Failure
States	[A 2 3 1 6] [B 4 1 1 4] F1(B A) F2(A B)	[A 2 2 1 4] [B 4 1 1 4] F1(B A) F2(A B)

Table 10.6 Defining new relations for explanation.

exists ($4 \not> 4$). The fact that there is no predefined relation on the fourth feature gives us a hint that such a relation should be defined in order to discriminate these two states. Just as it defines new predicates during rule creation (see Chapter 9), LIVE will define a new relation as follows:

$$F4(x\ y) \Longleftrightarrow (\text{elt } x\ 4) > (\text{elt } y\ 4)$$

and return F4(A B) as the difference between these two states.

In general, when comparing two states that have no relational differences, LIVE checks whether there are any differences between those features that have no predefined relations. If differences can be found according to the given constructors on these features, LIVE will define the new and necessary relational predicates as outlined above. Since creating new relations here is the same as defining new relations during rule creation, we will have no further discussion here. Interested readers can see Chapter 9 for more examples and a detailed description.

10.2.5 When Overly Specific Rules Are Learned

Although LIVE's discrimination method has returned the correct reasons for each of the surprises we have talked about so far, sometimes wrong reasons are found and overly specific rules are learned. Fortunately, LIVE will detect such faulty rules as it uses them in the problem solving and then correct them. In this section, we give an example of how a faulty rule is learned; in Section 10.3 we indicate how the faulty rule is corrected when we discuss LIVE's method for learning from experiments.

Suppose LIVE learns the following Rule1 while putting DISK1 on PEG2 in the state shown in Figure 10.4:

RuleID:	Rule1
Condition:	$\text{INHAND}(x) \wedge \neg\text{ON}(x\ p)$
Action:	$\text{Put}(x\ p)$
Prediction:	$\text{ON}(x\ p) \wedge \neg\text{INHAND}(x)$

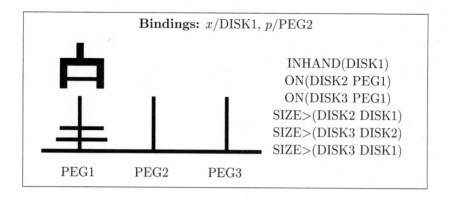

Figure 10.4   A successful application of Rule1.

In order to put DISK2 on PEG2 in the state shown in Figure 10.5, Rule1 is applied with x bound to DISK2 and p bound to PEG2. LIVE is surprised after Put(DISK2 PEG2) is applied, because DISK2 is not on PEG2 but is still in hand.

As before, the two states are compared to find relational differences. The inner circles do not reveal any differences because in each state INHAND(x) is the only relation in the inner circle. However, since the outer circle of the successful state, SIZE>(DISK2 x) and SIZE>(DISK3 x), is different from the outer circle of the failed state, ON(DISK1 p), SIZE>(DISK2 x), and SIZE>(DISK3 x), LIVE finds the difference to be ¬ON(y p) and splits Rule1 into Rule2 and Rule4 as follows:

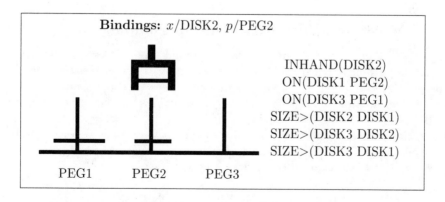

Figure 10.5   A failed application of Rule1.

RuleID: Rule2
Condition: INHAND(x) $\wedge$ $\neg$ON(x p) $\wedge$ $\neg$ON(y p)
Action: Put(x p)
Prediction: ON(x p) $\wedge$ $\neg$INHAND(x)
Sibling: Rule4

RuleID: Rule4
Condition: INHAND(x) $\wedge$ $\neg$ON(x p)$\wedge$ ON(y p)
Action: Put(x p)
Prediction: INHAND(x) $\wedge$ $\neg$ON(x p)
Sibling: Rule2

However, Rule2 is a faulty rule. It says that in order to put a disk on a peg, that peg must be empty. According to the actual rules of the Tower of Hanoi, this rule is overly specific because it prevents LIVE from putting smaller disks on bigger ones.

In previous methods of learning by discrimination, as Bundy and others pointed out [12], it is very hard to recover from situations like this. Fortunately, LIVE's learning does not suffer fatally from this kind of error because the overly specific rule has an overly general sibling. As we will see in the next section, LIVE can detect such faulty rules and correct them by experimentation.

10.3   Experimentation: Seeking Surprises

Up to now, we have said only that faulty rules are detected during execution and that they are corrected based on the information derived from surprises. In fact, faulty rules, especially those that are overly specific, can also be detected during planning. In that case we need to seek surprises in order to correct such rules.

10.3.1   Detecting Faulty Rules During Planning

LIVE can detect two kinds of faulty rules at planning time: the rules that make given goals impossible to reach (called *goal contradiction*) and the rules that repeatedly propose subgoals that are already in the goal stack (called *subgoal looping*). We will give an example of each kind of faulty rule and explain how the errors are detected.

Goal contradiction is an error wherein no plan can be proposed because subgoals prevent a goal from being attained no matter how they are arranged. As an example, suppose LIVE is given the following goals to reach:

ON(DISK1 PEG3) $\wedge$ ON(DISK2 PEG3) $\wedge$ ON(DISK3 PEG3)

Also assume that Rule2 has already been learned (see Section 10.2.5), which says that in order to put x on p successfully, p must be empty (i.e., no y can be on p). As we described in Chapter 8, to construct a solution for the given goals, LIVE first selects a rule for each goal. It then orders the goals according to their corresponding rules so that goals achieved earlier in the sequence do not violate the conditions for the goals to be achieved later. Suppose Rule2 is chosen for all the goals in this example (with different bindings). When LIVE tries to order these goals, it discovers that no matter how the goals are arranged, they cannot all be achieved. For example, assume ON(DISK3 PEG3) is achieved first; in order to achieve ON(DISK2 PEG3), the condition of its rule requires ¬ON(y PEG3) to be satisfied. This condition is violated by the achieved goal ON(DISK3 PEG3) because the free variable y can be bound to DISK3. At this point, LIVE reports a goal contradiction error and returns the rule as an erroneous rule to be fixed.

Unlike goal contradiction, subgoal looping is an error whereby planning goes into an infinite loop. Suppose LIVE has learned a rule, Rule M, as follows:

Condition:	ON(x p) $\wedge\neg$INHAND(x) $\wedge \neg$ON(y p)
Action:	Pick(x p)
Prediction:	INHAND(x) $\wedge \neg$ON(x p)

and wants to pick up DISK3 in the state shown in Figure 10.6.

Since Rule M predicts INHAND(x), it is chosen to accomplish INHAND(DISK3) with x bound to DISK3 and p bound to PEG2. However, since one of its conditions, ¬ON(y p), is not true in the current state, the rule is not immediately applicable. (The reason that ¬ON(y p) is false in the state is that p is bound to PEG2 where DISK3 is and y is bound to DISK1 by the matcher because it is on PEG2.) So LIVE proposes ¬ON(DISK1 PEG2) as a new subgoal to achieve and continues its

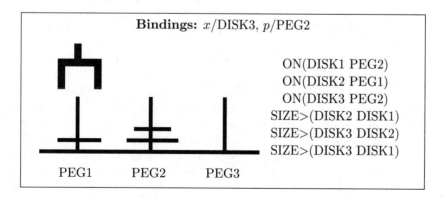

Figure 10.6 A state in which a subgoal loop occurs.

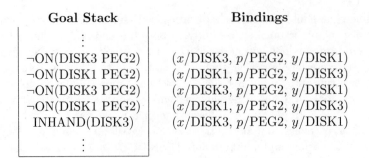

Figure 10.7   A subgoal loop.

planning. To achieve this new goal, Rule M is again chosen because it predicts ¬ON(DISK1 PEG2) with bindings x/DISK1 and p/PEG2. Unfortunately, in order to apply this new rule instance in the current state, subgoal ¬ON(DISK3 PEG2) is proposed again for the same reason explained above. To achieve this subgoal, Rule M is chosen again, and the subgoal ¬ON(DISK1 PEG2) is proposed again. At this point, we loop back to where we started (see the goal stack in Figure 10.7). Clearly, such a subgoal loop will iterate forever if not detected and stopped.

In general, LIVE detects subgoal loop errors by comparing a newly proposed subgoal to the goals that are already on the goal stack. Suppose a new subgoal G_0 is proposed and the existing goals are $(G_1, \ldots, G_i, G_{i+1}, \ldots)$. LIVE will report a subgoal loop error as soon as it finds that $G_0 = G_i$ and $G_1 = G_{i+1}$. The rule responsible for proposing these subgoals will be returned as the faulty rule.

10.3.2   What Is an Experiment?

Unlike faulty rules detected at the time of a surprise, faulty rules detected during planning do not come with information about how to fix them. In order to find out why they are faulty, LIVE must design and perform experiments in the hope that they will yield surprises.

Before we present LIVE's experiments, let us first examine one such faulty rule to get some hints on how we should proceed. Recall that Rule2 causes a goal contradiction. The rule says that in order to put a disk on a peg, the target peg must be empty. We assume that LIVE's goals are not impossible to reach and that the rule has been proven wrong by the goal contradiction error. We can now draw the conclusion that there must be situations in which a disk *can* be put on a nonempty peg. We need experiments because we must find out more about such situations, although we already know that in this case the target peg should be nonempty. Such a conclusion tells us not only that Rule2 is wrong but also that its sibling, Rule4, is wrong because the sibling says that if a peg is not empty, no disk can be put on it.

Since our primary learning method is learning from surprises, experiments must have predictions based on our knowledge; without predictions LIVE can never be surprised. By putting all these considerations together, three constraints for experimental design become clear. First, we want a situation where the target peg is not empty; second, we want to use Put to place a disk on that target peg; third, we must have predictions because we want to learn from any surprises that might occur after the action.

Given these constraints, we find Rule4, the sibling of the faulty rule Rule2, is a good candidate for the experiment. This is because (1) Rule4 is applicable in the states where the target peg is not empty (while Rule2 is not); (2) Rule4 has the same action as Rule2 so the desired action, Put, will be performed; (3) predictions can be made because Rule4 is applicable when the target peg is not empty and its prediction reflects LIVE's existing knowledge.

Therefore, an experiment in LIVE is nothing but an instantiation of the faulty rule's sibling rule. Its condition specifies a situation in which LIVE must put itself, and its action specifies an action that LIVE must perform once it is in that situation. LIVE carries out an experiment as if it were a new problem to be solved. In particular, the problem solver will make and execute a plan to achieve the experiment's condition. Once the condition is satisfied, the problem solver will perform the required action and observe the outcome. An experiment succeeds if the outcome of its action produces a surprise; that is, the outcome violates the experiment's prediction. In that case, the explanation derived from the surprise is used to revise the faulty rule and its sibling. If the experiment's action does not produce any surprises, then LIVE proposes another experiment using the same rule instantiated differently.

Let us now reconsider our goal contradiction example. Once Rule2 is identified as the faulty rule, LIVE instantiates Rule4, the sibling of Rule2, to construct an experiment:

Experiment:	For Rule4
Condition:	INHAND(DISK2) $\land$ ¬ON(DISK2 PEG1) $\land$ ON(DISK3 PEG1)
Action:	Put(DISK2 PEG1)
Prediction:	INHAND(DISK2) $\land$ ¬ON(DISK2 PEG1)
Sibling:	Rule2
Bindings:	x/DISK2, p/PEG1, y/DISK3

Since LIVE is currently in the state pictured in Figure 10.5, where Rule2 and Rule4 are created and the goal contradiction error is detected, the condition of this experiment is satisfied, and the action can be performed immediately. The experiment is successful because its outcome, ON(DISK2 PEG1), surprises the prediction ¬ON(DISK2 PEG1).

Surprises in experiments are explained as described in Section 10.2. In this example, LIVE will compare the success, Figure 10.5 with bindings x/DISK2, p/PEG2, and y/DISK1, with the failure, Figure 10.5 with bindings x/DISK2, p/PEG1, and

y/DISK3. These two applications are in the same state but have different bindings. The comparison yields the explanation $ON(y\ p) \wedge SIZE > (x\ y)$, which is true in the successful case but false in the failed case. Thus, Rule4 is revised into the new Rule6, and its sibling Rule2 is revised into the new Rule8:

RuleID:	Rule6
Condition:	$INHAND(x) \wedge \neg ON(x\ p) \wedge ON(y\ p) \wedge SIZE > (x\ y)$
Action:	$Put(x\ p)$
Prediction:	$INHAND(x) \wedge \neg ON(x\ p)$
Sibling:	Rule8

RuleID:	Rule8
Condition:	$INHAND(x) \wedge \neg ON(x\ p) \wedge \neg(ON(y\ p) \wedge SIZE > (x\ y))$
Action:	$Put(x\ p)$
Prediction:	$ON(x\ p) \wedge \neg INHAND(x)$
Sibling:	Rule6

Rule8 says that in order to put a disk (x) on a peg (p), the peg should not contain any smaller disks (y). After the experiment, LIVE has learned the correct rules about when a disk can be put on a peg and when it cannot be. In a similar way, although details will not be given here, the rules that cause subgoal looping errors are also corrected by LIVE's learning from experiments.

10.3.3   Experiment Design and Execution

From the above example and the analysis, we can see that LIVE's experimentation method, which is based on the representation of prediction rules and complementary discrimination learning, is quite simple. When an incorrect rule is detected, LIVE first retrieves the sibling of that rule. Then it instantiates the sibling to seek surprises as easily and as quickly as possible. The instantiation is implemented as a set of heuristics that will be described shortly. Once the instantiation is completed, an experiment is designed, and it is the problem solver's job to bring LIVE into the state specified by the conditions of the experiment. Thus an experiment can be viewed as a new goal generated by the learner itself. Finally, the experiment's action is executed in that state, and the outcome is compared to the experiment's prediction. If the experiment succeeds, learning will be triggered as if LIVE had met a normal surprise in its plan execution; otherwise, a new instantiation from the same sibling rule will be generated, and LIVE will continue its experiments.

From the description of experiments, it is not hard to see what makes a good experiment. First, since the purpose of an experiment is to seek surprises for a given rule, an experiment is better if its action is instantiated in such a way that it is likely to produce surprises. Second, since the condition of an experiment must be satisfied before the real experiment can begin and such preparation involves both planning and execution, an experiment should have a condition that is easily satisfied from the current state. Ideally, the condition is already satisfied in the current state. These two criteria give us the following procedure, which is used by LIVE's experimental module:

1. Given a rule, experiments are instantiated from the rule by alternately assigning different objects to the parameters of the action. For instance, if the experiment rule's action is Pick(x p), then different disks will be assigned to the variable x, while different pegs will be assigned to p.

2. An experiment's action must be different from all actions that have been done successfully by its sibling rule (because such actions will not produce any surprises) and different from all actions that were performed in previous experiments instantiated from the same rule that did not produce any surprises.

3. An experiment is preferred if its condition is true in the current state or can easily be reached from the current state.

10.3.4   Related Work on Learning from Experiments

In the context of concept learning, experimental design is equivalent to the learner selecting its own training instances. An early system of this kind is by Mitchell and others, LEX [70], which generates problems autonomously with two heuristics. One heuristic produces problems that refine existing, partially learned rules, and the other creates problems that lead to proposing new rules. Although the underlying rule representation in LEX is very different from that in LIVE, its heuristics are very similar to those used in LIVE's experiment module and exploration module.

Carbonell and Gil [13] have also studied learning from experiments. In their program, when an operator does not produce the expected results, the program applies the operator to different objects to find the missing preconditions. Kulkarni and Simon [48] have focused on the strategy of experimentation in scientific discovery; their work has identified a set of heuristics for autonomously collecting data for discovering scientific laws.

10.4   Comparison with Previous Rule-Learning Methods

We have already seen from some examples that complementary discrimination differs from version space in that a generalization is accomplished by discriminating a concept's complement. This provides the advantage that no initial concept hierarchy is necessary. If we view the initial concept hierarchy as a bias for learning [123] (for example, in Section 4.5 the version space cannot learn $(y = circle) \lor (y = square)$ because the concept is not included in the initial concept hierarchy), then complementary discrimination does not introduce any bias aside from that inherent in the initial concept description language itself. This property plus the fact that the method is data driven suggests that it can construct new terms if the current language is inadequate for describing the whole phenomenon of the environment (as we will see in Chapter 11). Complementary discrimination can also deal with noisy data to some extent because the method will not throw away concepts when training instances are not consistent (see examples in Sections 4.8 and 4.9). As for the time needed for LIVE to converge to the correct concept, it seems that complementary discrimination will do no worse than version space, as demonstrated by the examples in this book.

From the examples of rule revision, we see that complementary discrimination extends Brazdil's and Langley's pure discrimination methods because it can recover from overly specific errors and learn disjunctive rules without depending solely on far misses. Unlike decision trees [87] and the ID3 learning algorithm, complementary discrimination is an incremental method that splits or revises a concept according to differences found in comparing failures and successes. Thus the revision is based on an expression of multiple features instead of any particular feature as in a decision tree.

Compared to other one-way generalization learning methods such as Winston [135], our method utilizes both generalization and specialization and uses counterexamples in a constructive way. Vere's excellent paper [128] is the most closely related work to complementary discrimination. His "counterfactual" is very similar to our learning from mistakes. Our approaches share the same spirit, but Vere's is not incremental, it does not keep track of complementary concepts, and its method for finding differences is less sophisticated.

Although the final concepts are somewhat like a decision tree, LIVE's method is incremental and does not require that all the training instances be given before learning. This important characteristic makes it possible for LIVE to interleave its learning with problem solving.

10.5   Discussion

In all the examples so far, LIVE revises only the conditions of the rules and not the predictions, as does Carbonell and Gil's work [13]. However, if we share their assumption that all differences caused by an action can be seen and remembered even if they are not used in the rules, then LIVE can easily handle Carbonell and Gil's telescope task. For example, as we pointed out in Chapter 9, the missing prediction ¬IS-CLEAN(obj) in their initial Operator-3 will be included by LIVE during rule creation because there is a condition IS-CLEAN(obj) that has been changed by the action ALUMINIZE. Similarly, the missing predictions ¬IS-POLISHED(obj) and ¬IS-REFLECTIVE(obj) in their initial Operator-1 will also be included if the action GRIND-CONCAVE is applied to a POLISHED and REFLECTIVE object for the first time. If it is not, then in the future LIVE will notice that the action GRIND-CONCAVE produces more changes than predicted and will remember these extra changes. If these changes violate the conditions of some later rules in the plan execution, LIVE will then insert the changes into the rule's prediction.

In the examples of detecting faulty rules during planning, LIVE was lucky in that only one faulty rule was found at a time. When more than one faulty rule is found, LIVE faces a credit assignment problem. At present, we have not implemented any mechanisms to deal with this difficult problem, but any good method for credit assignment, such as Shapiro's contradiction backtracking [99], can be employed here.

There is one potential difficulty in LIVE's method of learning from experiments. Experiments can be beyond the problem-solving ability of LIVE's existing knowledge. For example, during the execution of an experiment for correcting a faulty rule, another faulty rule may be detected or the same faulty rule may be required in order to carry out the experiment. Although LIVE can make sure that unsuccessful experiments are not repeated, no general solution for this problem has been identified other than totally giving up on the current experiment and exploring the environment further to learn better rules.

Although complementary discrimination is best for learning a single concept and its complement, the method can also be used to learn multiple concepts if the concept description language has the predicates that can divide the set of concepts correctly. For example, in order to learn the rules that predict the result of releasing the balance beam [112] (see Section 11.3), LIVE must have a predicate that can distinguish the concept of balancing and the concept of not balancing (i.e., tilting left or right). We have also investigated a method that always splits the faulty rule even if the rule already has siblings [110]. This method learns multiple concepts, but it is not as complete as complementary discrimination in general.

In principle, complementary discrimination has the potential for dealing with noisy data because it is incremental and does not throw away concepts even if the training instances are not consistent. For example, if (*large square*) is a positive instance at time t but becomes a negative instance at time $t + i$, complementary discrimination should be able to recover from the earlier commitment by revising the complement concept. Here we would like to point out a philosophical difficulty which applies to any learning method for noisy data, including methods based on statistics. The problem is that when errors are made, it is very difficult to decide whether the learner should believe in itself or the environment. Although there are only two possibilities (either the learning data are bad or the existing knowledge is wrong), it is extremely difficult to distinguish one from the other. A naive solution would be to remember all instances in which the learner chose to believe in itself, which means that the learner refuses to adapt itself to the environment's feedback. Then when it discovers it was really wrong, the history can be used to do the adaptation. This method is very expensive, and we do not know any existing learning programs that can do the task smoothly or flawlessly.

CHAPTER 11

DISCOVERING HIDDEN FEATURES

This chapter extends the application of complementary discrimination to the discovery of hidden features in environments. We first outline the extension and then illustrate it by two examples: one for discovering hidden features by constructing new terms in the existing concept language, the other for discovering hidden features that are not in the concept language but in the combination of the action language and the concept language. We also relate the hidden features to the theoretical terms long used in the philosophy of science and point out some interesting aspects of theoretical terms that have not been studied before. Finally, we compare our discovery method with some previous discovering programs, such as AM [54], BACON [52], ARE [102], and STABB [123].

11.1   What Are Hidden Features?

In discrimination learning, many methods have been developed for finding the critical difference between two states, but what if the two states have no difference at all, as when two pairs of green peas look exactly the same but produce different offspring? In this case, we say that the environment has *hidden features*, something unobservable that yet can discriminate two states that appear identical.

Although they cannot be observed, hidden features are necessary for predicting the outcomes of actions. For example, suppose a learner has an action Push(*obj*) and can perceive only objects' shapes, volumes, densities, and locations. If *weight*

249

was the feature that determines whether an object can be pushed or not, then *weight* would be a hidden feature.

Hidden features are commonly called *theoretical terms* in the philosophy of science and *new terms* in artificial intelligence. They are terms that are missing in the initial concept description language but necessary for describing the target concepts. Since terms can be either variables, constants, or the result of functions on other terms (see the definition of *term* in Section 8.3), hidden features in a particular concept language C can be further divided into two different classes: those that can be defined as $f_i^n(t_1, \ldots, t_n)$ (where f_i^n is a function given in C and $t_1, \ldots, t_n$ are existing terms in C), and those that are variables and constants themselves and cannot be defined in terms of existing terms and functions unless actions are considered or temporal concepts are introduced. In our current example, if the function $*$ is known, then *weight* can be defined as a new term because $weight = volume * density$; otherwise, *weight* cannot be defined except by executing Push(*obj*) (here we assume the action is not in the language C). A more natural example of undefinable terms is discussed in Section 11.4.

Hidden features have been studied from different aspects for different reasons. For example, all the new concepts defined by AM [54] and ARE [102] can be regarded as hidden features, but they are defined merely because they are "interesting." BACON [52] defines hidden features for constructing laws that explain a given set of data. Utgoff studied hidden features as a problem of bias [123] and proposed a framework for shifting bias during the process of learning.

11.2   How LIVE Discovers Hidden Features

Using CDL+ framework, LIVE discovers hidden features in three steps:

1. Detecting the existence of hidden features by noticing the failure of a discrimination

2. Identifying hidden features that enable LIVE to discriminate further

3. Assimilating the hidden features into the existing language and continuing the discrimination process

The first step is to decide when hidden features must be discovered. Since LIVE learns through discrimination, this step can be made in a straightforward manner. That is, if the discrimination process cannot find any difference between the current failure and previous successes, then hidden features must be discovered. When such situations arise, LIVE goes to the second step by determining the failure and the success (each with a state and a set of bindings) that are indistinguishable in the current language.

Given two indistinguishable cases, the task of the second step is to search for a set of new terms that can distinguish them. As we said earlier, such terms can be defined either by existing terms and functions or through actions. Consequently, discovering hidden features can be done in two different ways, depending on whether an environment is time dependent or not. In an action-independent environment, where states do not depend on previous actions, LIVE discovers hidden features by applying its m-constructor functions to the existing features and testing whether the result discriminates the ambiguous states. For example, when predicting whether a balance beam will tip or balance [112], LIVE discovers the invisible *torque* concept by multiplying *distance* and *weight* (see Section 11.3). In action-dependent environments, where states depend on previous actions, LIVE discovers hidden features by searching the history for differences in the states preceding the two indistinguishable states. Details of such a search are given in Section 11.4.

Identifying hidden features does not complete the discovery process; these features must be assimilated into the system to be useful in the future. In an action-independent environment, since hidden features are defined in terms of observable features, the system can simply use the newly defined features as if they were visible because they can be computed from the observable features. For example, when the concept of *torque* is discovered by a system that perceives only objects' distances and weights, the concept will simply be added as another object feature. Any rule that needs *torque* to discriminate its condition can obtain it by computing the value *weight*distance*. In an action-dependent environment, since hidden features determine the observable features, two additional tasks must be performed before these features can be used: determining how the hidden features define the observable features and determining how the hidden features are inherited through actions. One strategy is used for both tasks: testing all the m-constructor functions to find one that is consistent with all the examples collected.

11.3   Using Existing Functions and Terms

As an example of how LIVE discovers hidden features in an action-independent environment, we will consider the balance beam (Figure 11.1), a research experiment in child development. It was first studied by Inhelder and Piaget [38]. Siegler [112] hypothesized a set of production rules used by children from ages 2 to 15 to demonstrate how knowledge influences learning. Flinn and Newell [76] used the balance beam to test Soar's cognitive theory. In the experiment, children are shown a type of seesaw with pegs at either end on which weights can be placed. The task is to predict, after the beam is released, whether the beam will tip to the left, tip to the right, or balance. From the point of view of learning from the environment, we can define a learner as shown in Table 11.1. One simplification is made in the definition: Weights on one side are always put on a single peg, so that each side of the beam can be viewed as a single object with three features: *weight*, *distance*, and *altitude*. In addition to these features, we assume that the learner has two primitive relations, = and >, and two simple functions, + and *. A state in this

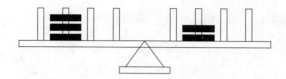

Figure 11.1   The balance beam experiment.

Percepts	two objects L and R, each of which is a feature vector [*objID weight distance altitude*]; six relational predicates: WEQ (*weight* =), WGR (*weight* >), DEQ (*distance* =), DGR (*distance* >), AEQ (*altitude* =), and AGR (*altitude* >)
Action	Release(*obj$_x$ obj$_y$*)
M-constructors	Two primitive relations, = and >, and two functions, + and ∗
Goal	to predict AEQ or AGR after an action
Environment	the balance beam in Figure 11.1

Table 11.1   A learner in the balance beam environment.

environment is perceived as two objects, L and R ("left" and "right," respectively), represented as feature vectors and a set of relations between them.

In our experiment, LIVE is given a sequence of tasks (see Figure 11.2) taken directly from Siegler's paper [112]. When the first task is given, LIVE observes the state

$$[L\ 3\ 1\ 0]\ [R\ 3\ 1\ 0]\ \text{WEQ(L R) DEQ(L R) AEQ(L R)}$$

but has nothing to predict because its internal rule base is empty (recall from Chapter 8 that at this point LIVE's problem solver would report a *No Rule* error). So it decides to explore the action Release(L R) (this can be thought of as a single-action explorative plan). After observing that nothing is changed by the action, LIVE creates the first and the most general rule from this environment as follows:

RuleID: Rule1
Condition: [*obj$_x$ w$_x$ d$_x$ a$_x$*] [*obj$_y$ w$_y$ d$_y$ a$_y$*] AEQ(*obj$_x$ obj$_y$*)
Action: Release(*obj$_x$ obj$_y$*)
Prediction: AEQ(*obj$_x$ obj$_y$*)

(Note that because the goal is to predict AEQ or AGR, the rule's prediction includes the relation AEQ even though nothing has changed in this task.)

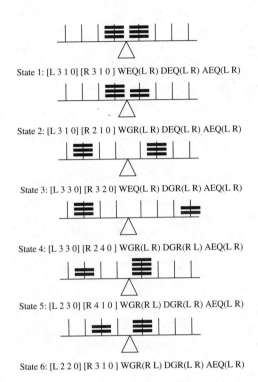

State 1: [L 3 1 0] [R 3 1 0] WEQ(L R) DEQ(L R) AEQ(L R)

State 2: [L 3 1 0] [R 2 1 0] WGR(L R) DEQ(L R) AEQ(L R)

State 3: [L 3 3 0] [R 3 2 0] WEQ(L R) DGR(L R) AEQ(L R)

State 4: [L 3 3 0] [R 2 4 0] WGR(L R) DGR(R L) AEQ(L R)

State 5: [L 2 3 0] [R 4 1 0] WGR(R L) DGR(L R) AEQ(L R)

State 6: [L 2 2 0] [R 3 1 0] WGR(R L) DGR(L R) AEQ(L R)

Figure 11.2 A series of beam tasks.

In the second task, because Rule1's condition is satisfied in the state

$$[L\ 3\ 1\ 0]\ [R\ 2\ 1\ 0]\ WGR(L\ R)\ DEQ(L\ R)\ AEQ(L\ R)$$

LIVE predicts AEQ(L R). Unfortunately, the prediction is proven false by the result AGR(R L). By comparing this task with the first task, a reason is found for the surprise, WEQ(L R) $\wedge$ ¬WGR(L R), which was true in the first task but false in the second. Thus the rule is split into the following two (see Section 10.2.1 for the procedure):

RuleID:	Rule1
Condition:	$[obj_x\ w_x\ d_x\ a_x]\ [obj_y\ w_y\ d_y\ a_y]$ AEQ($obj_x\ obj_y$)
	WEQ($obj_x\ obj_y$) ¬WGR($obj_x\ obj_y$)
Action:	Release($obj_x\ obj_y$)
Prediction:	AEQ($obj_x\ obj_y$)
Sibling:	Rule2

RuleID: Rule2
Condition: $[obj_x\ w_x\ d_x\ a_x]\ [obj_y\ w_y\ d_y\ a_y]$ AEQ$(obj_x\ obj_y)$
              $\neg$(WEQ$(obj_x\ obj_y)\ \neg$WGR$(obj_x\ obj_y))$
Action: Release$(obj_x\ obj_y)$
Prediction: AGR$(obj_y\ obj_x)$
Sibling: Rule1

With these two rules, LIVE has learned to pay attention to the objects' *weight* feature. When working on the third task, which has the state

$$[\text{L } 3\ 3\ 0]\ [\text{R } 3\ 2\ 0]\ \text{WEQ(L R)}\ \text{DGR(L R)}\ \text{AEQ(L R)}$$

Rule1 is employed because L and R have the same weight. Again, LIVE's prediction AEQ(L R) is wrong because the beam tips to the left, AGR(R L). After comparing the current state to the first task and finding the explanation, DEQ(L R) $\wedge$ $\neg$DGR(L R), Rule1 is modified into the following new Rule1, and Rule2 is modified to be the complement of the new Rule1 (see Section 10.2.1 for the procedure):

RuleID: Rule1
Condition: $[obj_x\ w_x\ d_x\ a_x]\ [obj_y\ w_y\ d_y\ a_y]$ AEQ$(obj_x\ obj_y)$
              WEQ$(obj_x\ obj_y)\ \neg$WGR$(obj_x\ obj_y)$ DEQ$(obj_x\ obj_y)$
              $\neg$DGR$(obj_x\ obj_y)$
Action: Release$(obj_x\ obj_y)$
Prediction: AEQ$(obj_x\ obj_y)$
Sibling: Rule2

RuleID: Rule2
Condition: $[obj_x\ w_x\ d_x\ a_x]\ [obj_y\ w_y\ d_y\ a_y]$ AEQ$(obj_x\ obj_y)$
              $\neg$(WEQ$(obj_x\ obj_y)\ \neg$WGR$(obj_x\ obj_y)$ DEQ$(obj_x\ obj_y)$
              $\neg$DGR$(obj_x\ obj_y))$
Action: Release$(obj_x\ obj_y)$
Prediction: AGR$(obj_y\ obj_x)$
Sibling: Rule1

With these two new rules, LIVE will predict that the beam will be balanced when both sides have the same weight and distance. However, LIVE believes that weight and distance are independent when it determines which side will tip. Rule2 says that the side that has either greater weight or greater distance will tip down.

When the fourth task comes along, Rule2 is invoked because in the state

$$[\text{L } 3\ 3\ 0]\ [\text{R } 2\ 4\ 0]\ \text{WGR(L R)}\ \text{DGR(R L)}\ \text{AEQ(L R)}$$

both weight and distance are different. Since the condition WGR precedes DGR, L will be bound to obj_x and R will be bound to obj_y, so LIVE predicts AGR(R L). This time the prediction is correct and no rule is changed.

So far, learning by discrimination has worked smoothly. However, trouble now begins. In the fifth task Rule2 is invoked again but with obj_x bound to R and obj_y bound to L. Because WGR(R L), LIVE predicts AGR(L R). As usual, after the prediction is proven false by the result AGR(R L), LIVE begins to compare the current application with Rule2's last successful application, task 4:

Task 4 State: [L 3 3 0] [R 2 4 0] WGR(L R) DGR(R L) AEQ(L R)
Task 4 Bindings: obj_x/L, obj_y/R

Task 5 State: [L 2 3 0] [R 4 1 0] WGR(R L) DGR(L R) AEQ(L R)
Task 5 Bindings: obj_x/R, obj_y/L

Comparing these two applications, LIVE cannot find any relational difference because WGR(obj_x obj_y), DGR(obj_x obj_y), and AEQ(obj_x obj_y) are all true in both cases.

At this point, LIVE becomes convinced that hidden features exist in this environment and decides to use its m-constructor functions, $+$ and $*$, to search for a new feature that can discriminate these two look-alike states. Since each object has three features w (weight), d (distance), and a (altitude), there are six possible hidden features: $w + d$, $w * d$, $w + a$, $w * a$, $d + a$, and $d * a$. LIVE finds that $w * d$ is the only one that can distinguish the two states because in task 4, obj_x's $w * d$ ($3 * 3$) is greater then obj_y's $w * d$ ($2 * 4$), while in task 5, obj_x's ($4 * 1$) is less than obj_y's ($2 * 3$). LIVE concludes that ($w * d$) is the hidden feature it is looking for. Since this new feature is defined in terms of existing functions and features, it is added as a fourth feature for the objects in this environment, and a new relation TGR (*torque* $>$) is defined with respect to the greater-than function $>$ and index 4 of the new feature vector (see Chapter 9 for details):

$$\text{TGR}(obj_x\ obj_y) : \text{TRUE} \iff (\text{elt } obj_x\ 4) > (\text{elt } obj_y\ 4)$$

Rule2 is then split according to the relational difference made possible by the new feature and its relation (Rule1's condition is modified to become the complement of Rule2's condition):

RuleID: Rule1
Condition: [obj_x w_x d_x a_x w_x*d_x] [obj_y w_y d_y a_y w_y*d_y] AEQ(obj_x obj_y)
              $\neg(\neg(\neg(\text{WEQ}(obj_x\ obj_y)\ \neg\text{WGR}(obj_x\ obj_y)\ \text{DEQ}(obj_x\ obj_y)$
              $\neg\text{DGR}(obj_x\ obj_y))\ \text{TGR}(obj_x\ obj_y))$
Action: Release(obj_x obj_y)
Prediction: AEQ(obj_x obj_y)
Sibling: Rule2

RuleID: Rule2
Condition: $[obj_x\ w_x\ d_x\ a_x\ w_x{*}d_x]$ $[obj_y\ w_y\ d_y\ a_y\ w_y{*}d_y]$ AEQ$(obj_x\ obj_y)$
              $\neg$(WEQ$(obj_x\ obj_y)$ $\neg$WGR$(obj_x\ obj_y)$ DEQ$(obj_x\ obj_y)$
              $\neg$DGR$(obj_x\ obj_y)$) TGR$(obj_x\ obj_y)$
Action: Release$(obj_x\ obj_y)$
Prediction: AGR$(obj_y\ obj_x)$
Sibling: Rule1

Note that the last condition for Rule1 is a disjunctive expression; that is, it is equivalent to

$$(\text{WEQ}(obj_x\ obj_y)\ \neg\text{WGR}(obj_x\ obj_y)\ \text{DEQ}(obj_x\ obj_y)\ \neg\text{DGR}(obj_x\ obj_y))$$

or

$$\neg\text{TGR}(obj_x obj_y)$$

Therefore, when the the sixth task comes, Rule1's condition is true in the state

$$[\text{L 2 2 0 4}]\ [\text{R 4 1 0 4}]\ \text{WGR(R L) DGR(L R) AEQ(L R)}$$

because $\neg$TGR$(obj_x obj_y)$ is true. So LIVE predicts AEQ(L R) and the prediction succeeds. Up to this point, LIVE has learned the correct rules to predict the behavior of the beam in this environment. In this example, the hidden feature is the concept of *torque*, defined by $(weight * distance)$.

In general, the discovery of action-independent hidden features is triggered when the normal discrimination process fails, that is, when no difference can be found between a failure and a success. LIVE searches for the hidden feature by applying all its m-constructors to the existing features and testing whether the result can discriminate the indistinguishable states. This process can be summarized as the algorithm listed in Figure 11.3.

Relating this procedure to the example above, the relation r specified in the algorithm is $>$, the function f is $*$, and feature functions are $p_1 = weight$ and $p_2 = distance$. The new term discovered is $torque(x) \equiv distance(x) * weight(x)$. Notice that all the terms defined in this fashion are action independent, for they can be defined without actions.

11.4   Using Actions as Well as Percepts

In the balance beam environment, the hidden feature $w{*}d$, although defined in the process of learning, is already inside the concept language because the function $*$ and the features *weight* and *distance* exist in the language. In fact, this is the kind of hidden feature that previous discovery systems and constructive induction programs have most often studied. But sometimes hidden features can be harder to find, and to discover them, one must use not only the system's percepts (the concept description language) but also its actions.

Procedure Search-Rel-Terms(S, T):
1   Let *Difference* = Search-Action-Independent-Rel-Terms(S, T),
2   Return *Difference* to the rule reviser (see Section 10.2.1).

Procedure Search-Action-Independent-Rel-Terms(S, T):
1   Select a relation r, which takes n parameters, and a function f, which takes m parameters,
2   Select m unary functions $p_1, p_2, \ldots, p_m$ whose domains are features,
3   If there exist n objects $o_1, o_2, \ldots, o_n$ such that $r[v_1^S, v_2^S, \ldots, v_n^S] \neq r[v_1^T, v_2^T, \ldots, v_n^T]$ where $v_i^S = f[p_1(o_i), p_2(o_i), \ldots, p_m(o_i)]$ in state S, and $v_i^T = f[p_1(o_i), p_2(o_i), \ldots, p_m(o_i)]$ in state T,
    Then return $r[v_1^S, v_2^S, \ldots, v_n^S]$,
4   If all sections are exhausted, then return FAIL, else goto step 1.

Figure 11.3   Searching for action-independent relations and terms.

In this section, we describe how to discover hidden features that involve both percepts and actions. In particular, we will look at the task of discovering genes by breeding garden peas as Mendel reported in his classic paper [62].

Mendel's experiments start with a set of purebred peas. All their ancestors are known to have the same characteristics. The peas are divided into classes according to their observable features. For example, one class of peas is green and has wrinkles, and another class is yellow and has long stems. The experiments are very well controlled so that the characteristics of hybridized peas are determined solely by their parents and not by other factors such as weather or temperature (we shall refer to this as the "relevancy assumption"). We have redone Mendel's experiments (see Figure 11.4) with two simplifications: (1) a pea's color is the only observable feature, and (2) if two peas are fertilized, then they will produce exactly four children.

In these experiments, the first generation is a set of purebreds P_1 through P_8. Four of them are green and four are yellow. From these purebreds, three more generations are produced by the action Artificial Fertilization, or AF, which takes two peas and produces four children. As reported in his paper, Mendel noticed that purebreds produce only purebreds (for example, all the children of AF$((P_9\,0), (P_{10}\,0))$ are yellow and all the children of AF$((P_{13}\,1), (P_{14}\,1))$ are green), but hybrids produce both green and yellow offspring (for example, AF$((P_{17}\,1), (P_{18}\,1))$ produces one yellow child and three green children, as does AF$((P_{21}\,1), (P_{22}\,1))$).

Furthermore, Mendel also noticed some regularity in the colors of the children of hybrids. The yellow children of hybrids (e.g., AF$((P_{33}\,0), (P_{40}\,0))$) produce only yellow grandchildren, but green children of hybrids produce yellow grandchildren in the following proportion: one-third of the green children (see AF$((P_{36}\,1), P_{37}\,1))$)

Let AF(pea_x pea_y) stand for the action Artificial Fertilization.
Let a pea be denoted as (P_i $color$), where P_i is the pea's identifier, and $color$ can
be either 1 (for green), or 0 (for yellow).

Generation 1:   (P_1 0), (P_2 0), (P_3 1), (P_4 1), (P_5 0), (P_6 1), (P_7 1), (P_8 0)

Generation 2:
AF((P_1 0), (P_2 0)) $\Longrightarrow$ {(P_9 0), (P_{10} 0), (P_{11} 0), (P_{12} 0)}
AF((P_3 1), (P_4 1)) $\Longrightarrow$ {(P_{13} 1), (P_{14} 1), (P_{15} 1), (P_{16} 1)}
AF((P_5 0), (P_6 1)) $\Longrightarrow$ {(P_{17} 1), (P_{18} 1), (P_{19} 1), (P_{20} 1)}
AF((P_7 1), (P_8 0)) $\Longrightarrow$ {(P_{21} 1), (P_{22} 1), (P_{23} 1), (P_{24} 1)}

Generation 3:
AF((P_9 0), (P_{10} 0)) $\Longrightarrow$ {(P_{25} 0), (P_{26} 0), (P_{27} 0), (P_{28} 0)}
AF((P_{13} 1), (P_{14} 1)) $\Longrightarrow$ {(P_{29} 1), (P_{30} 1), (P_{31} 1), (P_{32} 1)}
AF((P_{17} 1), (P_{18} 1)) $\Longrightarrow$ {(P_{33} 0), (P_{34} 1), (P_{35} 1), (P_{36} 1)}
AF((P_{21} 1), (P_{22} 1)) $\Longrightarrow$ {(P_{37} 1), (P_{38} 1), (P_{39} 1), (P_{40} 0)}

Generation 4:
AF((P_{33} 0), (P_{40} 0)) $\Longrightarrow$ {(P_{41} 0), (P_{42} 0), (P_{43} 0), (P_{44} 0)}
AF((P_{34} 1), (P_{38} 1)) $\Longrightarrow$ {(P_{45} 1), (P_{46} 0), (P_{47} 1), (P_{48} 1)}
AF((P_{35} 1), (P_{39} 1)) $\Longrightarrow$ {(P_{49} 1), (P_{50} 1), (P_{51} 0), (P_{52} 1)}
AF((P_{36} 1), (P_{37} 1)) $\Longrightarrow$ {(P_{53} 1), (P_{54} 1), (P_{55} 1), (P_{56} 1)}

Figure 11.4 A simplification of Mendel's pea experiments.

produce only green grandchildren, and the other two-thirds (AF((P_{34} 1), (P_{38} 1))
and AF((P_{35} 1), (P_{39} 1))) produce three green grandchildren and one yellow grand-
child.

From these regularities, Mendel hypothesized that a pea's color is determined by
some invisible entities (now known as genes), and the regularity in the color display
of the children of hybrids is determined by the combinations of these entities. In his
hypothesis of how these entities determine color, Mendel also believed that some
entities are dominant (such as green here) and others are recessive (yellow). When
both are present at the same time, only the dominant characteristic shows up.

In order to simulate Mendel's discovery with LIVE's learning and discovery
methods, we have formalized, in Table 11.2, his experiments as a problem of learning
from the environment. In addition to the assumptions that a pea's color is the only
observable feature and that two peas produce exactly four children when fertilized,
this definition also makes two other important assumptions. First, it assumes that
the genes of the parents are evenly distributed into their four children according to
the function $EvenDistr$ (in other words, we are not concerned with statistics). This
assumption puts a very strong bias on the discovery task because LIVE is given a
small set of m-constructor functions, of which $EvenDistr$ is one. If there were a large
set of m-constructors, LIVE might have to make a lengthier search, but the present

Percepts	a set of peas, each of which is a feature vector (P_i *color*), where P_i is the identifier of the pea and *color* can be 1 (green) or 0 (yellow)
Actions	AF(pea_x, pea_y)
M-constructors	two primitive relations, $=$ and $>$, and three functions, max (maximum), min (minimum), and an evenly distributed pairing function $EvenDistr((a\ b)\ (c\ d)) = ((a\ c)\ (a\ d)\ (b\ c)\ (b\ d))$
Goal	to predict the colors of hybridized children

Table 11.2   A learner in the environment of pea hybridization.

set will illustrate the process. Second, we will not deal with the problem of how to choose peas for fertilization, although this might have been another important part of Mendel's discovery.

In the following description, we assume that LIVE remembers the whole history of its actions in this environment, and each memorized historic element has four parts: the ruleID, the state, the bindings, and the results of the action. In this way LIVE can recall what were the parents of a given pea.

Following the experiments in Figure 11.4, LIVE starts with a set of purebred peas as the first generation. To make the second generation, the system fertilizes yellow with yellow, green with green, yellow with green, and green with yellow. When applying AF($(P_1\ 0), (P_2\ 0)$) (with no prediction), the system observes that all the offspring, $(P_9\ 0), (P_{10}\ 0), (P_{11}\ 0)$, and $(P_{12}\ 0)$, are yellow; thus a new rule is constructed as follows:

RuleID:	Rule1
Condition:	$(P_i\ c_i)\ (P_j\ c_j)$
Action:	AF($(P_i\ c_i), (P_j\ c_j)$)
Prediction:	$(P_k\ c_i)\ (P_l\ c_i)\ (P_m\ c_i)\ (P_n\ c_i)$

This rule is created using the technique described in Chapter 9. In accordance with the relevancy assumption mentioned earlier, the rule's only condition pertains to the peas, not other facts such as the weather, the soil, and so on. The rule predicts that all the children will have the same color as P_i because when correlating the predictions with the action in this rule, LIVE examines c_i before c_j.

For the next two actions, this rule successfully predicts that the hybrids of green $(P_3\ 1)$ with green $(P_4\ 1)$ will be all green—$(P_{13}\ 1), (P_{14}\ 1), (P_{15}\ 1)$, and $(P_{16}\ 1)$—but it fails to predict that the hybrids of yellow $(P_5\ 0)$ with green $(P_6\ 1)$ will all be green too—$(P_{17}\ 1), (P_{18}\ 1), (P_{19}\ 1)$, and $(P_{20}\ 1)$. The incorrect prediction is made because c_i is bound to yellow. This surprise causes LIVE to compare this application with the last one (green with green), and it finds a difference that $c_i = c_j$ was true previously but is false now. (Following the method described in Section 9.2.1, $c_i = c_j$ is in fact defined as a new relation RELxxx, such that

$$\text{RELxxx}(P_i\,P_j) \iff (\text{elt}\,P_i\,1) = (\text{elt}\,P_j\,1)$$

where 1 is the index for the color feature and $=$ is a given m-constructor, but we will use the shorthand $c_i = c_j$ in the description of the rules.) With this relational difference, Rule1 is then split into two new rules as follows:

RuleID:	Rule1
Condition:	$(P_i\,c_i)\,(P_j\,c_j)\,(c_i = c_j)$
Action:	$\text{AF}((P_i\,c_i), (P_j\,c_j))$
Prediction:	$(P_k\,c_i)\,(P_l\,c_i)\,(P_m\,c_i)\,(P_n\,c_i)$
Sibling:	Rule2

RuleID:	Rule2
Condition:	$(P_i\,c_i)\,(P_j\,c_j)\,\neg(c_i = c_j)$
Action:	$\text{AF}((P_i\,c_i), (P_j\,c_j))$
Prediction:	$(P_k\,c_j)\,(P_l\,c_j)\,(P_m\,c_j)\,(P_n\,c_j)$
Sibling:	Rule1

Rule2 is then applied to predict that all hybrids of green ($P_7\,1$) with yellow ($P_8\,0$) will be yellow (because c_j is bound to yellow), but the result is again a surprise: $(P_{21}\,1)$, $(P_{22}\,1)$, $(P_{23}\,1)$, and $(P_{24}\,1)$ are all green. After comparing the two cases, LIVE finds that the reason for the surprise is $(c_j > c_i)$ (obtained by the same technique used for creating the relation $(c_i = c_j)$), and it revises Rule2's condition as follows (Rule1's condition is modified to become the complement of Rule2's condition):

RuleID:	Rule1
Condition:	$(P_i\,c_i)\,(P_j\,c_j)\,\neg(\neg(c_i = c_j)\,(c_j > c_i))$
Action:	$\text{AF}((P_i\,c_i), (P_j\,c_j))$
Prediction:	$(P_k\,c_i)\,(P_l\,c_i)\,(P_m\,c_i)\,(P_n\,c_i)$
Sibling:	Rule2

RuleID:	Rule2
Condition:	$(P_i\,c_i)\,(P_j\,c_j)\,\neg(c_i = c_j)\,(c_j > c_i)$
Action:	$\text{AF}((P_i\,c_i), (P_j\,c_j))$
Prediction:	$(P_k\,c_j)\,(P_l\,c_j)\,(P_m\,c_j)\,(P_n\,c_j)$
Sibling:	Rule1

These two new rules reflect the fact that the green color dominates the yellow color and that together they account for the results in the second generation. The third generation of the experiment is made by self-fertilizing the second generation. We assume the pairs to be hybridized are the same as the third generation in Figure 11.4. When fertilizing $(P_9\ 0)$ with $(P_{10}\ 0)$ and $(P_{13}\ 1)$ with $(P_{14}\ 1)$, Rule1 successfully predicts that the children will be $\{(P_{25}\ 0), (P_{26}\ 0), (P_{27}\ 0), (P_{28}\ 0)\}$ and $\{(P_{29}\ 1), (P_{30}\ 1), (P_{31}\ 1), (P_{32}\ 1)\}$, respectively.   However, the hybridization of $(P_{17}\ 1)$ with $(P_{18}\ 1)$ surprises LIVE because the children have different colors: $\{(P_{33}\ 1), (P_{34}\ 1), (P_{35}\ 1), (P_{36}\ 0)\}$. In explaining the surprise, the last application $\mathrm{AF}((P_{13}\ 1), (P_{14}\ 1))$ is brought in to compare with the current application, but the system fails to find any relational difference because both pairs are green. This is the point where hidden features must be discovered. Since the environment is action dependent, LIVE traces the history and searches for differences in previous states. Fortunately, a difference is found when comparing the parents of these two indistinguishable states: $c_i = c_j$ was true for the parents of $(P_{13}\ 1)$ and $(P_{14}\ 1)$, namely $(P_3\ 1)$ and $(P_4\ 1)$, but not for the parents of $(P_{17}\ 1)$ and $(P_{18}\ 1)$, namely $(P_5\ 0)$ and $(P_6\ 1)$. Since each pea has one "mother" and one "father," this difference indicates the existence of two hidden features from the grandparents, denoted as m and f, respectively. These features are invisible in the parental generation but necessary to determine the grandchildren's color. The representation of the pea is thus extended to include three features: *color*, m, and f.

As noted before, we must now do two things to use the hidden features. One is to figure out how m and f are related to the *color* feature, and the other is to figure out how m and f are inherited through the action AF.

For the first task, LIVE begins to collect examples. Since the first-generation peas are known to be purebred—that is, all their ancestors have the same color—their m and f must be the same as their color. Thus all the peas in the first generation are the relevant examples:

$(P_1\ 0\ 0\ 0), (P_2\ 0\ 0\ 0), (P_3\ 1\ 1\ 1), (P_4\ 1\ 1\ 1), (P_5\ 0\ 0\ 0), (P_6\ 1\ 1\ 1), (P_7\ 1\ 1\ 1),$ $(P_8\ 0\ 0\ 0)$

The second-generation peas are also examples of how m and f determine color. This is because their parents, the first generation, all have a single value for m, f, and *color*, and no matter how m and f are inherited, each parent has only one possible value to inherit. For example, $(P_9\ 0)$'s m and f can only be 0 because its parents $(P_1\ 0\ 0\ 0)$ and $(P_2\ 0\ 0\ 0)$ have only 0s to inherit. $(P_{17}\ 1)$'s m and f can only be 0 and 1, respectively, because its mother, $(P_5\ 0\ 0\ 0)$, has only 0s and its father, $(P_6\ 1\ 1\ 1)$, has only 1s. Therefore, the examples from the second generation are as follows:

$(P_9\ 0\ 0\ 0), (P_{10}\ 0\ 0\ 0), (P_{11}\ 0\ 0\ 0), (P_{12}\ 0\ 0\ 0), (P_{13}\ 1\ 1\ 1), (P_{14}\ 1\ 1\ 1),$ $(P_{15}\ 1\ 1\ 1), (P_{16}\ 1\ 1\ 1), (P_{17}\ 1\ 0\ 1), \ldots, (P_{21}\ 1\ 1\ 0), \ldots$

Some of the peas in the third generation are also examples, such as $(P_{25}\ 0\ 0\ 0)$ and $(P_{29}\ 0\ 0\ 0)$, because their parents are still purebreds. But others may not be, such as $(P_{33}\ 0\ 0\ 0)$ or $(P_{37}\ 0\ 0\ 0)$, because their parents are hybrids and it is uncertain at this point how the m's and f's are inherited from hybrids.

With the examples collected, it is straightforward for LIVE to search through the m-constructor functions and see that the following formula is consistent with all the examples:

$$color = \max(m\ f) \tag{11.1}$$

where $\max(0\ 0) = 0$, $\max(1\ 1) = 1$, $\max(1\ 0) = 1$, and $\max(0\ 1) = 1$. This formula is a restatement of Mendel's hypothesis that a pea's color is determined by the dominant color, green.

For the second task, we know that the parents' m and f are passed on to all four children's m and f, and the actions LIVE has done can be used as examples. Here we list some of the examples that show how the third generation is produced from the second generation (where surprises arise):

$$\text{AF}((P_9\ 0\ 0\ 0)\ (P_{10}\ 0\ 0\ 0)) \implies \{(P_{25}\ 0\ 0\ 0), (P_{26}\ 0\ 0\ 0)(P_{27}\ 0\ 0\ 0), (P_{28}\ 0\ 0\ 0)\}$$
$$\text{AF}((P_{13}\ 1\ 1\ 1)\ (P_{14}\ 1\ 1\ 1)) \implies \{(P_{29}\ 1\ 1\ 1), (P_{30}\ 1\ 1\ 1), (P_{31}\ 1\ 1\ 1), (P_{32}\ 1\ 1\ 1)\}$$
$$\text{AF}((P_{17}\ 1\ 0\ 1)\ (P_{18}\ 1\ 0\ 1)) \implies \{(P_{33}\ 1\ x_1\ x_2), (P_{34}\ 1\ x_3\ x_4), (P_{35}\ 1\ x_5\ x_6),$$
$$(P_{36}\ 0\ x_7\ x_8)\}$$

These examples, together with the formula $color = \max(m\ f)$, specify an unknown function, *Inherit*, that must satisfy the following equations:

$$
\begin{aligned}
Inherit((0\ 0)(0\ 0)) &= ((0\ 0)(0\ 0)(0\ 0)(0\ 0)) \\
Inherit((1\ 1)(1\ 1)) &= ((1\ 1)(1\ 1)(1\ 1)(1\ 1)) \\
Inherit((0\ 1)(0\ 1)) &= ((x_1\ x_2)(x_3\ x_4)(x_5\ x_6)(x_7\ x_8)) \\
\max(x_1\ x_2) &= 1 \\
\max(x_3\ x_4) &= 1 \\
\max(x_5\ x_6) &= 1 \\
\max(x_7\ x_8) &= 0
\end{aligned}
$$

Searching through the m-constructor functions, LIVE finds that *EvenDistr* fits the data (i.e. *EvenDistr* can replace *Inherit*); thus it concludes that if the mother has $(m_i\ f_i)$ and the father has $(m_j\ f_j)$, then the m and f for the four children will be determined as follows:

$$EvenDistr((m_i\ f_i)(m_j\ f_j)) = ((m_i\ m_j)(m_i\ f_j)(f_i\ m_j)(f_i\ f_j)) \tag{11.2}$$

Note that m and f are not defined in terms of any observable features but in terms of m and f recursively. With equations 11.1 and 11.2, LIVE now modifies Rule1 (the one that is surprised) and Rule2 as follows (Rule2's condition is the complement of Rule1's):

RuleID: Rule1
Condition: $(P_i \; c_i \; m_i \; f_i) \; (P_j \; c_j \; m_j \; f_j)$
             $\neg(\neg(c_i = c_j) \; (c_j > c_i)) \; (m_i = f_i) \; (m_j = f_j)$
Action: $AF((P_i \; c_i \; m_i \; f_i), (P_j \; c_j \; m_j \; f_j))$
Prediction: $(P_k \; \max(m_i \, m_j) \; m_i \; m_j) \; (P_l \; \max(m_i \, f_j) \; m_i \; f_j)$
             $(P_m \; \max(f_i \, m_j) \; f_i \; m_j) \; (P_n \; \max(f_i \, f_j) \; f_i \; f_j)$
Sibling: Rule2

RuleID: Rule2
Condition: $(P_i \; c_i \; m_i \; f_i) \; (P_j \; c_j \; m_j \; f_j)$
             $\neg(\neg(\neg(c_i = c_j) \; (c_j > c_i)) \; (m_i = f_i) \; (m_j = f_j))$
Action: $AF((P_i \; c_i \; m_i \; f_i), (P_j \; c_j \; m_j \; f_j))$
Prediction: $(P_k \; \max(m_i \, m_j) \; m_i \; m_j) \; (P_l \; \max(m_i \, f_j) \; m_i \; f_j)$
             $(P_m \; \max(f_i \, m_j) \; f_i \; m_j) \; (P_n \; \max(f_i, f_j) \; f_i \; f_j)$
Sibling: Rule1

Note that Rule1 and Rule2 now make the same prediction. This is because the newly defined m and f determine a pea's color, and they are distributed into the prediction in the same way (by the function *EvenDistr*) no matter what the condition is.

With these two new rules, LIVE is now ready to predict the color of other hybrids. When $(P_{21} \; 1)$ and $(P_{22} \; 1)$ are hybridized, LIVE determines that they are really $(P_{21} \; 1 \; 1 \; 0)$ and $(P_{22} \; 1 \; 1 \; 0)$ by tracing their ancestry. Rule2 correctly predicts that among their four children, three will be green and one will be yellow.

At this point, it is interesting to compare the hidden features that have been revealed with Mendel's experiments, shown in Figure 11.5. This time, the addition of m and f provides a much clearer picture.

The procedure for discovering action-dependent hidden features, given in Figure 11.6, is an extension of the algorithm in Figure 11.3. Because the hidden feature is action dependent (i.e., it cannot be defined without actions), the procedure Search-Action-Independent-Rel-Terms(S_0, T_0) returns FAIL. In this case, the learner must search back into the history of S_0 and T_0 to find differences. New terms must be defined not only in terms of percepts but also in terms of actions. These terms are defined to carry the difference to the present so that the learner can predict the future.

In Figure 11.6, the procedure Search-Rel-Terms is modified to search both action-independent and action-dependent terms. When the procedure Search-Action-Independent-Rel-Terms(S_0, T_0) returns FAIL, this new procedure searches into the history of S_0 and T_0, finds the difference there, and returns the difference in terms of some newly defined action-dependent predicates. This procedure will be further illustrated in Section 12.2.

Finally, there are some differences between LIVE's behavior and Mendel's experiments. First, LIVE defined the hidden features when fertilizing the third gener-

Generation 1: $(P_1\ 0\ 0\ 0), (P_2\ 0\ 0\ 0), (P_3\ 1\ 1\ 1), (P_4\ 1\ 1\ 1),$
                $(P_5\ 0\ 0\ 0), (P_6\ 1\ 1\ 1), (P_7\ 1\ 1\ 1), (P_8\ 0\ 0\ 0)$

Generation 2: $\text{AF}((P_1\ 0\ 0\ 0), (P_2\ 0\ 0\ 0)) \Longrightarrow \{(P_9\ 0\ 0\ 0), (P_{10}\ 0\ 0\ 0), (P_{11}\ 0\ 0\ 0), (P_{12}\ 0\ 0\ 0)\}$
                $\text{AF}((P_3\ 1\ 1\ 1), (P_4\ 1\ 1\ 1)) \Longrightarrow \{(P_{13}\ 1\ 1\ 1), (P_{14}\ 1\ 1\ 1), (P_{15}\ 1\ 1\ 1), (P_{16}\ 1\ 1\ 1)\}$
                $\text{AF}((P_5\ 0\ 0\ 0), (P_6\ 1\ 1\ 1)) \Longrightarrow \{(P_{17}\ 1\ 0\ 1), (P_{18}\ 1\ 0\ 1), (P_{19}\ 1\ 0\ 1), (P_{20}\ 1\ 0\ 1)\}$
Generation 3: $\text{AF}((P_7\ 1\ 1\ 1), (P_8\ 0\ 0\ 0)) \Longrightarrow \{(P_{21}\ 1\ 1\ 0), (P_{22}\ 1\ 1\ 0), (P_{23}\ 1\ 1\ 0), (P_{24}\ 1\ 1\ 0)\}$

                $\text{AF}((P_9\ 0\ 0\ 0), (P_{10}\ 0\ 0\ 0)) \Longrightarrow \{(P_{25}\ 0\ 0\ 0), (P_{26}\ 0\ 0\ 0), (P_{27}\ 0\ 0\ 0), (P_{28}\ 0\ 0\ 0)\}$
                $\text{AF}((P_{13}\ 1\ 1\ 1), (P_{14}\ 1\ 1\ 1)) \Longrightarrow \{(P_{29}\ 1\ 1\ 1), (P_{30}\ 1\ 1\ 1), (P_{31}\ 1\ 1\ 1), (P_{32}\ 1\ 1\ 1)\}$
                $\text{AF}((P_{17}\ 1\ 0\ 1), (P_{18}\ 1\ 0\ 1)) \Longrightarrow \{(P_{33}\ 0\ 0\ 0), (P_{34}\ 1\ 0\ 1), (P_{35}\ 1\ 1\ 0), (P_{36}\ 1\ 1\ 1)\}$
                $\text{AF}((P_{21}\ 1\ 1\ 0), (P_{22}\ 1\ 1\ 0)) \Longrightarrow \{(P_{37}\ 1\ 1\ 1), (P_{38}\ 1\ 1\ 0), (P_{39}\ 1\ 0\ 1), (P_{40}\ 0\ 0\ 0)\}$

Generation 4: $\text{AF}((P_{33}\ 0\ 0\ 0), (P_{40}\ 0\ 0\ 0)) \Longrightarrow \{(P_{41}\ 0\ 0\ 0), (P_{42}\ 0\ 0\ 0), (P_{43}\ 0\ 0\ 0), (P_{44}\ 0\ 0\ 0)\}$
                $\text{AF}((P_{34}\ 1\ 0\ 1), (P_{38}\ 1\ 1\ 0)) \Longrightarrow \{(P_{45}\ 1\ 0\ 1), (P_{46}\ 0\ 0\ 0), (P_{47}\ 1\ 1\ 1), (P_{48}\ 1\ 1\ 0)\}$
                $\text{AF}((P_{35}\ 1\ 1\ 0), (P_{39}\ 1\ 0\ 1)) \Longrightarrow \{(P_{49}\ 1\ 1\ 0), (P_{50}\ 1\ 1\ 1), (P_{51}\ 0\ 0\ 0), (P_{52}\ 1\ 0\ 1)\}$
                $\text{AF}((P_{36}\ 1\ 1\ 1), (P_{37}\ 1\ 1\ 1)) \Longrightarrow \{(P_{53}\ 1\ 1\ 1), (P_{54}\ 1\ 1\ 1), (P_{55}\ 1\ 1\ 1), (P_{56}\ 1\ 1\ 1)\}$

Figure 11.5 Mendel's pea experiments with hidden features. A pea is represented as $(P_i\ color\ m\ f)$.

Procedure Search-Rel-Terms(S, T):

1   Let *Difference* = Search-Action-Independent-Rel-Terms(S, T),
2   If *Difference* $\neq$ FAIL,
3   Then return *Difference* to the rule reviser,
4   Else identify the relevant history of S and T,
5   Define new predicates based on the difference between the histories of S and T,
6   Return the difference so found to the rule reviser.

Figure 11.6 Search for both action-independent and action-dependent terms.

ation, while Mendel's experiments lasted eight years. Of course, he might have had the idea very early in his experiments and used the later experiments to verify his hypothesis. Second, when defining hidden features, LIVE assumes that children's color is determined only by their ancestors' color. Mendel may have considered many more features and their combinations. If children's color is determined by parents' height, LIVE's discovery method will not always work.

Nevertheless, the discovery of genes is a natural example of hidden features that lie outside a given concept language (or an axiomatic system). Unlike their construction in previous discovery systems, such as BACON [52] and STABB [123], these hidden features are not functional combinations of any observable terms inside the language; rather, they stand by themselves. In this example, even though the first generation's m and f are equivalent to their observable color, they are by no means *determined* by the colors. Some interesting characteristics will become clear in the next section, as we compare hidden features with theoretical terms.

11.5 The Recursive Nature of Theoretical Terms

By definition, theoretical terms are those terms that cannot be observed directly but are derived from observable features. The concept of *torque* in the balance beam environment and genes in Mendel's experiments are two examples. However, whether such terms can be defined based on given experiments and observable features depends on how such terms are defined.

Lesniewski has proposed that definitions should satisfy two conditions, which Suppes [118, p. 153] has described intuitively:

> Two criteria which make more specific ... intuitive ideas about the character of definitions are that (i) a defined symbol should always be eliminable from any formula of the theory, and (ii) a new definition does not permit the proof of relationships among the old symbols which were previously unprovable; that is, it does not function as a creative axiom.

Following Suppes, we will refer to these two criteria as *eliminability* and *noncreativity*. Tarski [122, pp. 301–302] has proven a theorem that a term can be defined from existing terms if and only if its definition can be derived from the primitive terms and axioms. These criteria and theorem, often repeated in works of logic, stem from the notion that definitions are mere notational abbreviations, allowing theory to be stated in a more compact form without changing its content.

More recently, Simon [113] has proposed a somewhat weaker condition called *general definability*, which says that a term can generally be defined by means of other terms if it can be defined when a sufficient number of observations are taken. His argument is based on the analysis that some theoretical terms that should be defined cannot be under Tarski's criteria, and if observations are sufficient then theoretical terms can be both eliminable and creative simultaneously. Here we briefly repeat his axiomatization of Ohm's law, for it is the best example to illustrate his argument.

Γ is a system of Ohmic observations if and only if there exist D, r, and c such that

1. $\Gamma = \langle D, r, c \rangle$;

2. D is a nonempty set;

3. r and c are functions from D into the real numbers; and

4. for all $x \in D, r(x) > 0$ and $c(x) > 0$.

Γ' is an Ohmic circuit if and only if there exist D, r, c, b, and v such that

5. $\Gamma' = \langle D, r, c, b, v \rangle$;

6. $\Gamma = \langle D, r, c \rangle$ is a system of Ohmic observations;

7. v and b are real numbers;

8. for all $x \in D$,

$$c(x) = \frac{v}{b + r(x)} \qquad (11.3)$$

In this system, r and c are the observables (the external resistance and the current, respectively), and b and v are theoretical terms (the internal resistance and the voltage of the battery, respectively). However, according to the method of Padoa [122, pp. 304–305], v and b are not definable in the system above, as they should be, unless the following condition is added:

9. D contains at least two members with distinct r's and c's.

This is because after two such observations, (c_1, r_1) and (c_2, r_2), b and v can be uniquely defined as follows:

$$b = \frac{c_2 r_2 - c_1 r_1}{c_1 - c_2} \qquad (11.4)$$

$$v = \frac{c_2 r_2 - c_1 r_1}{c_1 - c_2} \qquad (11.5)$$

Furthermore, if we substitute these values for v and b in equation 11.3, and substitute a third observation (c_3, r_3) for $c(x)$ and $r(x)$, respectively, then we obtain a relation among three pairs of observations. Thus, the system becomes creative because the relation can hold among any three pairs of observations. Simon's general definability includes the condition that a sufficient number of observations must be made to uniquely determine the values of theoretical terms like v and b.

However, Simon did not make any further distinctions among observations. His approach is suitable for time-independent environments, such as an Ohmic circuit and a balance beam, because the values of theoretical terms depend only on the values of observable features regardless of when and in which order the observations are made. In the Ohmic circuit, for example, the values of b and v depend only on the values of the r's and c's; thus any two observations in the circuit can be used to define b and v. Examining equations 11.4 and 11.5 carefully, we can see that (1) no theoretical terms appear on the righthand side of the equations and (2) the equations do not incorporate any element of time.

In action-dependent environments, the situation is not as simple because of the order of the actions. The values of theoretical terms can be different at different times even though the values of observable features at those times may appear the same. For example, in Mendel's experiments, the values of m and f are different for P_3 and P_{17} even though they are both green. If we examine how m and f are defined, we can see that the theoretical terms are defined recursively; the definition has a clear sense of time because they are linked by the action AF:

Before AF (parent's m and f): $((m_i\ f_i)(m_j\ f_j))$
After AF (children's m and f): $((m_i\ m_j)(m_i\ f_j)(f_i\ m_j)(f_i\ f_j))$

In general, theoretical terms might have to be defined recursively in time-dependent environments. These terms do not depend on the values of observable features at the current time but on the history of the observable features and the actions; for example, the m and f for purebred peas depend on their ancestors' color. Furthermore, these terms also depend on their own history. For example, the m and f of hybrids depend on their parent's m and f.

In order to both define and use a set of theoretical terms T in an action-dependent environment, the following three functions might have to be determined:

$D()$, how T is computed from existing terms, if possible;

$U()$, how T is used to determine the values of observable features; and

$I()$, how T is inherited by the actions.

Since theoretical terms in a action-dependent environment are defined recursively on themselves, the first *definition* function $D()$ requires knowing where the first generation of theoretical terms came from. This function cannot always be defined because it is equivalent to asking where the first egg came from. However, in Mendel's experiments, we assume that the purebreds' m and f are the same as their color because all their ancestors are known to have the same color. (Having such a fact is not equal to having $D()$ because m and f may differ from the color of the peas if the peas are not purebred.) Nevertheless, in that environment, the time line between the purebreds and the hybrids provides a starting point for using the recursive definitions. However, whether such starting points always exist and are identifiable in any action-dependent environment is an open question. Furthermore, if no such starting point exists, that is, if no $D()$ exists, then whether or not these recursive theoretical terms are identifiable is another unresolved question.

The second *utilize* function, $U()$, tells us how the theoretical terms are used at a particular time. If $U()$ exists, then the theoretical terms are *meaningful* (see [113]) because they determine, and thus predict, the values of observable features. For example, in Mendel's experiments, a pea's m and f determine its color. This may suggest that, at any particular time, these recursively defined theoretical terms may not be eliminable because they not only determine the values of observable features at that time but also preserve historical information. This is another deviation from previous definitions of identifiability, which applied only to time-independent environments.

Finally, the third function $I()$ is the useful definition of recursive theoretical terms. This *inherit* function tells us how such terms are developed and, once they are identified, how they change with time (actions can also be viewed as time). In some sense, once we know the function $I()$ and the current values of theoretical terms T, then we can use T without knowing the actual definition of T. The function $I()$ also indicates that actions may play important roles in defining recursive theoretical terms in action-dependent environments. Further study is needed to utilize such "floating" definitions in our attempts to form scientific theories computationally.

Using this analysis, we can safely say that theoretical terms can be recursive, that is, not defined in a concrete sense but defined by how they are inherited through actions. It is important to note that theoretical terms can be derived from observable features, but also that they can be derived and defined from themselves. These recursive terms add some interesting extensions to the concept of the identifiability of theoretical terms [111].

11.6 Comparison with Other Discovery Systems

11.6.1 Closed-Eye versus Open-Eye Discovery

Compared with previous discovery systems in mathematics, like AM [54] and ARE [102], learning from the environment has an interesting difference. It not only thinks but also interacts with the surrounding environment. This property is very important if a system is to discover novel things that are unknown to its designer. We shall call systems with such an ability *open-eye* discovery systems and those that lack this ability *closed-eye* discovery systems.

AM is a system designed to discover "interesting" mathematical concepts and functions. It starts with a small set of primitive concepts and functions, and then launches a search with a set of powerful concept-manipulating operators. The search is guided by how interesting a concept is, which is determined solely by a set of fixed heuristics. Since AM does not interact with any external environment, it is a closed-eye discovery system.

In learning from the environment, how interesting new concepts are is determined by evaluation in the environment, not by the learner itself. In different environments, different concepts are learned. In a sense, the environment plays the role of teacher; the learner asks questions through predictions. Thus, any system that learns from the environment is open-eye.

Compared to previous open-eye discovery systems like BACON, LIVE's discovery is more autonomous. Our system not only finds the regularity in a given set of data, as BACON did, but also detects when a discovery is needed and collects examples itself.

11.6.2 Discrimination and the STABB System

Besides their use in discovery, hidden features are also studied as a problem of shifting biases in learning. Utgoff [123, 124] has designed a program called STABB for automating such a process in inductive concept learning when the initial concept space is biased. In his framework, the learner starts with a restricted hypothesis space (a bias) and shifts to a better one using the following three steps:

1. recommending (via heuristics) a new concept description to be added to the concept description language,

2. translating recommendations into new concept descriptions that are formally expressed in the concept description language, and

3. assimilating any new concepts into the restricted space of hypotheses so that the organization of the hypothesis space is maintained.

However, since it does not compare failures with successes for learning, STABB has encountered some difficulty in properly assimilating newly defined terms into its restricted hypothesis space. An example of this kind is the term "even integer," defined in STABB when the system notices that the same sequence of operators leads the state $\int(\cos^7 x)dx$ to a success but the state $\int(\cos^6 x)dx$ to a failure. When describing how his "constraints back-propagation" procedure assimilates a new term, Utgoff [124, p. 134] writes, "the procedure assimilates a new description NS by adding a new grammar rule of the form $d \Rightarrow NS$. The description d is the unconstrained description that was used in the domain of the corresponding operator." Thus, the term "even integer" has to be assimilated under the real numbers instead of the integers because the domain of the corresponding operator is the real numbers.

During the construction of "even integer," STABB only considers the successful problem-solving trace from the state $\int(\cos^7 x)dx$ but ignores the failure trace from the state $\int(\cos^6 x)dx$. From our point of view, the new term "even integer" is necessary only because $\int(\cos^7 x)dx$ and $\int(\cos^6 x)dx$ are indistinguishable in the current language yet yield different results when the same sequence of operators is applied. If we compare these two states, it is easy to see that 6 and 7 are indistinguishable in the current language because the least general concept, *integer*, includes both 6 and 7, and that all concepts that are more specific than *integer* exclude both 6 and 7. Thus, it is the concept of *integer*, not anything else, that needs further discrimination. Naturally, after "even integer" is defined, it should be assimilated for the purpose of discriminating integers, not real numbers.

11.6.3   LIVE as an Integrated Discovery System

In their book on scientific discovery, Langley and others [53] have outlined a system that infers Mendel's model by integrating two separate systems: GLAUBER, a data-driven system that can form classes from instances, and DALTON, a theory-driven system that can infer internal structures based on reactions between classes. Using a given high-level predicate *child-has-quality* and Mendel's data, the first system, GLAUBER, can divide the peas into three classes, G (pure greens), G'

(hybrid greens), and Y (pure yellow), and constructs four rules to describe the reactions between these classes:

$$(GG) \rightarrow (G)$$
$$(YY) \rightarrow (Y)$$
$$(GY) \rightarrow (G')$$
$$(G'G') \rightarrow (GG'Y)$$

The first two rules state that pure green peas produce only pure green offspring and that pure yellow peas produce only pure yellow offspring. The third rule states that crossing pure green and pure yellow peas produces only mixed green offspring. The fourth rule states that breeding hybrid green peas generates offspring in all three classes.

Given these rules, the second system, DALTON, can infer that two primitive traits (say, g and y) are required and decide that the genotype G can be modeled by the pair $(g\ g)$, that Y can be modeled by the pair $(y\ y)$, and that G' can be modeled by the pair $(g\ y)$. These structural inferences are then passed back to GLAUBER to form a law stating that g is the dominant trait of peas' color.

Although the pipeline of GLAUBER and DALTON seems capable of inferring Mendel's model, these two systems are still separate programs. Neither has any procedure to use if the information flow contains errors, nor can one system's search help the other. For example, if the classes or the laws generated by GLAUBER are incorrect, then DALTON's search for substructures may fail or return fruitless results. Moreover, this pipeline style of integration cannot explain convincingly why GLAUBER thinks that *child-has-quality* is the key feature to consider or why DALTON must infer the particular substructures g and y.

Unlike GLAUBER and DALTON, LIVE integrates the search for new laws (classes) and the search for new terms (substructures) naturally. As we have seen in this chapter, if a law's prediction fails, LIVE searches for hidden features, and the resulting features help LIVE form better laws. At any stage, neither the laws nor the hidden features are required to be completely correct. The discovery process in LIVE is an interaction between these two search spaces.

CHAPTER 12

LIVE'S PERFORMANCE

This chapter describes the performance of LIVE on experiments chosen from several environments: the Tower of Hanoi environment with different learners, the balance beam experiments, Mendel's pea hybridization experiments, and the HAND-EYE version of the Tower of Hanoi. In some of the environments, LIVE is tested with various conditions. The results obtained from experiments demonstrate the strengths and weaknesses of LIVE.

LIVE is currently implemented in Common Lisp and runs on any Sun workstation or IBM PC. The times recorded in this chapter are obtained from an IBM PC with 10 megabytes of primary memory. When running, LIVE interacts with an "environment" process, which is specified in separate Lisp files (see Appendix A); the communication is conducted through symbols exported from the environment. Thus, when changing domains or conditions within a particular environment, only the environment files need be replaced.

12.1   LIVE as LOGIC1

The LOGIC1 learner is defined in Section 2.4, and the implementation of its environment is in Appendix A.1. There are three kinds of experiments in this section: experiments with different goals, experiments with different exploration plans, and experiments using different numbers of disks in the Tower of Hanoi environment.

As we pointed out in Section 8.4.3, LIVE's problem solving in this environment is guided by a given domain-specific heuristic, namely, whenever LIVE faces the decision of where to put the disk presently in hand, it always chooses the "other" peg (the one not mentioned in the most recent goal).

12.1.1 Experiments with Different Goals

Table 12.1 shows LIVE's performance in the environment with different goals. In the experiments, three disks were used, all were initially on PEG1, and the exploration plan was to pick DISK1 from PEG1 and put it down on PEG2. Table 12.1 (and all the tables in this section) is set up as follows: The first column shows expressions of the goals, the second column shows the total number of steps (including both actions and subgoal proposing) LIVE spent on the problem and, in parentheses, the last step at which LIVE revised its rules; the third column shows the CPU time (LIVE was not compiled when these experiments were run); the fourth column shows the number of exploring actions made; the fifth lists the num-

Goal Expression	No. of Steps*	CPU Time (sec.)	No. of Exploring Actions	No. of Surprises	No. of Experiments	No. of Rules Learned
ON(DISK1 PEG3) ON(DISK2 PEG3) ON(DISK3 PEG3)	32 (15)	191.59	2	4	1	4
ON(DISK3 PEG3) ON(DISK2 PEG3) ON(DISK1 PEG3)	40 (12)	231.48	2	4	1	4
ON(DISK2 PEG3) ON(DISK1 PEG3) ON(DISK3 PEG3)	52 (38)	273.23	2	4	1	4
ON(DISK3 PEG1) ON(DISK2 PEG3) ON(DISK1 PEG3)	8 (2)	37.31	2	0	0	2
ON(DISK3 PEG3) ON(DISK2 PEG1) ON(DISK1 PEG3)	36 (12)	201.87	2	4	1	4
ON(DISK1 PEG1) ON(DISK2 PEG1) ON(DISK3 PEG3)	65 (30)	348.61	2	5	2	4

* The number in parentheses is the last step at which LIVE revised its rules.

The testing conditions were as follows:
   Number of disks: 3
   Initial state: ON(DISK1 PEG1) ON(DISK2 PEG1) ON(DISK3 PEG1)
   Exploration plan: Pick(DISK1 PEG1) Put(DISK1 PEG2)

Table 12.1 Experiments with different goals.

ber of surprises that arose in the plan execution; the sixth shows the number of
experiments conducted by LIVE (which is equal to the number of errors detected
at the planning time; see Section 10.2); and the last column shows the total number
of rules learned.

The first three experiments listed in Table 12.1 test how LIVE behaves when the
same goals are expressed in a different order. As we can see, the learning results
are the same, but the total time (including both learning and problem solving) is
inversely proportional to the correctness of the given goal expression. For example,
the first goal expression is the worst (for it implies that smaller disks are always
put on the target peg before larger ones), but LIVE's running time is the shortest.
These experiments indicate that LIVE prefers to have surprises or errors happen
early in problem solving; it can then learn the correct rules before wasting too
much time trying to solve the goals with a set of incorrect rules. For example,
LIVE spends the longest time in the third experiment because it does not meet any
surprise or error until both DISK1 and DISK2 are already on the target peg. These
experiments suggest that learning correct rules is more important than making
progress in problem solving.

The remaining experiments show LIVE's performance when the goals themselves
are different. The fourth experiment shows that if the goal is too trivial to achieve,
LIVE might not learn all the rules in one run (but it will when new and more difficult
goals are given). In this particular experiment, the goals and the exploration plan
are so well arranged that LIVE has no chance to make any mistakes, and it is happy
to learn two incomplete rules in the exploration.

The last experiment is also interesting; it shows that learning is sensitive to
different problem-solving situations. In this run, the particular arrangement of the
goals causes LIVE to make more mistakes and hence make more experiments to
learn the correct rules. Consequently, both learning time and problem-solving time
in this problem are longer than in the other experiments. Since this test run is the
most typical of LIVE's behavior and thus the most informative, we have included
its detailed running trace in Appendix B.

Note that in all these experiments, four rules are always learned, two rules for
the action Pick and two for the action Put. This is because the actions employed in
the exploration are so informative that LIVE does not create any unfruitful rules.
In the next section, we will see how LIVE behaves if the exploration plan is not so
perfect.

12.1.2   Experiments with Different Explorations

This section presents some experiments in which LIVE used imperfect exploration
plans. The set of experiments in Table 12.2 was conducted under the same testing
conditions as in Table 12.1 except for the exploration plans; the set of experiments
in Table 12.3 had different initial states, goals, and exploration plans from the
experiments in Table 12.1 and 12.2.

Goal Expression	No. of Steps*	CPU Time (sec.)	No. of Exploring Actions	No. of Surprises	No. of Experiments	No. of Rules Learned
ON(DISK1 PEG3) ON(DISK2 PEG3) ON(DISK3 PEG3)	32 (15)	188.23	4	4	1	5
ON(DISK3 PEG3) ON(DISK2 PEG1) ON(DISK1 PEG3)	36 (12)	206.53	4	4	1	5
ON(DISK1 PEG1) ON(DISK2 PEG1) ON(DISK3 PEG3)	57 (22)	299.26	4	4	1	5

* The number in parentheses is the last step at which LIVE revised its rules.

The testing conditions were as follows:
   Number of disks: 3
   Initial state: ON(DISK1 PEG1) ON(DISK2 PEG1) ON(DISK3 PEG1)
   Exploration plan 1: Pick(DISK3 PEG1) Put(DISK3 PEG2)
   Exploration plan 2: Pick(DISK1 PEG1) Put(DISK1 PEG2)

Table 12.2   Some experiments from Table 12.1 with different exploration plans.

In each set of experiments, there were two exploration plans. Note that the first exploration plan was not effective because picking up DISK3, which was underneath DISK1 and DISK2, had no effect in the environment. To run these tests, we forced LIVE to use this plan first. In doing so, LIVE created two no-change rules in the exploration and attempted to use them to achieve the given goals. Since these two new rules did not specify any changes in the environment, planning for a solution failed and LIVE was forced to do some more exploration using the second exploration plan. These simple experiments demonstrate that the quality of an exploration plan has a large impact on LIVE's problem-solving performance.

Comparing these experiments with those in Table 12.1 shows that although different explorations do not affect LIVE's behavior very much, two things do change: (1) LIVE learns five rules instead of four, and (2) LIVE takes less time to solve problems if it explores the environment more thoroughly before it starts to attack the given goals.

The extra rule is created during the ineffective exploration when LIVE does the Put action when nothing is in hand. The rules look like the following:

Goal Expression	No. of Steps*	CPU Time (sec.)	No. of Exploring Actions	No. of Surprises	No. of Experiments	No. of Rules Learned
ON(DISK1 PEG3) ON(DISK2 PEG3) ON(DISK3 PEG3)	8 (25)	160.00	4	3	0	5
ON(DISK3 PEG2) ON(DISK2 PEG3) ON(DISK1 PEG1)	10 (29)	178.59	4	3	0	5
ON(DISK1 PEG2) ON(DISK2 PEG2) ON(DISK3 PEG2)	14 (31)	193.24	4	4	1	5
ON(DISK1 PEG2) ON(DISK2 PEG1) ON(DISK3 PEG3)	16 (45)	252.29	4	3	0	5

* The number in parentheses is the last step at which LIVE revised its rules.

The testing conditions were as follows:

Number of disks: 3
Initial state: ON(DISK1 PEG2) ON(DISK2 PEG1) ON(DISK3 PEG1)
Exploration plan 1: Pick(DISK3 PEG1) Put(DISK3 PEG1)
Exploration plan 2: Pick(DISK2 PEG1) Put(DISK2 PEG1)

Table 12.3 Experiments with different initial states, goals, and exploration plans from Table 12.1.

Condition:	ON(x p) [x] [p]
Action:	Put(x p)
Predict:	ON(x p) [x] [p]

This rule is useless in problem solving because it does not specify any changes in the environment. However, it does no harm to the learning and problem solving either. Instead, such a dummy rule prevents LIVE from creating similar rules again if its future exploration includes more actions like putting nothing down.

A third difference is that if LIVE does more exploration, then the total time for solving a given problem may be reduced. For example, the third problem in Table 12.2, which took LIVE 348.61 CPU seconds to solve in Table 12.1, is solved in 299.26 seconds here. This phenomenon is consistent with the idea that LIVE prefers early errors to late errors; the ineffective exploration enables LIVE to be surprised in the effective exploration.

Regarding concept learning, doing ineffective exploration before effective exploration is like presenting a learning program with negative examples before any positive examples. The fact that LIVE's behavior in this case is no worse than the cases in Table 12.1 demonstrates again that the complementary discrimination learning method is less sensitive to the order in which the training instances are presented.

12.1.3   Experiments with Different Numbers of Disks

Table 12.4 lists the results when the environment has four disks; Table 12.5 lists results for five disks. All other testing conditions are the same as those in Table 12.1. Except for a longer time required to solve the problems, LIVE's learning behavior remains the same. For learning the same number of rules, LIVE requires approximately the same number of steps, surprises, and experiments.

One may wonder why the size of the problem does not increase the difficulty of learning. The reason is that the rules learned by LIVE are developed for the most general cases; they do not depend on how many disks are on a peg, but how the disk in the action is related to the others. In fact, the rules are not only useful for a larger number of disks but also transferable from one experiment to another. In other words, rules learned in one problem work in other related problems as well.

Goal Expression	No. of Steps*	CPU Time (sec.)	No. of Exploring Actions	No. of Surprises	No. of Experiments	No. of Rules Learned
ON(DISK4 PEG3) ON(DISK3 PEG3) ON(DISK2 PEG3) ON(DISK1 PEG3)	116 (14)	1035.49	2	4	1	4
ON(DISK1 PEG2) ON(DISK2 PEG1) ON(DISK3 PEG1) ON(DISK4 PEG2)	127 (20)	1125.58	2	4	1	4

* The number in parentheses is the last step at which LIVE revised its rules.

The testing conditions were as follows:
   Number of disks: 4
   Initial state: ON(DISK1 PEG1) ON(DISK2 PEG1) ON(DISK3 PEG1) ON(DISK4 PEG1)
   Exploration plan: Pick(DISK1 PEG1) Put(DISK1 PEG2)

Table 12.4   Experiments with different four disks.

Goal Expression	No. of Steps[*]	CPU Time (sec.)	No. of Exploring Actions	No. of Surprises	No. of Experiments	No. of Rules Learned
ON(DISK1 PEG3) ON(DISK2 PEG3) ON(DISK3 PEG3) ON(DISK4 PEG3) ON(DISK5 PEG3)	340 (16)	4630.75	2	4	1	4

[*] The number in parentheses is the last step at which LIVE revised its rules.

The testing conditions were as follows:

Number of disks: 5

Initial state: ON(DISK1 PEG1) ON(DISK2 PEG1) ON(DISK3 PEG1)
ON(DISK4 PEG1) ON(DISK5 PEG1)

Exploration plan: Pick(DISK1 PEG1) Put(DISK1 PEG2)

Table 12.5   Experiments with different five disks.

12.2   LIVE as LOGIC2 (Translucent Environments)

In this section, LIVE is instantiated as the LOGIC2 learner defined in Section 2.4. To make the task more vivid, we gave the elements in the Tower of Hanoi environment different physical meanings. In particular, we defined an environment called the "Plates of Hanoi" as follows: There are three balls and three plates. The balls have different sizes and they can be moved from one plate to another according to the following rules:

1. Only one ball can be picked up at a time.

2. A ball can be put onto a plate only if that ball is smaller than all the balls on that plate. (Attempts to put a ball onto a plate that contains a smaller ball will cause the ball in hand to be popped onto the table.)

3. A ball can be picked up from a plate only if it is the smallest on that plate. (Note that if a ball is on the table, no ball can be picked up from any plate.)

The Plate of Hanoi environment differs from the standard Tower of Hanoi environment in two ways. First, when the learner does an illegal Put action, the ball in hand is dropped onto the table (so the table is another object in the environment) instead of staying in hand. This change makes the environment more realistic: Actions always change the environment regardless of whether they are legal or not.

Second, balls in a plate do not stack, and so there are no particular spatial relations between balls. Balls on a plate can only be distinguished by size. When the percept *size* is taken away from the learner, the environment becomes translucent.

Before going to the LOGIC2 learner, let us first discuss two variants of LOGIC1 and see how they behave in this more realistic environment. The first variant is called LOGIC-PUT, which is the same as LOGIC1 except that its percepts and actions allow TABLE as a parameter and its Put action drops a ball on the table if the action is illegal. LOGIC-PUT performs just as well as LOGIC1. The only difference is that the rule for the action Put is different from Rule4 in Chapter 10. The new Rule4 is as follows:

RuleID: Rule4
Condition: $INHAND(x) \land \neg ON(x\ p) \land ON(y\ p)$
Action: $Put(x\ p)$
Prediction: $ON(x\ TABLE) \land \neg INHAND(x)$
Sibling: Rule2

Notice the difference in the prediction. Instead of saying the ball is still in hand, the prediction is that the ball will be on the table. (Here we assume that the learner knows TABLE is a permanent object; thus when the rule is created, TABLE is not generalized into a variable.) Since the rules for the Pick action are the same as in LOGIC1, balls on TABLE are picked up in the process of reaching the goals.

The second variant of LOGIC1 is called LOGIC-FEATURE. It is exactly the same as LOGIC-PUT except that it cannot perceive the relation SIZE>; instead it perceives a feature of object called *size* (e.g., $size(BALL3) = 3$). In addition, it is given two relations, $>$ and $=$, as m-constructors of its mental language.

To LOGIC-FEATURE, the two states in Figure 10.5 that enable LOGIC1 to create Rule6 and Rule8 are perceived as follows (replace DISK with BALL and PEG with PLATE, respectively):

$S_0 =$ {BALL1, BALL2, BALL3, PLATE1, PLATE2, PLATE3, $INHAND(x)$, $ON(y\ \ p)$, $ON(BALL1\ PLATE2)$, $size(y) = 3$, $size(x) = 2$, $size(BALL1) = 1$}
Bindings: $x/BALL2, p/PLATE1, y/BALL3$

$T_0 =$ {BALL1, BALL2, BALL3, PLATE1, PLATE2, PLATE3, $INHAND(x)$, $ON(BALL3\ PLATE1)$, $ON(y\ p)$, $size(BALL3) = 3$, $size(x) = 2$, $size(y) = 1$}
Bindings: $x/BALL2, p/PLATE2, y/BALL1$

Since SIZE> is not perceivable, LOGIC-FEATURE cannot find any relational difference between S_0 and T_0 according to the incremental enlargement heuristic discussed in Section 10.2.1.

However, as we saw in Section 11.3, new action-independent relations may be defined in terms of existing features and mental m-constructors. Specifically, when given two states that the learner's percepts cannot distinguish, the learner applies its mental relations and functions to the objects in these two states to see if any new relations or terms can be defined to distinguish them. In the current example, since LOGIC-FEATURE has mental relations $>$ and $=$, applying them to S_0 and T_0 results in the following expanded states:

$S_0 =$ {BALL1, BALL2, BALL3, PLATE1, PLATE2, PLATE3, INHAND(x), ON(y p), ON(BALL1 PLATE2), $size(y) = 3$, $size(x) = 2$, $size$(BALL1) $= 1$, SGR(y x), SGR(y BALL1), SGR(x BALL1)}

Bindings: x/BALL2, p/PLATE1, y/BALL3

$T_0 =$ {BALL1, BALL2, BALL3, PLATE1, PLATE2, PLATE3, INHAND(x), ON(BALL3 PLATE1), ON(y p), $size$(BALL3) $=$ 3, $size(x) = 2$, $size(y) = 1$, SGR(BALL3 x), SGR(BALL3 y), SGR(x y)}

Bindings: x/BALL2, p/PLATE2, y/BALL1

where the relation SGR(x y) is defined as $>(size(x)\ size(y))$. (We note here that all the plates are the same size, which is larger than any of balls. For simplicity, however, these relations are not included in the description.)

Corresponding to the algorithm in Figure 11.3, the relation r is $>$, the function f is identity, and the feature functions are $p_1 = size$ and $p_2 = size$, respectively. From these two enlarged states, the difference can be found easily. The relation $>(size(x)\ size(y))$ is true in T_0 but false in S_0. Since it is the relation $>(size(x)\ size(y))$ that makes the difference, a new relation SGR(x y) is defined as $>(size(x)\ size(y))$, and the difference SGR(x y) is then returned to the rule reviser. Subsequently, LOGIC-FEATURE will always apply the relation SGR to objects. Since this new relation is equivalent to the relation SIZE$>$, LOGIC-FEATURE is now functionally equivalent to LOGIC-PUT.

We now turn our attention to LOGIC2. The main point is to see if LIVE can learn from a translucent environment and discover hidden features. Technically speaking, LOGIC2 is just a restricted version of LOGIC-FEATURE: It cannot see the size of objects. To LOGIC2, balls are of the same size and the states S_0 and T_0 are perceived as follows:

$S_0 =$ {BALL1, BALL2, BALL3, PLATE1, PLATE2, PLATE3, INHAND(x), ON(y p), ON(BALL1 PLATE2)}

Bindings: x/BALL2, p/PLATE1, y/BALL3

$T_0 =$ {BALL1, BALL2, BALL3, PLATE1, PLATE2, PLATE3, INHAND(x), ON(BALL3 PLATE1), ON(y p)}

Bindings: x/BALL2, p/PLATE2, y/BALL1

Since LOGIC2 cannot perceive any features of objects, applying the mental functions and relations does not reveal any differences between these two states.

When situations like this arise, as specified in Figure 11.6, the learner must search the history of S_0 and T_0 and find differences there. New terms must be defined using not only percepts but also actions. These terms are defined to carry the difference to the present so that the learner can predict the future. In the current example, the hidden predicates that must be discovered by LOGIC2 are the following conditions for the actions Pick and Put, which we shall define as shown:

$$\text{Pickable}(x\ p)_t \equiv$$
$$\text{ON}(x\ p)_t \wedge \neg\text{INHAND}(z)_t \wedge$$
$$\neg(\text{ON}(y\ p)_t \wedge y\text{-was-put-on-}p\text{-more-recently-than-}x)$$

$$y\text{-was-put-on-}p\text{-more-recently-than-}x \equiv$$
$$\forall(n)\exists(n')(\text{Put}(x\ p)_{t-n} \wedge \text{Put}(y\ p)_{t-n'} \wedge (n' < n))$$

$$\text{Putable}(x\ p)_t \equiv$$
$$\text{INHAND}(x)_t \wedge$$
$$\neg(\text{ON}(y\ p)_t \wedge y\text{-was-pickable-from-}q\text{-when-}x\text{-on-}q)$$

$$y\text{-was-pickable-from-}q\text{-when-}x\text{-on-}q \equiv$$
$$\exists(n)(\text{ON}(y\ q)_{t-n} \wedge \text{ON}(x\ q)_{t-n} \wedge \text{Pick}(x\ q)_{t-n} \wedge \text{INHAND}(y)_{t-n+1})$$

The predicate $\text{Pickable}(x\ p)_t$ says that x can be picked up from p at time t if x is on p, the hand is empty, and there is no y on p such that y was put on p more recently than x. The predicate $\text{Putable}(x\ p)_t$ says that x can be put on p at time t if x is in hand and there is no y on p such that y was pickable from a plate q at a previous time when x was on q. From these definitions, one can see that action-dependent terms are defined in terms of both actions and percepts. Moreover, their values may depend on values in previous states and on actions taken. (In this sense, they are also known as *recursive theoretical terms*, see [111].)

To discover action-dependent terms, LIVE searches the history of S_0 and T_0 when Search-Action-Independent-Rel-Terms(S_0, T_0) returns FAIL. It then identifies two relevant historical sequences of S_0 and T_0 and finds the difference between them. This difference then becomes the definition of a new predicate that is returned to the rule reviser.

In the current example, the history of LIVE is listed in the first column of Table 12.6. As described in Section 10.2.1, each historical item contains a ruleID (omitted in this column), a state observation to which the rule's action was applied, and a set of variable bindings (also omitted in this column). As we can see, the item t_6 is what we call T_0. It is the current state in which the application of Rule4 resulted in a prediction failure. The item t_4 is what we call S_0, for it was the last successful application of Rule4 in the history. The second and third columns in Table 12.6 are the ancestor states of S_0 and T_0, respectively. They are "views" of

History	S_0's Ancestors Bindings: x/BALL2,p/PLATE2,y/BALL1	T_0's Ancestors Bindings: x/BALL2,p/PLATE1,y/BALL3
t_1: ON(BALL1 PLATE1) ON(BALL2 PLATE1) ON(BALL3 PLATE1) Pick(BALL1 PLATE1)	S_{-3} ON(y PLATE1) ON(x PLATE1) Pick(y PLATE1)	
t_2: INHAND(BALL1) ON(BALL2 PLATE1) ON(BALL3 PLATE1) Put(BALL1 PLATE2)	S_{-2} INHAND(y) ON(x PLATE1) Put(y p)	
t_3: ON(BALL1 PLATE2) ON(BALL2 PLATE1) ON(BALL3 PLATE1) Pick(BALL2 PLATE1)	S_{-1} ON(y p) ON(x PLATE1) Pick(x PLATE1)	T_{-3} ON(y p) ON(x p) Pick(x p)
t_4: INHAND(BALL2) ON(BALL1 PLATE2) ON(BALL3 PLATE1) Put(BALL2 PLATE2)	S_0 ON(y p) INHAND(x) Put(x p)	T_{-2} ON(y p) INHAND(x) Put(x PLATE2)
t_5: ON(BALL1 PLATE2) ON(BALL2 TABLE) ON(BALL3 PLATE1) Pick(BALL2 TABLE)		T_{-1} ON(y p) ON(x TABLE) Pick(x TABLE)
t_6: INHAND(BALL2) ON(BALL1 PLATE2) ON(BALL3 PLATE1) Put(BALL2 PLATE1)		T_0 ON(y p) INHAND(x) Put(x p)

Table 12.6 Search for historical differences.

the items in the first column of the same row through the variable bindings of S_0 and T_0 (listed in the top rows of these two columns). Such views are created by copying the corresponding items from the first column, replacing the balls and plates with the variables according to the bindings, and then deleting those elements that have no variables. For example, S_{-1} is a view of t_3, with the bindings (x/BALL2, p/PLATE2, y/BALL1), in which ON(BALL1 PLATE2) is replaced by ON(y p), ON(BALL2 PLATE1) is replaced by ON(x PLATE1), ON(BALL3 PLATE1) is deleted, and Pick(BALL2 PLATE1) is replaced by Pick(x PLATE1). Likewise, T_{-3} is also a view of t_3, but with the bindings (x/BALL2, p/PLATE1, y/BALL3).

This particular way of viewing ancestor states from a particular rule application is a general heuristic, and a very powerful one, for identifying relevant histories. It focuses the learner's attention on the history of objects related to the current action. When comparing two histories, LIVE identifies the relevant historical sequences, say from time t_{0-u} to t_{0-v}, where $(0 - u) < (0 - v)$, and finds the difference there.

The time t_{0-u} is identified by searching back from T_0 and S_0 to the first states, say $T_{t_{0-u}}$ and $S_{t_{0-u}}$, where the objects (now represented as variables) that do not have apparent relations in T_0 and S_0 had some visible relations. In our current example, searching back from T_0 in this way leads to T_{-3} because the objects x and y, which are not related in T_0, were both on plate p. Likewise, searching from S_0 in the same way leads to S_{-3}.

The time t_{0-v} is identified by searching back from T_0 and S_0 to the first states, say $T_{t_{0-v}}$ and $S_{t_{0-v}}$, where the difference between $T_{t_{0-v}}$ and $S_{t_{0-v}}$ first becomes visible. In our example, this leads to T_{-2} and S_{-2}, where INHAND(y) was true in S_{-2} while INHAND(x) was true in T_{-2}.

After $(S_{0-u}, \ldots, S_{0-v})$ and $(T_{0-u}, \ldots, T_{0-v})$ are identified, the difference between these two historical sequences are those relations and actions (except the action at time $0 - v$) that appear in $(S_{0-u}, \ldots, S_{0-v})$ but not in $(T_{0-u}, \ldots, T_{0-v})$. In our current example, this difference is

$$\text{ON}(y\ \text{PLATE1})_{0-3} \wedge \text{ON}(x\ \text{PLATE1})_{0-3} \wedge \text{Pick}(y\ \text{PLATE1})_{0-3}$$
$$\wedge\ \text{INHAND}(y)_{0-3+1} \wedge \text{ON}(x\ \text{PLATE1})_{0-3+1}$$

Generalizing this difference, say PLATE1 to q, time 0 to t, and time -3 to $-n$, we have the definition of a new predicate:

$$\text{ON}(y\ q)_{t-n} \wedge \text{ON}(x\ q)_{t-n} \wedge \text{Pick}(y\ q)_{t-n} \wedge \text{INHAND}(y)_{t-n+1} \wedge \text{ON}(x\ q)_{t-n+1}$$

which is equivalent to the predicate y-was-pickable-from-q-when-x-on-q described in the definition of Putable above. This new predicate is then returned to the rule reviser, and a correct rule for Put is built.

12.3   LIVE on the Balance Beam

In this section, we consider LIVE's behavior in the balance beam environment, which was defined in Section 11.3. The implementation of the environment is

presented in Appendix A.2. Our main purpose here is to demonstrate how the order
of training instances and the given m-constructors influence LIVE's performance
in discovering hidden features. Since the task in this environment is to predict the
correct outcome, LIVE's problem-solving components, although inseparable from
the system as a whole, are not employed.

12.3.1 Experiments with Training Instances in Different Orders

Table 12.7 summarizes the particular run of LIVE described in Section 11.3. The
m-constructors are listed as the testing condition. The table is set up as follows:
The first column are the indices of the training tasks; the second column is the state
seen by LIVE; the third is LIVE's prediction; the fourth is the reason for LIVE's
prediction; the fifth is the accuracy of the prediction; and the last column is what
LIVE learned from the mistakes. In the fourth column, the reasons are expressed
as predicates, and they should be read together with the objects and their order in
the state (second) column. For instance, the reason WGR in row 4 should be read
as WGR(L R) (because L precedes R in state 4), while the reason WGR in row
5 should be read as WGR(R L) (because R precedes L in state 5). The predicate
TGR is the relational predicate *torque-greater*.

No.	State	Prediction	Reason	Accuracy	Learned
1	[L 3 1 1][R 3 1 1]				
2	[L 3 1 1][R 2 1 1]	balance		wrong	WGR
3	[L 3 3 1][R 3 2 1]	balance	WEQ	wrong	DGR
4	[L 3 3 1][R 2 4 1]	left	WGR	correct	
5	[R 4 1 1][L 2 3 1]	right	WGR	wrong	TGR
6	[L 2 2 1][R 4 1 1]	balance	¬TGR	correct	
7	[R 3 1 1][L 2 1 1]	right	TGR	correct	
8	[R 3 3 1][L 3 2 1]	right	TGR	correct	
9	[R 3 3 1][L 2 4 1]	right	TGR	correct	
10	[R 2 3 1][L 4 1 1]	right	TGR	correct	
11	[L 4 1 1][R 2 2 1]	balance	¬TGR	correct	
12	[L 3 3 1][R 2 4 1]	left	TGR	correct	
13	[L 2 3 1][R 4 1 1]	left	TGR	correct	
14	[L 2 2 1][R 4 1 1]	balance	¬TGR	correct	
15	[L 4 1 1][R 2 2 1]	balance	¬TGR	correct	

The testing conditions were as follows:
Constructor functions: *, +
Constructor relations: >, =

Table 12.7   The effect of order of the training instances.

As we can see from Table 12.7, the sequence of training tasks does a good job of leading to the discovery of the torque feature W*D and the relation TGR. Although LIVE initially believes that weight and distance are adequate for predicting the results, it soon meets a surprise (row 5) where it is forced to define the torque feature and its relation (see Section 11.3 for details).

However, such a good surprise can come earlier or later in the training. Whether and when LIVE will discover the torque feature and its relation mainly depends on whether and when such surprises happen. For instance, in Table 12.8, LIVE is so lucky that the second training task is a good surprise, and the torque feature is discovered immediately. On the other hand, in Table 12.9, LIVE does not find the torque feature until task 9.

12.3.2   Experiments with the Constructors in Different Orders

As we pointed out in Chapter 11, one of the weak points in LIVE's discovery method is that the necessary constructors must be given and they must be presented in some favorable order. The experiments in this section show the effects of constructors on LIVE's performance. First we give LIVE the same constructors as in Table 12.9 but in a different order; then we see how LIVE acts when given a larger set of constructors.

Table 12.10 shows a set of experiments conducted under the same testing conditions as those used in the last section except for the order of the constructor relations, which were presented in reverse order, = and then >.

No.	State	Prediction	Reason	Accuracy	Learned
1	[L 2 4 1][R 3 3 1]				
2	[L 2 2 1][R 4 1 1]	right		wrong	¬TGR
3	[L 3 1 1][R 3 1 1]	balance	¬TGR	correct	
4	[L 3 3 1][R 3 2 1]	left	TGR	correct	
5	[R 3 3 1][L 3 2 1]	right	TGR	correct	
6	[L 3 1 1][R 2 1 1]	left	TGR	correct	
7	[L 2 3 1][R 4 1 1]	left	TGR	correct	
8	[R 3 1 1][L 2 1 1]	right	TGR	correct	
9	[R 2 2 1][L 4 1 1]	balance	¬TGR	correct	

The testing conditions were as follows:

Constructor functions: *, +

Constructor relations: >, =

Table 12.8   An experiment with an early good surprise.

No.	State	Prediction	Reason	Accuracy	Learned
1	[L 3 2 1][R 3 3 1]				
2	[L 3 1 1][R 3 1 1]	right		wrong	DEQ
3	[R 2 4 1][L 3 3 1]	right	DGR	wrong	WGR
4	[L 3 1 1][R 2 1 1]	balance	DEQ	wrong	¬WEQ
5	[L 2 3 1][R 4 1 1]	left	¬WEQ DGR	correct	
6	[L 3 3 1][R 4 1 1]	left	¬WEQ DGR	correct	
7	[R 2 3 1][L 4 1 1]	right	¬WEQ DGR	correct	
8	[R 2 5 1][L 4 2 1]	right	¬WEQ DGR	correct	
9	[L 2 2 1][R 4 1 1]	left	¬WEQ DGR	wrong	¬TGR
10	[L 2 1 1][R 3 1 1]	right	TGR	correct	

The testing conditions were as follows:

Constructor functions: ∗, +

Constructor relations: >, =

Table 12.9   An experiment with a late good surprise.

No.	State	Prediction	Reason	Accuracy	Learned
1	[L 3 2 1][R 3 3 1]				
2	[L 3 1 1][R 3 1 1]	right		wrong	DEQ
3	[L 2 2 1][R 4 1 1]	left	DGR	wrong	WGR
4	[L 3 3 1][R 2 4 1]	balance	WGR ¬DGR	wrong	¬WGR
5	[L 3 1 1][R 2 1 1]	left	WGR	wrong	DEQ
6	[L 2 3 1][R 4 1 1]	left	DGR	correct	
7	[L 2 2 1][R 4 1 1]	left	DGR	wrong	W∗D=
8	[L 3 1 1][R 2 1 1]	left	¬(W∗D=)	correct	
9	[L 2 1 1][R 3 1 1]	left	¬(W∗D=)	wrong	WGR
10	[R 3 3 1][L 3 2 1]	left	¬(W∗D=)	wrong	WEQ DGR
11	[R 3 3 1][L 2 4 1]	balance	WGR ¬DGR	wrong	TGR
12	[R 2 3 1][L 4 1 1]	right	TGR	correct	
13	[R 2 2 1][L 4 1 1]	balance	¬TGR	correct	
14	[L 3 3 1][R 2 4 1]	left	TGR	correct	
15	[L 2 3 1][R 4 1 1]	left	TGR	correct	
16	[L 2 2 1][R 4 1 1]	balance	¬TGR	correct	
17	[L 4 1 1][R 2 2 1]	balance	¬TGR	correct	

The testing conditions were as follows:

Constructor functions: ∗, +

Constructor relations: =, >

Table 12.10   Experiments with the constructor relations in a different order.

No.	State	Prediction	Reason	Accuracy	Learned
1	[L 3 2 1][R 3 3 1]				
2	[L 3 1 1][R 3 1 1]	right		wrong	DEQ
3	[L 2 2 1][R 4 1 1]	left	DGR	wrong	WGR
4	[L 3 3 1][R 2 4 1]	balance	WGR ¬DGR	wrong	¬WGR
5	[L 3 1 1][R 2 1 1]	left	WGR	wrong	DEQ
6	[L 2 3 1][R 4 1 1]	left	DGR	correct	
7	[L 2 2 1][R 4 1 1]	left	DGR	wrong	W+D>
8	[L 3 1 1][R 2 1 1]	balance	W+D>	wrong	DEQ
9	[R 3 1 1][L 2 1 1]	right	DEQ W+D>	correct	
10	[R 3 3 1][L 3 2 1]	left	¬(W+DGR)	wrong	WEQ DGR
11	[R 3 3 1][L 2 4 1]	balance	WGR ¬DGR	wrong	DGR ¬WGR
12	[L 1 4 1][R 2 3 1]	right	DGR ¬WGR	correct	
13	[R 2 2 1][L 4 1 1]	right	DGR ¬WGR	wrong	W+D>
14	[L 3 3 1][R 2 4 1]	left	¬(W+D>)	correct	
15	[R 3 1 1][L 2 2 1]	right	¬(W+D>)	wrong	TGR
16	[L 2 2 1][R 4 1 1]	balance	¬TGR	correct	
17	[L 3 2 1][R 2 2 1]	left	TGR	correct	

The testing conditions were as follows:
  Constructor functions: +, *
  Constructor relations: >, =

Table 12.11   Experiments with the constructor functions in a different order.

As we can see in Table 12.10, because the relation = precedes >, LIVE considers = before > when defining a hidden feature W∗D. Therefore, at row 7, the relation W∗D= is constructed instead of TGR (W∗D>). As a result, LIVE continues to make mistakes on the following experiments (rows 8 through 11) until another unresolvable surprise (row 11) happens and TGR is defined.

Similarly, if we switch the order of constructor functions, as shown in Table 12.11, then LIVE constructs the hidden feature W+D (at row 7) before it discovers W∗D (at row 15). Consequently, it takes longer to learn the torque concept.

In general, when the order of constructors is not favorable for constructing the desired features and relations first, LIVE spends more time searching. When the training instances do not provide good surprises, LIVE sometimes defines many useless hidden features and can even fail to find any hidden features that can discriminate two indistinguishable states, as shown in step 13 of Table 12.12.

Note that the only difference between Table 12.11 and Table 12.12 is task 12. The reason LIVE fails in Table 12.12 is that when LIVE is surprised at step 15, whose state is ([R 3 1 1] [L 2 2 1]) with bindings x/L and y/R, step 12, whose state

No.	State	Prediction	Reason	Accuracy	Learned
1	[L 3 2 1][R 3 3 1]				
2	[L 3 1 1][R 3 1 1]	right		wrong	DEQ
3	[L 2 2 1][R 4 1 1]	left	DGR	wrong	WGR
4	[L 3 3 1][R 2 4 1]	balance	WGR ¬DGR	wrong	¬WGR
5	[L 3 1 1][R 2 1 1]	left	WGR	wrong	DEQ
6	[L 2 3 1][R 4 1 1]	left	DGR	correct	
7	[L 2 2 1][R 4 1 1]	left	DGR	wrong	W+D>
8	[L 3 1 1][R 2 1 1]	balance	W+D>	wrong	DEQ
9	[R 3 1 1][L 2 1 1]	right	DEQ W+D>	correct	
10	[R 3 3 1][L 3 2 1]	left	¬(W+D>)	wrong	WEQ DGR
11	[R 3 3 1][L 2 4 1]	balance	WGR ¬DGR	wrong	DGR ¬WGR
12	[R 2 3 1][L 4 1 1]	right	DGR ¬WGR	correct	
13	[R 2 2 1][L 4 1 1]	right	DGR ¬WGR	wrong	W+D>
14	[L 3 3 1][R 2 4 1]	left	¬(W+D>)	correct	
15	[R 3 1 1][L 2 2 1]	right	¬(W+D>)	wrong	FAIL
16	[L 2 2 1][R 4 1 1]				
17	[L 3 2 1][R 2 2 1]				

The testing conditions were as follows:

Constructor functions: +, *

Constructor relations: >, =

Table 12.12   An experiment where LIVE fails.

is ([R 2 3 1] [L 4 1 1]) with bindings x/R and y/L, is brought in for comparison. Unfortunately, with all the given constructors and features (including W+D and W*D), LIVE cannot find any new features that can discriminate these two states. One possible solution to this problem is to keep multiple hypothetical hidden features so that LIVE can backtrack when earlier hidden features cannot discriminate states that cause surprises.

12.3.3   Experiments with Larger Sets of Constructors

Just as the order of the given constructors affects LIVE's learning performance, so does the number of constructors. In this section, we give LIVE a larger set of constructors to try.

When the constructors are given in a favorable order as in Table 12.13, LIVE's learning performance is not affected. The reader can see that the experiments in Table 12.13 are the same as those in Table 12.7; even though the set of constructors is much larger here, LIVE's learning results are the same.

No.	State	Prediction	Reason	Accuracy	Learned
1	[L 3 1 1][R 3 1 1]				
2	[L 3 1 1][R 2 1 1]	balance		wrong	WGR
3	[L 3 3 1][R 3 2 1]	balance	WEQ	wrong	DGR
4	[L 3 3 1][R 2 4 1]	left	WGR	correct	
5	[R 4 1 1][L 2 3 1]	right	WGR	wrong	TGR
6	[L 2 2 1][R 4 1 1]	balance	¬TGR	correct	
7	[R 3 1 1][L 2 1 1]	right	TGR	correct	
8	[R 3 3 1][L 3 2 1]	right	TGR	correct	
9	[R 3 3 1][L 2 4 1]	right	TGR	correct	
10	[R 2 3 1][L 4 1 1]	right	TGR	correct	
11	[L 4 1 1][R 2 2 1]	balance	¬TGR	correct	
12	[L 3 3 1][R 2 4 1]	left	TGR	correct	
13	[L 2 3 1][R 4 1 1]	left	TGR	correct	
14	[L 2 2 1][R 4 1 1]	balance	¬TGR	correct	
15	[L 4 1 1][R 2 2 1]	balance	¬TGR	correct	

The testing conditions were as follows:

Constructor functions: $*, +, x^y, -, \max, \min$

Constructor relations: $>, =, <, \leq, \geq$

Table 12.13   An experiment with a larger set of constructors.

However, if the constructors are not given in a favorable order, then LIVE is swallowed in the vast space of possible hidden features and often fails to find any that are useful. Table 12.14 shows that when the constructor functions are given in a very bad order, LIVE is desperate to find the right hidden feature. In 15 steps, the system defines features like $\max(W\ D)$, and W^D. Continued running defines other features, like $(W^D)^{\max(WD)}$ and $(W + D)^{(W+D)}$. Since $*$ is far back in the constructor list, LIVE does not find the feature *torque* in these experiments.

12.4   LIVE's Discovery in Action-Dependent Environments

So far LIVE has been tested in two action-dependent environments. One is the artificial Plates of Hanoi environment defined for LOGIC2 in Section 12.2; the other is the simulation of Mendel's pea hybridization experiments in Section 11.4, in which LIVE discovers the concept of gene. The implementation of the pea hybridization environment is in Appendix A.3, and LIVE's performance is described in Section 11.4. Unfortunately, we have not found other natural action-dependent

No.	State	Prediction	Reason	Accuracy
1	[L 3 1 1][R 3 1 1]			
2	[L 3 1 1][R 2 1 1]	balance		wrong
3	[L 3 3 1][R 3 2 1]	balance	WEQ	wrong
4	[L 3 3 1][R 2 4 1]	left	WGR	correct
5	[L 2 3 1][R 4 1 1]	right	WGR	wrong
6	[L 2 2 1][R 4 1 1]	right	$\max(DW) >$	wrong
7	[R 3 1 1][L 2 1 1]	balance	$\neg(\max(DW) >)$	wrong
8	[R 3 3 1][L 3 2 1]	balance	WEQ	wrong
9	[R 3 3 1][L 2 4 1]	left	$\max(DW) >$	wrong
10	[R 2 3 1][L 4 1 1]	balance	WGR	wrong
11	[R 2 2 1][L 4 1 1]	right	DGR	wrong
12	[L 3 3 1][R 2 4 1]	right	$W^D >$	wrong
13	[L 2 3 1][R 4 1 1]	right	$W^D >$	wrong
14	[L 2 2 1][R 4 1 1]	balance	WGR	correct
15	[R 2 2 1][L 4 1 1]	balance	WGR	correct

The testing conditions were as follows:

Constructor functions: max, min, x^y, $-$, $+$, $*$

Constructor relations: $>$, $=$, $<$, $\leq$, $\geq$

Table 12.14 An experiment with many constructors in an unfavorable order.

environments for testing LIVE further, and even within the pea environment, we do not have other conditions to consider. This is because in its present form LIVE can only deal with features that are inherited independently. For instance, although we can provide LIVE with more features of pea plants, such as the length of stems and the position of the flowers, if these are features inherited independently, then the tests will be no more than a collection of runs similar to those described in Section 11.4.

However, when experimenting with LIVE's learning method in the pea hybridization experiments, two new issues arise that seem common to any action-dependent environment. We list them below and point out how LIVE is adjusted correspondingly. First, as we point out in Section 11.5, in order to assimilate newly defined hidden features in an action-dependent environment, the utilize function $U()$ and the inherit function $I()$ must be determined. To do so, examples for each function must be collected, and in the pea hybridization experiments, LIVE receives help from some given domain-dependent knowledge. In particular, the system is told that the first-generation peas are purebred and so their hidden features are equal to their color. Fortunately, since such additional knowledge is used only for collecting examples, their presence does not affect LIVE's performance in other domains (of course, for different domains, different additional knowledge may be required). Thus we see that domain-dependent knowledge may be necessary for LIVE to discover hidden features in some action-dependent environments.

The second and perhaps more important issue is that the representation of the history in LIVE is determined by the nature of time (whether linear or branching [20]) in the environment. In the Tower of Hanoi environment, time is linear because a state at any time t_i is the result of the state and action at time t_{i-1}; in the pea hybridization experiments, time is branching because a state at time t_i need not depend on time t_{i-1} but on its ancestor states through the inheritance line. To preserve the inheritance line, LIVE is adjusted to remember, for each element of history, not only the state (the parents), the action, and the variable bindings, but also the result state (the children) after the action. Furthermore, instead of remembering just one history element for each rule, LIVE now remembers a complete history back to a certain point (20 elements in LIVE's present form). Thus, when searching for the parents of a pea, LIVE can go through the remembered history and find a history element whose result state contains the pea. Of course, there are more efficient ways to remember the inheritance line, but we find the current method to be the most compatible with the requirement that LIVE work in both action-dependent and action-independent environments.

12.5   LIVE as a HAND-EYE Learner

To illustrate LIVE's performance as the HAND-EYE learner in the Tower of Hanoi environment, we include here a problem-solving trace. The environment is defined in Section 2.4, and its implementation is shown in Appendix A.4. This section does not present a large number of experiments in this environment; instead, it shows how lower-level percepts and actions are used to solve the puzzle.

In this problem, there are seven objects in the environment: three disks, three pegs, and LIVE's hand. Objects are represented as the feature vectors

$$[objID\ shape\ size\ direction\ distance\ altitude]$$

as described in Section 9.2. LIVE is given the following initial state:

[OBJ5 PEG 3.1 38.0 32.0 8.0]
[OBJ6 PEG 3.1 -38.0 32.0 8.0]
[OBJ7 PEG 3.1 0.0 40.0 8.0]
[OBJ4 DISK 3.0 -38.0 32.0 2.0]
[OBJ3 DISK 2.5 0.0 40.0 2.0]
[OBJ2 DISK 2.0 0.0 40.0 4.0]
[OBJ1 HAND 3.5 0.0 40.0 23.0]

The goals in this problem are the following:

[GOAL-OBJ2 DISK 2.0 -38.0 32.0 (< 20)]
[GOAL-OBJ3 DISK 2.5 -38.0 32.0 (< 20)]
[GOAL-OBJ4 DISK 3.0 -38.0 32.0 (< 20)]

Although the goals are expressed as feature vectors, they are not real objects. Therefore, for each goal, LIVE has assigned a name so that the goals can be compared to the real disks for differences.

Given these goals in the initial state, LIVE first computes the differences between the goals and the current state, which yields the following list:

[GOAL-OBJ3 DISK 2.5 -38.0 32.0 (< 20)]
[GOAL-OBJ2 DISK 2.0 -38.0 32.0 (< 20)]

However, since LIVE does not know anything about the environment, no rule can be found to construct any solution plans. So LIVE proposes an exploration plan and explores the environment as follows (Section 9.3 gives details of how predicates and rules are created):

1. Pick(): This action picks up OBJ2, which happens to be under the hand at the moment. Since the altitude of the disk changes, LIVE creates a new relation ALTITUDE= and a rule about picking up an object.

2. Rotate(-10): This action changes the direction of HAND, so that LIVE creates a new relation DIR= and a rule about rotating HAND (while holding an object) away from some object (e.g. OBJ7).

3. Slide(5): This action changes the distance of HAND, so that LIVE creates a new relation DIST= and a rule about sliding HAND (holding an object) away from some objects.

4. Slide(-5): LIVE creates a new rule about sliding HAND (holding an object) back to some objects.

5. Rotate(10): LIVE creates a new rule about rotating HAND (holding an object) back to some objects.

6. Put(): This action puts the object in HAND, so that LIVE creates a new rule about putting an object.

7. Rotate(10): LIVE is surprised that this action does not change the other object's direction as it did in the last application, so the rule about rotating is split into two rules: Rotate-with-object and Rotate-without-object.

8. Slide(-5): LIVE is surprised that this action does not change the other objects' distance as it did in the last application, so the rule about sliding is split into two rules: Slide-with-object and Slide-without-object.

9. Slide(5): LIVE creates a new rule about sliding an empty HAND back to some objects.

10. Rotate(-10): LIVE creates a new rule about rotating an empty HAND back to some objects.

After these explorations, LIVE plans the following solution for the given goals:

DIR=(OBJ3 GOAL-OBJ3); to be achieved by Rotate-with-object
DIST=(OBJ3 GOAL-OBJ3); to be achieved by Slide-with-object
DIR=(OBJ2 GOAL-OBJ2); to be achieved by Rotate-with-object
DIST=(OBJ2 GOAL-OBJ2); to be achieved by Slide-with-object

In order to apply Rotate-with-object to rotate OBJ3 to GOAL-OBJ3, the rule proposes the following goals:

ALTITUDE=(OBJ3 HAND); to be achieved by Pick
DIST=(OBJ3 GOAL-OBJ3); to be achieved by Slide-with-object

In order to pick up OBJ3, the Pick rule proposes these new goals:

¬DIR=(HAND GOAL-OBJ3); to be achieved by Rotate-without-object
DIR=(HAND OBJ3); to be achieved by Rotate-without-object

So LIVE first rotates its HAND from GOAL-OBJ3, then rotates its HAND to OBJ3. But when it does pick up OBJ3, it is surprised that OBJ3 is not in hand by encountering OBJ2. Comparing this failure to a previous success, LIVE creates a new relation SIZE> and finds that the reason for the failure is that there is a smaller disk at the same spot as the disk to be picked up. LIVE is lucky here because it finds the right reason in one step. This is the result of the failure and the success being in the same state but with different bindings.

After this surprise, a new solution plan is constructed:

(No smaller disk, such as OBJ2, should have the same direction and distance as OBJ3); to be achieved by the rule Rotate-with-object to rotate OBJ2 away
ALTITUDE=(OBJ3 HAND); to be achieved by Pick
DIST=(OBJ3 GOAL-OBJ3); to be achieved by Slide-with-object
DIR=(OBJ3 GOAL-OBJ3); to be achieved by Rotate-with-object
ALTITUDE=(OBJ3 GOAL-OBJ3); to be achieved by Put
DIST=(OBJ2 GOAL-OBJ2); to be achieved by Slide-with-object
DIR=(OBJ2 GOAL-OBJ2); to be achieved by Rotate-with-object
ALTITUDE=(OBJ2 GOAL-OBJ2); to be achieved by Put

To reach the first goal, LIVE turns its hand, which is holding OBJ2, away from OBJ3. To achieve the second goal, one new goal is proposed by the rule of Pick:

DIR=(HAND OBJ3); to be achieved by Rotate-without-object

The rule of Rotate-without-object, in turn, requires the following conditions:

¬DIST=(OBJ2 OBJ3); to be achieved by Slide-with-object
¬ALTITUDE=(OBJ2 HAND); to be achieved by Put

So LIVE slides OBJ2 away from OBJ3 and does the Put action. Unfortunately, LIVE is surprised that OBJ2 is still in its hand after the Put action! (This is because there is nothing under the hand. Comparing this failure to an earlier successful Put, LIVE learns that in order to put a disk successfully, something must be under the hand.

After this surprise, a new plan is constructed as follows:

DIR=(HAND OBJ3); to be achieved by Rotate-with-object
ALTITUDE=(OBJ3 HAND); to be achieved by Pick
DIST=(OBJ3 GOAL-OBJ3); to be achieved by Slide-with-object
DIR=(OBJ3 GOAL-OBJ3); to be achieved by Rotate-with-object
ALTITUDE=(OBJ3 GOAL-OBJ3); to be achieved by Put
DIST=(OBJ2 GOAL-OBJ2); to be achieved by Slide-with-object
DIR=(OBJ2 GOAL-OBJ2); to be achieved by Rotate-with-object
ALTITUDE=(OBJ2 GOAL-OBJ2); to be achieved by Put

To reach the first goal, LIVE rotates its hand, which is still holding OBJ2, away from OBJ3. To achieve the second goal, one new goal is proposed by the rule of Pick:

DIR=(HAND OBJ3); to be achieved by Rotate-without-object

So LIVE rotates to OBJ3 and performs a Pick action. Unfortunately, the Pick fails because HAND is not at the same distance as OBJ3 (not to mention that OBJ2 is still in hand). From this mistake, LIVE learns that in order to pick up an object successfully, HAND's distance must be equal to the object's distance. A new plan is constructed as follows:

DIST=(HAND OBJ3); to be achieved by Slide-with-object
ALTITUDE=(OBJ3 HAND); to be achieved by Pick
DIST=(OBJ3 GOAL-OBJ3); to be achieved by Slide-with-object
DIR=(OBJ3 GOAL-OBJ3); to be achieved by Rotate-with-object
ALTITUDE=(OBJ3 GOAL-OBJ3); to be achieved by Put
DIST=(OBJ2 GOAL-OBJ2); to be achieved by Slide-with-object
DIR=(OBJ2 GOAL-OBJ2); to be achieved by Rotate-with-object
ALTITUDE=(OBJ2 GOAL-OBJ2); to be achieved by Put

To reach the first goal, LIVE slides its hand, which is still holding OBJ2, back to OBJ3. To achieve the second goal, one new goal is proposed by the rule of Pick:

DIR=(HAND OBJ3); to be achieved by Rotate-without-object

So LIVE rotates its hand to OBJ3. But, in order to pick up OBJ3, the Pick rule now requires the following condition:

(No smaller disk, such as OBJ2, should have the same direction and distance as OBJ3); to be achieved by Rotate-with-object to move OBJ2 away

Thus LIVE rotates OBJ2 away from OBJ3. However, in order to pick up OBJ3, the Pick rule also requires the following condition:

DIR=(HAND OBJ3); to be achieved by Rotate-without-object

In order to apply the rule Rotate-without-object, the following conditions must be true:

¬DIST=(OBJ2 OBJ3); to be achieved by Slide-with-object
¬ALTITUDE=(OBJ2 HAND); to be achieved by Put

So LIVE slides OBJ2 away from OBJ3. But when applying the Put rule, the following condition must be true (OBJ5 is chosen to be the other peg):

DIR=(HAND OBJ5); to be achieved by Rotate-with-object
DIST=(HAND OBJ5); to be achieved by Slide-with-object

Thus LIVE rotates and slides its HAND to OBJ5 and puts OBJ2 there. Then, following the rest of the plan, LIVE rotates and slides its hand back to OBJ3's location, picks it up, slides and rotates to GOAL-OBJ3's location, and puts OBJ3 there. After that, OBJ2 is moved to the location of GOAL-OBJ2 in a similar way, and LIVE solves all the given goals.

12.6   Discussion

There are three principal advantages in the LIVE learning framework. First, it defines the problem of learning from the environment as constructing a model of the environment in the context of problem solving. The definition distinguishes between a learner's innate actions and the consequences of actions in the environment. An approximate model of the environment is extracted from an immense "raw" space determined by the learner's innate physical abilities and prior knowledge. This extraction process is guided by information gathered from interactions with the environment.

Second, the framework coordinates various activities, such as perception, action, exploration, experimentation, problem solving, learning, discovery, and constructing new terms. To my knowledge, LIVE is the first system implemented that incorporates so many activities. By viewing discovery as a form of learning from the environment, this integration provides some insights into what activities are involved in discovery processes and how they interact with each other.

Third, the keys to integration in the LIVE framework are prediction sequences and learning by complementary discrimination. Prediction sequences provide a unified view of planning, exploration, and experimentation. These activities are linked to learning and discovery by prediction failures. Learning by complementary discrimination enables a model from the environment to be abstracted and new terms to be readily constructed.

The framework is still in its early developmental stage, and several limitations must be overcome for the framework to become a general solution for learning from the environment. For example, the framework cannot deal with uncertain actions. A single noisy prediction failure will cause the model to be revised completely. It cannot react in real time: All its actions are deliberate and may be very time consuming.

The incremental enlargement heuristic is not the most general way to find the correct difference between two states. It relies on the hints that are inferred from the parameters of action. When actions do not have these parameters, the learner needs to determine how objects in the environment are related to actions. This is a question I have not addressed.

Perhaps the most severe limitation of LIVE is that the brute-force search method for discovering new terms is too naive and relies on two strong biases. One is that the set of useful mental relations and functions must be given beforehand. The other is that the current way of discovering action-dependent terms is limited to features and objects that are related to the current condition and action. For example, in defining gene in the pea hybridization experiments, LIVE must assume that the children's color is determined only by their ancestors' color. However, in the real world, features in one state may be determined by different features in previous states.

CHAPTER 13

THE FUTURE OF AUTONOMOUS LEARNING

The future of autonomous learning from the environment is both bright and challenging. The implications and the applications of this technology are profound and bounded only by our imagination. At the same time, many difficult problems lie ahead of us. In this final chapter, I shall address two of the major challenges we face.

13.1   The Gap Between Interface and Cognition

The first and perhaps most challenging problem today is to bridge the gap between physical and mental activities. Physical activities, as defined and used in this book, are perceptions and actions that interface directly with the environment. Mental activities, on the other hand, are high-level learning and reasoning processes that abstract and apply models of the environment. However, as we know from this book, correct models can be built by high-level processes only when necessary mental entities (such as mental attributes, objects, relations, and functions) are in place. However, these mental entities are not directly available in physical perceptions and actions. For example, the mental entities used in Dickmann's [19] autonomous vehicle (such as the edges of the road or the corners of a docking place) are given by the system designers (see Section 6.3), and they are much higher-level features than the pixels in the sensing images. Naturally, for systems to be truly autonomous, these features must be learned and created from physical activities in the current

297

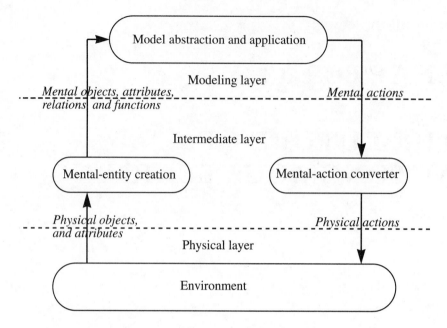

Figure 13.1   Three layers of information from interface to model.

environment. But the task is very difficult, because the amount of raw information and the number of actions that travel through the physical interface are tremendous. Although we touched on the issue of creating new features and relations in this book, we simplified the problem by giving the learner only a small number of necessary percepts, actions, mental relations, and mental functions. At present, there is no general solution for creating the necessary mental entities when the learner's percepts and actions are realistic (such as camera images or sonar readings).

To illustrate the problem, we can divide the learner's information flow into three layers, as shown in Figure 13.1. The bottom layer is the interface between the learner and the environment. This layer contains physical percepts observed directly from the environment and physical actions applied directly to the environment. The top layer is where models are generated and used. This layer contains the learning and reasoning processes discussed in this book. The building blocks required by this important layer (i.e., the mental entities) are not directly produced by the bottom layer. To fill in this void, we introduce the middle layer as a placeholder for the mental entities. As we can see in Figure 13.1, this layer contains the mental objects, mental attributes, mental relations, and mental functions required for building correct models. It also contains mental actions to create and compute these entities. Since different environments require different sets of mental entities, the information in this intermediate layer cannot be given completely at the outset and must be learned dynamically during the process of model abstraction. This is what we refer to as the gap between physical and mental activities.

To appreciate the difficulty of the problem, let us revisit the boat control problem, the Boat-Driver learner, defined in Chapter 2. It turns out that the mental entities required for this particular problem (at least for the system built by [4]) are very intricate, and it is not known how humans generate these entities autonomously. (Psychological protocols indicate that humans indeed create and use these mental entities in solving this problem.)

Recall that the Boat-Driver learner is to learn how to control the boat well enough to drive it through a series of gates. Following Anzai [4], we assume that the boat moves at constant speed V, and its position is viewed as a point (x, y) in a 2-dimensional space. With these simplifications, the equations that govern the action of the boat can be simplified as follows:

$$\frac{dx}{dt} = V \sin(g(t)), x(0) = x_0 \tag{13.1}$$

$$\frac{dy}{dt} = V \cos(g(t)), y(0) = y_0 \tag{13.2}$$

$$\frac{dg}{dt} = h(t), g(0) = g_0 \tag{13.3}$$

$$\frac{dh}{dt} = T(m(t) - h(t)), h(0) = h_0 \tag{13.4}$$

Equations 13.1 and 13.2 state that the next position of the boat (point) is determined by the rotation of the boat $g(t)$ at time t with respect to due north. (One can think of $g(t)$ as a combination of $a(t)$ and $r(t)$ in Figure 2.10.) Equation 13.3 states that the change of rotation $g(t)$ is determined by its velocity $h(t)$ (which is roughly equal to $u(t)$ in Figure 2.10). Finally, Equation 13.4 states that the change of rotational velocity is determined, with a "delay" constant T, $0 < T \leq 1$, by the current rotational velocity $h(t)$ and a controlled quantity $m(t)$, which is the steering action controlled by the learner.

With this example, the functions of the different layers become clear. At the physical layer, the information includes the percepts of the boat and the set of physical gates. These entities have physical attributes. For example, the boat has the location x_t and y_t and is moving in direction d_t. (Notice that d_t is the direction from (x_{t-1}, y_{t-1}) to (x_t, y_t), and is different from the boat's rotation $g(t)$.) Similarly, the gates have identifiers and locations. To represent these entities, we use the tuples $pboat(x_t, y_t, d_t)$ and $pgate(name, x_t, y_t)$ to denote the boat and the gates, respectively.

At the top modeling layer, the information includes the model, which in this case is a set of production rules. All these rules use mental objects and attributes that are not available at the physical layer. For example, one rule says that if you want the moving trajectory of the boat to be {*left, straight, right*}, then you should steer the rudder to {*left, straight, right*} for at least a time of duration d. The attribute

- Mental attributes and values
  symbolic-direction: $\{n, nne, ne, \ldots, ssw, s\}$
  symbolic-distance: $\{close, very\text{-}near, near, medium\text{-}near, medium,$
      medium-far, far, very-far, too-far$\}$
  moving-trajectory: $\{left, straight, right\}$
- Mental objects
  ship(x, y, *current-direction, moving-trajectory*)
  gate(x, y, *trajectory-to-be-realized-at-the-gate, type*),
      where *type* can have value *physical* or *mental*
- Mental relations
  next-gate($gate_i, gate_j$), where $gate_j$ is the gate immediately after $gate_i$
  current-goal(*gate*), where *gate* is a gate to go through now
- Mental functions
  relative-direction(a, b), which returns a symbolic direction value indicating
      the direction from object a to object b
  relative-distance(a, b), which returns a symbolic distance value indicating
      the distance from object a to object b
  direction-diff(*ship, gate*), defined as the difference between *relative-direction*
      (*gate, ship*) and the ship's current moving direction;
      the value can be either *positive, zero,* or *negative*
- Mental actions
  Compute-trajectory(), which computes the ship's current trajectory
  Msteering(*angle,duration*), where *angle* can be *left, straight,* or *right*, and
  duration is an integer

Figure 13.2   The mental entities required for solving the boat problem.

trajectory is mental. As another example, in order to go through a sequence of physical gates successfully, humans create mental gates and position these gates in between the physical gates.

A complete list of the mental entities required for solving the boat problem, derived from [4], is shown in Figure 13.2. Based on psychological protocols, these entities are apparently constructed and used by human subjects in solving this problem.

In Anzai's system, all these mental entities are either given or computed by prespecified basic procedures. In general, however, these entities must be learned autonomously, as we argued earlier. To do so, we must answer at least two basic questions: Which mental entities are necessary for the current problem and environment, and how are these entities constructed? At present, no one seems to know the answers.

For the first question, we seem to have a clue: The identification of these entities is driven by the need for abstracting correct models. That is, we must look for the answer in the modeling layer, where models are constructed and used. For the second question, humans must have a set of heuristics to guide the process of picking up the relations and functions relevant to constructing the mental entities. Identifying these heuristics seems to be a very important task.

13.2   Being Humans' Friends Forever

Another major challenge is how to keep these autonomous systems as our friends. This may not seem as urgent as the first challenge since we have not yet built any such system. But as systems become more autonomous, it is a difficult task to keep them always obeying and protecting humans. If attention is not paid at an early enough stage, it might be very costly to rectify this problem in the future.

There are two keys to making an autonomous system friendly. One is to build into these systems some lifetime goals of being friendly to humans. The other is to give these systems effective communications abilities so that they and humans can keep in touch with each other. In doing so, we can ask systems to do what we think is appropriate, and they can tell us what knowledge they have learned from their environment. Obviously, both approaches require much future research.

Communicating with an autonomous system involves a degree of authority. A communication can be a mandatory command or a negotiation. Both types of comunication are two-edged swords. On the one hand, mandatory commands give us control over a system, but they may disturb a system's mental state and even destroy its autonomous vitality. On the other hand, negotiations give a system more freedom, but we may face the danger of losing control when critical actions must be taken. There is much to learn to balance these trade-offs. At least one thing is clear: To communicate with autonomous systems, we cannot use "brain surgeries" as we have used today.

At present, the communications aspect of autonomous systems has not received the attention it deserves. Most of today's research has concentrated on perceptions and actions (as we do in this book). The question of how communication affects the learning and the behavior of autonomous systems must be taken seriously if we want them to stay our friends forever.

Appendix A

THE IMPLEMENTATIONS
OF THE ENVIRONMENTS

This appendix lists the implementations of the environments used in this book. Each environment is a LISP program (package) that provides a list of "export" symbols for learners to use as percepts and actions. However, the internal structures of these programs are not visible to learners.

A.1   The Tower of Hanoi Environment

```
(provide 'environment)
(in-package 'environment)

(export '(env-initiate observe
          *relations* on gr inhand disk1 disk2 disk3 peg1 peg2 peg3
          *actions* mpick mput
          *m-constructors*))

(defvar *actions* '((mpick d p) (mput d p)))
(defvar *relations* '(on gr inhand))
(defvar *feature-counter* 0)
(defvar *world* nil)

;;; ****************** Initiate and Observe ******************

(defun env-initiate ()
  (setq *actions* '((mpick d p) (mput d p)))
```

303

```
          *relations* '(on gr inhand) *cnst-funs* '() *cnst-rels* '()
          *time-depen* t *relations-to-predict* '() *feature-counter* 0)
  (setf (get 'disk1 'user::external-id) 'disk1)
  (setf (get 'disk2 'user::external-id) 'disk2)
  (setf (get 'disk3 'user::external-id) 'disk3)
  (setf (get 'peg1 'user::external-id) 'peg1)
  (setf (get 'peg2 'user::external-id) 'peg2)
  (setf (get 'peg3 'user::external-id) 'peg3)
  (setq *world*
        (copy-tree
         (list '(disk1 disk 1 1) '(disk2 disk 2 1) '(disk3 disk 3 1)
               '(peg1 peg 0 1) '(peg2 peg 0 2) '(peg3 peg 0 3)))))

(defun observe ()
  (list '(disk1) '(disk2) '(disk3) '(peg1) '(peg2) '(peg3)
        '(gr disk2 disk1) '(gr disk3 disk2) '(gr disk3 disk1)
        (on-or-inh (copy-list (elt *world* 0)))
        (on-or-inh (copy-list (elt *world* 1)))
        (on-or-inh (copy-list (elt *world* 2)))))


;;; ******************** Pre-Defined Relations ********************

(defun on (x y) nil)
(setf (get 'on 'constructor) '=)
(setf (get 'on 'fe-index) 0)
(defun gr (x y) nil)
(setf (get 'gr 'constructor) '>)
(setf (get 'gr 'fe-index) 0)
(defun inhand (x y)  nil)
(setf (get 'inhand 'constructor) 'eql)
(setf (get 'inhand 'fe-index) 0)

;;; ******************** Actions ********************

(defun mpick (disk peg)
  (format t "~%Pick ~S from ~S. ~%" disk peg)
  (let ((d (indexof disk)) (p (indexof peg)))
    (if (and (= (elt (elt *world* p) 3) (elt (elt *world* d) 3))
             (nothing-in-hand) (no-block d p))
        (setf (elt (elt *world* d) 3) 0))))

(defun mput (disk peg)
  (format t "~%Put ~S on ~S. ~%" disk peg)
  (let ((d (indexof disk)) (p (indexof peg)))
    (if (and (= 0 (elt (elt *world* d) 3)) (no-block d p))
        (setf (elt (elt *world* d) 3) (elt (elt *world* p) 3)))))


;;; ******************** Misc Functions ********************

(defun on-or-inh (d)
  (cond ((= 0 (elt d 3)) (list 'inhand (car d)))
        ((= 1 (elt d 3)) (list 'on (car d) 'peg1))
```

```
                ((= 2 (elt d 3)) (list 'on (car d) 'peg2))
                ((= 3 (elt d 3)) (list 'on (car d) 'peg3))))

(defun no-block (d p)
  (let ((peg (elt (elt *world* p) 3)) (size (elt (elt *world* d) 2)))
    (dolist (f *world* t)
            (if (and (eql 'disk (elt f 1))
                     (= peg (elt f 3))
                     (> size (elt f 2)))
                (return nil)))))

(defun nothing-in-hand ()
  (and (/= 0 (elt (elt *world* 0) 3))
       (/= 0 (elt (elt *world* 1) 3))
       (/= 0 (elt (elt *world* 2) 3))))

(defun indexof (dp)
  (case dp ('disk1 0) ('disk2 1) ('disk3 2) ('peg1 3) ('peg2 4) ('peg3 5)))
```

A.2   The Balance Beam Environment

```
(provide 'environment)
(in-package 'environment)

(export '(env-initiate observe
          *relations* wg= wg> dist= dist> alt= alt>
          *actions* release
          *m-constructors*))

(defvar *actions* '((release)))
(defvar *relations* '(wg= wg> dist= dist> alt= alt>))
(defvar *cnst-funs* '(* +))
(defvar *cnst-rels* '(> =))
(defvar *time-depen* nil)
(defvar *relations-to-predict* '(alt= alt>))
(defvar *feature-counter* 3)
(defvar *world* nil)
(defvar *trial* -1)

;;;   ****************** Initiate and Observe ******************

(defun env-initiate ()
  (setq *actions* '((release))
        *relations* '(wg= wg> dist= dist> alt= alt>)
        *cnst-funs* '(* +)
        *cnst-rels* '(> =)
        *time-depen* nil
        *relations-to-predict* '(alt= alt>)
        *feature-counter* 3
        *trial* -1)
  (setq *world*
```

```
(list '((L 3 1 1) (R 3 1 1)) '((L 3 1 1) (R 3 1 1))
      '((L 3 1 1) (R 2 1 1)) '((L 3 1 0) (R 2 1 2))
      '((L 3 3 1) (R 3 2 1)) '((L 3 3 0) (R 3 2 2))
      '((L 3 3 1) (R 2 4 1)) '((L 3 3 0) (R 2 4 2))
      '((L 2 3 1) (R 4 1 1)) '((L 2 3 0) (R 4 1 2))
      '((L 2 2 1) (R 4 1 1)) '((L 2 2 1) (R 4 1 1))
      '((R 3 1 1) (L 2 1 1)) '((R 3 1 0) (L 2 1 2))
      '((R 3 3 1) (L 3 2 1)) '((R 3 3 0) (L 3 2 2))
      '((R 3 3 1) (L 2 4 1)) '((R 3 3 0) (L 2 4 2))
      '((R 2 3 1) (L 4 1 1)) '((R 2 3 0) (L 4 1 2))
      '((R 2 2 1) (L 4 1 1)) '((R 2 2 1) (L 4 1 1))
      '((L 3 3 1) (R 2 4 1)) '((L 3 3 0) (R 2 4 2))
      '((L 2 3 1) (R 4 1 1)) '((L 2 3 0) (R 4 1 2))
      '((L 2 2 1) (R 4 1 1)) '((L 2 2 1) (R 4 1 1))
      '((L 2 2 1) (R 4 1 1)) '((L 2 2 1) (R 4 1 1)))))

(defun observe ()
  (setq *trial* (1+ *trial*))
  (copy-tree (elt *world* *trial*)))

;;; ****************** Pre-Defined Relations ******************

(defun wg= (x y)
  (unless (eql (car x) (car y))
          (if (eql (elt x 1) (elt y 1))
              (list 'wg= (car x) (car y)))))

(setf (get 'wg= 'constructor) '=)
(setf (get 'wg= 'fe-index) 1)

(defun wg> (x y)
  (unless (eql (car x) (car y))
          (if (> (cadr x) (cadr y))
              (list 'wg> (car x) (car y)))))

(setf (get 'wg> 'constructor) '>)
(setf (get 'wg> 'fe-index) 1)

(defun dist= (x y)
  (unless (eql (car x) (car y))
          (if (eql (elt x 2) (elt y 2))
              (list 'dist= (car x) (car y)))))

(setf (get 'dist= 'constructor) '=)
(setf (get 'dist= 'fe-index) 2)

(defun dist> (x y)
  (unless (eql (car x) (car y))
          (if (> (elt x 2) (elt y 2))
              (list 'dist> (car x) (car y)))))

(setf (get 'dist> 'constructor) '>)
(setf (get 'dist> 'fe-index) 2)
```

```
(defun alt= (x y)
  (unless (eql (car x) (car y))
          (if (eql (elt x 3) (elt y 3))
              (list 'alt= (car x) (car y)))))

(setf (get 'alt= 'constructor) '=)
(setf (get 'alt= 'fe-index) 3)

(defun alt> (x y)
  (unless (eql (car x) (car y))
          (if (> (elt x 3) (elt y 3))
              (list 'alt> (car x) (car y)))))

(setf (get 'alt> 'constructor) '>)
(setf (get 'alt> 'fe-index) 3)

;;; ****************** Actions ******************

(defun release ())
```

A.3   The Pea Hybridization Environment

```
(provide 'environment)
(in-package 'environment)
(export '(env-initiate observe
         *relations* *cnst-rels* *feature-counter*
         *actions* af
         *m-constructors*))

(defvar *actions* '((af x y)))
(defvar *relations* nil)
(defvar *cnst-funs* '(e-max e-min e-distr))
(defvar *cnst-rels* '(= >))
(defvar *purebreds* ())

(defvar *time-depen* t)
(defvar *predict-only* t)
(defvar *discret-events* t)
(defvar *relations-to-predict* nil)
(defvar *feature-counter* 1)
(defvar *world* nil)
(defvar *trial* -1)


;;; ****************** Initiate and Observe ******************

(defun env-initiate ()
  (setq *actions* '((af x y))
        *relations* nil
        *cnst-funs* '(e-max e-min e-distr)
        *cnst-rels* '(= >)
        *time-depen* t *predict-only* t *discret-events* t
```

```
            *relations-to-predict* nil
            *feature-counter* 1
            *trial* -1
            *purebreds* '(P1 P2 P3 P4 P5 P6 P7 P8))
    (setq *world*
          (list '((P1 0 0 0) (P2 0 0 0))
                '((P9 0 0 0) (P10 0 0 0) (P11 0 0 0) (P12 0 0 0))
                '((P3 1 1 1) (P4 1 1 1))
                '((P13 1 1 1) (P14 1 1 1) (P15 1 1 1) (P16 1 1 1))
                '((P5 0 0 0) (P6 1 1 1))
                '((P17 1 0 1) (P18 1 0 1) (P19 1 0 1) (P20 1 0 1))
                '((P7 1 1 1) (P8 0 0 0))
                '((P21 1 1 0) (P22 1 1 0) (P23 1 1 0) (P24 1 1 0))

                '((P9 0 0 0) (P10 0 0 0))
                '((P25 0 0 0) (P26 0 0 0) (P27 0 0 0) (P28 0 0 0))
                '((P13 1 1 1) (P14 1 1 1))
                '((P29 1 1 1) (P30 1 1 1) (P31 1 1 1) (P32 1 1 1))
                '((P17 1 0 1) (P18 1 0 1))
                '((P33 0 0 0) (P34 1 0 1) (P35 1 1 0) (P36 1 1 1))
                '((P21 1 1 0) (P22 1 1 0))
                '((P37 1 1 1) (P38 1 1 0) (P39 1 0 1) (P40 0 0 0))

                '((P33 0 0 0) (P40 0 0 0))
                '((P41 0 0 0) (P42 0 0 0) (P43 0 0 0) (P44 0 0 0))
                '((P34 1 0 1) (P38 1 1 0))
                '((P45 1 0 1) (P46 0 0 0) (P47 1 1 1) (P48 1 1 0))
                '((P35 1 1 0) (P39 1 0 1))
                '((P49 1 1 0) (P50 1 1 1) (P51 0 0 0) (P52 1 0 1))
                '((P36 1 1 1) (P37 1 1 1))
                '((P53 1 1 1) (P54 1 1 1) (P55 1 1 1) (P56 1 1 1)))))


(defun observe ()
   (setq *trial* (1+ *trial*))
   (mapcar \#'(lambda (x) (subseq x 0 2))
      (copy-tree (elt *world* *trial*))))



;;; ******************** Actions ********************

(defun af (x y))

;;; ******************** Misc Functions ********************

(defun e-distr (a b)
   (if (and (listp a) (listp b) (= (length a) 2) (= (length b) 2))
       '((,(car a) ,(car b)) (,(car a) ,(cadr b))
       (,(cadr a) ,(car b)) (,(cadr a) ,(cadr b)))))

(defun e-max (&rest a)
   (if (every \#'numberp a) (apply \#'max a)))

(defun e-min (&rest a)
   (if (every \#'numberp a) (apply \#'min a)))
```

A.4   The HAND-EYE Environment

```
(provide 'environment)
(in-package 'environment)
(export '(env-initiate observe
          peg disk
          *relations*
          *actions* rotate slide pick put
          *cnst-funs* *cnst-rels* constructor fe-index *feature-counter*))

(defvar *actions* '((rotate g) (slide d) (pick) (put)))
(defvar *relations* '())
(defvar *cnst-funs* '())
(defvar *cnst-rels* '())
(defvar *time-depen* t)
(defvar *feature-counter* 6)
(defvar *world* nil)

;;; ******************** Initiate and Observe ********************

(defun env-initiate ()
  (setq *world*
    (copy-tree '((0 cylinder 3.5   0.0   40.0  23.0)  ; the hand
                 (1 disk    2.0   0.0   40.0  4.002)   ; disk1
                 (2 disk    2.5   0.0   40.0  2.001)   ; disk2
                 (3 disk    3.0  38.0   32.0  2.001)   ; disk3
                 (4 peg 3.1   0.0   40.0   8.0)        ; peg-c
                 (5 peg 3.1 -38.0   32.0   8.0)        ; peg-b
                 (6 peg 3.1  38.0   32.0   8.0)))))    ; peg-a


(defun observe () (copy-tree *world*))


;;; *********************** Actions ***********************

(defun rotate (theta)
  (format t "~%Hand attempts to ROTATE ~S.~%" theta)
  (setf (fourth (car *world*)) (+ theta (fourth (car *world*))))
  (let ((id (thing-in-hand)))
    (if id
        (setf (fourth (elt *world* id))
              (+ theta (fourth (elt *world* id)))))))

(defun slide (dis)
  (format t "~%Hand attempts to SLIDE ~S.~%" dis)
  (setf (fifth (car *world*)) (+ dis (fifth (car *world*))))
  (let ((id (thing-in-hand)))
    (if id
        (setf (fifth (elt *world* id))
              (+ dis (fifth (elt *world* id)))))))

(defun pick ()
```

```
         (format t "~%Hand attempts to PICK.~%")
         (unless (thing-in-hand)
                 (let ((th (top-disk-under-hand)))
                    (if th (setf (sixth (elt *world* th)) 23.0)))))

(defun put ()
  (format t "~%Hand attempts to PUT. ~%")
  (let (in-hand under alt)
    (when (and (setq in-hand (thing-in-hand)) (peg-under-hand))
          (multiple-value-setq (under alt) (top-disk-under-hand))
          (if (null under)
              (setf (sixth (elt *world* in-hand)) 2.001)
            (if (< (third (elt *world* in-hand))
                   (third (elt *world* under)))
                (setf (sixth (elt *world* in-hand)) (+ alt 2.001)))))))


;;; ************************ Misc Functions  ************************

(defun thing-in-hand ()
  (position 23.0 (list* nil (cdr *world*)) :key \#'sixth))

(defun peg-under-hand ()
  (let ((hand-dir (fourth (car *world*)))
        (hand-dis (fifth (car *world*)))
        (temp nil))
    (do ((i 1 (1+ i)))
        ((> i 6) nil)
        (setq temp (elt *world* i))
        (if (and (eq (second temp) 'peg)
                 (= (third temp) 3.1)
                 (= hand-dir (fourth temp))
                 (= hand-dis (fifth temp)))
            (return t)))))

(defun top-disk-under-hand ()
  (let ((hand-dir (fourth (car *world*)))
        (hand-dis (fifth (car *world*)))
        (top-altitude -500)
        (top-disk nil))
    (do ((i 1 (1+ i)))
        ((> i 6) (values top-disk top-altitude))
        (if (and (eq (second (elt *world* i)) 'disk)
                 (= hand-dir (fourth (elt *world* i)))
                 (= hand-dis (fifth (elt *world* i)))
                 (> (sixth (elt *world* i)) top-altitude)
                 (< (sixth (elt *world* i)) 20)) ; not in hand
            (setq top-disk i top-altitude (sixth (elt *world* i)))))))
```

Appendix B

LIVE'S RUNNING TRACE IN THE TOWER OF HANOI ENVIRONMENT

This appendix gives a detailed trace of the LOGIC1 learner described in the book. The environment is as listed in Appendix A.1, and the initial state and goals are given as shown in the Table 12.1.1. The trace is printed as LIVE goes through its internal cycle of revising, planning, and acting. Each cycle is marked by a line "Think and Act (x)," where x is the number of cycle. Whenever LIVE revises its model, the trace also prints out a set of prediction rules.

———— LIVE ————

The Initial Rules: ( )
Observe: ON(DISK3 PEG1) ON(DISK2 PEG1) ON(DISK1 PEG1) SIZE>(DISK3 DISK1) SIZE>(DISK3 DISK2) SIZE>(DISK2 DISK1) [PEG3] [PEG2] [PEG1] [DISK3] [DISK2] [DISK1]
The Goals Given:
ON(DISK1 PEG1) ON(DISK2 PEG1) ON(DISK3 PEG3)
Planning for the remaining goals:
ON(DISK1 PEG1) ON(DISK2 PEG1) ON(DISK3 PEG3)
Differences towards the goal ON(DISK3 PEG3) are:
ON(DISK3 PEG3)
Find rules for the differences and sort them ...
To achieve ON(DISK3 PEG3), Rules NIL can be used.

———— Think or Act (1) ————

311

Observe: ON(DISK3 PEG1) ON(DISK2 PEG1) ON(DISK1 PEG1) SIZE>(DISK3 DISK1)
SIZE>(DISK3 DISK2) SIZE>(DISK2 DISK1) [PEG3] [PEG2] [PEG1] [DISK3] [DISK2] [DISK1]
Current Differences: ON(DISK3 PEG3)
Proposing explore plan ...
(PICK(DISK1 PEG1) PUT(DISK1 PEG2))
Given the action PICK(DISK1 PEG1), rules NIL can predict.
Useful-Rule-Instance: NIL
Decide to do PICK(DISK1 PEG1).
Execute PICK DISK1 from PEG1.
Waiting for responses from the environment ...
Observe: ON(DISK3 PEG1) ON(DISK2 PEG1) INHAND(DISK1) SIZE>(DISK3 DISK1)
SIZE>(DISK3 DISK2) SIZE>(DISK2 DISK1) [PEG3] [PEG2] [PEG1] [DISK3] [DISK2] [DISK1]
Creating a new rule ...
**** BEGIN PRINTING MODEL ****

Index: 0
Sibling: NIL
State: ON(*disk peg*) ¬INHAND(*disk*) [*peg*] [*disk*]
Action: PICK(*disk peg*)
Predict: INHAND(*disk*) ¬ON(*disk peg*) [*peg*] [*disk*]

**** END PRINTING MODEL ****
Given the action PUT(DISK1 PEG2), rules NIL can predict.
Useful-Rule-Instance: NIL
Decide to do PUT(DISK1 PEG2).
Execute Put DISK1 on PEG2.
Waiting for responses from the environment ...
Observe: ON(DISK3 PEG1) ON(DISK2 PEG1) ON(DISK1 PEG2) SIZE>(DISK3 DISK1)
SIZE>(DISK3 DISK2) SIZE>(DISK2 DISK1) [PEG3] [PEG2] [PEG1] [DISK3] [DISK2] [DISK1]
Creating new rules ...
**** BEGIN PRINTING MODEL ****

Index: 0
Sibling: NIL
State: ON(*disk peg*) ¬INHAND(*disk*) [*peg*] [*disk*]
Action: PICK(*disk peg*)
Predict: INHAND(*disk*) ¬ON(*disk peg*) [*peg*] [*disk*]

Index: 1
Sibling: NIL
State: INHAND(*disk*) ¬ON(*disk peg*) [*peg*] [*disk*]
Action: PUT(*disk peg*)
Predict: ON(*disk peg*) ¬INHAND(*disk*) [*peg*] [*disk*]

**** END PRINTING MODEL ****
Planning for the remaining goals:
ON(DISK1 PEG1) ON(DISK2 PEG1) ON(DISK3 PEG3)
Differences towards the goal ON(DISK1 PEG1) are: ON(DISK1 PEG1)
Differences towards the goal ON(DISK3 PEG3) are: ON(DISK3 PEG3)
Find rules for the differences and sort them ...
To achieve ON(DISK1 PEG1), Rules (1) can be used.
To achieve ON(DISK3 PEG3), Rules (1) can be used.

——————— Think or Act (2) ———————

Observe: ON(DISK3 PEG1) ON(DISK2 PEG1) ON(DISK1 PEG2) SIZE>(DISK3 DISK1)
SIZE>(DISK3 DISK2) SIZE>(DISK2 DISK1) [PEG3] [PEG2] [PEG1] [DISK3] [DISK2] [DISK1]
Current Differences: ON(DISK1 PEG1)

Useful-Rule-Instance:
State: INHAND(DISK1) ¬ON(DISK1 PEG1) [PEG1] [DISK1]
Action: PUT(DISK1 PEG1)
Predict: ON(DISK1 PEG1) ¬INHAND(DISK1) [PEG1] [DISK1]
Index: 1
Bindings: (*disk*/DISK1, *peg*/PEG1)

Decide to do Propose new subgoals.
New differences to achieve: INHAND(DISK1)
Find rules for the differences and sort them ...
To achieve INHAND(DISK1), Rules (0) can be used.
New plan for the differences: INHAND(DISK1) by applying Rule0

———————— Think or Act (3) ————————

Observe: ON(DISK3 PEG1) ON(DISK2 PEG1) ON(DISK1 PEG2) SIZE>(DISK3 DISK1)
SIZE>(DISK3 DISK2) SIZE>(DISK2 DISK1) [PEG3] [PEG2] [PEG1] [DISK3] [DISK2] [DISK1]
Current Differences: INHAND(DISK1)
Rule's action has free variable: *peg* is bound to PEG2.

Useful-Rule-Instance:
State: ON(DISK1 PEG2) ¬INHAND(DISK1) [PEG2] [DISK1]
Action: PICK(DISK1 PEG2)
Predict: INHAND(DISK1) ¬ON(DISK1 PEG2) [PEG2] [DISK1]
Index: 0
Bindings: (*peg*/PEG2, *disk*/DISK1)

Decide to do PICK(DISK1 PEG2).
Execute Pick DISK1 from PEG2.
Waiting for responses from the environment ...
Observe: ON(DISK3 PEG1) ON(DISK2 PEG1) INHAND(DISK1) SIZE>(DISK3 DISK1)
SIZE>(DISK3 DISK2) SIZE>(DISK2 DISK1) [PEG3] [PEG2] [PEG1] [DISK3] [DISK2] [DISK1]
Goal INHAND(DISK1) accomplished!

———————— Think or Act (4) ————————

Observe: ON(DISK3 PEG1) ON(DISK2 PEG1) INHAND(DISK1) SIZE>(DISK3 DISK1)
SIZE>(DISK3 DISK2) SIZE>(DISK2 DISK1) [PEG3] [PEG2] [PEG1] [DISK3] [DISK2] [DISK1]
Current Differences: ON(DISK1 PEG1)

Useful-Rule-Instance:
State: INHAND(DISK1) ¬ON(DISK1 PEG1) [PEG1] [DISK1]
Action: PUT(DISK1 PEG1)
Predict: ON(DISK1 PEG1) ¬INHAND(DISK1) [PEG1] [DISK1]
Index: 1
Bindings: (*disk*/DISK1, *peg*/PEG1)

Decide to do PUT(DISK1 PEG1).
Execute Put DISK1 on PEG1.
Waiting for responses from the environment ...
Observe: ON(DISK3 PEG1) ON(DISK2 PEG1) ON(DISK1 PEG1) SIZE>(DISK3 DISK1)
SIZE>(DISK3 DISK2) SIZE>(DISK2 DISK1) [PEG3] [PEG2] [PEG1] [DISK3] [DISK2] [DISK1]
Goal ON(DISK1 PEG1) accomplished!

———————— Think or Act (5) ————————

Observe: ON(DISK3 PEG1) ON(DISK2 PEG1) ON(DISK1 PEG1) SIZE>(DISK3 DISK1)
SIZE>(DISK3 DISK2) SIZE>(DISK2 DISK1) [PEG3] [PEG2] [PEG1] [DISK3] [DISK2] [DISK1]
Current Differences: ON(DISK3 PEG3)

Useful-Rule-Instance:
State: INHAND(DISK3) ¬ON(DISK3 PEG3) [PEG3] [DISK3]
Action: PUT(DISK3 PEG3)
Predict: ON(DISK3 PEG3) ¬INHAND(DISK3) [PEG3] [DISK3]
Index: 1
Bindings: (*disk*/DISK3, *peg*/PEG3)

Decide to do Propose new subgoals.
New differences to achieve: INHAND(DISK3)
Find rules for the differences and sort them ...
To achieve INHAND(DISK3), Rules (0) can be used.
New plan for the differences: INHAND(DISK3) by Rule0

——————— Think or Act (6) ———————

Observe: ON(DISK3 PEG1) ON(DISK2 PEG1) ON(DISK1 PEG1) SIZE>(DISK3 DISK1)
SIZE>(DISK3 DISK2) SIZE>(DISK2 DISK1) [PEG3] [PEG2] [PEG1] [DISK3] [DISK2] [DISK1]
Current Differences: INHAND(DISK3)
Rule's action has free variable: *peg* is bound to PEG1.

Useful-Rule-Instance:
State: ON(DISK3 PEG1) ¬INHAND(DISK3) [PEG1] [DISK3]
Action: PICK(DISK3 PEG1)
Predict: INHAND(DISK3) ¬ON(DISK3 PEG1) [PEG1] [DISK3]
Index: 0
Bindings: (*peg*/PEG1, *disk*/DISK3)

Decide to do PICK(DISK3 PEG1).
Execute PICK DISK3 from PEG1.
Waiting for responses from the environment ...
Observe: ON(DISK3 PEG1) ON(DISK2 PEG1) ON(DISK1 PEG1) SIZE>(DISK3 DISK1)
SIZE>(DISK3 DISK2) SIZE>(DISK2 DISK1) [PEG3] [PEG2] [PEG1] [DISK3] [DISK2] [DISK1]
Wrong prediction: INHAND(DISK3) ¬ON(DISK3 PEG1) [PEG1] [DISK3] by Rule0 with bindings
(*peg*/PEG1, *disk*/DISK3).
Explain the surprise by comparing with the last successful application viewed by the current relations.
(ON(DISK3 PEG1) ON(DISK2 PEG1) ON(DISK1 PEG2) SIZE>(DISK3 DISK1) SIZE>(DISK3
DISK2) SIZE>(DISK2 DISK1) [PEG3] [PEG2] [PEG1] [DISK3] [DISK2] [DISK1] (NIL NIL) PICK
(DISK1 PEG2) ((*peg*/PEG2) (*disk*/DISK1)))
Explanation 1: Relation differences inside bindings.
Rel-Then: NIL
Rel-Now: NIL
Creating relations on the bound things ...
Explanation 2: Middle circle relation differences.
Rel-Then: (SIZE>(DISK2 DISK1) SIZE>(DISK3 DISK1))
Rel-Now: (SIZE>(DISK3 DISK2) SIZE>(DISK3 DISK1) ON(DISK1 PEG1) ON(DISK2 PEG1))
WHY: ON(*diskM peg*)
Splitting Rule0 with WHY
**** BEGIN PRINTING MODEL ****

Index: 0
Sibling: 2
State: ON(*disk peg*) ¬ON(*diskM peg*) ¬INHAND(*disk*) [*disk*] [*peg*]
Action: PICK(*disk peg*)
Predict: INHAND(*disk*) ¬ON(*disk peg*) [*peg*] [*disk*]

Index: 1
Sibling: NIL
State: INHAND(*disk*) ¬ON(*disk peg*) [*peg*] [*disk*]
Action: PUT(*disk peg*)
Predict: ON(*disk peg*) ¬INHAND(*disk*) [*peg*] [*disk*]

Index: 2
Sibling: 0
State: ¬ON(*diskM peg*) ON(*disk peg*) ¬INHAND(*disk*) [*peg*] [*disk*]
Action: PICK(*disk peg*)
Predict: ON(*disk peg*)

**** END PRINTING MODEL ****
Planning for the remaining goals: ON(DISK1 PEG1) ON(DISK2 PEG1) ON(DISK3 PEG3)
Differences towards the goal ON(DISK3 PEG3) are: ON(DISK3 PEG3)
Find rules for the differences and sort them ...
To achieve ON(DISK3 PEG3), Rules (1) can be used.

——————— Think or Act (7) ———————

Observe: ON(DISK3 PEG1) ON(DISK2 PEG1) ON(DISK1 PEG1) SIZE>(DISK3 DISK1)
SIZE>(DISK3 DISK2) SIZE>(DISK2 DISK1) [PEG3] [PEG2] [PEG1] [DISK3] [DISK2] [DISK1]
    Current Differences: ON(DISK3 PEG3)

Useful-Rule-Instance:
State: INHAND(DISK3) ¬ON(DISK3 PEG3) [PEG3] [DISK3]
Action: PUT(DISK3 PEG3)
Predict: ON(DISK3 PEG3) ¬INHAND(DISK3) [PEG3] [DISK3]
Index: 1
Bindings: ((*disk*/DISK3) (*peg*/PEG3))

    Decide to do Propose new subgoals.
    New differences to achieve: INHAND(DISK3)
    Find rules for the differences and sort them ...
    To achieve INHAND(DISK3), Rules (0) can be used.
    New plan for the differences: INHAND(DISK3) by Rule0

——————— Think or Act (8) ———————

Observe: ON(DISK3 PEG1) ON(DISK2 PEG1) ON(DISK1 PEG1) SIZE>(DISK3 DISK1)
SIZE>(DISK3 DISK2) SIZE>(DISK2 DISK1) [PEG3] [PEG2] [PEG1] [DISK3] [DISK2] [DISK1]
    Current Differences: INHAND(DISK3)
    Rule's action has free variable: *peg* is bound to PEG1.

Useful-Rule-Instance:
State: ON(DISK3 PEG1) ¬ON(*diskM* PEG1) ¬INHAND(DISK3) [DISK3] [PEG1]
Action: PICK(DISK3 PEG1)
Predict: INHAND(DISK3) ¬ON(DISK3 PEG1) [PEG1] [DISK3]
Index: 0
Bindings: ((*peg*/PEG1) (*disk*/DISK3))

    Decide to do Propose new subgoals.
    New differences to achieve: ¬ON(DISK2 PEG1)
    Find rules for the differences and sort them ...
    To achieve ¬ON(DISK2 PEG1), Rules (0) can be used.
    New plan for the differences: ¬ON(DISK2 PEG1) by Rule0

——————— Think or Act (9) ———————

Observe: ON(DISK3 PEG1) ON(DISK2 PEG1) ON(DISK1 PEG1) SIZE>(DISK3 DISK1)
SIZE>(DISK3 DISK2) SIZE>(DISK2 DISK1) [PEG3] [PEG2] [PEG1] [DISK3] [DISK2] [DISK1]
    Current Differences: ¬ON(DISK2 PEG1)

Useful-Rule-Instance:
State: ON(DISK2 PEG1) ¬ON(*diskM* PEG1) ¬INHAND(DISK2) [DISK2] [PEG1]
Action: PICK(DISK2 PEG1)
Predict: INHAND(DISK2) ¬ON(DISK2 PEG1) [PEG1] [DISK2]
Index: 0
Bindings: ((*disk*/DISK2) (*peg*/PEG1))

    Decide to do Propose new subgoals.
    New differences to achieve: ¬ON(DISK3 PEG1)
    Find rules for the differences and sort them ...
    To achieve ¬ON(DISK3 PEG1), Rules (0) can be used.
    New plan for the differences: ¬ON(DISK3 PEG1) by Rule0

——————— Think or Act (10) ———————

Observe: ON(DISK3 PEG1) ON(DISK2 PEG1) ON(DISK1 PEG1) SIZE>(DISK3 DISK1)
SIZE>(DISK3 DISK2) SIZE>(DISK2 DISK1) [PEG3] [PEG2] [PEG1] [DISK3] [DISK2] [DISK1]
    Current Differences: ¬ON(DISK3 PEG1)

Useful-Rule-Instance:
State: ON(DISK3 PEG1) ¬ON(*diskM* PEG1) ¬INHAND(DISK3) [DISK3] [PEG1]
Action: PICK(DISK3 PEG1)
Predict: INHAND(DISK3) ¬ON(DISK3 PEG1) [PEG1] [DISK3]
Index: 0
Bindings: ((*disk*/DISK3) (*peg*/PEG1))

    Decide to do Propose new subgoals.
    New differences to achieve: ¬ON(DISK2 PEG1)
    Find rules for the differences and sort them ...
    To achieve ¬ON(DISK2 PEG1), Rules (0) can be used.
    New plan for the differences: ¬ON(DISK2 PEG1) by Rule0

                  ——————— Think or Act (11) ———————

    Observe: ON(DISK3 PEG1) ON(DISK2 PEG1) ON(DISK1 PEG1) SIZE>(DISK3 DISK1)
SIZE>(DISK3 DISK2) SIZE>(DISK2 DISK1) [PEG3] [PEG2] [PEG1] [DISK3] [DISK2] [DISK1]
    Current Differences: ¬ON(DISK2 PEG1)

Useful-Rule-Instance:
State: ON(DISK2 PEG1) ¬ON(*diskM* PEG1) ¬INHAND(DISK2) [DISK2] [PEG1]
Action: PICK(DISK2 PEG1)
Predict: INHAND(DISK2) ¬ON(DISK2 PEG1) [PEG1] [DISK2]
Index: 0
Bindings: ((*disk*/DISK2) (*peg*/PEG1))

    Decide to do Propose new subgoals.
    Rule 0 causes SUBGOAL-LOOP.
    Generating an experiment for it.

                  ——————— Think or Act (12) ———————

    Observe: ON(DISK3 PEG1) ON(DISK2 PEG1) ON(DISK1 PEG1) SIZE>(DISK3 DISK1)
SIZE>(DISK3 DISK2) SIZE>(DISK2 DISK1) [PEG3] [PEG2] [PEG1] [DISK3] [DISK2] [DISK1]
    Current Differences: (EXPERIMENT)

Useful-Rule-Instance:
State: ON(DISK3 PEG1) ON(DISK1 PEG1) ¬INHAND(DISK1) [PEG1] [DISK1]
Action: PICK(DISK1 PEG1)
Predict: ON(DISK1 PEG1)
Index: 2
Bindings: ((*disk*/DISK1) (*peg*/PEG1) (*diskM*/DISK3))

    Decide to do PICK(DISK1 PEG1).
    Execute PICK DISK1 from PEG1.
    Waiting for responses from the environment ...
    Observe: ON(DISK3 PEG1) ON(DISK2 PEG1) INHAND(DISK1) SIZE>(DISK3 DISK1)
SIZE>(DISK3 DISK2) SIZE>(DISK2 DISK1) [PEG3] [PEG2] [PEG1] [DISK3] [DISK2] [DISK1]
    Wrong prediction: (ON(DISK1 PEG1)) 2 ((*disk*/DISK1) (*peg*/PEG1) (*diskM*/DISK3))
    Explain the surprise by comparing with the last successful application viewed by the current rela-
tions.
    (ON(DISK3 PEG1) ON(DISK2 PEG1) ON(DISK1 PEG1) SIZE>(DISK3 DISK1) SIZE>(DISK3
DISK2) SIZE>(DISK2 DISK1) [PEG3] [PEG2] [PEG1] [DISK3] [DISK2] [DISK1] (NIL NIL) PICK
(DISK3 PEG1) ((*diskM*/DISK2) (*peg*/PEG1) (*disk*/DISK3)))
    Explanation 1: Relation differences inside bindings.
    Rel-Then: NIL
    Rel-Now: NIL
    Creating relations on the bound things ...
    Explanation 2: Middle circle relation differences.
    Rel-Then: (SIZE>(DISK3 DISK2) SIZE>(DISK3 DISK1) ON(DISK1 PEG1) ON(DISK2 PEG1))
    Rel-Now: (SIZE>(DISK2 DISK1) SIZE>(DISK3 DISK1) ON(DISK2 PEG1) ON(DISK3 PEG1))
    WHY: ¬(SIZE>(*disk diskM*) ON(*diskM peg*))
    Update the wrong rule and complement its sibling.
    **** BEGIN PRINTING MODEL ****

Index: 0
Sibling: 2
State: ¬(SIZE>(*disk diskM*) ON(*diskM peg*)) ON(*disk peg*) ¬INHAND(*disk*) [*peg*] [*disk*]
Action: PICK(*disk peg*)
Predict: INHAND(*disk*) ¬ON(*disk peg*) [*peg*] [*disk*]

Index: 1
Sibling: NIL
State: INHAND(*disk*) ¬ON(*disk peg*) [*peg*] [*disk*]
Action: PUT(*disk peg*)
Predict: ON(*disk peg*) ¬INHAND(*disk*) [*peg*] [*disk*]

Index: 2
Sibling: 0
State: ON(*diskM peg*) SIZE>(*disk diskM*) [*disk*] [*peg*] ON(*disk peg*) ¬INHAND(*disk*)
Action: PICK(*disk peg*)
Predict: ON(*disk peg*)

**** END PRINTING MODEL ****
    Experiment done.
    Planning for the remaining goals: ON(DISK1 PEG1) ON(DISK2 PEG1) ON(DISK3 PEG3)
    Differences towards the goal ON(DISK1 PEG1) are: ON(DISK1 PEG1)
    Differences towards the goal ON(DISK3 PEG3) are: ON(DISK3 PEG3)
    Find rules for the differences and sort them ...
    To achieve ON(DISK1 PEG1), Rules (1) can be used.
    To achieve ON(DISK3 PEG3), Rules (1) can be used.

———————— Think or Act (13) ————————

    Observe: ON(DISK3 PEG1) ON(DISK2 PEG1) INHAND(DISK1) SIZE>(DISK3 DISK1)
SIZE>(DISK3 DISK2) SIZE>(DISK2 DISK1) [PEG3] [PEG2] [PEG1] [DISK3] [DISK2] [DISK1]
    Current Differences: ON(DISK1 PEG1)

Useful-Rule-Instance:
State: INHAND(DISK1) ¬ON(DISK1 PEG1) [PEG1] [DISK1]
Action: PUT(DISK1 PEG1)
Predict: ON(DISK1 PEG1) ¬INHAND(DISK1) [PEG1] [DISK1]
Index: 1
Bindings: ((*disk*/DISK1) (*peg*/PEG1))

    Decide to do PUT(DISK1 PEG1).
    Execute PUT DISK1 on PEG1.
    Waiting for responses from the environment ...
    Observe: ON(DISK3 PEG1) ON(DISK2 PEG1) ON(DISK1 PEG1) SIZE>(DISK3 DISK1)
SIZE>(DISK3 DISK2) SIZE>(DISK2 DISK1) [PEG3] [PEG2] [PEG1] [DISK3] [DISK2] [DISK1]
    Goal ON(DISK1 PEG1) accomplished!

———————— Think or Act (14) ————————

    Observe: ON(DISK3 PEG1) ON(DISK2 PEG1) ON(DISK1 PEG1) SIZE>(DISK3 DISK1)
SIZE>(DISK3 DISK2) SIZE>(DISK2 DISK1) [PEG3] [PEG2] [PEG1] [DISK3] [DISK2] [DISK1]
    Current Differences: ON(DISK3 PEG3)

Useful-Rule-Instance:
State: INHAND(DISK3) ¬ON(DISK3 PEG3) [PEG3] [DISK3]
Action: PUT(DISK3 PEG3)
Predict: ON(DISK3 PEG3) ¬INHAND(DISK3) [PEG3] [DISK3]
Index: 1
Bindings: ((*disk*/DISK3) (*peg*/PEG3))

    Decide to do Propose new subgoals.
    New differences to achieve: INHAND(DISK3)
    Find rules for the differences and sort them ...
    To achieve INHAND(DISK3), Rules (0) can be used.
    New plan for the differences: INHAND(DISK3) by Rule0

——————— Think or Act (15) ———————

Observe: ON(DISK3 PEG1) ON(DISK2 PEG1) ON(DISK1 PEG1) SIZE>(DISK3 DISK1)
SIZE>(DISK3 DISK2) SIZE>(DISK2 DISK1) [PEG3] [PEG2] [PEG1] [DISK3] [DISK2] [DISK1]
    Current Differences: INHAND(DISK3)
    Rule's action has free variable: *peg* is bound to PEG1.

Useful-Rule-Instance:
State: ¬(SIZE>(DISK3 *diskM*) ON(*diskM* PEG1)) ON(DISK3 PEG1)
        ¬INHAND(DISK3) [PEG1] [DISK3]
Action: PICK(DISK3 PEG1)
Predict: INHAND(DISK3) ¬ON(DISK3 PEG1) [PEG1] [DISK3]
Index: 0
Bindings: ((*peg*/PEG1) (*disk*/DISK3))

    Decide to do Propose new subgoals.
    New differences to achieve: ¬(SIZE>(DISK3 DISK1) ON(DISK1 PEG1))
    Find rules for the differences and sort them ...
    To achieve ¬SIZE>(DISK3 DISK1), Rules NIL can be used.
    To achieve ¬ON(DISK1 PEG1), Rules (0) can be used.
    New plan for the differences: ¬(SIZE>(DISK3 DISK1) ON(DISK1 PEG1)) by Rule0

——————— Think or Act (16) ———————

Observe: ON(DISK3 PEG1) ON(DISK2 PEG1) ON(DISK1 PEG1) SIZE>(DISK3 DISK1)
SIZE>(DISK3 DISK2) SIZE>(DISK2 DISK1) [PEG3] [PEG2] [PEG1] [DISK3] [DISK2] [DISK1]
    Current Differences: ¬(SIZE>(DISK3 DISK1) ON(DISK1 PEG1))

Useful-Rule-Instance:
State: ¬(SIZE>(DISK1 *diskM*) ON(*diskM* PEG1)) ON(DISK1 PEG1)
        ¬INHAND(DISK1) [PEG1] [DISK1]
Action: PICK(DISK1 PEG1)
Predict: INHAND(DISK1) ¬ON(DISK1 PEG1) [PEG1] [DISK1]
Index: 0
Bindings: ((*disk*/DISK1) (*peg*/PEG1))

    Decide to do PICK(DISK1 PEG1).
    Execute PICK DISK1 from PEG1.
    Waiting for responses from the environment ...
    Observe: ON(DISK3 PEG1) ON(DISK2 PEG1) INHAND(DISK1) SIZE>(DISK3 DISK1)
SIZE>(DISK3 DISK2) SIZE>(DISK2 DISK1) [PEG3] [PEG2] [PEG1] [DISK3] [DISK2] [DISK1]
    Goal ¬(SIZE>(DISK3 DISK1) ON(DISK1 PEG1)) accomplished!

——————— Think or Act (17) ———————

Observe: ON(DISK3 PEG1) ON(DISK2 PEG1) INHAND(DISK1) SIZE>(DISK3 DISK1)
SIZE>(DISK3 DISK2) SIZE>(DISK2 DISK1) [PEG3] [PEG2] [PEG1] [DISK3] [DISK2] [DISK1]
    Current Differences: INHAND(DISK3)

Useful-Rule-Instance:
State: ¬(SIZE>(DISK3 *diskM*) ON(*diskM* PEG1)) ON(DISK3 PEG1)
        ¬INHAND(DISK3) [PEG1] [DISK3]
Action: PICK(DISK3 PEG1)
Predict: INHAND(DISK3) ¬ON(DISK3 PEG1) [PEG1] [DISK3]
Index: 0
Bindings: ((*peg*/PEG1) (*disk*/DISK3))

    Decide to do Propose new subgoals.
    New differences to achieve: ¬(SIZE>(DISK3 DISK2) ON(DISK2 PEG1))
    Find rules for the differences and sort them ...
    To achieve ¬SIZE>(DISK3 DISK2), Rules NIL can be used.
    To achieve ¬ON(DISK2 PEG1), Rules (0) can be used.
    New plan for the differences: ¬(SIZE>(DISK3 DISK2) ON(DISK2 PEG1)) by Rule0

———————— Think or Act (18) ————————

Observe: ON(DISK3 PEG1) ON(DISK2 PEG1) INHAND(DISK1) SIZE>(DISK3 DISK1) SIZE>(DISK3 DISK2) SIZE>(DISK2 DISK1) [PEG3] [PEG2] [PEG1] [DISK3] [DISK2] [DISK1]
Current Differences: ¬(SIZE>(DISK3 DISK2) ON(DISK2 PEG1))

Useful-Rule-Instance:
State: ¬(SIZE>(DISK2 *diskM*) ON(*diskM* PEG1)) ON(DISK2 PEG1)
    ¬INHAND(DISK2) [PEG1] [DISK2]
Action: PICK(DISK2 PEG1)
Predict: INHAND(DISK2) ¬ON(DISK2 PEG1) [PEG1] [DISK2]
Index: 0
Bindings: ((*disk*/DISK2) (*peg*/PEG1))

Decide to do PICK(DISK2 PEG1).
Execute PICK DISK2 from PEG1.
Waiting for responses from the environment ...
Observe: ON(DISK3 PEG1) ON(DISK2 PEG1) INHAND(DISK1) SIZE>(DISK3 DISK1) SIZE>(DISK3 DISK2) SIZE>(DISK2 DISK1) [PEG3] [PEG2] [PEG1] [DISK3] [DISK2] [DISK1]
Wrong prediction: (INHAND(DISK2) ¬ON(DISK2 PEG1)) [PEG1] [DISK2] Rule0 (*disk*/DISK2, *peg*/PEG1)
Explain the surprise by comparing with the last successful application viewed by the current relations.
(ON(DISK3 PEG1) ON(DISK2 PEG1) ON(DISK1 PEG1) SIZE>(DISK3 DISK1) SIZE>(DISK3 DISK2) SIZE>(DISK2 DISK1) [PEG3] [PEG2] [PEG1] [DISK3] [DISK2] [DISK1] (NIL NIL) PICK (DISK1 PEG1) ((*disk*/DISK1) (*peg*/PEG1)))
Explanation 1: Relation differences inside bindings.
Rel-Then: NIL
Rel-Now: (INHAND(DISK1))
WHY: INHAND(*diskN*)
Update the wrong rule and complement its sibling.
**** BEGIN PRINTING MODEL ****

Index: 0
Sibling: 2
State: ON(*disk peg*)
    ¬(SIZE>(*disk diskM*) ON(*diskM peg*))
    ¬INHAND(*diskN*) ¬INHAND(*disk*) [*disk*] [*peg*]
Action: PICK(*disk peg*)
Predict: INHAND(*disk*) ¬ON(*disk peg*) [*peg*] [*disk*]

Index: 1
Sibling: NIL
State: INHAND(*disk*) ¬ON(*disk peg*) [*peg*] [*disk*]
Action: PUT(*disk peg*)
Predict: ON(*disk peg*) ¬INHAND(*disk*) [*peg*] [*disk*]

Index: 2
Sibling: 0
State: ¬(¬INHAND(*diskN*) ¬(SIZE>(*disk diskM*) ON(*diskM peg*)))
    ON(*disk peg*) ¬INHAND(*disk*) [*peg*] [*disk*]
Action: PICK(*disk peg*)
Predict: ON(*disk peg*)

**** END PRINTING MODEL ****
Planning for the remaining goals: ON(DISK1 PEG1) ON(DISK2 PEG1) ON(DISK3 PEG3)
Differences towards the goal ON(DISK1 PEG1) are: ON(DISK1 PEG1)
Differences towards the goal ON(DISK3 PEG3) are: ON(DISK3 PEG3)
Find rules for the differences and sort them ...
To achieve ON(DISK1 PEG1), Rules (1) can be used.
To achieve ON(DISK3 PEG3), Rules (1) can be used.

———————— Think or Act (19) ————————

    Observe: ON(DISK3 PEG1) ON(DISK2 PEG1) INHAND(DISK1) SIZE>(DISK3 DISK1)
SIZE>(DISK3 DISK2) SIZE>(DISK2 DISK1) [PEG3] [PEG2] [PEG1] [DISK3] [DISK2] [DISK1]
    Current Differences: ON(DISK1 PEG1)

Useful-Rule-Instance:
State: INHAND(DISK1) ¬ON(DISK1 PEG1) [PEG1] [DISK1]
Action: PUT(DISK1 PEG1)
Predict: ON(DISK1 PEG1) ¬INHAND(DISK1) [PEG1] [DISK1]
Index: 1
Bindings: ((*disk*/DISK1) (*peg*/PEG1))

    Decide to do PUT(DISK1 PEG1).
    Execute PUT DISK1 on PEG1.
    Waiting for responses from the environment ...
    Observe: ON(DISK3 PEG1) ON(DISK2 PEG1) ON(DISK1 PEG1) SIZE>(DISK3 DISK1)
SIZE>(DISK3 DISK2) SIZE>(DISK2 DISK1) [PEG3] [PEG2] [PEG1] [DISK3] [DISK2] [DISK1]
    Goal ON(DISK1 PEG1) accomplished!

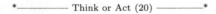
                    ———————— Think or Act (20) ————————

    Observe: ON(DISK3 PEG1) ON(DISK2 PEG1) ON(DISK1 PEG1) SIZE>(DISK3 DISK1)
SIZE>(DISK3 DISK2) SIZE>(DISK2 DISK1) [PEG3] [PEG2] [PEG1] [DISK3] [DISK2] [DISK1]
    Current Differences: ON(DISK3 PEG3)

Useful-Rule-Instance:
State: INHAND(DISK3) ¬ON(DISK3 PEG3) [PEG3] [DISK3]
Action: PUT(DISK3 PEG3)
Predict: ON(DISK3 PEG3) ¬INHAND(DISK3) [PEG3] [DISK3]
Index: 1
Bindings: ((*disk*/DISK3) (*peg*/PEG3))

    Decide to do Propose new subgoals.
    New differences to achieve: INHAND(DISK3)
    Find rules for the differences and sort them ...
    To achieve INHAND(DISK3), Rules (0) can be used.
    New plan for the differences: INHAND(DISK3) by Rule0

                    ———————— Think or Act (21) ————————

    Observe: ON(DISK3 PEG1) ON(DISK2 PEG1) ON(DISK1 PEG1) SIZE>(DISK3 DISK1)
SIZE>(DISK3 DISK2) SIZE>(DISK2 DISK1) [PEG3] [PEG2] [PEG1] [DISK3] [DISK2] [DISK1]
    Current Differences: INHAND(DISK3)
    Rule's action has free variable: *peg* is bound to PEG1.

Useful-Rule-Instance:
State: ON(DISK3 PEG1)
       ¬(SIZE>(DISK3 *diskM*) ON(*diskM* PEG1))
       ¬INHAND(*diskN*) ¬INHAND(DISK3) [DISK3] [PEG1]
Action: PICK(DISK3 PEG1)
Predict: INHAND(DISK3) ¬ON(DISK3 PEG1) [PEG1] [DISK3]
Index: 0
Bindings: ((*peg*/PEG1) (*disk*/DISK3))

    Decide to do Propose new subgoals.
    New differences to achieve: ¬(SIZE>(DISK3 DISK1) ON(DISK1 PEG1))
    Find rules for the differences and sort them ...
    To achieve ¬SIZE>(DISK3 DISK1), Rules NIL can be used.
    To achieve ¬ON(DISK1 PEG1), Rules (0) can be used.
    New plan for the differences: ¬(SIZE>(DISK3 DISK1) ON(DISK1 PEG1)) by Rule0

                    ———————— Think or Act (22) ————————

Observe: ON(DISK3 PEG1) ON(DISK2 PEG1) ON(DISK1 PEG1) SIZE>(DISK3 DISK1)
SIZE>(DISK3 DISK2) SIZE>(DISK2 DISK1) [PEG3] [PEG2] [PEG1] [DISK3] [DISK2] [DISK1]
Current Differences: ¬(SIZE>(DISK3 DISK1) ON(DISK1 PEG1))

Useful-Rule-Instance:
State: ON(DISK1 PEG1)
      ¬(SIZE>(DISK1 *diskM*) ON(*diskM* PEG1))
      ¬INHAND(*diskN*) ¬INHAND(DISK1) [DISK1] [PEG1]
Action: PICK(DISK1 PEG1)
Predict: INHAND(DISK1) ¬ON(DISK1 PEG1) [PEG1] [DISK1]
Index: 0
Bindings: ((*disk*/DISK1) (*peg*/PEG1))

Decide to do PICK(DISK1 PEG1).
Execute PICK DISK1 from PEG1.
Waiting for responses from the environment ...
Observe: ON(DISK3 PEG1) ON(DISK2 PEG1) INHAND(DISK1) SIZE>(DISK3 DISK1)
SIZE>(DISK3 DISK2) SIZE>(DISK2 DISK1) [PEG3] [PEG2] [PEG1] [DISK3] [DISK2] [DISK1]
Goal ¬(SIZE>(DISK3 DISK1) ON(DISK1 PEG1)) accomplished!

——————— Think or Act (23) ———————

Observe: ON(DISK3 PEG1) ON(DISK2 PEG1) INHAND(DISK1) SIZE>(DISK3 DISK1)
SIZE>(DISK3 DISK2) SIZE>(DISK2 DISK1) [PEG3] [PEG2] [PEG1] [DISK3] [DISK2] [DISK1]
Current Differences: INHAND(DISK3)

Useful-Rule-Instance:
State: [DISK3] [PEG1] ON(DISK3 PEG1)
      ¬(SIZE>(DISK3 *diskM*) ON(*diskM* PEG1))
      ¬INHAND(*diskN*) ¬INHAND(DISK3)
Action: PICK(DISK3 PEG1)
Predict: INHAND(DISK3) ¬ON(DISK3 PEG1) [PEG1] [DISK3]
Index: 0
Bindings: ((*peg*/PEG1) (*disk*/DISK3))

Decide to do Propose new subgoals.
New differences to achieve: ¬(SIZE>(DISK3 DISK2) ON(DISK2 PEG1)) ¬INHAND(DISK1)
Find rules for the differences and sort them ...
To achieve ¬SIZE>(DISK3 DISK2), Rules NIL can be used.
To achieve ¬ON(DISK2 PEG1), Rules (0) can be used.
To achieve ¬INHAND(DISK1), Rules (1) can be used.
New plan for the differences:
¬(SIZE>(DISK3 DISK2) ON(DISK2 PEG1)) by Rule0
¬INHAND(DISK1) by Rule1

——————— Think or Act (24) ———————

Observe: ON(DISK3 PEG1) ON(DISK2 PEG1) INHAND(DISK1) SIZE>(DISK3 DISK1)
SIZE>(DISK3 DISK2) SIZE>(DISK2 DISK1) [PEG3] [PEG2] [PEG1] [DISK3] [DISK2] [DISK1]
Current Differences: ¬(SIZE>(DISK3 DISK2) ON(DISK2 PEG1))

Useful-Rule-Instance:
State: [DISK2] [PEG1] ON(DISK2 PEG1)
      ¬(SIZE>(DISK2 *diskM*) ON(*diskM* PEG1))
      ¬INHAND(*diskN*) ¬INHAND(DISK2)
Action: PICK(DISK2 PEG1)
Predict: INHAND(DISK2) ¬ON(DISK2 PEG1) [PEG1] [DISK2]
Index: 0
Bindings: ((*disk*/DISK2) (*peg*/PEG1))

Decide to do Propose new subgoals.
New differences to achieve: ¬INHAND(DISK1)
Find rules for the differences and sort them ...
To achieve ¬INHAND(DISK1), Rules (1) can be used.
New plan for the differences: ¬INHAND(DISK1) by Rule1

————— Think or Act (25) —————

Observe: ON(DISK3 PEG1) ON(DISK2 PEG1) INHAND(DISK1) SIZE>(DISK3 DISK1)
SIZE>(DISK3 DISK2) SIZE>(DISK2 DISK1) [PEG3] [PEG2] [PEG1] [DISK3] [DISK2] [DISK1]
Current Differences: ¬INHAND(DISK1)
Rule's action has free variable: *peg* is bound to PEG2.

Useful-Rule-Instance:
State: INHAND(DISK1) ¬ON(DISK1 PEG2) [PEG2] [DISK1]
Action: PUT(DISK1 PEG2)
Predict: ON(DISK1 PEG2) ¬INHAND(DISK1) [PEG2] [DISK1]
Index: 1
Bindings: ((*peg*/PEG2) (*disk*/DISK1))

Decide to do PUT(DISK1 PEG2).
Execute PUT DISK1 on PEG2.
Waiting for responses from the environment ...
Observe: ON(DISK3 PEG1) ON(DISK2 PEG1) ON(DISK1 PEG2) SIZE>(DISK3 DISK1)
SIZE>(DISK3 DISK2) SIZE>(DISK2 DISK1) [PEG3] [PEG2] [PEG1] [DISK3] [DISK2] [DISK1]
Goal ON(DISK1 PEG2) accomplished!
Goal ¬INHAND(DISK1) accomplished!

————— Think or Act (26) —————

Observe: ON(DISK3 PEG1) ON(DISK2 PEG1) ON(DISK1 PEG2) SIZE>(DISK3 DISK1)
SIZE>(DISK3 DISK2) SIZE>(DISK2 DISK1) [PEG3] [PEG2] [PEG1] [DISK3] [DISK2] [DISK1]
Current Differences: ¬(SIZE>(DISK3 DISK2) ON(DISK2 PEG1))

Useful-Rule-Instance:
State: [DISK2] [PEG1] ON(DISK2 PEG1)
      ¬(SIZE>(DISK2 *diskM*) ON(*diskM* PEG1))
      ¬INHAND(*diskN*) ¬INHAND(DISK2)
Action: PICK(DISK2 PEG1)
Predict: INHAND(DISK2) ¬ON(DISK2 PEG1) [PEG1] [DISK2]
Index: 0
Bindings: ((*disk*/DISK2) (*peg*/PEG1))

Decide to do PICK(DISK2 PEG1).
Execute PICK DISK2 from PEG1.
Waiting for responses from the environment ...
Observe: ON(DISK3 PEG1) INHAND(DISK2) ON(DISK1 PEG2) SIZE>(DISK3 DISK1)
SIZE>(DISK3 DISK2) SIZE>(DISK2 DISK1) [PEG3] [PEG2] [PEG1] [DISK3] [DISK2] [DISK1]
Goal ¬(SIZE>(DISK3 DISK2) ON(DISK2 PEG1)) accomplished!
Goal ¬INHAND(DISK1) accomplished!

————— Think or Act (27) —————

Observe: ON(DISK3 PEG1) INHAND(DISK2) ON(DISK1 PEG2) SIZE>(DISK3 DISK1)
SIZE>(DISK3 DISK2) SIZE>(DISK2 DISK1) [PEG3] [PEG2] [PEG1] [DISK3] [DISK2] [DISK1]
Current Differences: INHAND(DISK3)

Useful-Rule-Instance:
State: [DISK3] [PEG1] ON(DISK3 PEG1)
      ¬(SIZE>(DISK3 *diskM*) ON(*diskM* PEG1))
      ¬INHAND(*diskN*) ¬INHAND(DISK3)
Action: PICK(DISK3 PEG1)
Predict: INHAND(DISK3) ¬ON(DISK3 PEG1) [PEG1] [DISK3]
Index: 0
Bindings: ((*peg*/PEG1) (*disk*/DISK3))

Decide to do Propose new subgoals.
New differences to achieve: ¬INHAND(DISK2)
Find rules for the differences and sort them ...
To achieve ¬INHAND(DISK2), Rules (1) can be used.
New plan for the differences: ¬INHAND(DISK2) by Rule1

——————— Think or Act (28) ———————

Observe: ON(DISK3 PEG1) INHAND(DISK2) ON(DISK1 PEG2) SIZE>(DISK3 DISK1)
SIZE>(DISK3 DISK2) SIZE>(DISK2 DISK1) [PEG3] [PEG2] [PEG1] [DISK3] [DISK2] [DISK1]
Current Differences: ¬INHAND(DISK2)
Rule's action has free variable: *peg* is bound to PEG2.

Useful-Rule-Instance:
State: INHAND(DISK2) ¬ON(DISK2 PEG2) [PEG2] [DISK2]
Action: PUT(DISK2 PEG2)
Predict: ON(DISK2 PEG2) ¬INHAND(DISK2) [PEG2] [DISK2]
Index: 1
Bindings: ((*peg*/PEG2) (*disk*/DISK2))

Decide to do PUT(DISK2 PEG2).
Execute PUT DISK2 on PEG2.
Waiting for responses from the environment ...
Observe: ON(DISK3 PEG1) INHAND(DISK2) ON(DISK1 PEG2) SIZE>(DISK3 DISK1)
SIZE>(DISK3 DISK2) SIZE>(DISK2 DISK1) [PEG3] [PEG2] [PEG1] [DISK3] [DISK2] [DISK1]
Wrong prediction: ON(DISK2 PEG2) ¬INHAND(DISK2) [PEG2] [DISK2] Rule1 ((*peg*/PEG2)
(*disk*/DISK2))
Explain the surprise by comparing with the last successful application viewed by the current rela-
tions.
(ON(DISK3 PEG1) ON(DISK2 PEG1) INHAND(DISK1) SIZE>(DISK3 DISK1) SIZE>(DISK3
DISK2) SIZE>(DISK2 DISK1) [PEG3] [PEG2] [PEG1] [DISK3] [DISK2] [DISK1] (NIL NIL) PUT(DISK1
PEG2) ((*peg*/PEG2) (*disk*/DISK1)))
Explanation 1: Relation differences inside bindings.
Rel-Then: INHAND(*disk*)
Rel-Now: INHAND(*disk*)
Creating relations on the bound things ...
Explanation 2: Middle circle relation differences.
Rel-Then: (SIZE>(DISK2 DISK1) SIZE>(DISK3 DISK1))
Rel-Now: (SIZE>(DISK2 DISK1) SIZE>(DISK3 DISK2) ON(DISK1 PEG2))
WHY: ON(*diskP peg*)
Splitting Rule1 with WHY.
**** BEGIN PRINTING MODEL ****

Index: 0
Sibling: 2
State: [*disk*] [*peg*] ON(*disk peg*)
        ¬(SIZE>(*disk diskM*) ON(*diskM peg*))
        ¬INHAND(*diskN*) ¬INHAND(*disk*)
Action: PICK(*disk peg*)
Predict: INHAND(*disk*) ¬ON(*disk peg*) [*peg*] [*disk*]

Index: 1
Sibling: 3
State: [*disk*] [*peg*] INHAND(*disk*) ¬ON(*diskP peg*)
        ¬ON(*disk peg*)
Action: PUT(*disk peg*)
Predict: ON(*disk peg*) ¬INHAND(*disk*) [*peg*] [*disk*]

Index: 2
Sibling: 0
State: ¬(¬INHAND(*diskN*) ¬(SIZE>(*disk diskM*) ON(*diskM peg*)))
        ON(*disk peg*) ¬INHAND(*disk*) [*peg*] [*disk*]
Action: PICK(*disk peg*)
Predict: ON(*disk peg*)

Index: 3
Sibling: 1
State: ON(*diskP peg*) INHAND(*disk*) ¬ON(*disk peg*) [*peg*] [*disk*]
Action: PUT(*disk peg*)
Predict: INHAND(*disk*)

**** END PRINTING MODEL ****
Planning for the remaining goals: ON(DISK1 PEG1) ON(DISK2 PEG1) ON(DISK3 PEG3)
Differences towards the goal ON(DISK1 PEG1) are: ON(DISK1 PEG1)
Differences towards the goal ON(DISK2 PEG1) are: ON(DISK2 PEG1)
Differences towards the goal ON(DISK3 PEG3) are: ON(DISK3 PEG3)
Find rules for the differences and sort them ...
To achieve ON(DISK1 PEG1), Rules (1) can be used.
To achieve ON(DISK2 PEG1), Rules (1) can be used.
To achieve ON(DISK3 PEG3), Rules (1) can be used.
Rule1 causes GOAL-CONFLICT.
Generating an experiment for it.
Generating an Experiment ...

——————— Think or Act (29) ———————

Observe: ON(DISK3 PEG1) INHAND(DISK2) ON(DISK1 PEG2) SIZE>(DISK3 DISK1)
SIZE>(DISK3 DISK2) SIZE>(DISK2 DISK1) [PEG3] [PEG2] [PEG1] [DISK3] [DISK2] [DISK1]
Current Differences: (EXPERIMENT)

Useful-Rule-Instance:
State: ON(DISK3 PEG1) INHAND(DISK2) ¬ON(DISK2 PEG1) [PEG1] [DISK2]
Action: PUT(DISK2 PEG1)
Predict: INHAND(DISK2)
Index: 3
Bindings: ((*disk*/DISK2) (*peg*/PEG1) (*diskP*/DISK3))

Decide to do PUT(DISK2 PEG1).
Execute PUT DISK2 on PEG1.
Waiting for responses from the environment ...
Observe: ON(DISK3 PEG1) ON(DISK2 PEG1) ON(DISK1 PEG2) SIZE>(DISK3 DISK1)
SIZE>(DISK3 DISK2) SIZE>(DISK2 DISK1) [PEG3] [PEG2] [PEG1] [DISK3] [DISK2] [DISK1]
Wrong prediction: INHAND(DISK2) Rule3 ((*disk*/DISK2) (*peg*/PEG1) (*diskP*/DISK3))
Explain the surprise by comparing with the last successful application viewed by the current relations.
(ON(DISK3 PEG1) INHAND(DISK2) ON(DISK1 PEG2) SIZE>(DISK3 DISK1) SIZE>(DISK3
DISK2) SIZE>(DISK2 DISK1) [PEG3] [PEG2] [PEG1] [DISK3] [DISK2] [DISK1] (NIL NIL) PUT(DISK2
PEG2) ((*diskP*/DISK1) (*peg*/PEG2) (*disk*/DISK2)))
Explanation 1: Relation differences inside bindings.
Rel-Then: INHAND(*disk*)
Rel-Now: INHAND(*disk*)
Creating relations on the bound things ...
Explanation 2: Middle circle relation differences.
Rel-Then: (SIZE>(DISK2 DISK1) SIZE>(DISK3 DISK2) ON(DISK1 PEG2))
Rel-Now: (SIZE>(DISK2 DISK1) SIZE>(DISK3 DISK2) ON(DISK3 PEG1))
WHY: ¬(SIZE>(*disk diskP*) ON(*diskP peg*))
Update the wrong rule and complement its sibling.
**** BEGIN PRINTING MODEL ****

Index: 0
Sibling: 2
State: [*disk*] [*peg*] ON(*disk peg*)
       ¬(SIZE>(*disk diskM*) ON(*diskM peg*))
       ¬INHAND(*diskN*) ¬INHAND(*disk*)
Action: PICK(*disk peg*)
Predict: INHAND(*disk*) ¬ON(*disk peg*) [*peg*] [*disk*]

Index: 1

Sibling: 3
State: ¬(SIZE>(*disk diskP*) ON(*diskP peg*))
  INHAND(*disk*) ¬ON(*disk peg*) [*peg*] [*disk*]
Action: PUT(*disk peg*)
Predict: ON(*disk peg*) ¬INHAND(*disk*) [*peg*] [*disk*]

Index: 2
Sibling: 0
State: ¬(SIZE>(*disk diskM*) ON(*diskM peg*))
  INHAND(*diskN*) ON(*disk peg*) ¬INHAND(*disk*) [*peg*] [*disk*]
Action: PICK(*disk peg*)
Predict: ON(*disk peg*)

Index: 3
Sibling: 1
State: ON(*diskP peg*) SIZE>(*disk diskP*) [*disk*] [*peg*]
  INHAND(*disk*) ¬ON(*disk peg*)
Action: PUT(*disk peg*)
Predict: INHAND(*disk*)

  **** END PRINTING MODEL ****
Experiment done.
Planning for the remaining goals: ON(DISK1 PEG1) ON(DISK2 PEG1) ON(DISK3 PEG3)
Differences towards the goal ON(DISK1 PEG1) are: ON(DISK1 PEG1)
Differences towards the goal ON(DISK3 PEG3) are: ON(DISK3 PEG3)
Find rules for the differences and sort them ...
To achieve ON(DISK1 PEG1), Rules (1) can be used.
To achieve ON(DISK3 PEG3), Rules (1) can be used.

    ——————— Think or Act (30) ———————

  Observe: ON(DISK3 PEG1) ON(DISK2 PEG1) ON(DISK1 PEG2) SIZE>(DISK3 DISK1)
SIZE>(DISK3 DISK2) SIZE>(DISK2 DISK1) [PEG3] [PEG2] [PEG1] [DISK3] [DISK2] [DISK1]
  Current Differences: ON(DISK1 PEG1)

Useful-Rule-Instance:
State: ¬(SIZE>(DISK1 *diskP*) ON(*diskP* PEG1)) INHAND(DISK1)
  ¬ON(DISK1 PEG1) [PEG1] [DISK1]
Action: PUT(DISK1 PEG1)
Predict: ON(DISK1 PEG1) ¬INHAND(DISK1) [PEG1] [DISK1]
Index: 1
Bindings: ((*disk*/DISK1) (*peg*/PEG1))

  Decide to do Propose new subgoals.
New differences to achieve: INHAND(DISK1)
Find rules for the differences and sort them ...
To achieve INHAND(DISK1), Rules (0) can be used.
New plan for the differences: INHAND(DISK1) by Rule0

    ——————— Think or Act (31) ———————

  Observe: ON(DISK3 PEG1) ON(DISK2 PEG1) ON(DISK1 PEG2) SIZE>(DISK3 DISK1)
SIZE>(DISK3 DISK2) SIZE>(DISK2 DISK1) [PEG3] [PEG2] [PEG1] [DISK3] [DISK2] [DISK1]
  Current Differences: INHAND(DISK1)
  Rule's action has free variable: *peg* is bound to PEG2.

Useful-Rule-Instance:
State: [DISK1] [PEG2] ON(DISK1 PEG2)
  ¬(SIZE>(DISK1 *diskM*) ON(*diskM* PEG2))
  ¬INHAND(*diskN*) ¬INHAND(DISK1)
Action: PICK(DISK1 PEG2)
Predict: INHAND(DISK1) ¬ON(DISK1 PEG2) [PEG2] [DISK1]
Index: 0
Bindings: ((*peg*/PEG2) (*disk*/DISK1))

Decide to do PICK(DISK1 PEG2).
Execute PICK DISK1 from PEG2.
Waiting for responses from the environment ...
Observe: ON(DISK3 PEG1) ON(DISK2 PEG1) INHAND(DISK1) SIZE>(DISK3 DISK1)
SIZE>(DISK3 DISK2) SIZE>(DISK2 DISK1) [PEG3] [PEG2] [PEG1] [DISK3] [DISK2] [DISK1]
Goal INHAND(DISK1) accomplished!

————— Think or Act (32) —————

Observe: ON(DISK3 PEG1) ON(DISK2 PEG1) INHAND(DISK1) SIZE>(DISK3 DISK1)
SIZE>(DISK3 DISK2) SIZE>(DISK2 DISK1) [PEG3] [PEG2] [PEG1] [DISK3] [DISK2] [DISK1]
Current Differences: ON(DISK1 PEG1)

Useful-Rule-Instance:
State: ¬(SIZE>(DISK1 $diskP$) ON($diskP$ PEG1)) INHAND(DISK1)
        ¬ON(DISK1 PEG1) [PEG1] [DISK1]
Action: PUT(DISK1 PEG1)
Predict: ON(DISK1 PEG1) ¬INHAND(DISK1) [PEG1] [DISK1]
Index: 1
Bindings: (($disk$/DISK1) (peg/PEG1))

Decide to do PUT(DISK1 PEG1).
Execute PUT DISK1 on PEG1.
Waiting for responses from the environment ...
Observe: ON(DISK3 PEG1) ON(DISK2 PEG1) ON(DISK1 PEG1) SIZE>(DISK3 DISK1)
SIZE>(DISK3 DISK2) SIZE>(DISK2 DISK1) [PEG3] [PEG2] [PEG1] [DISK3] [DISK2] [DISK1]
Goal ON(DISK1 PEG1) accomplished!

————— Think or Act (33) —————

Observe: ON(DISK3 PEG1) ON(DISK2 PEG1) ON(DISK1 PEG1) SIZE>(DISK3 DISK1)
SIZE>(DISK3 DISK2) SIZE>(DISK2 DISK1) [PEG3] [PEG2] [PEG1] [DISK3] [DISK2] [DISK1]
Current Differences: ON(DISK3 PEG3)

Useful-Rule-Instance:
State: ¬(SIZE>(DISK3 $diskP$) ON($diskP$ PEG3)) INHAND(DISK3)
        ¬ON(DISK3 PEG3) [PEG3] [DISK3]
Action: PUT(DISK3 PEG3)
Predict: ON(DISK3 PEG3) ¬INHAND(DISK3) [PEG3] [DISK3]
Index: 1
Bindings: (($disk$/DISK3) (peg/PEG3))

Decide to do Propose new subgoals.
New differences to achieve: INHAND(DISK3)
Find rules for the differences and sort them ...
To achieve INHAND(DISK3), Rules (0) can be used.
New plan for the differences: INHAND(DISK3) by Rule0

————— Think or Act (34) —————

Observe: ON(DISK3 PEG1) ON(DISK2 PEG1) ON(DISK1 PEG1) SIZE>(DISK3 DISK1)
SIZE>(DISK3 DISK2) SIZE>(DISK2 DISK1) [PEG3] [PEG2] [PEG1] [DISK3] [DISK2] [DISK1]
Current Differences: INHAND(DISK3)
Rule's action has free variable: peg is bound to PEG1.

Useful-Rule-Instance:
State: [DISK3] [PEG1] ON(DISK3 PEG1)
        ¬(SIZE>(DISK3 $diskM$) ON($diskM$ PEG1))
        ¬INHAND($diskN$) ¬INHAND(DISK3)
Action: PICK(DISK3 PEG1)
Predict: INHAND(DISK3) ¬ON(DISK3 PEG1) [PEG1] [DISK3]
Index: 0
Bindings: ((peg/PEG1) ($disk$/DISK3))

Decide to do Propose new subgoals.
New differences to achieve: ¬(SIZE>(DISK3 DISK1) ON(DISK1 PEG1))
Find rules for the differences and sort them ...
To achieve ¬SIZE>(DISK3 DISK1), Rules NIL can be used.
To achieve ¬ON(DISK1 PEG1), Rules (0) can be used.
New plan for the differences: ¬(SIZE>(DISK3 DISK1) ON(DISK1 PEG1)) by Rule0

——————— Think or Act (35) ———————

Observe: ON(DISK3 PEG1) ON(DISK2 PEG1) ON(DISK1 PEG1) SIZE>(DISK3 DISK1)
SIZE>(DISK3 DISK2) SIZE>(DISK2 DISK1) [PEG3] [PEG2] [PEG1] [DISK3] [DISK2] [DISK1]
   Current Differences: ¬(SIZE>(DISK3 DISK1) ON(DISK1 PEG1))

Useful-Rule-Instance:
State: [DISK1] [PEG1] ON(DISK1 PEG1)
       ¬(SIZE>(DISK1 diskM) ON(diskM PEG1))
       ¬INHAND(diskN) ¬INHAND(DISK1)
Action: PICK(DISK1 PEG1)
Predict: INHAND(DISK1) ¬ON(DISK1 PEG1) [PEG1] [DISK1]
Index: 0
Bindings: ((disk/DISK1) (peg/PEG1))

Decide to do PICK(DISK1 PEG1).
Execute PICK DISK1 from PEG1.
Waiting for responses from the environment ...
Observe: ON(DISK3 PEG1) ON(DISK2 PEG1) INHAND(DISK1) SIZE>(DISK3 DISK1)
SIZE>(DISK3 DISK2) SIZE>(DISK2 DISK1) [PEG3] [PEG2] [PEG1] [DISK3] [DISK2] [DISK1]
   Goal ¬(SIZE>(DISK3 DISK1) ON(DISK1 PEG1)) accomplished!

——————— Think or Act (36) ———————

Observe: ON(DISK3 PEG1) ON(DISK2 PEG1) INHAND(DISK1) SIZE>(DISK3 DISK1)
SIZE>(DISK3 DISK2) SIZE>(DISK2 DISK1) [PEG3] [PEG2] [PEG1] [DISK3] [DISK2] [DISK1]
   Current Differences: INHAND(DISK3)

Useful-Rule-Instance:
State: [DISK3] [PEG1] ON(DISK3 PEG1)
       ¬(SIZE>(DISK3 diskM) ON(diskM PEG1))
       ¬INHAND(diskN) ¬INHAND(DISK3)
Action: PICK(DISK3 PEG1)
Predict: INHAND(DISK3) ¬ON(DISK3 PEG1) [PEG1] [DISK3]
Index: 0
Bindings: ((peg/PEG1) (disk/DISK3))

Decide to do Propose new subgoals.
New differences to achieve: ¬(SIZE>(DISK3 DISK2) ON(DISK2 PEG1)) ¬INHAND(DISK1)
Find rules for the differences and sort them ...
To achieve ¬SIZE>(DISK3 DISK2), Rules NIL can be used.
To achieve ¬ON(DISK2 PEG1), Rules (0) can be used.
To achieve ¬INHAND(DISK1), Rules (1) can be used.
New plan for the differences:
¬(SIZE>(DISK3 DISK2) ON(DISK2 PEG1)) by Rule0
¬INHAND(DISK1) by Rule1

——————— Think or Act (37) ———————

Observe: ON(DISK3 PEG1) ON(DISK2 PEG1) INHAND(DISK1) SIZE>(DISK3 DISK1)
SIZE>(DISK3 DISK2) SIZE>(DISK2 DISK1) [PEG3] [PEG2] [PEG1] [DISK3] [DISK2] [DISK1]
   Current Differences: ¬(SIZE>(DISK3 DISK2) ON(DISK2 PEG1))

Useful-Rule-Instance:
State: [DISK2] [PEG1] ON(DISK2 PEG1)
      ¬(SIZE>(DISK2 *diskM*) ON(*diskM* PEG1))
      ¬INHAND(*diskN*) ¬INHAND(DISK2)
Action: PICK(DISK2 PEG1)
Predict: INHAND(DISK2) ¬ON(DISK2 PEG1) [PEG1] [DISK2]
Index: 0
Bindings: ((*disk*/DISK2) (*peg*/PEG1))

    Decide to do Propose new subgoals.
    New differences to achieve: ¬INHAND(DISK1)
    Find rules for the differences ...
    To achieve ¬INHAND(DISK1), Rules (1) can be used.
    New plan for the differences: ¬INHAND(DISK1) by Rule1

——————— Think or Act (38) ———————

    Observe: ON(DISK3 PEG1) ON(DISK2 PEG1) INHAND(DISK1) SIZE>(DISK3 DISK1)
SIZE>(DISK3 DISK2) SIZE>(DISK2 DISK1) [PEG3] [PEG2] [PEG1] [DISK3] [DISK2] [DISK1]
    Current Differences: ¬INHAND(DISK1)
    Rule's action has free variable: *peg* is bound to PEG2.

Useful-Rule-Instance:
State: ¬(SIZE>(DISK1 *diskP*) ON(*diskP* PEG2)) INHAND(DISK1)
      ¬ON(DISK1 PEG2) [PEG2] [DISK1]
Action: PUT(DISK1 PEG2)
Predict: ON(DISK1 PEG2) ¬INHAND(DISK1) [PEG2] [DISK1]
Index: 1
Bindings: ((*peg*/PEG2) (*disk*/DISK1))

    Decide to do PUT(DISK1 PEG2).
    Execute PUT DISK1 on PEG2.
    Waiting for responses from the environment ...
    Observe: ON(DISK3 PEG1) ON(DISK2 PEG1) ON(DISK1 PEG2) SIZE>(DISK3 DISK1)
SIZE>(DISK3 DISK2) SIZE>(DISK2 DISK1) [PEG3] [PEG2] [PEG1] [DISK3] [DISK2] [DISK1]
    Goal ON(DISK1 PEG2) accomplished!
    Goal ¬INHAND(DISK1) accomplished!

——————— Think or Act (39) ———————

    Observe: ON(DISK3 PEG1) ON(DISK2 PEG1) ON(DISK1 PEG2) SIZE>(DISK3 DISK1)
SIZE>(DISK3 DISK2) SIZE>(DISK2 DISK1) [PEG3] [PEG2] [PEG1] [DISK3] [DISK2] [DISK1]
    Current Differences: ¬(SIZE>(DISK3 DISK2) ON(DISK2 PEG1))

Useful-Rule-Instance:
State: [DISK2] [PEG1] ON(DISK2 PEG1)
      ¬(SIZE>(DISK2 *diskM*) ON(*diskM* PEG1))
      ¬INHAND(*diskN*) ¬INHAND(DISK2)
Action: PICK(DISK2 PEG1)
Predict: INHAND(DISK2) ¬ON(DISK2 PEG1) [PEG1] [DISK2]
Index: 0
Bindings: ((*disk*/DISK2) (*peg*/PEG1))

    Decide to do PICK(DISK2 PEG1).
    Execute PICK DISK2 from PEG1.
    Waiting for responses from the environment ...
    Observe: ON(DISK3 PEG1) INHAND(DISK2) ON(DISK1 PEG2) SIZE>(DISK3 DISK1)
SIZE>(DISK3 DISK2) SIZE>(DISK2 DISK1) [PEG3] [PEG2] [PEG1] [DISK3] [DISK2] [DISK1]
    Goal ¬(SIZE>(DISK3 DISK2) ON(DISK2 PEG1)) accomplished!
    Goal ¬INHAND(DISK1) accomplished!

——————— Think or Act (40) ———————

Observe: ON(DISK3 PEG1) INHAND(DISK2) ON(DISK1 PEG2) SIZE>(DISK3 DISK1)
SIZE>(DISK3 DISK2) SIZE>(DISK2 DISK1) [PEG3] [PEG2] [PEG1] [DISK3] [DISK2] [DISK1]
Current Differences: INHAND(DISK3)

Useful-Rule-Instance:
State: [DISK3] [PEG1] ON(DISK3 PEG1)
     ¬(SIZE>(DISK3 *diskM*) ON(*diskM* PEG1))
     ¬INHAND(*diskN*) ¬INHAND(DISK3)
Action: PICK(DISK3 PEG1)
Predict: INHAND(DISK3) ¬ON(DISK3 PEG1) [PEG1] [DISK3]
Index: 0
Bindings: ((*peg*/PEG1) (*disk*/DISK3))

Decide to do Propose new subgoals.
New differences to achieve: ¬INHAND(DISK2)
Find rules for the differences and sort them ...
To achieve ¬INHAND(DISK2), Rules (1) can be used.
New plan for the differences: ¬INHAND(DISK2) by Rule1

——————— Think or Act (41) ———————

Observe: ON(DISK3 PEG1) INHAND(DISK2) ON(DISK1 PEG2) SIZE>(DISK3 DISK1)
SIZE>(DISK3 DISK2) SIZE>(DISK2 DISK1) [PEG3] [PEG2] [PEG1] [DISK3] [DISK2] [DISK1]
Current Differences: ¬INHAND(DISK2)
Rule's action has free variable: *peg* is bound to PEG2.

Useful-Rule-Instance:
State: ¬(SIZE>(DISK2 *diskP*) ON(*diskP* PEG2)) INHAND(DISK2)
     ¬ON(DISK2 PEG2) [PEG2] [DISK2]
Action: PUT(DISK2 PEG2)
Predict: ON(DISK2 PEG2) ¬INHAND(DISK2) [PEG2] [DISK2]
Index: 1
Bindings: ((*peg*/PEG2) (*disk*/DISK2))

Decide to do Propose new subgoals.
New differences to achieve: ¬(SIZE>(DISK2 DISK1) ON(DISK1 PEG2))
Find rules for the differences and sort them ...
To achieve ¬SIZE>(DISK2 DISK1), Rules NIL can be used.
To achieve ¬ON(DISK1 PEG2), Rules (0) can be used.
New plan for the differences: ¬(SIZE>(DISK2 DISK1) ON(DISK1 PEG2)) by Rule0

——————— Think or Act (42) ———————

Observe: ON(DISK3 PEG1) INHAND(DISK2) ON(DISK1 PEG2) SIZE>(DISK3 DISK1)
SIZE>(DISK3 DISK2) SIZE>(DISK2 DISK1) [PEG3] [PEG2] [PEG1] [DISK3] [DISK2] [DISK1]
Current Differences: ¬(SIZE>(DISK2 DISK1) ON(DISK1 PEG2))

Useful-Rule-Instance:
State: [DISK1] [PEG2] ON(DISK1 PEG2)
     ¬(SIZE>(DISK1 *diskM*) ON(*diskM* PEG2))
     ¬INHAND(*diskN*) ¬INHAND(DISK1)
Action: PICK(DISK1 PEG2)
Predict: INHAND(DISK1) ¬ON(DISK1 PEG2) [PEG2] [DISK1]
Index: 0
Bindings: ((*disk*/DISK1) (*peg*/PEG2))

Decide to do Propose new subgoals.
New differences to achieve: ¬INHAND(DISK2)
Find rules for the differences and sort them ...
To achieve ¬INHAND(DISK2), Rules (1) can be used.
New plan for the differences: ¬INHAND(DISK2) by Rule1

——————— Think or Act (43) ———————

Observe: ON(DISK3 PEG1) INHAND(DISK2) ON(DISK1 PEG2) SIZE>(DISK3 DISK1)
SIZE>(DISK3 DISK2) SIZE>(DISK2 DISK1) [PEG3] [PEG2] [PEG1] [DISK3] [DISK2] [DISK1]
    Current Differences: ¬INHAND(DISK2)
    Rule's action has free variable: *peg* is bound to PEG3.

Useful-Rule-Instance:
State: ¬(SIZE>(DISK2 *diskP*) ON(*diskP* PEG3)) INHAND(DISK2)
        ¬ON(DISK2 PEG3) [PEG3] [DISK2]
Action: PUT(DISK2 PEG3)
Predict: ON(DISK2 PEG3) ¬INHAND(DISK2) [PEG3] [DISK2]
Index: 1
Bindings: ((*peg*/PEG3) (*disk*/DISK2))

    Decide to do PUT(DISK2 PEG3).
    Execute PUT DISK2 on PEG3.
    Waiting for responses from the environment ...
    Observe: ON(DISK3 PEG1) ON(DISK2 PEG3) ON(DISK1 PEG2) SIZE>(DISK3 DISK1)
SIZE>(DISK3 DISK2) SIZE>(DISK2 DISK1) [PEG3] [PEG2] [PEG1] [DISK3] [DISK2] [DISK1]
    Goal ON(DISK2 PEG3) accomplished!
    Goal ¬INHAND(DISK2) accomplished!

——————— Think or Act (44) ———————

Observe: ON(DISK3 PEG1) ON(DISK2 PEG3) ON(DISK1 PEG2) SIZE>(DISK3 DISK1)
SIZE>(DISK3 DISK2) SIZE>(DISK2 DISK1) [PEG3] [PEG2] [PEG1] [DISK3] [DISK2] [DISK1]
    Current Differences: ¬(SIZE>(DISK2 DISK1) ON(DISK1 PEG2))

Useful-Rule-Instance:
State: [DISK1] [PEG2] ON(DISK1 PEG2)
        ¬(SIZE>(DISK1 *diskM*) ON(*diskM* PEG2))
        ¬INHAND(*diskN*) ¬INHAND(DISK1)
Action: PICK(DISK1 PEG2)
Predict: INHAND(DISK1) ¬ON(DISK1 PEG2) [PEG2] [DISK1]
Index: 0
Bindings: ((*disk*/DISK1) (*peg*/PEG2))

    Decide to do PICK(DISK1 PEG2).
    Execute PICK DISK1 from PEG2.
    Waiting for responses from the environment ...
    Observe: ON(DISK3 PEG1) ON(DISK2 PEG3) INHAND(DISK1) SIZE>(DISK3 DISK1)
SIZE>(DISK3 DISK2) SIZE>(DISK2 DISK1) [PEG3] [PEG2] [PEG1] [DISK3] [DISK2] [DISK1]
    Goal ¬(SIZE>(DISK2 DISK1) ON(DISK1 PEG2)) accomplished!

——————— Think or Act (45) ———————

Observe: ON(DISK3 PEG1) ON(DISK2 PEG3) INHAND(DISK1) SIZE>(DISK3 DISK1)
SIZE>(DISK3 DISK2) SIZE>(DISK2 DISK1) [PEG3] [PEG2] [PEG1] [DISK3] [DISK2] [DISK1]
    Current Differences: ON(DISK2 PEG2)

Useful-Rule-Instance:
State: ¬(SIZE>(DISK2 *diskP*) ON(*diskP* PEG2)) INHAND(DISK2)
        ¬ON(DISK2 PEG2) [PEG2] [DISK2]
Action: PUT(DISK2 PEG2)
Predict: ON(DISK2 PEG2) ¬INHAND(DISK2) [PEG2] [DISK2]
Index: 1
Bindings: ((*peg*/PEG2) (*disk*/DISK2))

    Decide to do Propose new subgoals.
    New differences to achieve: INHAND(DISK2)
    Find rules for the differences and sort them ...
    To achieve INHAND(DISK2), Rules (0) can be used.
    New plan for the differences: INHAND(DISK2) by Rule0

——————— Think or Act (46) ———————

Observe: ON(DISK3 PEG1) ON(DISK2 PEG3) INHAND(DISK1) SIZE>(DISK3 DISK1)
SIZE>(DISK3 DISK2) SIZE>(DISK2 DISK1) [PEG3] [PEG2] [PEG1] [DISK3] [DISK2] [DISK1]
     Current Differences: INHAND(DISK2)
     Rule's action has free variable: *peg* is bound to PEG3.

Useful-Rule-Instance:
State: [DISK2] [PEG3] ON(DISK2 PEG3)
      ¬(SIZE>(DISK2 *diskM*) ON(*diskM* PEG3))
      ¬INHAND(*diskN*) ¬INHAND(DISK2)
Action: PICK(DISK2 PEG3)
Predict: INHAND(DISK2) ¬ON(DISK2 PEG3) [PEG3] [DISK2]
Index: 0
Bindings: ((*peg*/PEG3) (*disk*/DISK2))

     Decide to do Propose new subgoals.
     New differences to achieve: ¬INHAND(DISK1)
     Find rules for the differences and sort them ...
     To achieve ¬INHAND(DISK1), Rules (1) can be used.
     New plan for the differences: ¬INHAND(DISK1) by Rule1

——————— Think or Act (47) ———————

Observe: ON(DISK3 PEG1) ON(DISK2 PEG3) INHAND(DISK1) SIZE>(DISK3 DISK1)
SIZE>(DISK3 DISK2) SIZE>(DISK2 DISK1) [PEG3] [PEG2] [PEG1] [DISK3] [DISK2] [DISK1]
     Current Differences: ¬INHAND(DISK1)
     Rule's action has free variable: *peg* is bound to PEG1.

Useful-Rule-Instance:
State: ¬(SIZE>(DISK1 *diskP*) ON(*diskP* PEG1)) INHAND(DISK1)
      ¬ON(DISK1 PEG1) [PEG1] [DISK1]
Action: PUT(DISK1 PEG1)
Predict: ON(DISK1 PEG1) ¬INHAND(DISK1) [PEG1] [DISK1]
Index: 1
Bindings: ((*peg*/PEG1) (*disk*/DISK1))

     Decide to do PUT(DISK1 PEG1).
     Execute PUT DISK1 on PEG1.
     Waiting for responses from the environment ...
     Observe: ON(DISK3 PEG1) ON(DISK2 PEG3) ON(DISK1 PEG1) SIZE>(DISK3 DISK1)
SIZE>(DISK3 DISK2) SIZE>(DISK2 DISK1) [PEG3] [PEG2] [PEG1] [DISK3] [DISK2] [DISK1]
     Goal ON(DISK1 PEG1) accomplished!
     Goal ¬INHAND(DISK1) accomplished!

——————— Think or Act (48) ———————

Observe: ON(DISK3 PEG1) ON(DISK2 PEG3) ON(DISK1 PEG1) SIZE>(DISK3 DISK1)
SIZE>(DISK3 DISK2) SIZE>(DISK2 DISK1) [PEG3] [PEG2] [PEG1] [DISK3] [DISK2] [DISK1]
     Current Differences: INHAND(DISK2)

Useful-Rule-Instance:
State: [DISK2] [PEG3] ON(DISK2 PEG3)
      ¬(SIZE>(DISK2 *diskM*) ON(*diskM* PEG3))
      ¬INHAND(*diskN*) ¬INHAND(DISK2)
Action: PICK(DISK2 PEG3)
Predict: INHAND(DISK2) ¬ON(DISK2 PEG3) [PEG3] [DISK2]
Index: 0
Bindings: ((*peg*/PEG3) (*disk*/DISK2))

Decide to do PICK(DISK2 PEG3).
Execute PICK DISK2 from PEG3.
Waiting for responses from the environment ...
Observe: ON(DISK3 PEG1) INHAND(DISK2) ON(DISK1 PEG1) SIZE>(DISK3 DISK1)
SIZE>(DISK3 DISK2) SIZE>(DISK2 DISK1) [PEG3] [PEG2] [PEG1] [DISK3] [DISK2] [DISK1]
Goal INHAND(DISK2) accomplished!

——————— Think or Act (49) ———————

Observe: ON(DISK3 PEG1) INHAND(DISK2) ON(DISK1 PEG1) SIZE>(DISK3 DISK1)
SIZE>(DISK3 DISK2) SIZE>(DISK2 DISK1) [PEG3] [PEG2] [PEG1] [DISK3] [DISK2] [DISK1]
Current Differences: ON(DISK2 PEG2)

Useful-Rule-Instance:
State: ¬(SIZE>(DISK2 $diskP$) ON($diskP$ PEG2)) INHAND(DISK2)
       ¬ON(DISK2 PEG2) [PEG2] [DISK2]
Action: PUT(DISK2 PEG2)
Predict: ON(DISK2 PEG2) ¬INHAND(DISK2) [PEG2] [DISK2]
Index: 1
Bindings: ((peg/PEG2) ($disk$/DISK2))

Decide to do PUT(DISK2 PEG2).
Execute PUT DISK2 on PEG2.
Waiting for responses from the environment ...
Observe: ON(DISK3 PEG1) ON(DISK2 PEG2) ON(DISK1 PEG1) SIZE>(DISK3 DISK1)
SIZE>(DISK3 DISK2) SIZE>(DISK2 DISK1) [PEG3] [PEG2] [PEG1] [DISK3] [DISK2] [DISK1]
Goal ON(DISK2 PEG2) accomplished!
Goal ¬INHAND(DISK2) accomplished!

——————— Think or Act (50) ———————

Observe: ON(DISK3 PEG1) ON(DISK2 PEG2) ON(DISK1 PEG1) SIZE>(DISK3 DISK1)
SIZE>(DISK3 DISK2) SIZE>(DISK2 DISK1) [PEG3] [PEG2] [PEG1] [DISK3] [DISK2] [DISK1]
Current Differences: INHAND(DISK3)

Useful-Rule-Instance:
State: [DISK3] [PEG1] ON(DISK3 PEG1)
       ¬(SIZE>(DISK3 $diskM$) ON($diskM$ PEG1))
       ¬INHAND($diskN$) ¬INHAND(DISK3)
Action: PICK(DISK3 PEG1)
Predict: INHAND(DISK3) ¬ON(DISK3 PEG1) [PEG1] [DISK3]
Index: 0
Bindings: ((peg/PEG1) ($disk$/DISK3))

Decide to do Propose new subgoals.
New differences to achieve: ¬(SIZE>(DISK3 DISK1) ON(DISK1 PEG1))
Find rules for the differences and sort them ...
To achieve ¬SIZE>(DISK3 DISK1), Rules NIL can be used.
To achieve ¬ON(DISK1 PEG1), Rules (0) can be used.
New plan for the differences: ¬(SIZE>(DISK3 DISK1) ON(DISK1 PEG1)) by Rule0

——————— Think or Act (51) ———————

Observe: ON(DISK3 PEG1) ON(DISK2 PEG2) ON(DISK1 PEG1) SIZE>(DISK3 DISK1)
SIZE>(DISK3 DISK2) SIZE>(DISK2 DISK1) [PEG3] [PEG2] [PEG1] [DISK3] [DISK2] [DISK1]
Current Differences: ¬(SIZE>(DISK3 DISK1) ON(DISK1 PEG1))

Useful-Rule-Instance:
State: [DISK1] [PEG1] ON(DISK1 PEG1)
       ¬(SIZE>(DISK1 $diskM$) ON($diskM$ PEG1))
       ¬INHAND($diskN$) ¬INHAND(DISK1)
Action: PICK(DISK1 PEG1)
Predict: INHAND(DISK1) ¬ON(DISK1 PEG1) [PEG1] [DISK1]
Index: 0
Bindings: (($disk$/DISK1) (peg/PEG1))

Decide to do PICK(DISK1 PEG1).
Execute PICK DISK1 from PEG1.
Waiting for responses from the environment ...
Observe: ON(DISK3 PEG1) ON(DISK2 PEG2) INHAND(DISK1) SIZE>(DISK3 DISK1)
SIZE>(DISK3 DISK2) SIZE>(DISK2 DISK1) [PEG3] [PEG2] [PEG1] [DISK3] [DISK2] [DISK1]
Goal ¬(SIZE>(DISK3 DISK1) ON(DISK1 PEG1)) accomplished!

——————— Think or Act (52) ———————

Observe: ON(DISK3 PEG1) ON(DISK2 PEG2) INHAND(DISK1) SIZE>(DISK3 DISK1)
SIZE>(DISK3 DISK2) SIZE>(DISK2 DISK1) [PEG3] [PEG2] [PEG1] [DISK3] [DISK2] [DISK1]
Current Differences: INHAND(DISK3)

Useful-Rule-Instance:
State: [DISK3] [PEG1] ON(DISK3 PEG1)
        ¬(SIZE>(DISK3 *diskM*) ON(*diskM* PEG1))
        ¬INHAND(*diskN*) ¬INHAND(DISK3)
Action: PICK(DISK3 PEG1)
Predict: INHAND(DISK3) ¬ON(DISK3 PEG1) [PEG1] [DISK3]
Index: 0
Bindings: ((*peg*/PEG1) (*disk*/DISK3))

Decide to do Propose new subgoals.
New differences to achieve: ¬INHAND(DISK1)
Find rules for the differences and sort them ...
To achieve ¬INHAND(DISK1), Rules (1) can be used.
New plan for the differences: ¬INHAND(DISK1) by Rule1

——————— Think or Act (53) ———————

Observe: ON(DISK3 PEG1) ON(DISK2 PEG2) INHAND(DISK1) SIZE>(DISK3 DISK1)
SIZE>(DISK3 DISK2) SIZE>(DISK2 DISK1) [PEG3] [PEG2] [PEG1] [DISK3] [DISK2] [DISK1]
Current Differences: ¬INHAND(DISK1)
Rule's action has free variable: *peg* is bound to PEG2.

Useful-Rule-Instance:
State: ¬(SIZE>(DISK1 *diskP*) ON(*diskP* PEG2)) INHAND(DISK1)
        ¬ON(DISK1 PEG2) [PEG2] [DISK1]
Action: PUT(DISK1 PEG2)
Predict: ON(DISK1 PEG2) ¬INHAND(DISK1) [PEG2] [DISK1]
Index: 1
Bindings: ((*peg*/PEG2) (*disk*/DISK1))

Decide to do PUT(DISK1 PEG2).
Execute PUT DISK1 on PEG2.
Waiting for responses from the environment ...
Observe: ON(DISK3 PEG1) ON(DISK2 PEG2) ON(DISK1 PEG2) SIZE>(DISK3 DISK1)
SIZE>(DISK3 DISK2) SIZE>(DISK2 DISK1) [PEG3] [PEG2] [PEG1] [DISK3] [DISK2] [DISK1]
Goal ON(DISK1 PEG2) accomplished!
Goal ¬INHAND(DISK1) accomplished!

——————— Think or Act (54) ———————

Observe: ON(DISK3 PEG1) ON(DISK2 PEG2) ON(DISK1 PEG2) SIZE>(DISK3 DISK1)
SIZE>(DISK3 DISK2) SIZE>(DISK2 DISK1) [PEG3] [PEG2] [PEG1] [DISK3] [DISK2] [DISK1]
Current Differences: INHAND(DISK3)

Useful-Rule-Instance:
State: [DISK3] [PEG1] ON(DISK3 PEG1)
        ¬(SIZE>(DISK3 *diskM*) ON(*diskM* PEG1))
        ¬INHAND(*diskN*) ¬INHAND(DISK3)
Action: PICK(DISK3 PEG1)
Predict: INHAND(DISK3) ¬ON(DISK3 PEG1) [PEG1] [DISK3]
Index: 0
Bindings: ((*peg*/PEG1) (*disk*/DISK3))

Decide to do PICK(DISK3 PEG1).
Execute PICK DISK3 from PEG1.
Waiting for responses from the environment ...
Observe: INHAND(DISK3) ON(DISK2 PEG2) ON(DISK1 PEG2) SIZE>(DISK3 DISK1)
SIZE>(DISK3 DISK2) SIZE>(DISK2 DISK1) [PEG3] [PEG2] [PEG1] [DISK3] [DISK2] [DISK1]
Goal INHAND(DISK3) accomplished!

——————— Think or Act (55) ———————

Observe: INHAND(DISK3) ON(DISK2 PEG2) ON(DISK1 PEG2) SIZE>(DISK3 DISK1)
SIZE>(DISK3 DISK2) SIZE>(DISK2 DISK1) [PEG3] [PEG2] [PEG1] [DISK3] [DISK2] [DISK1]
Current Differences: ON(DISK3 PEG3)

Useful-Rule-Instance:
State: ¬(SIZE>(DISK3 *diskP*) ON(*diskP* PEG3)) INHAND(DISK3)
        ¬ON(DISK3 PEG3) [PEG3] [DISK3]
Action: PUT(DISK3 PEG3)
Predict: ON(DISK3 PEG3) ¬INHAND(DISK3) [PEG3] [DISK3]
Index: 1
Bindings: ((*disk*/DISK3) (*peg*/PEG3))

Decide to do PUT(DISK3 PEG3).
Execute PUT DISK3 on PEG3.
Waiting for responses from the environment ...
Observe: ON(DISK3 PEG3) ON(DISK2 PEG2) ON(DISK1 PEG2) SIZE>(DISK3 DISK1)
SIZE>(DISK3 DISK2) SIZE>(DISK2 DISK1) [PEG3] [PEG2] [PEG1] [DISK3] [DISK2] [DISK1]
Goal ON(DISK3 PEG3) accomplished!
Planning for the remaining goals: ON(DISK1 PEG1) ON(DISK2 PEG1) ON(DISK3 PEG3)
Differences towards the goal ON(DISK1 PEG1) are: ON(DISK1 PEG1)
Differences towards the goal ON(DISK2 PEG1) are: ON(DISK2 PEG1)
Find rules for the differences and sort them ...
To achieve ON(DISK1 PEG1), Rules (1) can be used.
To achieve ON(DISK2 PEG1), Rules (1) can be used.

——————— Think or Act (56) ———————

Observe: ON(DISK3 PEG3) ON(DISK2 PEG2) ON(DISK1 PEG2) SIZE>(DISK3 DISK1)
SIZE>(DISK3 DISK2) SIZE>(DISK2 DISK1) [PEG3] [PEG2] [PEG1] [DISK3] [DISK2] [DISK1]
Current Differences: ON(DISK2 PEG1)

Useful-Rule-Instance:
State: ¬(SIZE>(DISK2 *diskP*) ON(*diskP* PEG1)) INHAND(DISK2)
        ¬ON(DISK2 PEG1) [PEG1] [DISK2]
Action: PUT(DISK2 PEG1)
Predict: ON(DISK2 PEG1) ¬INHAND(DISK2) [PEG1] [DISK2]
Index: 1
Bindings: ((*disk*/DISK2) (*peg*/PEG1))

Decide to do Propose new subgoals.
New differences to achieve: INHAND(DISK2)
Find rules for the differences and sort them ...
To achieve INHAND(DISK2), Rules (0) can be used.
New plan for the differences: INHAND(DISK2) by Rule0

——————— Think or Act (57) ———————

Observe: ON(DISK3 PEG3) ON(DISK2 PEG2) ON(DISK1 PEG2) SIZE>(DISK3 DISK1)
SIZE>(DISK3 DISK2) SIZE>(DISK2 DISK1) [PEG3] [PEG2] [PEG1] [DISK3] [DISK2] [DISK1]
Current Differences: INHAND(DISK2)
Rule's action has free variable: *peg* is bound to PEG2.

Useful-Rule-Instance:
State: [DISK2] [PEG2] ON(DISK2 PEG2)
       ¬(SIZE>(DISK2 *diskM*) ON(*diskM* PEG2))
       ¬INHAND(*diskN*) ¬INHAND(DISK2)
Action: PICK(DISK2 PEG2)
Predict: INHAND(DISK2) ¬ON(DISK2 PEG2) [PEG2] [DISK2]
Index: 0
Bindings: ((*peg*/PEG2) (*disk*/DISK2))

    Decide to do Propose new subgoals.
    New differences to achieve: ¬(SIZE>(DISK2 DISK1) ON(DISK1 PEG2))
    Find rules for the differences and sort them ...
    To achieve ¬SIZE>(DISK2 DISK1), Rules NIL can be used.
    To achieve ¬ON(DISK1 PEG2), Rules (0) can be used.
    New plan for the differences: ¬(SIZE>(DISK2 DISK1) ON(DISK1 PEG2)) by Rule0

——————— Think or Act (58) ———————

    Observe: ON(DISK3 PEG3) ON(DISK2 PEG2) ON(DISK1 PEG2) SIZE>(DISK3 DISK1)
SIZE>(DISK3 DISK2) SIZE>(DISK2 DISK1) [PEG3] [PEG2] [PEG1] [DISK3] [DISK2] [DISK1]
    Current Differences: ¬(SIZE>(DISK2 DISK1) ON(DISK1 PEG2))

Useful-Rule-Instance:
State: [DISK1] [PEG2] ON(DISK1 PEG2)
       ¬(SIZE>(DISK1 *diskM*) ON(*diskM* PEG2))
       ¬INHAND(*diskN*) ¬INHAND(DISK1)
Action: PICK(DISK1 PEG2)
Predict: INHAND(DISK1) ¬ON(DISK1 PEG2) [PEG2] [DISK1]
Index: 0
Bindings: ((*disk*/DISK1) (*peg*/PEG2))

    Decide to do PICK(DISK1 PEG2).
    Execute PICK DISK1 from PEG2.
    Waiting for responses from the environment ...
    Observe: ON(DISK3 PEG3) ON(DISK2 PEG2) INHAND(DISK1) SIZE>(DISK3 DISK1)
SIZE>(DISK3 DISK2) SIZE>(DISK2 DISK1) [PEG3] [PEG2] [PEG1] [DISK3] [DISK2] [DISK1]
    Goal ¬(SIZE>(DISK2 DISK1) ON(DISK1 PEG2)) accomplished!

——————— Think or Act (59) ———————

    Observe: ON(DISK3 PEG3) ON(DISK2 PEG2) INHAND(DISK1) SIZE>(DISK3 DISK1)
SIZE>(DISK3 DISK2) SIZE>(DISK2 DISK1) [PEG3] [PEG2] [PEG1] [DISK3] [DISK2] [DISK1]
    Current Differences: INHAND(DISK2)

Useful-Rule-Instance:
State: [DISK2] [PEG2] ON(DISK2 PEG2)
       ¬(SIZE>(DISK2 *diskM*) ON(*diskM* PEG2))
       ¬INHAND(*diskN*) ¬INHAND(DISK2)
Action: PICK(DISK2 PEG2)
Predict: INHAND(DISK2) ¬ON(DISK2 PEG2) [PEG2] [DISK2]
Index: 0
Bindings: ((*peg*/PEG2) (*disk*/DISK2))

    Decide to do Propose new subgoals.
    New differences to achieve: ¬INHAND(DISK1)
    Find rules for the differences and sort them ...
    To achieve ¬INHAND(DISK1), Rules (1) can be used.
    New plan for the differences: ¬INHAND(DISK1) by Rule1

——————— Think or Act (60) ———————

Observe: ON(DISK3 PEG3) ON(DISK2 PEG2) INHAND(DISK1) SIZE>(DISK3 DISK1)
SIZE>(DISK3 DISK2) SIZE>(DISK2 DISK1) [PEG3] [PEG2] [PEG1] [DISK3] [DISK2] [DISK1]
    Current Differences: ¬INHAND(DISK1)
    Rule's action has free variable: *peg* is bound to PEG3.

Useful-Rule-Instance:
State: ¬(SIZE>(DISK1 *diskP*) ON(*diskP* PEG3)) INHAND(DISK1)
      ¬ON(DISK1 PEG3) [PEG3] [DISK1]
Action: PUT(DISK1 PEG3)
Predict: ON(DISK1 PEG3) ¬INHAND(DISK1) [PEG3] [DISK1]
Index: 1
Bindings: ((*peg*/PEG3) (*disk*/DISK1))

    Decide to do PUT(DISK1 PEG3).
    Execute PUT DISK1 on PEG3.
    Waiting for responses from the environment ...
    Observe: ON(DISK3 PEG3) ON(DISK2 PEG2) ON(DISK1 PEG3) SIZE>(DISK3 DISK1)
SIZE>(DISK3 DISK2) SIZE>(DISK2 DISK1) [PEG3] [PEG2] [PEG1] [DISK3] [DISK2] [DISK1]
    Goal ON(DISK1 PEG3) accomplished!
    Goal ¬INHAND(DISK1) accomplished!

——————— Think or Act (61) ———————

Observe: ON(DISK3 PEG3) ON(DISK2 PEG2) ON(DISK1 PEG3) SIZE>(DISK3 DISK1)
SIZE>(DISK3 DISK2) SIZE>(DISK2 DISK1) [PEG3] [PEG2] [PEG1] [DISK3] [DISK2] [DISK1]
    Current Differences: INHAND(DISK2)

Useful-Rule-Instance:
State: [DISK2] [PEG2] ON(DISK2 PEG2)
      ¬(SIZE>(DISK2 *diskM*) ON(*diskM* PEG2))
      ¬INHAND(*diskN*) ¬INHAND(DISK2)
Action: PICK(DISK2 PEG2)
Predict: INHAND(DISK2) ¬ON(DISK2 PEG2) [PEG2] [DISK2]
Index: 0
Bindings: ((*peg*/PEG2) (*disk*/DISK2))

    Decide to do PICK(DISK2 PEG2).
    Execute PICK DISK2 from PEG2.
    Waiting for responses from the environment ...
    Observe: ON(DISK3 PEG3) INHAND(DISK2) ON(DISK1 PEG3) SIZE>(DISK3 DISK1)
SIZE>(DISK3 DISK2) SIZE>(DISK2 DISK1) [PEG3] [PEG2] [PEG1] [DISK3] [DISK2] [DISK1]
    Goal INHAND(DISK2) accomplished!

——————— Think or Act (62) ———————

Observe: ON(DISK3 PEG3) INHAND(DISK2) ON(DISK1 PEG3) SIZE>(DISK3 DISK1)
SIZE>(DISK3 DISK2) SIZE>(DISK2 DISK1) [PEG3] [PEG2] [PEG1] [DISK3] [DISK2] [DISK1]
    Current Differences: ON(DISK2 PEG1)

Useful-Rule-Instance:
State: ¬(SIZE>(DISK2 *diskP*) ON(*diskP* PEG1)) INHAND(DISK2)
      ¬ON(DISK2 PEG1) [PEG1] [DISK2]
Action: PUT(DISK2 PEG1)
Predict: ON(DISK2 PEG1) ¬INHAND(DISK2) [PEG1] [DISK2]
Index: 1
Bindings: ((*disk*/DISK2) (*peg*/PEG1))

    Decide to do PUT(DISK2 PEG1).
    Execute PUT DISK2 on PEG1.
    Waiting for responses from the environment ...
    Observe: ON(DISK3 PEG3) ON(DISK2 PEG1) ON(DISK1 PEG3) SIZE>(DISK3 DISK1)
SIZE>(DISK3 DISK2) SIZE>(DISK2 DISK1) [PEG3] [PEG2] [PEG1] [DISK3] [DISK2] [DISK1]
    Goal ON(DISK2 PEG1) accomplished!

———————— Think or Act (63) ————•——

Observe: ON(DISK3 PEG3) ON(DISK2 PEG1) ON(DISK1 PEG3) SIZE>(DISK3 DISK1) SIZE>(DISK3 DISK2) SIZE>(DISK2 DISK1) [PEG3] [PEG2] [PEG1] [DISK3] [DISK2] [DISK1]
Current Differences: ON(DISK1 PEG1)

Useful-Rule-Instance:
State: ¬(SIZE>(DISK1 *diskP*) ON(*diskP* PEG1)) INHAND(DISK1)
     ¬ON(DISK1 PEG1) [PEG1] [DISK1]
Action: PUT(DISK1 PEG1)
Predict: ON(DISK1 PEG1) ¬INHAND(DISK1) [PEG1] [DISK1]
Index: 1
Bindings: ((*disk*/DISK1) (*peg*/PEG1))

Decide to do Propose new subgoals.
New differences to achieve: INHAND(DISK1)
Find rules for the differences and sort them ...
To achieve INHAND(DISK1), Rules (0) can be used.
New plan for the differences: INHAND(DISK1) by Rule0

———————— Think or Act (64) ————————

Observe: ON(DISK3 PEG3) ON(DISK2 PEG1) ON(DISK1 PEG3) SIZE>(DISK3 DISK1) SIZE>(DISK3 DISK2) SIZE>(DISK2 DISK1) [PEG3] [PEG2] [PEG1] [DISK3] [DISK2] [DISK1]
Current Differences: INHAND(DISK1)
Rule's action has free variable: *peg* is bound to PEG3.

Useful-Rule-Instance:
State: [DISK1] [PEG3] ON(DISK1 PEG3)
     ¬(SIZE>(DISK1 *diskM*) ON(*diskM* PEG3))
     ¬INHAND(*diskN*) ¬INHAND(DISK1)
Action: PICK(DISK1 PEG3)
Predict: INHAND(DISK1) ¬ON(DISK1 PEG3) [PEG3] [DISK1]
Index: 0
Bindings: ((*peg*/PEG3) (*disk*/DISK1))

Decide to do PICK(DISK1 PEG3).
Execute PICK DISK1 from PEG3.
Waiting for responses from the environment ...
Observe: ON(DISK3 PEG3) ON(DISK2 PEG1) INHAND(DISK1) SIZE>(DISK3 DISK1) SIZE>(DISK3 DISK2) SIZE>(DISK2 DISK1) [PEG3] [PEG2] [PEG1] [DISK3] [DISK2] [DISK1]
Goal INHAND(DISK1) accomplished!

———————— Think or Act (65) ————————

Observe: ON(DISK3 PEG3) ON(DISK2 PEG1) INHAND(DISK1) SIZE>(DISK3 DISK1) SIZE>(DISK3 DISK2) SIZE>(DISK2 DISK1) [PEG3] [PEG2] [PEG1] [DISK3] [DISK2] [DISK1]
Current Differences: ON(DISK1 PEG1)

Useful-Rule-Instance:
State: ¬(SIZE>(DISK1 *diskP*) ON(*diskP* PEG1)) INHAND(DISK1)
     ¬ON(DISK1 PEG1) [PEG1] [DISK1]
Action: PUT(DISK1 PEG1)
Predict: ON(DISK1 PEG1) ¬INHAND(DISK1) [PEG1] [DISK1]
Index: 1
Bindings: ((*disk*/DISK1) (*peg*/PEG1))

Decide to do PUT(DISK1 PEG1).
Execute PUT DISK1 on PEG1.
Waiting for responses from the environment ...
Observe: ON(DISK3 PEG3) ON(DISK2 PEG1) ON(DISK1 PEG1) SIZE>(DISK3 DISK1) SIZE>(DISK3 DISK2) SIZE>(DISK2 DISK1) [PEG3] [PEG2] [PEG1] [DISK3] [DISK2] [DISK1]
Goal ON(DISK1 PEG1) accomplished!
Planning for the remaining goals: ON(DISK1 PEG1) ON(DISK2 PEG1) ON(DISK3 PEG3)
Time Report on clock *GTIME*: 348.61 sec.
All given goals accomplished!

*

BIBLIOGRAPHY

[1] Angluin, D. 1987. Learning regular sets from queries and counter-examples. *Information and Computation*, 75(2):87–106.

[2] Angluin, D. 1990. Negative results for equivalence queries. *Machine Learning*, 5(2):121–150.

[3] Angluin, D., and C. H. Smith. 1983. Inductive inference: Theory and methods. *Computing Surveys*, 15(3):237–269.

[4] Anzai, Y. 1984. Cognitive control of real-time event-driven systems. *Cognitive Science*, 8:221–254.

[5] Anzai, Y., and H. A. Simon. 1979. The theory of learning by doing. *Psychological Review*, 86:124–140.

[6] Atkeson, C. G. 1989. Learning arm kinematics and dynamics. *Annual Review of Neuroscience*, 12:157–183.

[7] Barto, A. G. 1985. Learning by statistical cooperation of self-interested neuron-like computing elements. *Human Neurobiology*, 4:229–256.

[8] Baum, L. E., T. Petrie, G. Soules, and N. Weiss. 1970. A maximization technique occurring in the statistical analysis of probabilistic functions of Markov chains. *Annals of Mathematical Statistics*, 41(1):164–171.

[9] Bellman, R. E., and S. E. Dreyfus. 1962. *Applied dynamic programming*. RAND Corporation.

[10] Brazdil, P. 1981. A model for error detection and correction. Ph.D. thesis, University of Edinburgh.

[11] Breiman, L., L. H. Fredman, R. A. Olshen, and C. J. Stone. 1984. *Classification and regression trees*. Wadsworth.

[12] Bundy, A., B. Silver, and D. Plummer. 1985. An analytical comparison of some rule-learning programs. *Artificial Intelligence*, 27:137–181.

[13] Carbonell, J. G., and Y. Gil. 1987. Learning by experimentation. In *Proceedings of International Conference on Machine Learning*, ed. P. Langley. Morgan Kaufmann.

[14] Chapman, D., and L. P. Kaelbling. 1991. Input generalization in delayed reinforcement learning: An algorithm and performance comparisons. In *Proceedings of International Joint Conference on Artificial Intelligence*, ed. J. Mylopoulos and R. Reiter. Morgan Kaufmann.

[15] Cheeseman, P., J. Kelly, M. Self, J. Stutz, W. Taylor, and D. Freeman. 1988. Autoclass: A Bayesian classification system. In *Proceedings of International Conference on Machine Learning*, ed. J. Laird. Morgan Kaufmann.

[16] Chrisman, L. 1992. Reinforcement learning with perceptual aliasing: The perceptual distinctions approach. In *Proceedings of National Conference on Artificial Intelligence*. MIT Press.

[17] Cox, R. T. 1946. Probability, frequency, and reasonable expectation. *American Journal of Physics*, 17:1–13.

[18] Crutchfield, J. P., J. D. Farmer, N. H. Packard, and R. S. Shaw. 1986. Chaos. *Scientific American*, 254:46–57.

[19] Dickmanns, E. D., and V. Graefe. 1988. Dynamic monocular machine vision and applications. Technical Report UniBwM/LRT/WE 13, Department of Air and Space Technology, University of Bundeswehr, Munich.

[20] Emerson, E. A., and J. Y. Halpern. 1986. "Sometimes" and "not never" revisited: On branching versus linear time temporal logic. *Journal of the Association of Computing Machinery*, 33(1):151–178.

[21] Falkenhainer, B. 1988. The utility of difference-based reasoning. In *Proceedings of National Conference on Artificial Intelligence*. MIT Press.

[22] Feigenbaum, E. A., and H. A. Simon. 1984. EPAM-like models of recognition and learning. *Cognitive Science*, 8:305–336.

[23] Fikes, R. E., and N. J. Nilsson. 1971. STRIPS: A new approach to the application of theorem proving to problem solving. *Artificial Intelligence*, 2:189–208.

[24] Fisher, D. H. 1987. Knowledge acquisition via incremental conceptual clustering. *Machine Learning*, 2:139–172.

[25] Fisher, D. H. 1989. Noise-tolerant conceptual clustering. In *Proceedings of International Joint Conference on Artificial Intelligence*, ed. N. Sridharan. Morgan Kaufmann.

[26] Garey, M., and D. Johnson. 1979. *Computers and intractability: A guide to the theory of NP-completeness.* W. H. Freeman.

[27] Gibson, J. 1979. *The ecological approach to visual perception.* Houghton Mifflin.

[28] Gil, Y. 1992. Acquiring domain knowledge for planning by experimentation. Ph.D. thesis, School of Computer Science, Carnegie Mellon University.

[29] Goodwin, G. C., and K. S. Sin. 1984. *Adaptive filtering, prediction, and control.* Prentice–Hall.

[30] Gross, K. P. 1991. Concept acquisition through attribute evolution and experiment selection. Ph.D. thesis, School of Computer Science, Carnegie Mellon University.

[31] Harris, N. L., L. Hunter, and D. J. States. 1992. Mega-classification: Discovering motifs in massive datastreams. In *Proceedings of National Conference on Artificial Intelligence.* MIT Press.

[32] Hartman, E., and J. Keeler. 1990. Neural net solves process control problem for Kodak. *Neural Network News.* August.

[33] Haussler, D. 1988. Quantifying inductive bias: AI learning algorithms and Valiant's learning framework. *Artificial Intelligence*, 36:177–221.

[34] Haussler, D. 1989. Learning conjunctive concepts in structural domains. *Machine Learning*, 4(1):7–40.

[35] Hayes, J. R., and H. A. Simon. 1974. Understanding written problem instructions. In *Knowledge and cognition*, ed. L. Gregg. Lawrence Erlbaum.

[36] Hopcroft, J. E., and J. D. Ullman. 1979. *Introduction to automata theory, languages, and computation.* Addison-Wesley.

[37] Hornik, K., M. Stinchcombe, and H. White. 1990. Universal approximation of an unknown mapping and its derivatives using multilayer feedforward networks. *Neural Networks*, 3:551–560.

[38] Inhelder, B., and J. Piaget. 1958. *The growth of logical thinking from childhood to adolescence.* Basic Books.

[39] Jaynes, E. T. In press. *Probability theory—the logic of science.* Publisher unknown. (Contact the author via email etj@wuphys.wustl.edu for more information.)

[40] Jeffery, H. 1939. *Theory of probability.* Clarendon Press.

[41] Jordan, M. I., and D. E. Rumelhart. 1991. Forward models: Supervised learning with a distal teacher. Technical Report OP-40, MIT Center for Cognitive Science.

[42] Kohavi, Z. 1978. *Switching and finite automata theory.* McGraw-Hill.

[43] Korf, R. E. 1983. Learning to solve problems by searching for macro-operators. Ph.D. thesis, Carnegie Mellon University.

[44] Korf, R. E. 1990. Real-time heuristic search. *Artificial Intelligence,* 42:189–211.

[45] Kosko, B. 1990. *Neural networks and fuzzy systems.* Prentice–Hall.

[46] Koslowski, B., and J. Bruner. 1972. Learning to use a lever. *Child Development,* 43:790–799.

[47] Kuipers, B., and Y. T. Byun. 1988. A robust, qualitative method for robot spatial reasoning. In *Proceedings of National Conference on Artificial Intelligence.* MIT Press.

[48] Kulkarni, D., and H. A. Simon. 1988. The processes of scientific discovery: The strategy of experimentation. *Cognitive Science,* 12(2):103–119.

[49] Langley, P. 1983. Learning search strategies through discrimination. *International Journal on Man-Machine Studies,* 18:513–541.

[50] Langley, P. 1985. Learning to search: From weak method to domain-specific heuristics. *Cognitive Science,* 9:217–260.

[51] Langley, P. 1987. A general theory of discrimination learning. In *Production System Models of Learning and Development,* ed. D. Klahr, P. Langley, and R. Neches. MIT Press.

[52] Langley, P., H. A. Simon, and G. L. Bradshaw. 1983. Rediscovering chemistry with the BACON system. In *Machine Learning,* ed. R. Michalski, J. Carbonell, and T. Mitchell. Morgan Kaufmann.

[53] Langley, P., H. A. Simon, G. L. Bradshaw, and J. M. Zytkow. 1987. *Scientific discovery—computational explorations of the creative processes.* MIT Press.

[54] Lenat, D. 1976. AM: An AI approach to discovery in mathematics as heuristic search. Ph.D. thesis, Computer Science Department, Stanford University.

[55] Lin, L. J. 1992. Self-improving reactive agents based on reinforcement learning, planning and teaching. *Machine Learning*, 8(3/4):293–321.

[56] Loredo, T. J. 1989. From Laplace to supernova SN 1987A: Bayesian inference in astrophysics. In *Maximum entropy and Bayesian methods*, ed. P. Fougere. Kluwer Academic.

[57] Lovejoy, W. S. 1991. A survey of algorithmic methods for partially observable Markov decision processes. *Annals of Operations Research*, 28:47–66.

[58] MacKay, D. J. C. 1991. *Bayesian methods for adaptive models*. Ph.D. thesis, California Institute of Technology.

[59] Mahadevan, S., and J. Connell. 1991. Automatic programming of behavior-based robots using reinforcement learning. In *Proceedings of National Conference on Artificial Intelligence*. MIT Press.

[60] Manahan, G. E. 1982. A survey of partially observable Markov decision processes: Theory, models, and algorithms. *Management Science*, 28:1–16.

[61] McClelland, J. L., D. E. Rumelhart, and the PDP Research Group. 1986. *Parallel distributed processing*. MIT Press.

[62] Mendel, G. 1976. Experiments in plant-hybridization. (Originally published 1865.) In *Classic papers in genetics*, ed. J. Peters. Prentice–Hall.

[63] McCarthy, J., and P. Hayes. 1969. Some philosophical problems from the standpoint of Artificial Intelligence. *Machine Intelligence*, 4:463–502. Edinburgh University Press.

[64] Michalski, R. S. 1983. A theory and methodology of inductive learning. *Artificial Intelligence*, 20:111–161.

[65] Michalski, R. S., I. Mozetic, J. Hong, and N. Lavrac. 1986. The multi-purpose incremental learning system AQ15 and its testing application to three medical domains. In *Proceedings of National Conference on Artificial Intelligence*. MIT Press.

[66] Minton, S. N. 1988. *Learning effective search control knowledge: An explanation-based approach*. Kluwer Academic.

[67] Mitchell, T. M. 1978. Version space: An approach to concept learning. Ph.D. thesis, Stanford University.

[68] Mitchell, T. M. 1980. The need for biases in learning generalizations. Technical Report CBM-TR-117, Rutgers University.

[69] Mitchell, T. M. 1982. Generalization as search. *Artificial Intelligence*, 18:203–226.

[70] Mitchell, T. M., P. E. Utgoff, and R. B. Banerji. 1983. Learning by experimentation: Acquiring and refining problem-solving heuristics. In *Machine Learning*, ed. R. Michalski, J. Carbonell, and T. Mitchell. Morgan Kaufmann.

[71] Moravec, H. 1988. Certainty grids for sensor fusion in mobile robots. *AI Magazine* (Summer), 61–74.

[72] Moravec, H., and D. W. Cho. 1988. A Bayesian method for certainty grids. Technical report, Mobile Robot Laboratory, Carnegie Mellon University.

[73] Mozer, M. C., and J. Bachrach. 1990. Discovering the structure of a reactive environment by exploration. In *Advances in neural information processing*, ed. D. Touretzky. Morgan Kaufmann.

[74] Nagel, E. 1950. *John Stuart Mill's* Philosophy of the Scientific Method. Hafner.

[75] Narendra, K., and M. A. L. Thathachar. 1989. *Learning automata.* Prentice–Hall.

[76] Newell, A. 1987. Unified theories of cognition. William James lecture, Harvard University.

[77] Newell, A., and H. A. Simon. 1972. *Human problem solving.* Prentice–Hall.

[78] Nguyen, D., and B. Widrow. 1989. The truck backer-upper: An example of self-learning in neural networks. In *Proceedings of International Joint Conference on Neural Networks*. IEEE Press.

[79] Nikolskii, S. M. 1963. *Approximations of functions*, Chap. 12. MIT Press.

[80] Nilsson, N. 1980. *Principles of artificial intelligence.* Tioga.

[81] Pagallo, G., and D. Haussler. 1990. Boolean feature discovery in empirical learning. *Machine Learning*, 5(1):71–100.

[82] Piaget, J. 1952. *The origins of intelligence in children.* Norton.

[83] Piaget, J. 1954. *The construction of reality in the child.* Ballantine.

[84] Pitt, L., and L. G. Valiant. 1988. Computational limitations on learning from examples. *Journal of the Association of Computing Machinery*, 35(4):965–984.

[85] Quinlan, R. J. 1983. Learning efficient classification procedures and their application to chess endgames. In *Machine Learning*, ed. R. Michalski, J. Carbonell, and T. Mitchell. Morgan Kaufmann.

[86] Quinlan, R. J. 1986. Induction of decision trees. *Machine Learning*, 1(1):81–106.

[87] Quinlan, R. J. 1987. Generating production rules from decision trees. In *Proceedings of International Joint Conference on Artificial Intelligence*, ed. J. McDermott. Morgan Kaufmann.

[88] Quinlan, R. J. 1987. Simplifying decision trees. *International Journal on Man-Machine Studies*, 27:221–234.

[89] Quinlan, R. J. 1990. Learning logical definitions from relations. *Machine Learning*, 5(3):239–266.

[90] Rabiner, L. R., and B. H. Juang. 1986. An introduction to hidden Markov models. *IEEE Acoustics, Speech, and Signal Processing Magazine* (January):4–16.

[91] Rivest, R. L. 1987. Learning decision lists. *Machine Learning*, 2:229–246.

[92] Rivest, R. L., and R. E. Schapire. 1987. Diversity-based inference of finite automata. In *Proceedings of Foundation of Computer Science*. ACM Press.

[93] Rivest, R. L., and R. E. Schapire. 1989. Inference of finite automata using homing sequences. In *Proceedings of 21st Annual ACM Symposium on Theory of Computing*. ACM Press.

[94] Rivest, R. L., and R. E. Schapire. In press. Inference of finite automata using homing sequences. *Information and Computation*.

[95] Rivest, R. L., and R. Sloan. 1988. Learning complicated concepts reliably and usefully. In *Proceedings of National Conference on Artificial Intelligence*. Morgan Kaufmann.

[96] Ross, S. 1983. *Introduction to stochastic dynamic programming*. Academic Press.

[97] Salzberg, S. 1991. A nearest hyperrectangle learning method. *Machine Learning*, 6(3):251–276.

[98] Schlimmer, J. C. 1987. Concept acquisition through representation adjustment. Ph.D. thesis, University of California, Irvine.

[99] Shapiro, E. 1981. An algorithm that infers theories from facts. In *Proceedings of International Joint Conference on Artificial Intelligence*. Morgan Kaufmann.

[100] Shen, W.-M. 1989. Learning from the environment based on actions and percepts. Ph.D. thesis, Computer Science Department, Carnegie Mellon University.

[101] Shen, W.-M. 1990. Complementary discrimination learning: A duality between generalization and discrimination. In *Proceedings of National Conference on Artificial Intelligence*. MIT Press.

[102] Shen, W.-M. 1990. Functional transformation in AI discovery systems. *Artificial Intelligence*, 41(3):257–272, 1990.

[103] Shen, W.-M. 1991. An architecture for autonomous learning from the environment. *Association of Computing Machinery, Special Interests Group of Artificial Intelligence Bulletin*, 2(4):151–155.

[104] Shen, W.-M. 1991. Discovering regularities from knowledge bases. In *Proceedings of International Conference on Machine Learning*, ed. L. Birnbuam and G. Collins. Morgan Kaufmann.

[105] Shen, W.-M. 1992. Complementary discrimination learning with decision lists. In *Proceedings of National Conference on Artificial Intelligence*. MIT Press.

[106] Shen, W.-M. 1992. Discovering regularities from knowledge bases. *International Journal of Intelligent Systems*, 7(7):623–636.

[107] Shen, W.-M. 1993. Discovery as autonomous learning from the environment. *Machine Learning*, 11(4):250–265.

[108] Shen, W.-M. 1993. Learning finite state automata using local distinguishing experiments. In *Proceedings of International Joint Conference on Artificial Intelligence*, ed. R. Bajcsy. Morgan Kaufmann.

[109] Shen, W.-M. Submitted for publication. Complementary discrimination learning. *Machine Learning*.

[110] Shen, W.-M., and H. A. Simon. 1989. Rule creation and rule learning through environmental exploration. In *Proceedings of International Joint Conference on Artificial Intelligence*, ed. N. Sridharan. Morgan Kaufmann.

[111] Shen, W.-M., and H. A. Simon. 1993. Fitness requirements for scientific theories containing recursive theoretical terms. *British Journal for the Philosophy of Science*, 44(4):504–520.

[112] Siegler, R. S. 1983. How knowledge influences learning. *American Scientist*, 71:631–638.

[113] Simon, H. A. 1970. The axiomatization of physical theories. *Philosophy of Science*, 37:16–26.

[114] Simon, H. A. 1975. The functional equivalence of problem solving skills. *Cognitive Psychology*, 7:268–288.

[115] Simon, H. A. 1981. *The sciences of the artificial*. MIT Press.

[116] Simon, H. A., and J. B. Kadane. 1975. Optimal problem-solving search: All-or-none solutions. *Artificial Intelligence*, 6:235–247.

[117] Simon, H. A., and G. Lea. 1974. Problem solving and rule induction: A unified view. In *Knowledge and cognition*, ed. L. Gregg. Lawrence Erlbaum.

[118] Suppes, P. 1957. *Introduction to logic*. Van Nostrand.

[119] Sussman, G. J. 1975. *A computer model of skill acquisition*. American Elsevier.

[120] Sutton, R. 1990. Integrated architectures for learning, planning, and reacting based on approximating dynamic programming. In *Proceedings of International Conference on Machine Learning*, ed. B. Porter. Morgan Kaufmann.

[121] Tan, M., and L. J. Eshelman. 1988. Using weighted networks to represent classification knowledge in noisy domains. In *Proceedings of International Conference on Machine Learning*, ed. J. Laird. Morgan Kaufmann.

[122] Tarski, A. 1956. *Some methodological investigations on the definability of concepts*, Chap. 10. Clarendon Press.

[123] Utgoff, P. E. 1986. *Machine learning of inductive bias*. Kluwer Academic.

[124] Utgoff, P. E. 1986. Shift of bias for inductive concept learning. In *Machine Learning*, vol. 2, ed. R. Michalski, J. Carbonell, and T. Mitchell. Morgan Kaufmann.

[125] Utgoff, P. E. 1988. ID5: An incremental ID3. In *Proceedings of International Conference on Machine Learning*. Morgan Kaufmann.

[126] Utgoff, P. E. 1989. Incremental induction of decision trees. *Machine Learning*, 4(2):161–186.

[127] Valiant, L. A theory of the learnable. *Communications of Association of Computing Machinery*, 27(11):1134–1142.

[128] Vere, S. A. 1980. Multilevel counterfactuals for generalizations of relational concepts and productions. *Artificial Intelligence*, 14:139–164.

[129] Waldinger, R. 1977. Achieving several goals simultaneously. In *Machine Intelligence 8*. Academic Press.

[130] Warren, W. H., Jr., and R. E. Shaw. 1985. *Persistence and change*. Lawrence Erlbaum.

[131] Waterman, D. A. 1975. Adaptive production systems. In *Proceedings of International Joint Conference on Artificial Intelligence*. Morgan Kaufmann.

[132] Watkins, C. 1989. Learning from delayed rewards. Ph.D. thesis, Cambridge University.

[133] Watkins, C., and P. Dayan. 1992. Technical note: *Q*-learning. *Machine Learning*, 8(3/4):279–292.

[134] Wilson, S. L. 1987. Classifier systems and the animat problem. *Machine Learning*, 2:199–288.

[135] Winston, P. H. 1975. Learning structural descriptions from examples. In *The psychology of computer vision*, ed. P. Winston, McGraw-Hill.

INDEX